How a City Learned to Improve Its Schools

ANTHONY S. BRYK
SHARON GREENBERG
ALBERT BERTANI
PENNY SEBRING
STEVEN E. TOZER
TIMOTHY KNOWLES

HARVARD EDUCATION PRESS
CAMBRIDGE, MA

Continuous Improvement in Education Series

Paperback ISBN 978-1-68253-822-7

Library of Congress Cataloging-in-Publication Data is on file.

Published by Harvard Education Press,
an imprint of the Harvard Education Publishing Group

Harvard Education Press
8 Story Street
Cambridge, MA 02138

Cover Design: Wilcox Design
Cover Image: FrankRamspott@DigitalVisionVectors via Getty Images
Photo by Zehua Chen on Unsplash

The typefaces in this book are Minion Pro and ITC Stone Sans.

Contents

Acknowledgments:
The People and the Process

How A City Learned to Improve Its Schools is the result of an intensive, three-year collaboration that built on the distinctive academic strengths, hands-on experiences, and professional knowledge of its six authors. It involved a synthesis of research on Chicago's reform, extensive interviews with key actors across this thirty-year history, supplemental analyses of extant data resources, and multiple convenings of additional Chicagoans who made significant contributions to the developments described here.

We highlight below the background and relevant experiences that each author brought to this effort and how we worked together to develop the manuscript. We also acknowledge and thank many others who graciously shared their time, insights, and reflections and offered critical feedback as the work progressed. This was an orchestrated process that melded research evidence together with the insights and reflections offered by many individuals into one shared account.

WHO WE ARE

Anthony S. Bryk served as the ninth president of the Carnegie Foundation for the Advancement of Teaching from 2008 to 2020, where he is now a senior fellow. During his tenure at the Foundation, he pioneered efforts to bring the discipline of improvement science and the organization of improvement networks into education. Prior to that he was the Marshall Field Professor of Urban Education in the Departments of Education and Sociology at the University of Chicago (UChicago). Bryk's foundational writings on improving schooling include *Charting Chicago School Reform: Democratic Localism as a Lever for Change* (1998), *Trust in Schools: A Core Resource for Improvement* (2002), *Organizing Schools for Improvement: Lessons from Chicago* (2010), *Learning to Improve: How America's Schools Can Get Better at Getting Better* (2015), and *Improvement in Action: Advancing Quality in America's Schools* (2020).

Active in Chicago's reform from 1987 through 2004, Bryk led the formation of both the Center for School Improvement at the UChicago (subsequently expanded and operating as the Urban Education Institute) and the Consortium on Chicago School Research (now the UChicago Consortium on School Research).

Sharon Greenberg taught high school English and "remedial reading" in Chicago Public Schools (CPS) at the start of her career. She is now a quality improvement advisor and a literacy and education consultant who has worked with schools, districts, state boards of education, colleges of education, and nonprofits. Under the surname Rollow, she is an author of *Charting Chicago School Reform: Democratic Localism as a Lever for Change* and a contributing author to *Trust in Schools: A Core Resource for Improvement*. More recently she was a contributing author to the case study volume *Improvement in Action: Advancing Quality in America's Schools*.

Greenberg is a cofounder of the Center for School Improvement (the Center) at UChicago, where she was a senior research associate and director of research and director of literacy. Greenberg also played major roles in the development of the UChicago Consortium, the North Kenwood Oakland Professional Development Charter School, and the Urban Teacher Education Program—all started by the Center. In addition, Greenberg served as a cabinet member and literacy consultant to Barbara Eason-Watkins when she was the CPS chief education officer.

Albert Bertani is a senior fellow at the Carnegie Foundation for the Advancement of Teaching. He has worked as an elementary teacher, principal, assistant superintendent, college professor, university administrator, and senior researcher. Bertani has also consulted with schools, school districts, professional organizations, boards of education, colleges and universities, state departments, and ministries of education both domestically and internationally. He is a contributing author to *Redesigning Education: Shaping Learning Systems Around the Globe* (2013) and *Global Perspectives on Educational Leadership* (2016).

Bertani served in multiple roles, in different organizations, during reform. He was part of the Center team that developed Leading Change, the first leadership development program tailored to practicing CPS principals. At the Chicago Principals and Administrators Association, he designed and led programs that served school and district leaders at different career stages. In CPS, he established the Office of Professional Development. He has also taught courses and advised doctoral students in the Urban Educational Leadership Preparation program at the University of Illinois Chicago.

Penny Sebring is a senior research associate at the University of Chicago and a cofounder of the UChicago Consortium. She is an author of *Organizing Schools for Improvement: Lessons from Chicago* and *Charting Chicago School Reform: Democratic Localism as a Lever for Change*. Sebring has also contributed to numerous Consortium publications on school organization, leadership, and students' participation in digital media.

Sebring is president of the Lewis-Sebring Family Foundation, which funds actionable research and its dissemination in Chicago, educator professional training, and the UChicago Charter School. She also serves on the Policy Advisory Board for Northwestern's School of Education and Social Policy and governing boards for the Chicago Public Education Fund and Kids First Chicago.

Steven E. Tozer is professor and University Scholar Emeritus in Educational Policy Studies at the University of Illinois Chicago (UIC) and founding director of the Center for Urban Education Leadership. He is a senior research fellow of the Learning Policy Institute, lead author of a textbook for teachers (*School and Society: Historical and Contemporary Perspectives*, 8th edition [2021]), and lead editor of *The Handbook of Research in Social Foundations of Education* (2011). In addition, Tozer has authored or coauthored many articles and chapters on educational policy and leadership.

Specific to reform, Tozer chaired five statewide task forces on teacher and principal development that led to the passage of new licensure laws. In 1990 he began work on a PhD cohort program for Chicago school leaders. He also collaborated with the district and the Chicago Teachers Union to create a mentoring program for new teachers and is cofounder of the UIC EdD Program in Urban Education Leadership.

Timothy Knowles is president of the Carnegie Foundation for the Advancement of Teaching. Previously, he was the founder and managing partner of the Academy Group. His early career includes teaching African history in Botswana, founding Teach For America in New York City, starting and directing a public school in Bedford Stuyvesant, New York City, and serving as deputy superintendent of the Boston Public Schools. In Boston, Knowles started several nonprofit organizations, including the Boston Teacher Residency and the Boston Leadership Institute.

In Chicago, Knowles served as the John Dewey Clinical Professor in Education at the University of Chicago. He consolidated several university efforts focused on Chicago schools into the Urban Education Institute and served as its first director. He also established UChicago Urban Labs and served as an informal advisor to Mayor Emanuel and several of Chicago's CEOs. Knowles was active in the development of Renaissance 2010, helped initiate Advance Illinois, and served on several philanthropic and nonprofit boards in Chicago.

HOW WE WROTE THIS BOOK

This book is the culmination of a complex research and writing process that sought to integrate many different sources of knowledge into a coherent account of what happened in Chicago and how these developments came about. The six authors collaborated on this project for three years.

Bryk was responsible for the book's overall architecture, and members of the author group were responsible for individual chapters. Greenberg was the lead author on chapters 1 and 4, with early support on chapter 1 from Knowles. Bryk and Sebring were co-lead authors on chapter 2. Bertani and Tozer shared that responsibility for chapter 3. Bryk, with support from Greenberg, took responsibility for drafting the introduction and chapter 5.

Bryk designed an iterative process that engaged the six core authors in the development of all the chapters. The chapter lead(s) prepared outlines that were reviewed by the other authors. They were revised and then reviewed again by the full author group. A similar iterative process was used to develop first drafts, second drafts, and final revisions of each chapter based on critical commentary offered by a diverse group of Chicago reformers. Author discussions occurred through ninety-minute biweekly Zoom convenings where each chapter was considered individually. The writing and review cycle at each stage spanned several months.

Bertani assumed operational responsibility for the project and guided its evolving work. He led agenda development for various meetings, crafted activity protocols for our larger convenings, and facilitated all of them. Greenberg led the design of core interview protocols, participated in most of them, and developed thematic summaries of each. Interview teams were assembled to make the best use of each author's knowledge of the topical focus in each particular interview and their relationship to the person being interviewed. Bertani, Bryk, and Greenberg met weekly for the duration of the project to keep it on course.

Complementing this internal process was outreach to Chicagoans who had been active in school reform for an extended period during this thirty-year span. A convening in Chicago in January 2020 launched the project. It brought together the author group with about thirty other individuals from the eleven institutional sectors identified in the introduction. Following that, a series of smaller Zoom convenings and panels sustained these discussions with an expanding group of Chicago reformers over the next two years. Authors shared their emerging understandings as research and drafting were under way, and participants offered critical feedback. Bookending this process was a final large convening in January 2022. Participants read an early draft manuscript and again offered comments. That feedback set off the final round of chapter revisions. Our aim, through this extensive outreach, was to continually test and refine our story against the lived experiences of many individuals who were key to how Chicago learned to improve its schools.

Once penultimate drafts had been prepared in the spring of 2022, Bryk and Greenberg revised the final chapters to integrate the accounts and bring a coherent voice to the overall text.

OUR DEBT TO MANY OTHERS

As noted above, we sought to write a book that would ring true to many involved in moving school reform forward in Chicago. Toward that end we are deeply grateful to the seventy individuals who enriched the story by sitting for an interview and participating in one or more of our convenings. Appendix A enumerates all who participated in one or more ways. We are deeply grateful for their contributions. This book is much richer because of their insights and critical reactions.

We also wish to acknowledge those who contributed detailed notes on draft chapters, made time for conversations, and, in a few cases, undertook original analyses and penned memos on specific topics that added to and sometimes challenged our understandings. We are deeply appreciative of Paul Zavitovsky's analytic work that undergirded the data displays on student achievement outcomes shared in the introduction. The arc of chapter 1 was informed by commentary from several individuals. We wish to acknowledge John Ayers's narrative accounts about his own reform efforts, those of his father, Thomas Ayers, and those of his Civic Committee colleagues. Charles Payne was both provocative and gracious as he shared his insights and questioned some of our initial observations. Jesse Ruiz and Beth Swanson contributed to our understandings of the behind-the-scenes work of the Board of Education as it evolved in Era 4.

Especially pertinent to chapter 2, Elaine Allensworth contributed to our understanding of how the Consortium partnered with the CPS and about the ebb and flow of that partnership. She also shared with us how the Consortium worked with other organizations around the city. John Easton solidified our understanding of the Consortium's thirty-year history, his direct work with Arne Duncan and senior CPS leaders, and the nuances and challenges that inevitably arose from time to time in "speaking truth to power." Both John and Elaine pointed us to specific Consortium studies that merited mention in our account. In several cases they also offered commentary beyond what was published.

For chapter 3, we are indebted to our colleagues in the CPS central office who worked to reform the district's human capital and human development systems and were so generous with their time during interviews, follow-up conversations, and more. We include Heather Anichini, Ascención Juarez, Matt Lyons, Nancy Slavin, and Alicia Winkler.

Regarding chapter 4, we thank Barbara Eason-Watkins and Janice Jackson, who talked with us at length about their efforts and their own learnings as each took the district from where it was to a better place. We thank Marty Gartzman, whose work, and that of his colleagues, began the transition toward ambitious teaching and learning in math and science. Josie Yanguas and Gudelia Lopez enriched our understanding of the system's ethnic transition and Latino students' journey through that system.

We also acknowledge Emily Krone Phillips, who deepened our understanding of the changing role of Chicago's media over the years of reform. Her insights informed every chapter. Gudelia Lopez provided valuable background information on Chicago foundations' involvement with school reform. She interviewed foundation program officers, unearthed documents and reports, offered extensive comments on chapter drafts, and, as noted above, deepened our understanding of the district's evolving capability to serve its Latino students and their teachers.

Writing some thirty-five years after the start of Chicago's reform, we are also grateful to those who worked tirelessly during their lifetimes to improve public education in Chicago. We specifically mention those whose efforts strongly shaped our account, including Thomas Ayers, Fred Hess, John Kotsakis, Karen Lewis, Don Moore, Barbara Sizemore, Sara Spurlark, Harold Washington, and Arnold Weber. Each was a fierce advocate and dedicated colleague in the ambitious effort to transform Chicago's public schools.

We could not have documented CPS progress without new analyses provided by Consortium researchers. Todd Rosenkranz prepared extensive demographic information on students, teachers, and principals across the four eras. Chris Young analyzed thirty-year trends of key survey measures. Shelby Mahaffie tracked high school graduation rates from the late 1990s through 2017. Briana Diaz created a series of maps that illuminated the effects of historical racist public policies and the ongoing need, particularly in certain areas of the city, to significantly strengthen students' opportunities to learn and develop. We are also indebted to Jeff Hall, who skillfully crafted the visualizations that run through the book.

We express our appreciation to Pam George, who provided editorial assistance that included preparing the bibliography, formatting the manuscript, and checking quotes; to Cristina La, who provided research assistance for chapter 3; and to the knowledge workers/note-takers who worked with us at our initial January 2020 meeting in Chicago. This last group included Soulet Ali, Malak Arafa, Adrianna Barnett, and Sydney Jackson, as well as Andy Tousignant, who introduced these individuals to us.

We also thank Laverne Srinivasan at the Carnegie Corporation of New York, who believed in this effort when it was just an idea and encouraged us to push forward. We are grateful for the Corporation's support that underwrote the research activities necessary to complete the project, and for matching funding provided by Trustees of the Carnegie Foundation for the Advancement of Teaching. The Foundation's board continues to advocate for efforts to improve our nation's schools.

Finally, we express our appreciation to Caroline Chauncey at Harvard Education Press (HEP) for her initiation of the Continuous Improvement in Education series. We are especially thankful to Jayne Fargnoli, who took on this project just as she began her tenure as editor in chief at HEP. She was constant in her support, encouragement, and feedback as we worked through the development and completion of this manuscript. It was a privilege to call her our editor.

Introduction

It exploded on the pages of the *Chicago Tribune*:[1]

> Chicago Public Schools are hardly more than daytime warehouses for students, taught by disillusioned and inadequate teachers, presided over by a bloated, leaderless bureaucracy, and constantly undercut by a selfish single-minded teachers union.

This opened a series of articles, published in 1988, that was subsequently compiled into a book titled *Chicago Schools: Worst in America*. The label came courtesy of Bill Bennett, then the US Secretary of Education.

A focus of the series was life at William C. Goudy Elementary School. However, Goudy was emblematic of hundreds of Chicago neighborhood schools at that time. It was a mixed tale of both individual heroism and profound neglect: a principal who cared deeply about the students and their families but was quick to admit that he was a lousy administrator; the inspired efforts of a few teachers who were unable to compensate for their colleagues' indifference; and families who wanted to do right by their children but did not always know how.

Worst in America painted a picture of despair and hopelessness where even the best of intentions was overwhelmed by massive system failure. There had been nine teacher strikes in the previous eighteen years. Long-standing fiscal malfeasance had brought an independent School Finance Authority into existence to oversee the system's budget.

Figure I.1   Worst public school system in America

There was little public trust in the Chicago Board of Education, its central office, or the Chicago Teachers Union. These sentiments were captured in a *Tribune* cartoon. (See figure I.1.)

Student achievement data affirmed the bleak state of affairs: High school graduation rates hovered around 50 percent. When most school districts were living in the Lake Wobegon era of "everyone is above average," Chicago's standardized test scores were in the upper 20s to low 30s percentile range as judged against a very basic skills test.

The *Tribune* account was sensational, but it also galvanized a demand for change. Community leaders and advocacy groups had been pressing on these issues for years; now an elite city institution was amplifying their voices. Most important, Harold Washington, Chicago's first Black mayor, listened and stepped up. His sudden and untimely death afforded him little time to act, and no opportunity to see what his leadership would subsequently catalyze—the most "radical" urban education reform in the country.

THIRTY YEARS LATER: AMONG THE MOST IMPROVED

Chicago Public Schools (CPS) high school graduation rates, which had been stagnant for decades, began to creep up beginning around 2000. The climb continued through the early 2000s and then more rapidly after 2008.[2] System-wide, the graduation rate in Chicago rose to over 80 percent.[3] Importantly, the largest of these gains occurred for Black and Latino males.[4] (See figure I.2.)

Figure I.2 Continuing improvements in high school graduation rates

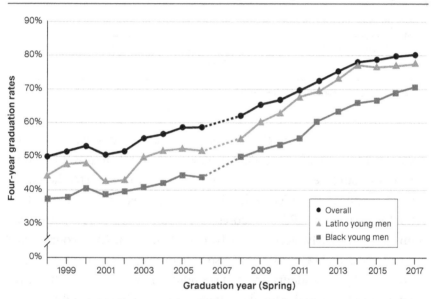

Source: UChicago Consortium on School Research.

Note: The 2007 results are incomparable to those in the years prior and after, due to an anomaly that existed in the CPS data system. For this reason, no results have been included for 2007. In addition, when examining estimates of high school graduation over long periods of time, discrepancies can arise due to the population of students included in the estimates, level of data quality, the emergence of different kinds of high schools, such as charter or alternative schools, and varying definitions of what it means to be a high school graduate. Consequently, variation in annual reports exists depending on the definitions adopted. The differences in these statistics, however, do not affect the overall shape of the high school graduation trends displayed here.

Figure I.3 Rising ACT scores in high schools

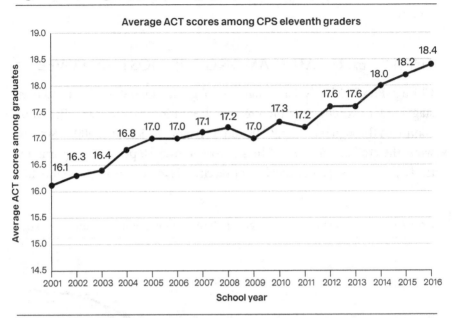

Average ACT scores among CPS eleventh graders

Source: UChicago Consortium on School Research.

Moreover, accompanying the changed graduation rates was actual improvement in high school student achievement. While improved graduation rates could be accomplished by lowering academic standards, the reverse happened in Chicago. In 2003 the ACT became a required high school assessment in CPS, and scores have been on the rise ever since.[5] (See figure I.3.) Similarly, access to Advanced Placement (AP) courses and student performance on AP tests also rose during this same period. (See figure I.4.) More students are college-bound now too. Since 2006, the proportion of CPS high school graduates enrolling in two- and four-year institutions rose from 49 percent to 70 percent.[6]

Substantial improvements occurred in the elementary schools as well. The best indicator of the productivity of an individual school, or system of schools, is the amount of learning that occurs for students from a year of instruction: if a school system is improving, these learning gains should

Figure I.4 Rising numbers of students enrolled and succeeding in advanced placement courses

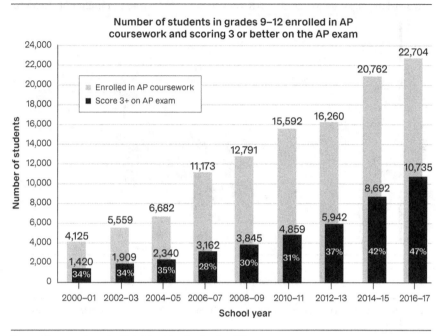

Number of students in grades 9–12 enrolled in AP coursework and scoring 3 or better on the AP exam

Source: Allensworth et al., *High School Graduation Rate,* 33.

Note: Additional data points provided by Allensworth.

be increasing in size over time.[7] Sean Reardon, director of the Educational Opportunity Project at Stanford University, brought this perspective to analyzing data from school districts across the country. Figure I.5 plots the relationship that was found between district poverty and amount of student learning. (The size of the bubble indicates the size of the school district.) We have superimposed earlier results from Chicago on the Educational Opportunity Project's findings from 2016.[8] In 1990, the average learning gain in Chicago across grades 3 through 8 in reading and math was 0.84, that is, just 0.84 years of learning for each year of instruction. By 1996 it rose to 0.94, by 2001 it crept up to 0.97, and then by 2016, in the Reardon data, it stood at 1.20. This translates into a whole extra year of learning for students as they moved through grades 4 to 8. This

Figure I.5 Chicago learning gains compared nationally and locally over time

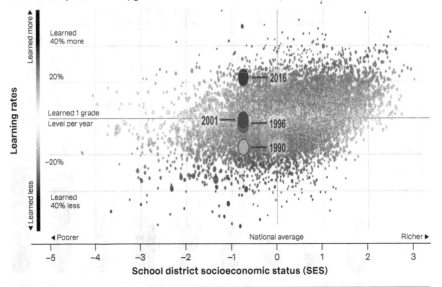

US districts, all students, grades 3–8 from 2009 to 2016, sized by number of students

Source: Base figure was created by the Educational Opportunity Project at Stanford University using SEDA 3.0 data.

accelerated rate of learning placed the CPS in 2016 above 96 percent of *all* school systems in the United States. Improvements for Black and Latino students were equal to or greater than those of white students, and Chicago's growth had become a key driver for Illinois's overall test score gains.[9]

These improvements in productivity of Chicago's elementary schools are reflected in National Assessment of Educational Progress (NAEP) results as well. NAEP began collecting data on individual urban districts in 2003. Figure I.6 documents substantial improvement in both reading and mathematics in Chicago at grade 8 relative to all other districts in the nation. The initial large gap in performance in 2003 shrank by about two-thirds over the next fourteen years. Even though the system's students remained educationally disadvantaged (see below), the improvement in academic productivity documented by Reardon translated into a

Figure I.6   NAEP data trends at grade 8: Chicago relative to all US schools

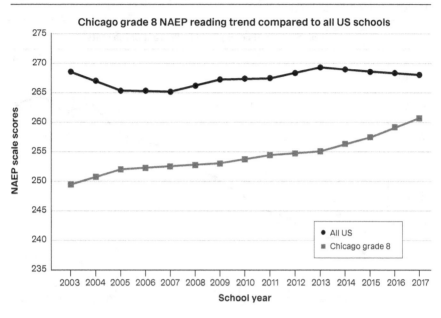

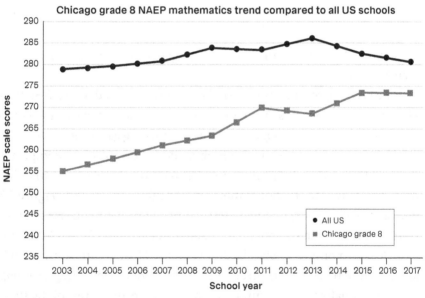

Figure I.7 Closing the gap in reading and mathematics at grade 3 from 2002 to 2017 (Illinois State Test)

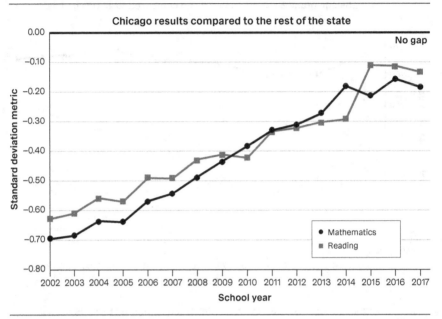

substantial reduction in the achievement gap at the end of students' elementary years.

Likewise, improvements occurred in the primary grades (preK–3). Regular annual assessments at each primary grade did not exist in Chicago during this historical period, and so annual learning gains cannot be computed. However, state testing results at grade 3 show substantial improvements in the "outputs" of primary instruction. Comparable data with other districts across the state of Illinois exists beginning in 2001. Figure I.7 indicates that in 2001, Chicago's test scores lagged behind those of other districts in the state by about 0.65 standard deviations. By 2017 that gap had closed to only 0.15 standard deviations. Most significant by 2015, low-income African American and Latino third graders in Chicago, a group who traditionally lagged behind their counterparts in the rest of the state, now outperformed similar students in both reading and mathematics.[10] (See figure I.8.)

Figure I.8 Improving performance of low-income African American and Latino third graders in Chicago compared with those of their counterparts statewide

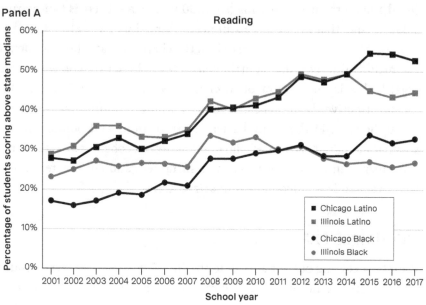

Panel A

Reading

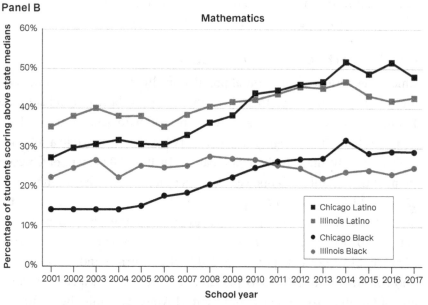

Panel B

Mathematics

In sum, across a diverse set of indicators at both the elementary and high school levels, a school system that was among the worst in America in 1988 stood among the best at getting better 30 years later. Even as Chicagoans acknowledge that much more still needs to be done, it is also clear that remarkable changes have occurred. In the chapters that follow, we detail the major initiatives that contributed to these better outcomes. In this regard, this is an account of *what* improvements came forward. But most distinctive about this Chicago story is *how and why* all of this came about: how, amid the many leadership transitions and political maelstrom that characterized CPS during this time, a coherent system of improvements emerged, developed, was sustained, and culminated in the improved student outcomes summarized above.

NO SIMPLE EXPLANATIONS

Prior to sketching out our answer to the "how" question, we first consider a set of plausible alternate explanations for these results. Each turns out to be only a minor contributor to the large-scale improvements witnessed in Chicago. They are part of the story, but they are not *the* story.

A Shifting School System Population

Chicago experienced substantial population shifts both prior to and during reform. As in many other cities, there was a suburban exodus in the 1950s, 60s, and 70s and then a more recent shift with gentrification. However, the changing demographics of the city have not resulted in a substantially more advantaged school population. In 1991, 80 percent of Chicago elementary school students were low income; in 2017 that number was 82 percent.[11] The combined population of white and Asian students has remained steady over these three decades at approximately 15 percent.[12] A major shift did occur, however, as African Americans declined from 57 percent in 1991 to 37 percent in 2017, with a corresponding rise in Latino enrollment from 28 to 47 percent. The latter reflects a continued influx of families from Mexico and Central America, while the decline in African American enrollment resulted from both an out-migration by low-income families, largely driven by the demolition of Chicago's public housing projects, and an exodus by middle-class African American families to private, parochial, and suburban schools.

While a significant compositional shift did occur, there is no evidence that it accounts for the large improvements in student outcomes noted above. Reardon and colleagues specifically examined this and discounted it as a plausible explanation for the large learning gains they found.[13] Locally, Paul Zavitkovsky at the University of Illinois at Chicago (UIC), who compiled the Illinois and NAEP trends presented above, found large average test score improvements in these two different sources of data for all ethnic subgroups.[14] Still other research documents that the improvements in high school graduation rates are broad-based and include nonselective neighborhood high schools.[15] In short, voluminous extant evidence points to a large overall improvement in Chicago school outcomes with only a small portion, at most, attributable to demographic changes.

Charters and Choice

Chicago is a choice district. In 2017 some 75 percent of students did not attend their neighborhood high school, and 50 percent did not attend their neighborhood elementary school.[16] This is not a recent phenomenon. Choice options in CPS date back to the 1960s when desegregation efforts created magnet and themed schools.[17] As early as 1990, 25 percent of elementary students and 50 percent of high schoolers attended schools other than their neighborhood assignments. While parental choice expanded over the 30 years of reform, it has been part of the system for a long time.

Turning specifically to charter schools, a small number opened in Chicago beginning in the late 1990s, with a major expansion occurring between 2003 and 2010. Even so, in 2017 only 22 percent of high school students and 12 percent of elementary students attended charter schools. So options expanded, but most families continued to send their children to schools directly operated by the district.

There is evidence that ACT scores were slightly higher, by 0.25 points, in charter high schools, compared to the outcomes from the neighborhood schools that these students otherwise would have attended.[18] However, the districtwide improvement on ACT scores between 2003 and 2016 was much larger, 1.9 points. When factoring in the modest size of the charter school effect and the fact that only 22 percent of students were enrolled in these schools, their contribution to the overall districtwide improvement in ACT scores is minimal. Graduation rates also improved in charter schools, but similar improvements occurred in neighborhood-based high schools as well.[19] Charter high schools did make a significant contribution to four-year college enrollment rates. These increased system-wide from 29 percent in 2005 to 42 percent in 2016, and about a third of this overall increase is attributable to charters.[20] But again, the rest of the system was improving at the same time.

As for Chicago's charter elementary schools, two external evaluations reported only small or no incremental effects for them. These findings are also consistent with descriptive reports used by the CPS in its school accountability system. While a few individual charter elementary schools have been successful, there is no evidence that Chicago's charter elementary schools, as a group, generated substantially better learning gains.[21] And representing only 12 percent of the system, they clearly do not account for the overall system-wide improvements documented above.

In short, Chicago's expansion of charter schools increased choice options in what was seen by many as a good unto itself. But it is not a major explanatory factor for the overall improvement in student outcomes.

Mayoral Control, Charismatic Leaders, and Strategic Plans

Strengthening mayoral control over the school system was another major change introduced starting in 1995. As discussed in chapter 1, actions by Chicago's mayors were significant determinants in how Chicago's reforms evolved, but not in the simple ways that advocates for this policy might have envisioned. In theory, a mayor with authority to appoint the school board and recruit and support a visionary superintendent can sustain attention to a transformative strategic plan. The mayor working with the board and superintendent can assure that every resource and instrument under their control is deployed to implement a blueprint for change across the entire school system.

It is a sensible argument, but it relates only modestly to Chicago's actual story. Prior to the state legislative action that granted expanded authorities to the mayor in 1995, there had been substantial leadership churn in Chicago, with five different superintendents over the previous seven years. Mayoral control under Richard M. Daley did stabilize the system for a fifteen-year period from 1995 to 2010. However, when Rahm Emanuel was elected in 2010, churn returned with six different system leaders in the next seven years. And interestingly, during the one period where the most meaningful improvements evolved, between 2001 and 2009, there was no widely visible strategic plan, and central command and control was used in circumscribed ways.[22]

To be clear, mayoral control was important in Chicago. From 1995 through 2010, it secured labor management peace and resolved budget shortfalls that had plagued the district for decades. Schools opened on time each fall, and tangible investments were made in renovated buildings, playgrounds, and some new school construction. There was also some increased coordination of efforts between CPS and select city departments, including human services, sanitation, and police. However, the major catalysts for most educational improvements took their early roots, not in the central bureaucracy, but in local schools and among individuals and organizations in Chicago's civic and community spaces. Several national groups were drawn in as well.

SETTING THE CONTEXT: A CONTEST AROUND POWER AND CONTROL

Issues of Race, Class, and Ethnic Succession

By design, public schools sit between the aspirations that families hold for their children and broad societal aims for public education. Across time and place, these public aims have been framed in a variety of ways—to increase economic prosperity, to afford more equitable individual opportunity, and to sustain a civil democratic society. Adjudicating among these aims, and also the more particular wishes of families and local communities, makes public education an intrinsically contested political space. This is especially so in an urban district that serves low-income children of color and where system leaders are typically making decisions about and for "other people's children."[23] Chicago's reforms took place inside one of the nation's most segregated cities. White men led both the school district and the city through most of this thirty-year period.

A century of institutional racism in the CPS and the city created reform's backdrop. Discussed in chapter 1, just as African Americans began to take over the leadership of traditional centers of power—the school board, superintendency, teacher union, and city hall—in the mid 1980s authority shifted away from that group toward parents and community members in local schools. This sowed class division between those who had climbed the political ladder to gain control over jobs and contracts with the school system, and consequently had something to lose, and those who believed that the district was so rotten that fundamental change was needed regardless of who sat at the top.

In addition, both race and class differences operated as powerful interpretative lenses for the myriad of social interactions that played out all along the way. Questions about who holds the reins of control, what their intentions are, who is benefiting and who is not, abounded. These concerns were especially manifest in major policy issues around school closings, the advent of charter and contract schools, the changing demographics of the workforce, where new buildings were built, and what curricula and special programs were offered (and where they were offered). The ongoing influence of civic and business leaders was continually scrutinized through this lens.

Ethnic succession over the control of the public school system is a critical part of every big city's education story, as it was in Chicago. Noted above, African Americans had wrested control of the school system by the mid-1980s, but African American student enrollment was starting to decline. By 2011 Latino students were the largest group, even though Latino representation at most senior district leadership levels lagged behind. As enrollments grew in Latino communities, overcrowding and organizing for new neighborhood schools became major issues. CPS leaders were slow to respond to Latino students' distinct educational needs, and especially those of the English learners among them. Amplifying this contested terrain were competing ideas nationally about how best to educate English learners. As discussed in chapter 4, early leadership for improvement in this domain emerged not from the central office but rather in local Latino school communities. Some of these individuals would move into senior leadership roles over time.

Competing Domains of Power

Chicago's reform was decades in the making. Pressure from the "bottom up" emanated from parents, community-based groups, and citywide advocacy organizations in the run-up to reform. Their efforts culminated in state legislative action, the School Reform Act of 1988, that ushered in local control of neighborhood schools. Many of the individuals and groups who were central to its passage stayed involved in the years that followed. In 1989, almost six thousand parents and community members were elected to the local school councils (LSCs) created by this law and greatly expanded Chicago's base of democratic localism. And unprecedented anywhere, undocumented parents and community members were able to vote for their LSC representatives and become council members themselves.

In addition, local institutions, including Chicago's media, advocacy and community groups, and business-led organizations, were pressing on the school system from the "outside in." Over time, this space expanded as new organizations came into being and new centers of work emerged in local colleges of education and in many of the city's cultural institutions. The Chicago Teachers Union (CTU), which previously had been vilified as an obstacle to reform, grew a progressive movement within it. Several national organizations, each with distinct human capacity development missions, became increasingly important as well. This opening up of the system set Chicago's development on a distinctive course. Local and national philanthropy fueled much of this activity—another powerful force from the outside in.

Noted earlier, the central office was discredited, and its staff was deliberately eviscerated as part of the initiating reforms in 1988. Efforts to rebuild capacities in the central office began in the mid-1990s and continued to develop over the next two decades. At its best, district leaders constructively used their role authority to advance improvements. They also, however, stood behind some of the system's most controversial initiatives. Many of the most impactful uses of "top-down" power came from the Illinois legislature and Illinois State Board of Education. Two major acts passed by the Illinois legislature, which applied only to Chicago, stand out in this regard. The first was the 1988 School Reform Act, which decentralized the system with local school councils, and the second was the 1995 Amendatory Act, which sought to address problems left unresolved in 1988 by extending considerable authority to the mayor. Moreover, the second law did not displace the first one but rather was layered on top. Several other smaller, but still significant, regulatory actions by the legislature and Illinois State Board of Education shaped Chicago's reform effort as well.

In sum, Chicago's reform set in motion a complex dynamic among competing sources of power—top-down, bottom-up, and outside-in—that challenged the base dysfunction of a parochial system by opening it to new energies, new pressures, new people, and new ideas. Figure I.9 offers a

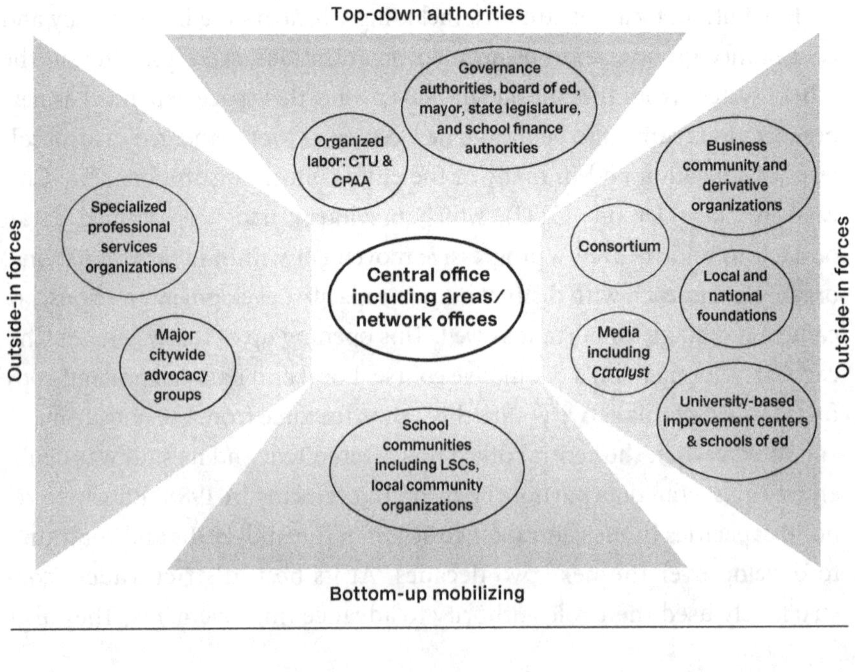

Figure I.9   The institutional map for change in Chicago

visual display of the multiple institutions, and various sources of power, that came into play in this thirty-year period. As will be seen in the pages ahead, an array of organizations nested within this institutional frame eventually joined in the fray.

Competing Ideas About How to Control Public School Systems

Over Chicago's thirty years of reform, any number of policy arguments raged nationally about transforming the governance of public education, and Chicago was drawn into all of them. At the outset, however, Chicago chose its own distinctive path—a "radical" vision of *community control*. While the roots of local community control date back to frontier America, the Chicago Black Panthers revived it in the 1960s when they stepped in to provide many of the services that the city refused to offer to schools and families on the south and west sides.[24] A few Afrocentric schools also were started, premised on the idea that those closest to the children should determine who should teach them and what and how they should be taught. The Chicago School Reform Act of 1988, with its creation of elected LSCs composed primarily of parent and community members, drew heavily on this tradition.[25]

Enhanced *bureaucratic control* also played a role in Chicago. Historically, the introduction of professional bureaucracies was public education's response to the mass immigration, urbanization, and industrialization that took place in the late nineteenth century. It was heralded as the antidote to urban systems that had grown rife with patronage, and offered in its place an efficient model for running school systems, anchored in the management principles of the assembly line. The reality of urban districts fifty years later, however, belied whatever promise might have existed back then. By the 1980s, the city's business leaders were keenly aware of the need to transform how central bureaucracies worked as they were seeking to redress similar concerns in their own organizations. Improving the management of the school system's operations was a driving concern for them.[26] From early on, they sought to transform a dysfunctional CPS bureaucracy into a better-managed operation.

Also gaining steam in the 1980s was a turn toward *market control* of public service systems. Its answer to calcified public bureaucracies was the introduction of competition and choice. The theory, briefly put, was that families would vote with their feet if high-quality alternatives to the public system were available. Forced to compete, public schools, in turn, would become more responsive to families, students, and communities. Productive schools would flourish, and problematic ones would go out of business. An early policy instrument for advancing this was voucher systems—embraced because they would largely bypass the problem of fixing the central office. The invisible hand of the market would solve the problem instead. While voucher initiatives were favored elsewhere, they sputtered in Chicago and paved the way for charters to become the pathway of choice instead.[27] Interestingly, market control held an important element in common with community control: both viewed the individual school, rather than the district, as the principal unit to target in efforts aiming to achieve better outcomes.

A push to empower teachers also gained ground nationally in the 1980s. It tapped into a different set of conversations aimed at professionalizing teaching by granting teachers greater control over how their work was organized and carried out.[28] Initiatives emphasizing school-site management and school-based decision-making followed from this line of thinking. Although Chicago did not tack strongly in this direction, at a more general level these arguments were consistent with Chicago's push into decentralization, as they too demonstrated a preference for increased control at the school-site level.

Crosscutting all of this was the beginning of a national conversation that would eventually reshape understandings about the aims for public education. Up into the late 1980s, and as reflected in the stated goals of the 1988 School Reform Act, improved high school graduation rates and increased scores on basic skills tests were the desired aims. Over the next two decades an aspiration for higher and more ambitious educational outcomes, including every graduate being "college ready," would replace them. Schools were being asked to achieve universally what no one anywhere had done before. Taken to heart, these new aspirations called into question the traditional roles, routines, norms, and mindsets of public school educators. It would no longer be satisfactory to think of principals as compliance managers; they needed to become instructional leaders. Likewise, weakly trained teachers could no longer be plugged into classroom slots and seen largely as replaceable parts—as the industrial economy saw its workers. Rather, a true professional culture, characterized by *professional normative control*, would need to emerge. An embrace of such professional control, in turn, depended on a reconceived central office specifically organized to support such systemic change. And with this development, a major tension became manifest in Chicago: how to sustain a diverse and decentralized system of schools yet couple this to professionally guided systems reform?

Figure I.10 organizes Chicago's reform into chronological eras. It illustrates when each of the core ideas about alternative mechanisms

Figure I.10   The control mechanisms that shaped Chicago's reform over time

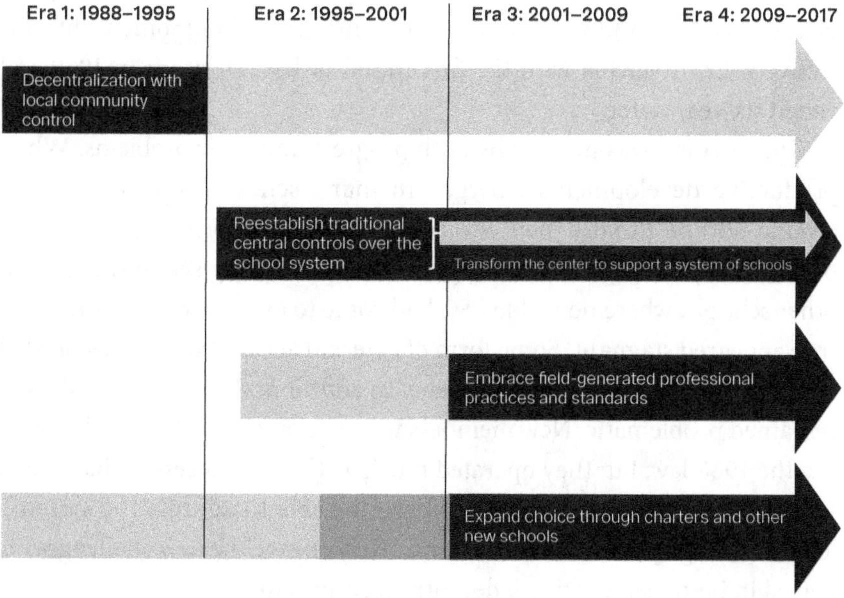

| Era 1: 1988–1995 | Era 2: 1995–2001 | Era 3: 2001–2009 | Era 4: 2009–2017 |

Decentralization with local community control

Reestablish traditional central controls over the school system

Transform the center to support a system of schools

Embrace field-generated professional practices and standards

Expand choice through charters and other new schools

Note: The gray/black density reflects the varying levels of centrality of each control mechanism throughout the thirty-year history.

for system control achieved salience, the intensity of its presence, and its persistence over time.

FOUR ERAS OF CHICAGO SCHOOL REFORM

As the discussion and figure I.10 attest, big transformative ideas were coming from the outside in, bottom up, and top down. Some never gained much traction, while others stuck and took on different levels of significance over time. This played out across four distinct reform eras over a thirty-year period. The opening salvo was the 1988 School Reform Act. It empowered LSCs at every school, composed of six parents, two community members, and two faculty representatives (and in high schools, a student representative). LSCs had authority to hire their principal on a four-year performance contract. And working with their principal, the LSC could determine the school's annual budget and improvement plan. Additionally, teachers were now hired by the principal (rather than assigned by central office) and without regard to seniority and bumping rights. Effectively, Era 1 started with the first round of LSC elections in 1989 and ended six years later.

This first era was marked by both progress and clear problems. While productive developments emerged in many schools, others struggled around how best to use their new resources and authorities. However, no organized system existed to support these struggling schools. And still other schools, where no viable LSC had come to exercise community control, appeared stagnant. Some form of external accountability was needed to identify these places and intervene. In addition, the school board itself remained problematic. New members were appointed to the board following the 1988 law, but they operated much as their predecessors had done. Few believed that the board would ever be able to address the system's long-standing operational issues nor actively engage the new challenges involved in better supporting a decentralized system.

This led to the passage of a second major piece of state legislation, the Amendatory Act of 1995. Its passage marked the beginning of Era 2. While the Amendatory Act preserved much of the original decentralization, it authorized the mayor to appoint a five-member board as well as the system's chief executive officer, who could in turn appoint a chief education officer. (These two new roles replaced the superintendency.) The act also contained provisions that aimed to address the school support and accountability needs mentioned above. Mayor Daley appointed Paul Vallas, then budget director for the city, as the district's first CEO. He and his administration, however, were quickly viewed as intent on weakening the authorities of LSCs—and particularly so when Vallas attempted to regain control over principal appointments. This created conflict between Vallas and the early reformers, who initially had organized around constraining the power of the system center. The introduction of a high-stakes test-based accountability system marked this era. The first efforts at raising standards, the introduction of charter schools, and the opening of new schools more generally also began in Era 2.

Subsequent eras coincided with changes in senior system leadership. Era 3, 2001–2009, was shaped by the team of Arne Duncan as chief executive officer and Barbara Eason-Watkins as chief education officer. They aimed to strengthen educators' skills and knowledge to achieve more-ambitious teaching and learning, and reorient the system toward greater professional normative control. They set out to rebuild the instructional capacities of the central office, which at that point in time were close to nil. Concurrent with this press was a simultaneous effort to expand school choice in Chicago. Renaissance 2010, a proposal of the Civic Committee of the Commercial Club, successfully advanced a plan for the opening of one hundred new schools during this period.

Era 4, 2009–2017, coincided with Duncan's departure. Daley's successor as mayor, Rahm Emanuel, championed progressive fiscal and educational reforms. A rapid turnover in senior district leadership marked this period, including two high-profile incidences of CEO corruption. The system again confronted severe budget shortfalls, a stronger and more adversarial teacher union, a return to strikes, and a highly contentious effort to close underutilized schools in the face of widespread community opposition. Even so, most of the constructive developments that were initiated in Era 3 persisted and continued to deepen in Era 4 despite these less

FIGURE I.11 At a glance: thirty years of Chicago school reform

Era 1: 1988–1995	Era 2: 1995–2001	Era 3: 2001–2009	Era 4: 2009–2017
Decentralization with local community control and downsizing the system center	"Vallas Years": reestablishing system center command-control	"Duncan + Eason-Watkins Years": partnering to develop professional capacity & expand choice	Churn in CEOs: District remains focused on key Era 3 initiatives, amid multiple challenges
Local school councils—primarily parents and community leaders • Authority to hire/fire principal • Teachers now hired at the local school • Substantial discretionary $$$ out to schools	High-stakes accountability for both students and schools • Numerous schools placed on probation with increased central office control • Promotion gates in elementary schools and increased academic courses required in high school	Central office attention to improving instruction • Instructional coaches and area instructional offices as part of literacy and math-science initiatives • District partners on community schools and arts initiatives	Instructional improvement continues • Embrace Common Core • Universal preschool and extended classroom time Area officers become "network chiefs" with accountability and support functions
		High school improvements focus on OnTrack and To&Through to college	High school improvements continue
	School cleanups, repairs, and new construction		
	First new charter schools	Choice expands with Ren2010: 100 new schools (mostly charters) and first school closings	Expanded school closings rolls CPS
	Initial attention to developing principalship as a key improvement	Major human capital initiatives for both teachers and principals	Human capital initiatives deepen • Improvement in teachers' evaluation and feedback
Rapid reduction in central office staff and span of control over schools	Rebuilding central office begins	Central office development continues Professional normative control emerges	A problematic performance management system evolves into a continuous improvement strategy
School board largely dysfunctional	Stable school board under mayoral control	Stability continues	Stability continues
District battles budget shortfalls and chronic labor unrest	Fiscal stability and multiyear contracts • Labor management peace	Fiscal stability and labor management peace continues	Budget and labor-management issues return

favorable conditions. Janice Jackson's appointment as CEO in 2017 marked the end of this era.

Figure I.11 provides an overview of each era's main initiatives—all discussed further in the chapters ahead. These are selective highlights from a much larger list of changes that occurred over this thirty-year period. To be clear, Chicago did not lack for initiatives. Interestingly, except for Chicago's community-control-based decentralization, most of the initiatives identified in figure I.10 occurred in numerous other school districts around the country. As a list of reform activities, they are not exceptionally innovative. However, the depth with which these developments took hold, and especially *how they came to cohere over time* into a broad system transformation, is distinctive to the Chicago story. Explaining how this came to be is central to the account that follows.

THE THEMES THAT RUN THROUGH IT

In the sections above we have sketched out a highly contested political space that framed a vast array of reform efforts in the CPS over three decades. Similar forces were at work in urban school districts across the country. Different groups vied for power, with winners advancing favored policies and programs. In some contexts like Chicago's, fundamental questions surfaced about how to govern public education systems better. Frequent transitions in school leadership typically accompanied this conflict, with each new leader layering on more changes. This highly contested political environment is often blamed for the seeming inability to transform public education in America.[29] These forces all were active in Chicago, yet over time and out of the protean, messy space of democracy in action, major improvements occurred. How and why did Chicago turn out differently?

In our effort to answer this question over the next four chapters, we describe how key changes came to exist initially, how they developed over time and came to cohere in the transformation of a major urban public school system. A set of core themes flow through each of these chapters and are introduced briefly below.

Opening Up the System to Change

The 1980s mobilization for reform and the accompanying press toward decentralization birthed and nurtured a movement that challenged the system's past parochialism with new ideas, new people, and new organizations, who in turn brought energy and hope to a calcified district. It created new pathways for individuals to take up work in the CPS, who would not have done so in the past, and to assume roles that previously would have been out of reach. Likewise, the engagement of many organizations across the city expanded as reform created new opportunities here too. Local and national philanthropy catalyzed much of this and supported these efforts for the long term.

As the system began to open up, institutional barriers that had walled it off before, broke down. Prior to reform, when CPS had belonged to bureaucrats housed at Pershing Road, business leaders largely grumbled among themselves about the system's failure to graduate students who were job ready, and academics mostly talked with each other about their research interests and favored programs. Educators in schools, and the students, parents, and communities they aimed to serve, were disconnected from these elite conversations and often felt disrespected. Yet as a diverse coalition mobilized for reform, social exchanges across divides began to grow, and long-held perspectives suddenly opened to examination. Many of the Chicagoans introduced in the pages ahead functioned as linkers in this newly forming social network. They became conduits for how new ideas to improve the system came to be more broadly understood and endorsed.

Fundamental change also began to grow organically inside the system itself as a new cadre of school-based educators were learning how to work and live in this evolving and gradually transforming environment. These individuals, some of whom would eventually become system leaders, were being formed by a very different set of experiences than those that had conditioned and constrained their predecessors.

The DNA of Decentralization

The starting place for Chicago's reform—a decentralization of the school system anchored in community control—set Chicago on a course that shaped its subsequent improvement journey. This remained the case even as reform evolved and supporting local school councils were no longer the most pressing issue confronting civic leaders. In essence, Chicago's story illustrates a path dependency. As is generally the case, where and how reform begins creates opportunities for change but also typically accepts some constraints in the status quo that remain unchallenged. The opening up of the CPS with its "radical" decentralization, in contrast, created possibilities for genuine challenges to the status quo across Chicago's public education landscape.

Critical in this regard was sustained attention to the *local school as the key context for change.* This shift eventually reframed the mission of the central office from *operating a school system* to *supporting a system of schools.* Decentralization also encouraged an innovation space in individual school communities and in new reform-oriented organizations that were springing up around the city. Many of the earliest improvement efforts began at a small scale in an individual school, a neighborhood, or a small network of schools. Through these efforts, participants learned about the actual work of school improvement and became more expert at addressing its challenges. The reach of these early innovators expanded over time as subsequent district leaders both brought these people into central office and *embraced partnerships* with their organizations as a strategy for scaling the most promising changes. All of this and more, as detailed in the pages ahead, is a manifestation of how the DNA of decentralization continually shaped change efforts that evolved in Chicago.

The Emergence of a New Civic Architecture

Most of the organizing that led to the legislative and regulatory actions noted above was catalyzed not by the school system itself, but rather through the efforts of diverse Chicago civic and community actors. These developments are consistent with a critical realist argument that the normal politics of a school system does not typically advance fundamental reform and that leadership for such change often comes from outside.[30] While this thesis about outside forces as catalytic agents rings true for the early phases of Chicago's reform, in later eras the central office itself was renewing. In tandem with this, a vibrant educational capacity had taken hold in many institutions across the city. Over time a distinctive civic architecture emerged in support of school improvement in Chicago. We adopted the imagery of an *exoskeleton* to characterize this architecture.[31]

In biology an exoskeleton is part of a living organism. As the needs of the organism change, the exoskeleton evolves to offer better protection, defense, support, nourishment, and structure, depending on need. The exoskeleton and the elements within it make up a system: one part cannot thrive without the others. As such, the concept of an exoskeleton offers a powerful metaphor that captures much of what emerged in Chicago. The exoskeleton was deeply embedded in the on-the-ground work of improving the city's schools while it also maintained connections to traditional sources of central power. Over time, the exoskeleton came to encompass the city's foundation and business communities, community-based and advocacy organizations, cultural institutions, colleges of education, and several new organizations that developed along the way. Different organizations in the exoskeleton partnered with the central office on specific improvement tasks. These partnerships in turn helped to sustain attention to high-leverage initiatives through periods when senior district leadership churned. In addition, many of those who enlivened this exoskeleton were pragmatists who adopted a learning-to-improve orientation. By doing so, they established a new institutional logic for district transformation.

An Evolutionary Dynamic

School system improvement typically is framed by multiyear strategic plans advanced by system leaders. Chicago had many such blueprints for reform as each new leadership team believed it was their professional obligation to create one. However, at no place in this story does such a plan become the primary explanation for what subsequently transpired.

In contrast, Chicago's reform history is better understood as following an evolutionary dynamic. As particular problems garnered attention, efforts to respond, often starting small, came forward. Some petered out—dead ends in an evolutionary chain—while others grew in significance, scaled, and emerged as defining elements in the system's overall transformation. These are the ones that organize the account that follows.

Looking back, it is easy now to see key forks in the road: places where Chicago's path dependency could have been breached but was not. In the moment of occurrence, however, many of those forks were not necessarily understood in these terms. Rather, they presented as problems that needed to be addressed and choices that needed to be made. At their best, the actions taken represented plausible next steps, while the exact path to the district's goals remained largely uncharted. The aspirations for improving student outcomes offered directional guidance, but how to constructively move toward improved outcomes meant learning from each current step how best to take the next step.

Social Learning at the Core

As the organizations directly engaged in improving Chicago's schools grew in number, new relationships formed across them, and the density of social interactions increased. It was not, however, merely the volume of those interactions that fueled improvement. Rather, distinctive learning processes characterized them. As individuals proximate to the actual work of improving the city's schools interacted with others, possibilities were created for new collective understandings to form around these shared tasks. Then, as more changes were tried and investigated, understandings deepened about the root causes of school and system failures, and conversations shifted around the actions needed next. In essence, a collective cognition was forming—what learning scientists call *social learning*. We illustrate throughout this book how a broad base of such learning developed in Chicago and functioned as a core driver for the evolution of its reform activity.

Chicago's social learning was grounded initially in the individual learning of early reformers. Prior to Era 1, teachers and principals had to accommodate a pathological command and control system that told them what to do. Given this socialization, few engaged in the mobilization for reform, and many remained passive early on. Some, however, took up the new opportunities afforded by the 1988 reform and embarked on ambitious professional learning-by-doing journeys. Along the way, they met like-minded colleagues in the school system, in the city, and in the neighborhoods where they worked. They learned from one another and contributed to others' learning as well.

A similar phenomenon was occurring within the exoskeleton itself. Individuals within these organizations were doing new things, learning new things, and forming new relationships—with each other, with other organizations, and directly with schools. The relationships and learnings became "the things they carried" as they moved over time into influential roles in central office and in organizations that comprised the exoskeleton. Because many of these individuals crossed institutional boundaries, they helped to break down the traditional silos of thinking and action that had previously constrained these separate organizations. Formally, these individuals operated as *boundary spanners*. Some began as school-community leaders, CPS teachers, and principals who eventually moved up into influential district roles. Some from within the school system brought their learnings into the exoskeleton. Others whose professional work initially located them in the exoskeleton, eventually went to work inside the central office, and a few were appointed to the board of education. Along the way, many learned through their experiences about the true challenges of improving schools in under-resourced neighborhoods. Being in the thick of it, and with responsibility for making things better, was different from the more passive stance of standing off to the side and criticizing the inadequacy of others' efforts. Such experiences forced a reconciliation between two compelling but very different ways of knowing—research- and policy-based theories about how to improve schools, and the lived experiences of students, local educators, parents, and community members actually trying to improve them.

A Supportive Civic Knowledge-Building Infrastructure

As years passed and reform advanced, it did so because a growing base of civic leadership—both individuals and organizations—kept learning from their evolving work about how to get better at advancing educational opportunities for Chicago's children. A key asset in this regard was the development of an innovative knowledge-building infrastructure.

Educational reform conversations in the United States, both now and when this story unfolded, tend to be characterized by a cacophony of ideas and new programmatic initiatives. While each may bring some important insight to bear, collectively they tend to exert a centrifugal force that pulls people in many different directions simultaneously. A district trying to absorb every new idea cannot focus and sustain attention on achieving any one well. A reasonable prediction about this thirty-year period is that it would have resulted in a welter of incoherent actions amounting to very little. But the evidence reported earlier affirms something different. A counterbalancing force had come into play.

The expanded civic space in Chicago gave life to two new innovative institutions that moderated these potential negative effects.[32] These institutions brought research evidence, rigorous analysis, and in-depth descriptive reporting to the table. Their reports deliberately sought to bring diverse voices into what was unfolding in the city's schools. Both organizations were external to the district, and while they sought to maintain a productive relationship with it, they also remained independent throughout.

The research programs and convenings conducted by the Consortium on Chicago School Research (later renamed UChicago Consortium on School Research and referred to in the book simply as the "Consortium") advanced an evolving line of data and argument about what needed to happen at each stage of reform for CPS to keep moving forward. A second new organization, *Catalyst Chicago*, was a monthly newsletter and education journal that told the stories of parents, students, and school educators experiencing reform. It aimed to bring to this audience the best of external ideas and emerging research and analysis. *Catalyst*'s mission to inform reform through the long and arduous process of institutional change carved a new role for what media can do.

In addition, neither *Catalyst* nor the Consortium focused primarily on backward-looking critiques. Instead, both placed primacy on identifying core issues that needed further attention, and they offered perspectives and evidence that added fuel to conversations occurring in diverse forums around the city about those issues. The origin and evolution of the Consortium is the central focus of chapter 2, and the contributions that both organizations made to how a city learned to improve are woven throughout all of the chapters.

OUR PERSPECTIVE AS ACTORS AND AUTHORS

How a City Learned to Improve Its Schools differs from most other chronicles of school district reforms, including those that introduced disruptive policy initiatives. Noted earlier, most efforts at this scale are typically organized around leaders' blueprints for change. In such contexts, the narrator's job is organized by these same blueprints and is typically framed around three questions: What was intended? How was it implemented, including the challenges that arose along the way? What effects were discerned? Excellent examples of this genre include accounts of instructional improvement reforms in San Diego, systems transformation efforts in New York City, and the introduction of a market-based strategy in New Orleans.[33] In fact, parts of each of these other cities' theories of change are embedded in the Chicago story, but none alone, or even taken together, capture it. In contrast, ours is an account spanning some three decades of how a vital civic community in partnership with formal school system and government leaders continued to learn through work on the ground and to develop their subsequent actions in response to that learning. As authors we have attended to what school system leaders were attempting to implement in each era; what central office staff and those in school communities were thinking, learning, and doing; and how an expanding exoskeleton came to catalyze, support, engage, inform, and provide resources for districtwide changes.

Many accounts about Chicago's reform have already been written, and likely more will come. Inquiry into one core question distinguishes this one: How did what was once described as the worst public school system in America become one of the most improving three decades later? The topics that receive major attention in the pages that follow, and those that are relegated to the background, are shaped by this question.

Our writing task resembled the frequently used analogy of describing the elephant: A thirty-year history of school reform in the nation's third-largest school district is a very large, unwieldy beast. Inevitably any one actor on the scene can only see part of it, and the part seen is very compelling. The scope of this enterprise, and the fact that it evolved over time, created a powerful tension for our author group as we tried to understand and tell this story within the confines of a modest length book. We have sought to do justice to the enormous range of actions attempted and actors involved, without sacrificing a coherent explanation of the transformations that occurred.

One way we came to think about our task was to identify the tributaries that flowed into a river of change. This led us to focus on identifying key actors (individuals and organizations), what they tried, what they learned from those trials, and what they carried into subsequent efforts. Consistent with the focus of *How a City Learned to Improve Its Schools*, we especially attended to those who functioned as linkers at given points in time and those who operated as boundary spanners across parts of the exoskeleton and the internal school system. Even so, many more individuals (and organizations) were active in Chicago than our account can introduce, and many more change efforts were attempted as well. The ones emphasized here generally met three criteria: (1) they generated learning that one can track forward into major subsequent actions; (2) there is evidence of specific linkers and boundary spanners who carried this learning outward and ahead; and (3) research evidence, either previously established or more recent, linked these developments to improved student outcomes at some scale. In addition, each had to pass a test of time; that is, the reform had to be in place long enough that its full range of effects were manifest and able to be assessed with some rigor. The latter constraint is especially salient for initiatives begun during the second half of Era 4. They have their champions in Chicago; they do pass a plausibility test that significant effects may emerge, but as our research activities concluded sufficient evidence of impact did not yet exist, and it just remained too early to tell. We trust that others will pursue these analyses in the years ahead.

Finally, each of the six authors was directly involved in this story for many years. As a group, our personal experiences span the full thirty-year period, and each of us has been a boundary spanner in some way. Consequently, our own learning journeys are woven into this account. This allows a depth of insight not otherwise available, but it also posed a challenge. We too see this system's evolution through particular roles and experiences and, more broadly, through the preexisting perspectives that we each brought into the work. Consequently, we had to attend to the potential biases that this can create. In response, we reached out to more than seventy others who also were active for long stretches in the reform effort as we developed this historical account. (See appendix A.) These individuals spanned the institutional domains and multiple sites of power mentioned earlier, and many were linkers and boundary spanners too. We conducted formal interviews with them, they participated in multiple convenings to help us test our initial understandings, several individuals wrote memos for us on specific topics, and many offered critical reactions to an early draft of this manuscript. We took as our challenges the crafting of a story that rings true to them too. We also attended to the extensive collection of research and historical reports from the Consortium, *Catalyst*, Chicago's other media, and numerous studies conducted by other researchers both local to Chicago and national. This combination of collective personal memoir and extensive historical documentation resourced our efforts to discern the evolution of Chicago's reforms and the learnings that were driving them.

Like any historical narrative, *How a City Learned to Improve Its Schools* reflects a point of view, but one that has been richly informed by the voices of many Chicagoans who have been on the ground improving the city's schools for so long. The core themes just introduced developed from this consultative process: We did not begin our research with most of them specifically in mind. In fact, the title for the book emerged in the course of an initial convening in Chicago that brought together over two dozen current and long-standing activists. We have benefited greatly from the insights generated by the many Chicago colleagues involved in this thirty-year improvement journey.

A few words about the writing itself. The text is crafted primarily as a historical narrative. We decided early on to organize it around four major subsystems that integrated in Chicago to form its improvement ecology. Each is a complex story unto itself, and this structure made the evolution in each of these domains more comprehendible than if we had attempted to interweave them in a simple chronological telling. The developments across these domains are tied together, however, through the social-learning infrastructure that evolved in Chicago, and we pause the narrative at times to point this out. We also occasionally interrupt the story to point out how a particular reform episode illustrates some larger lessons about school district improvement. We identify how select principles, tools, and methods of improvement science and networks were operating in the Chicago context, well before their formal specification in education. In fact, it was these firsthand improvement experiences in Chicago that largely laid the ground for what subsequently came forward in *Learning to Improve*.[34]

Chapter 1 details the civic context for reform. It introduces the key actors and institutions at work within Chicago's democratic polity pressing to improve the city's schools. It provides a window into the social conflicts that percolated in the background throughout this thirty-year period, occasionally surfaced, and sometimes took center stage. Chapter 2 takes us into the innovative information infrastructure that developed to broadly inform ongoing efforts across the city to improve schools and transform student outcomes. Central here is how this enterprise became deeply interwoven into the civic fabric of Chicago and operated as a force for coherence and alignment among the multiple, diverse changes simultaneously being attempted. Chapter 3 directs attention to the fact that schooling is a human-resource-intensive enterprise. It takes us into the transformation of what is arguably a school system's most essential resource—the quality of its people—and how efforts unfolded to improve the development, recruitment, ongoing professional learning, evaluation, and retention of educators at every level of the system: teachers, school-based leaders, network, and central office staff. Finally, chapter 4 delves directly into the technical core of improving teaching and learning in the city's 600-plus schools. In fact, this is the most challenging improvement problem of all: changing the quality of instruction every day, in every classroom, for every student. The book closes with an interpretative summary of the larger lessons that might be drawn from Chicago for school system improvement more broadly.

1

The Civic and Community Context for Reform

A CRISIS THAT SIMMERED UNTIL IT BURNED: A MOVEMENT CATALYZES A MOMENT

Parents lined up behind the microphones at each of ten parent community council (PCC) meetings convened across the city. They blamed teachers for the recent strike, for locking them out, and for not teaching their children. Parents booed whenever teachers rose to speak and slammed them for having "a fortress mentality . . . disrespecting us and our kids . . . having sick, incompetent minds . . . just in it for the money . . . and limiting us to selling taffy apples." Regardless of the teachers being Black or white, parents accused them of being "unprofessional . . . insensitive . . . disinterested . . . and ignorant of their children's educational, cultural, and emotional needs."[1] Parents demanded that unfit teachers be fired and had no patience with the union's remedial processes that sapped principals' time and energy and then usually failed on a technicality. Teachers were maligned at every forum, but the discontent was loudest at those convened in Chicago's poorest and most racially segregated communities. Principals and "the bloated bureaucracy" were criticized too but with less ferocity—largely because parents had less contact with principals and the professional bureaucrats housed just south of the stockyards on Pershing Road.[2]

The PCC that sponsored these events sat at the center of Mayor Harold Washington's education summit. Washington had planned a series of ten neighborhood forums for fall 1987, just weeks before his death, to ensure that parent and community members were heard in the clamor for school reform.

Parents' rage stemmed from three sources: their memories of being mistreated when they were CPS students a generation earlier; experiences with their children's current teachers; and a decades-old, smoldering fire. Patterns of discrimination trace back to the 1950s when Superintendent Benjamin Willis, appointed by and colluding with the first Mayor Daley, brought portable trailers onto the playgrounds and parking lots of overcrowded and dilapidated Black schools. Advertised as temporary, "Willis Wagons" lingered for years, even though seats in nearby white schools, some in brand-new buildings, sat empty. Keeping Black students segregated was part of the mayor's strategy to stem "white flight" and entice middle class families to stay in the city. The increased use of redlining and housing covenants restricted where African American families could live.[3] The new Dan Ryan Expressway divided and further isolated Black communities, and the high-rise housing projects that the Chicago Housing Authority was building, mostly on the south and west sides, corralled the poorest among them.

Activists called a school boycott in 1963. Half of CPS's students stayed home. A second boycott in 1964 kept a third home. By 1968 an alliance of Black and Puerto Rican high school students was organizing school walkouts. Boycotters protested underfunded, unequal, and inadequate conditions in their children's schools. Influenced by southern Freedom Schools, a growing Black Nationalist movement, Chicago's Black Panthers and Puerto Rican liberation groups, they demanded greater community control over their schools.[4] By the time local leaders asked Martin Luther King Jr. to come north to lend a hand, attention largely had shifted from inferior schools to inferior housing and pervasive unemployment. Nevertheless, King blasted Chicago's neglect of its school children in a speech he made at Soldier Field.[5]

While inadequate schools hurt the hearts and dimmed the future for children and their families every day, it was two more decades before demands for a system overhaul registered red hot again. There were many precipitating events that evidenced a system in free fall and caused leaders of the city's major institutions to rally around a shared premise: The status quo was unacceptable, and the traditional politics of the city and its school system were incapable of advancing fundamental change.

Local and National Reports Highlight Problems and the Need for Trustworthy Information

Don Moore came to Chicago in 1969 to join the group that was planning Metro High School. Chicago's first "school without walls," Metro was the system's most integrated school as soon as its doors opened. It embraced "small d" democracy as the means to empower students, parents, and community members in the life of the school.[6] Those same ideals were the heartbeat of Designs for Change (Designs), a small research and advocacy nonprofit that Moore started in 1977. It provided basic descriptive analyses on the progress (and mostly lack of progress) of CPS students and offered critical commentary on the limited reporting offered by the CPS. Following a 1979 fiscal crisis, a coalition of nineteen community and civic organizations founded the Chicago Panel on Public School Policy and Finance (the Panel) as another system watchdog. Fred Hess, an expert in school finance, became its executive director.[7] In 1985 both Designs and the Panel issued scathing reports about CPS truancy, dropout and achievement rates, and these followed an earlier Designs study that documented the misclassification of minority students into special education.[8] Another Panel analysis revealed how little CPS had done to integrate schools over the last two decades. Its inaction had resulted in a consent decree signed with the US Department of Justice in 1980 that sought to protect the civil rights of Black and Latino students.[9] Still another report documented that the system was retaining in its core budget "State Chapter 1" funds that were specifically designated for schools serving low-income students. One year this amounted to $42 million.[10] Moreover, this was business as usual—not a one-time misappropriation.

Picked up by Chicago's media, these studies gave veracity to the *Tribune*'s series Worst in America, which began our story. Efforts by Designs and the Panel had cast doubts about the information offered by district leaders, and in the process it exposed a problem endemic to dysfunctional districts: the maintenance of standard operating procedures that were simply indefensible, and the deliberate obfuscation of basic facts about system budgeting and performance.[11]

Sitting in the background to all of this was a major national report published in 1983, *A Nation at Risk*. Its powerful and widely cited rhetoric alarmed civic leaders in Chicago: "The educational foundations of our society are presently being eroded by a rising tide of mediocrity that threatens our very future as a Nation and a people. . . . If an unfriendly foreign power had attempted to impose on America the mediocre educational performance that exists today, we might well have viewed it as an act of war." Its authors noted that the problems of public education could be resolved, but only "if the people of our country, along with those with public responsibility for the matter, care enough and are courageous enough to do what is required."[12]

Strikes Ally Parents and Community Groups

Chicago had endured nine teacher strikes between 1969 and 1987. The nineteen-day strike in 1987 was the longest and most futile. Its duration gave parent groups with acronyms like PURE and CURE time and reason to unite across neighborhoods. With assistance from citywide groups including Designs and the Chicago Urban League, demonstrations brought thousands downtown for days to protest—in front of union headquarters, central office, and city hall. More-established community-based organizations, including Operation PUSH, The Woodlawn Organization (TWO), the Kenwood Oakland Community Organization (KOCO) on the south side, and the Heart of Uptown Coalition on the north side, joined in. The United Neighborhood Organization (UNO), which was a newer alliance of Mexican community groups, participated too.[13] In earlier eras these community groups had focused on civil rights, housing, and employment. In the late 1980s the right of every child to be educated was paramount, and these groups demanded that the strike end. Demonstrations in front of city hall pressured Mayor Washington to get involved.

Chicago's Business Community Reaches Its Limit

By the 1980s Chicago's business community also was disgusted by the district's lack of will and capacity to improve. The Commercial Club of Chicago was established in 1877 to take on "civic, social and economic projects for the city."[14] Fast forward to 1983 when it commissioned a report titled *Make No Little Plans: Jobs for Metropolitan Chicago*, which documented the region's economic decline as one hundred thousand manufacturing jobs moved overseas. The Civic Committee then formed within the Commercial Club, to "bolster core industries . . . pursue new economic opportunities" and develop regional strategies to combat the combined threats of Reaganomics, globalization, and job loss.[15] In 1985 the Financial Research and Advisory Committee (FRAC) was organized, at Mayor Washington's request, to advise regarding the city's chronic budget shortfalls. Shaken by *A Nation at Risk,* many of Chicago's corporate leaders felt a public responsibility to act.[16] Educational reform was identified as a core concern by both FRAC and the larger Civic Committee.[17] The status quo was hurting corporate Chicago's bottom line. CPS graduated less than half of its students, and many of these graduates were neither college nor job ready, even for basic entry-level positions.[18]

Following Mayor Daley's death in 1976, the depths of the school's financial problems came into view. A $500 million budget deficit was uncovered, along with some of the late mayor's questionable compromises with legislators downstate, and sweetheart deals with local businessmen. All of these starved the school system.[19] One corporate leader called it a "system cannibalizing its future to stay alive."[20] When Mayor Daley's successor, Jane Byrne, could not resolve the ensuing district fiscal crisis, the state legislature, the governor, and the business community imposed a solution. It strengthened each of their hands over the operations of a cash-strapped system that seemed incapable of self-improvement.

First, CPS was forced to restructure its debt and cut costs. This gutted about 8,500 positions in central office and the schools, which in turn increased class size, eliminated most enrichments and special programs, and forced central office to move from the Loop, where real estate was expensive, to Pershing Road, where it was cheap.[21]

Next, decision-making was restructured. The Chicago Board of Education was vacated, and the mayor was empowered to replace it. Byrne passed this responsibility to Chicago United—a multiracial group of civic, business, and nonprofit leaders organized after King's assassination—to avoid the racial blowback certain to follow appointments she made.[22]

Finally, the Chicago School Finance Authority (SFA) was created by the state legislature to oversee the CPS budget, approve budget plans and all major contracts, sell bonds, create a chief financial officer role, and appoint the CFO. The governor and the mayor could each make two appointments to this body, and jointly select the chair.[23] Their appointees were all white, corporate leaders. (One was a woman.) This came at a time when the presidents of the Chicago Board of Education and the Chicago Teachers Union (CTU) also were white. In a city where racial tension was ever present, and the majority of students and teachers were African American, this all-white cast smacked of a plantation politics revival.

With the budget under the SFA's control, business leaders tackled problems of daily management. Chicago United encouraged the mayor to replace the interim superintendent, Angeline Caruso, with someone who was business savvy, business friendly, and ideally, African American. Ruth Love, then superintendent in Oakland, California, was appointed in 1980.

Chicago United next conducted a district management audit, published in 1981, that highlighted internal problems, including mismanagement, fiscal malfeasance, patronage, misinformation, and corruption, as well as inadequate and inequitable state funding. Members of Chicago United offered to help Love implement its 253 recommendations.[24] She (and her successor, Manford Byrd) rebuffed the offer and ignored most of them. An evaluation conducted several years later documented that the central office had increased its administrative ranks rather than thin them; decision-making had further centralized; data continued to be sloppy, sometimes misleading and almost always closely held; and, in seeming defiance of the SFA, budgeting processes had become more opaque, not less.

In 1987, when Chicago United published its *Reassessment of the Report of the 1981 Special Task Force on Education*, Love was long gone.[25] By then, corporate leaders had moved beyond the management recommendations of their earlier report and lost hope that some other new district leader could solve the system's massive problems.

Alongside all of this, the business community was undergoing its own internal reckoning. The consequences of the deindustrialization that impacted Chicago and other midwestern Rust Belt cities were highly visible. Thomas Ayers (CEO of Commonwealth Edison), Mike Koldyke (venture capitalist), Don Perkins (CEO of Jewel-Osco), Harrison Steans (financier and philanthropist), Arnold Weber (Northwestern University president), and Warren Bacon (vice president of Inland Steel and head of Chicago United) were among that era's senior leaders who felt that the future of the region, the city, and their own businesses were in jeopardy. Revitalizing the CPS was deemed critical to that future.[26]

Also influencing their conversations were larger changes impacting industry at that time. Drawing on lessons from the Toyota Corporation in Japan, General Motors and other corporations were downsizing and aiming to bring decision-making closer to frontline workers. Internationally, the Cold War was defrosting, and glasnost and perestroika were putting pressure on societies and economies behind the Iron Curtain to engage new ideas and new ways of working. Stonewalled for years by a dysfunctional CPS bureaucracy and its leaders, Chicago's business leaders were warming to the idea of vesting more decision-making with education's frontline workers—principals and teachers.

The CPS Alienates Chicago's First African American Mayor

Mayor Harold Washington first won office in 1983. His victory was enabled by a massive grassroots effort that registered thousands of new African American and Latino voters. As a southsider himself, he had lived in segregated neighborhoods, attended segregated schools, and served in a segregated military unit. He also knew the Daley machine: he worked within it when he entered politics and supported a Daley-backed alderman, and then he opposed it when he later ran against machine-backed candidates for the Illinois house and senate. He also represented Illinois's first congressional district in the US House of Representatives.

Washington planned to focus on economic development and housing in his first term as mayor. He knew that the CPS was problematic and that his core constituents depended on it. However, the political cost of changing the Board of Education or SFA membership was high, and these appointments were his only authorities over the CPS.[27] Labor practices were beyond reach since the CPS negotiated directly with the CTU, and the state legislature determined collective bargaining rights.

Washington's stance changed toward the end of his first term when some downstate legislators threatened to "break" the CPS into smaller districts, "smash" the CTU, introduce vouchers, and justify draconian funding cuts based on students' abysmal academic achievement.[28] (Their logic was that CPS was a "black hole." Students could not learn, CPS teachers could not teach, so why fund CPS?)[29] Washington knew that each of these scenarios would splinter the district, minimize its clout, and hurt African American, Latino, and low-income families. Another concern was the potential to pit African American professionals employed by the CPS, and represented by the CTU, against the low-income families they served.[30] These were difficult waters for the city's first African American mayor to navigate, but by 1986 the discontent was such that Washington had no choice.

Washington convened his first education summit in 1986 to promote a "learn earn" partnership between CPS and the business community. If the CPS would produce more job-ready graduates, then corporate leaders pledged to hire them and secure additional funding for CPS.[31] When Superintendent Byrd demanded $100 million for the district up front and skipped a critical press conference, the partnership and the summit were declared dead.[32] Washington told confidants that Byrd's days were numbered.[33]

A City in Flux: Changing Demographics, Neighborhoods, and Leadership

Chicago has been a "city of big shoulders" since its incorporation in 1833. Waves of white ethnic immigrants came and clustered in enclaves. Each new group was mistreated by preceding ones, but fealty to an alderman or precinct captain could land a job in the CPS or city government and a pathway out of poverty and the neighborhood. A century later, the Great Migration brought African Americans to Chicago in search of a better world. Segregated on arrival on the south and west sides, they still created vibrant communities, including Bronzeville and Grand Boulevard. By the 1980s some were reaping the traditional rewards of patronage too, while others were contained in neighborhoods that were being systematically disinvested.

Latino students and educators were a small group in CPS in the 1980s. Segregated housing forced most Puerto Rican and Central American families into West Town and Humboldt Park, while Pilsen and Little Village became predominantly Mexican American. The Latino student population would grow rapidly over the next twenty years, and its growth signaled the next chapter in Chicago's story of ethnic succession. In the 1980s, however, few outside the Latino community were paying attention.

Garnering greater notice were shifts in the African American teaching force and student population. By 1987 both the CPS workforce and CTU membership had transitioned from majority white to majority African American. Student demographics changed even more as white enrollment declined by 50 percent from 1960 to 1980.[34] Operant here were both race and class differences. White flight was one factor. In addition, the city's neglect of schools and more generally the vitality of neighborhoods on the south and west sides motivated many African American families who could afford to live elsewhere, to leave. When the middle class left, bank branches, grocery stores, and other small businesses shuttered their doors too, pushing neighborhoods like Bronzeville and Grand Boulevard into decline.[35] Bodegas, payday lenders, and a thriving gang culture remained. All of this concentrated poverty among the children left behind. Children who needed more were served by schools and communities that had more to struggle against.

City leadership also changed across the decade as African Americans were appointed or elected to lead the CPS (Ruth Love, 1980), city hall (Harold Washington, 1983), the CTU (Jacqueline Vaughn, 1984), and the

Board of Education (Frank Gardner, 1988). This new leadership assumed responsibility for communities that were battered and a school district that was in ruins. They inherited responsibility for an overwhelming set of problems that had been a century in the making.

BUILDING ON AND BUILDING UP CIVIC CAPACITY: CHICAGO CHOOSES ITS PATH

Institutional racism in Chicago was like an ancient river running through. Its tributaries were long and deep and always creating worse conditions for children. But rising alongside this enduring tragedy, Chicago had built a reservoir of strong democratic activism. This resource was also a century in the making.

Chicago was home to the nation's first settlement house—the Community Renewal Society (1882). Hull House (1889) and Association House (1899) followed. The precursor to local 1 of the American Federation of Teachers (AFT) formed in 1901. Saul Alinsky started organizing in the Back of the Yards neighborhood in the 1930s. Fifty years later his proteges were still active, and a newcomer named Barack Obama was just cutting his teeth. Community-based groups and citywide advocacy organizations were strong. Chicago's activists focused on a range of injustices, but education malfeasance at central office, inequitable funding, and deplorable conditions in local schools almost always made the list. By the late 1980s, while there were new demographic currents stirring the water at its surface, and old injuries and injustices roiling underneath, the city had also fostered a civic capacity that would become part of reform, grow alongside it, and come to nurture, sustain, and defend it as needs changed over time.

The 1987 Education Summit: Outside Forces Deliver a Radical Bill

The settlement of the 1987 teachers' strike failed to alleviate the bitterness and distrust emanating from all sides. Teachers who were disappointed by their contract resigned from the CTU.[36] The press continued to blame the central office and the CTU for having a "stranglehold" on the system.[37]

The gulf between parents and school educators had never seemed wider. This rancor gave rise to renewed threats from downstate legislators and further parent mobilization even though the strike was over.

In response, Mayor Washington revived the education summit with a parent community council (PCC) at its center. Absent legal authority over the district or its labor negotiations, and stymied by Superintendent Byrd, whom he did not trust or respect following the learn-earn episode, Washington planned to use his "moral authority" to open a conversation about the future of public education in the city.[38] This summit would channel frustrations, defend against downstate, and ensure an inclusive decision-making process. Most importantly, Washington tasked the summit with writing a reform bill that he would introduce in the next legislative session.[39]

The PCC included many of the parent and community groups active in the mobilization for reform. Summit appointments also included representatives from the CPS, the CTU, the Chicago Principals Association, clergy, trade unions, the Commercial Club, its Civic Committee, and Chicago United, the archdiocese, citywide research and advocacy groups, foundations, and two university presidents.[40] Notably absent were Chicago's schools of education. Few of their faculty had worked in meaningful or sustained ways with the city's schools, and their deans had not shown interest in being part of the solution that the mayor hoped to forge.[41] To fill in for them, and because the mayor did not trust district leadership to be a source of professional expertise, he brought in Northwest Regional Education Lab (NWREL) as an external partner.[42]

In total, parents and community accounted for 44 percent of the seats on the summit, while professional educators held 19 percent (with the remainder sprinkled among the other groups listed). This composition afforded a strong voice for parents and community members who had been mistreated by CPS for so long. It also made visible a rift between the interests of lower-income parents and community members who wanted better schools for their children and middle-class African American educators who had a stake in the system as it was. In a town where the spoils of ethnic succession historically had been public jobs, followed by clout and contracts, some of the community-based organizations that had championed African Americans' rise in the school system were wary.[43] The potential for a schism had concerned Washington too. When power is viewed as a zero-sum game, a rising grassroots could easily diminish the grass tops.

Washington suffered a fatal heart attack days before the first forum was scheduled. His death cast doubt on the continuation of the summit process and the legislation that was supposed to be its outcome. Members hesitated, and then chose to advance his legacy by staying "in the room." The PCC convened all ten forums. Informed by that testimony, summit members then labored for months to develop a consensus draft bill.

Much has been written about these negotiations, with a few things noteworthy here.[44] One was the stance taken by the CPS. Its leaders confronted a hostile SFA, an unforgiving media, and now a summit that they perceived to be antagonistic as well. Given the years of strikes, budget shortfalls, and failing schools that never got better, central office leaders were powerless to defend against this onslaught of critics. They did not attempt to advance their own reform agenda.

CTU leaders, similarly, were protective of jobs and benefits, but otherwise disengaged. John Kotsakis was the exception. As special assistant to CTU president Vaughn, he tried to inject teachers' professional concerns into the conversation. He was effectively silenced, however, when Moore, from Designs for Change, pushed through a voting process that gave each institutional member one vote, rather than a weighted system based on the size of each organization's membership.[45] Schools of education, another source of professional expertise, remained missing in action. Also missing was NWREL, the West Coast education lab, which had already decamped.[46] Negotiations proceeded with little input from education professionals or academics.

The absence of a professional voice enabled stronger and better-organized advocacy groups to expand their influence and draft bills that promoted their versions of reform.[47] Moore shaped an agenda that would shift power away from leaders like Byrd and other CPS career bureaucrats and the CTU, and move it to parents and community members. Mayor Washington had opened up this path by structuring the summit as he did, and summit members took it from there. In negotiations Moore and other reformers argued that the only way schools would become more responsive to families is if parents and community members had meaningful authority over personnel, pedagogy, curriculum, and discretionary spending through a local school council (LSC) at every school.[48]

Many of Chicago's senior civic leaders, mentioned earlier, were on board with a power realignment, given the district's dismissal of their offers to assist, their experiences restructuring their own companies, and the salience of then trending ideas about downsizing and pushing decision-making out to frontline workers.[49] Their recommendations were not as radical as Moore's calls for local community control, but the two theories of change— one organizational downsizing and a second emanating from democratic localism—were not diametrically opposed. Both came from the outside in and were compatible under a broader umbrella of decentralization.

Of course, not all was copacetic. One influential business leader demanded an oversight group, in case "reform failed." PCC members pushed back against an "overseer" but lost the argument: a strengthened School Finance Authority followed.[50] Some community-based organizations expressed concern that local school control of discretionary spending would undermine the ability of a new group of Black entrepreneurs to win big system contracts.[51] They also championed the cause of Black educators in central office whose authorities were threatened.[52] These appeals resonated with no one, since central office had lost all credibility by that time. Similarly, a rumor that the new bill would strip teachers' seniority rights riled the CTU, but few sympathized.[53] Some African American and Latino parents and community members also resented what they perceived to be a power grab by largely white advocacy groups like Designs. When negotiations were getting stuck, summit leaders asked one of their own, Peter Martinez, to get it back on track.

Martinez represented the Latino Institute in the summit. He was also a southsider who had attended parochial schools and been active in the Catholic Church's Young Christian Workers movement. By the 1980s he was a seasoned Alinsky organizer. Prior to reform he had helped several schools win a dispute with central office over control of principal hiring and discretionary funds. His facilitation strategy, in simplest terms, was to help factions clarify points of consensus, act on them, and resolve the rest later. He credits Hess, director of the Panel, with winning the argument that State Chapter 1 money be disbursed directly to the schools that had generated the funds.[54] He called Moore "reform's MVP" for being clearest about what needed to be in the bill and relentless about pushing it through.[55] Business community support gave the proposed law credibility with lawmakers in Springfield. Still, they insisted that state funding for CPS would not increase (and the Reagan tax cuts ensured that no new federal dollars would flow either). Moreover, the law was written such that it would only impact Chicago schools—another factor that eased the way to voting yes. The legislation passed 98 to 8 in the house, and 56 to 1 in the senate.

Figure 1.1 offers a heuristic summary of the institutional map at play during the pre-reform organizing that culminated in the School Reform

Figure 1.1   The institutional map: organizing pre-reform

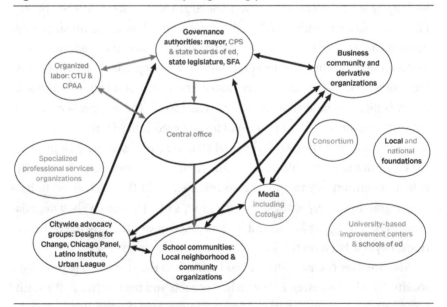

Note: Print gradient indicates intensity of action circa 1987. The lightest gradient (e.g., Consortium, *Catalyst*) indicates the organization did not exist yet. Medium gray indicates that it existed but was not a major player in the reform movement. Gray arrows represent traditional sources of authority. Black ones represent external press to reform the system.

Act of 1988. It highlights Chicago's unusual coalition of neighborhood and community activists joining with business leaders to press for change at the state level, and the catalytic role of local media reporting (discussed below). It also points outs the major institutional actors who largely stayed on the sidelines during this process. This institutional influence network would change dramatically in the years ahead.

The 1988 School Reform Act Realigns Coalitions and Shifts Centers of Power

As noted in our book's introduction, the School Reform Act granted significant authority to an elected local school council at every school comprising six parents, two community members, two teachers, and the principal. (High school LSCs included one student representative.) Principals would be hired by LSCs on four-year performance contracts. Additionally, principals could recruit and hire their own teachers and without regard for seniority rights. State Chapter 1 money now flowed directly to schools as discretionary funding to help them implement their annual school improvement plan (SIP). (The typical elementary school received about $500,000 annually. High schools, with larger enrollments, received two to three times that.) Each LSC was empowered to review and approve the SIP developed by their principal and an advisory faculty committee. This was their avenue to shape the school's mission, pedagogy, and curriculum through the school's use of discretionary funding.

Each of these provisions was considered revolutionary at the time and proved even more so *with* time.[56] The ramifications of these changes are explored in subsequent chapters.

Regarding city politics overall, the reform also had radical potential to realign coalitions and shift political and economic centers of power. Additionally, the right of undocumented parents and community members to vote in LSC elections and hold seats was an unprecedented and disrupting force. This provision followed on the heels of Latino participation in the voting drives that elected Mayor Washington. It enfranchised thousands and spurred a next wave of activism among Chicago's Latinos, whose power and organizing potential was unknown.[57]

Chicago's decentralization also took an innovative and unknown path on issues that prove controversial for districts to resolve—like the one best curriculum, or pedagogy, or approach to bilingual education. These were now redirected to the more intimate space of local school communities to decide. Rather than interest groups imposing their solutions, it was now possible for different paths to be tried in different communities, paths that responded to the pluralism of ideas operating in a metropolitan context. In principle, such decisions might be more easily resolved by people who knew each other and whose sole motivation was improving the education of their own children.[58] Whether this would actually sidestep squabbles among competing interest groups at the neighborhood level was an aspect of reform that would only become clear over time.[59] Moreover, Chicago had empowered local actors to recreate *every* school as a vibrant one.[60] At the time, this was best understood as a stimulus for expanding civic participation, and it was argued that this embrace of democratic localism would lead to more responsive schools. How this governance reform would actually enable instructional improvement, however, was entirely unknown.

Chicago in 1987 was not very different from a lot of urban districts in terms of the obstacles it faced and the resources it had. Warren Chapman was another southsider who, shortly after reform began, became a senior program officer at the Joyce Foundation. He reflected that legislators could have done what they had always done: "Passed legislation that in one form or another would have sounded good (to some), but in fact perpetuated inequities, an imbalance of power and vulnerabilities, and ushered in yet another rendition of Jim Crow." Instead, he mused that "Chicago chose a good path" when the "collective us stepped up for its poor, Black and brown children." If racism was an ancient river running through, Chicago responded by creating LSCs and deputizing their members to turn back its headwaters. Moreover, by trusting parents, community members, principals, and teachers in local schools to do right by their children, reform was premised on hope. It also had integrity, accountability to local parents and communities, and a chance at success.

ERA 1: 1988–1995
THIS IS WHAT DEMOCRACY LOOKS LIKE:
CHICAGO ENACTS GOVERNANCE REFORM

Seating and Training the First LSCs

The first LSC elections energized advocacy groups, community-based organizations, and neighborhood block clubs. Many had been part of the PCC, and they now encouraged and guided parents and community members to nominate themselves or each other, campaign for favorites, and get out the vote.[61] Activism was widespread.

Chicago's media did its part. The *Tribune* and *Sun-Times* sustained coverage; reporting by *Crain's Chicago Business* and the *Chicago Defender* spoke to different audiences but kept school reform on the front pages; and neighborhood periodicals and newsletters told parents and community members how to get involved. Television and radio stations like WBBM, WBEZ, and WVON were boosters, and this was especially true of local Spanish language radio and TV.[62]

Judged on the metrics of civic engagement, Chicago's first LSC election was a resounding success. There were 17,256 candidates, and the majority of parent and community seats were contested; 294,200 individuals voted; and the number of elected officials in the city increased by 5,940.[63] No city in the country came close to Chicago's count of elected officials of color.

Once the LSCs were seated, attention turned to the training they would need to evaluate their principals and retain or contract new ones: half the LSCs would do this in year one, and half in year two. LSCs also were charged to approve the annual school improvement plan (SIP) and budget developed by their principal with input from a teachers' advisory council. While this devolution of authorities to LSCs had been hard fought downstate, some new LSC members questioned their own expertise to weigh in on these matters and were reticent to get involved.[64] In response, groups that had mobilized for the elections now shifted gears and offered LSC training.

Because the School Reform Act allocated only $1,500 per school to support the law's early implementation, Chicago foundations filled the gap between what was available and what was needed for a strong start.[65] While several foundations had refused to fund the CPS in the recent past, they had supported the education summit process and the PCC. Now, quick grants to a multitude of advocacy and community-based organizations enabled much of the activity described above.[66] Across Chicago's philanthropic community, education spending increased by 90 percent in reform's first four years.[67] This group included small foundations, like the Woods Fund and the Polk Bros. Foundation, whose mission to support community empowerment aligned with the civic engagement aspects of reform. Larger support came from the Joyce and MacArthur Foundations and the Chicago Community Trust, even though some of their staff and board members questioned whether governance reform was a path to educational improvement. They still invested as a first step toward the changes that they did promote, and because this was the direction their city had chosen.[68]

Venture Investments in People, Ideas, and Innovation Organizations

Even as LSCs were being established in the first two years of reform, foundations began to expand their investments. They funded "smart, committed people" who were approaching them with thoughtful analyses of main problems that reform needed to solve and with plans for organizations that might help solve them.[69] None of these innovators promised a quick or certain payoff. Nor was it guaranteed that any of the proposed organizations would succeed over time. But each proposal was compelling because it targeted some specific capacity-building need critical to advancing reform. Moreover, the proposed work held potential to bring into the closed-off and dysfunctional school system new people and processes that might shape reform from the outside in. While it was not visible at the outset, these changes were the beginnings of a shift from strictly governance concerns to building an infrastructure for educational improvement.

The spending described above was both highly speculative and innovative.[70] Program officers Bill McKersie and Warren Chapman at Joyce, Peter Martinez, who was now at MacArthur, and John Barcroft at the

Spencer Foundation determined that the moment demanded a new strategy. Supported by their newly appointed presidents—Deborah Leff (Joyce), Adele Simmons (MacArthur), and Patricia Graham (Spencer)—the program officers teamed to get several promising new groups off the ground. In another break with tradition, they invited Chicago's small and family foundations to join them. This leveraged collective contributions and focused spending overall.

Over the first five years of reform, several existing and new organizations were funded by local Chicago foundations. Five from this larger group emerged as major contributors to much of what subsequently transpired. As investments, they proved to be "good bets."[71] Each is briefly introduced below; their methods, initiatives, and impacts are elaborated in subsequent chapters.

Catalyst was the brainchild of Linda Lenz, a veteran *Chicago Sun-Times* education reporter. She saw the need for a monthly publication, initially pitched to LSC members, that combined features of a newsletter and education journal so these newly elected leaders could learn about issues likely to be pertinent in their school communities.

Martinez, at MacArthur, provided start-up funds, and the Community Renewal Society housed it.[72] Lenz organized a diverse editorial board, and *Catalyst* debuted in 1990. In its inaugural issue Lenz committed *Catalyst* to deliver "news and analysis of the innovative ways Chicagoans are attempting to reform their schools" and to report a "variety of voices" so that "several audiences from policy makers to parents" could learn "what was working, what was not, and what was overlooked in classrooms, in neighborhoods across the city and in the circles where decisions are made." Additionally, *Catalyst* would "focus on issues of policy and the broad sweep of things" and be attentive to research and reform beyond Chicago but potentially informative to it.[73]

Over its twenty-five-year run, *Catalyst* was "the voice of Chicago's reform," and its audience expanded far beyond LSCs. An early Diaries series chronicled the experiences of twenty principals, teachers, paraprofessionals, and parents across the first years of reform. It amplified voices that were rarely heard and encouraged social learning across schools. This reporting also enabled decision-makers in other parts of the system to understand problems from the perspectives of school actors and the students and families they served.[74]

Catalyst also routinely reported on research and reform beyond Chicago, and in nonacademic language. In contrast to traditional media, *Catalyst* followed local and national education stories over time so that readers could see beyond the splash of a new effort, better understand the change (or lack of change) initiatives brought about, and see how they worked or partially succeeded or why they failed. *Catalyst* also focused each month's edition on a specific, timely concern such as the importance of principal leadership, teacher quality, different approaches to bilingual education, school closings, and charters and contract schools.

Catalyst generally refrained from investigative series like *Chicago Schools: Worst in America*, which the *Tribune* published, and forays into corruption that the *Sun-Times* exposed (discussed in chapter 2). It also avoided the "one and done" or "gotcha" formats of traditional media. These functions had been key to reform's mobilization and passage, and they would continue to be important as reform was implemented. In contrast, *Catalyst* pioneered what Martinez called "community journalism."[75] The decisions that Lenz and the editorial board made about what to cover and how to report and explain it, evidenced a keen understanding of the information and perspective that Chicagoans needed, at every stage, to move ahead.[76]

The Center for School Improvement (the Center) opened in 1989. Initial support came from Joyce; grants from MacArthur, Spencer, and the Chicago Community Trust (the Trust) followed. In the Trust's 1990 executive committee meeting book, program officers made the case for funding the Center by focusing on its ambition to improve "the way teachers teach and children learn." At that time, most other organizations were attending only to governance matters.[77] Over the first two eras of reform, the Center became an innovation engine for the district. Housed at the

University of Chicago (UChicago), the Center was founded by Anthony Bryk, Sharon Greenberg, and Sara Spurlark. Its work is discussed in chapters 3 and 4.

The Consortium on Chicago School Research.   McKersie, at the Joyce Foundation, also gave the Consortium its first planning grant in 1990, and three decades on, the Consortium continues to inform the improvement of public education in Chicago. The Consortium's origin story, its guiding principles, work processes, and the evolution of its major contributions are elaborated in chapter 2. Evidence of its influence and impact runs through the story overall.

The CTU Quest Center received its first funding from Martinez at the MacArthur Foundation. It too was aimed at bringing new ideas and people in, specifically to open up the teachers' union. John Kotsakis and Deborah Lynch launched Quest as a professional development center internal to the CTU. Kotsakis was the CTU leader who had tried to inject a dose of professional concern into summit negotiations. Lynch had recently returned to CPS following eight years in the education issues department of the AFT, where she had worked directly with Al Shanker and other progressive leaders. Lynch, Kotsakis, and Martinez hoped for Quest to be a transformative force that would broaden the union's mission to function as a "union of professionals" that "gave teachers voice [and was] empowered to shape the changes that need to be made, [to] make our schools, [and] our classrooms better."[78] This ambition was consonant with the national push in the 1980s and 1990s for teachers to have more authority over their work through school-based and shared decision-making. It also resonated with the business ethos of empowering frontline workers. The CTU had been minimally engaged in reform to date, but it was hard to imagine a road forward if progressive educators did not participate.

Through Quest the CTU entered the reform conversation, and because Quest's initial footprint within the union was small, it attracted minimal attention or hostility from the ranks.[79] Kotsakis died suddenly in

1993 just as Quest was finding its legs. That it became a Trojan horse would have delighted him: it snuck professional, progressive ideas into the local that Shanker had labeled the "most regressive, traditional local in the AFT [nationally]."[80] The nucleus that formed around Quest would later grow into the ProActive Chicago Teachers (PACT), led by Lynch. Its role promoting a professionalization agenda would also grow in the coming years, and especially when Lynch became CTU president.

A College of Education Reinvents Itself to Better Serve CPS. The organizations introduced above all got off the ground in 1990. The transformation of the College of Education at the University of Illinois Chicago (UIC) started in Era 2 and came about when its new dean, Vicki Chou, and Martinez engaged an extended conversation about the college's responsibility to serve the public schools and truly prepare urban educators to be successful in some of the city's most challenging contexts. Over the course of a decade, UIC's College of Education emerged as a critical part of the civic architecture that innovated to advance urban teacher and principal preparation and support in Chicago and nationally. Its journey and impacts are taken up in chapter 3.

None of these new organizations would have launched or persisted without Chicago philanthropy. While foundation money represented a minuscule portion of the city's total education spending, it was the lion's share of the discretionary money available to innovate.[81] The organizations described above each responded to a critical part of the infrastructure that needed to be built if CPS was to improve dramatically. *Catalyst* was the "fourth estate" that kept public attention focused on reform as it actually impacted daily life in schools. It also brought research-based insights into the mainstream as these were developing nationally. The Consortium complemented *Catalyst*'s public-informing role as an analytic arm that helped civic and district actors deepen their understanding about the current conditions of education in the city's schools, the progress of current reform initiatives, and the challenges ahead. The Center was an innovation hub that tested and developed ideas about how more ambitious teaching and learning might take hold in neighborhood schools, and how these schools more generally might become high-performing improvement communities. It also provided a strong practice-based grounding for much of the Consortium's early work. Quest raised the professional voice of teachers, contributed to their professional development needs, and brought the union into reform. And UIC's College of Education reinvented itself so that it might reinvent the preparation of Chicago teachers and school leaders. These organizations and the people who animated them all became influential through their direct work, through their social networks, and through the institutional boundaries they crossed as their careers evolved. Over the next three decades, these organizations became major elements in the larger exoskeleton that Chicago was developing to take its public education system from "worst in the nation" to a very different place.

ERA 2: 1995–2001
A UNITARY POLITICS TAKES HOLD:
MAYORAL CONTROL

The Amendatory Act of 1995

Republicans won the governor's seat and both houses of the Illinois state legislature in 1994. Their ascendance was part of a national Republican wave, and their agenda fit with the conservative ideology espoused in Newt Gingrich's 1994 "Contract with America." Chicago's business leaders saw opportunity in these new power arrangements. As discussed earlier, some business leaders had doubted from the outset whether LSCs dominated by parents and community members could actually lead to better outcomes, and at the start of Era 2 overall achievement scores and graduation rates remained low. Moreover, 600 LSCs were a harder group to influence than a mayor who always took their calls. Some wanted to do away with LSCs; others opposed organized labor and wanted to bludgeon the CTU. All agreed that the school board and central office remained dysfunctional. Another point of agreement was a "huge need" for more mayoral control over CPS.[82]

Mike Koldyke, an influential member of the Civic Committee, was among them. Beginning in 1986, he and his wife began developing what essentially evolved into a system for turning around chronically failing schools. In Koldyke's words, these places were a "tragedy for the children and teachers trapped in them . . . and a threat to our democracy."[83] When Koldyke was appointed SFA chair in 1992, its "negative power" to shut things down (rather than build them up) frustrated him. He and many of his peers were hamstrung by a Board of Education dominated by disagreeing factions unable to get anything done.[84] As discussed in chapter 2, they saw shortcomings in the 1988 legislation that had surfaced in the early implementation and needed redress, and they held lingering resentment toward superintendents—perhaps because superintendents had ignored their advice over the last fifteen years. The group split on unions: some were hostile, while Koldyke and others believed that labor was a necessary partner to business, even if the CTU "at that time was not focused on the betterment of the system." Moreover, this group trusted the second Mayor Daley to run the schools. John Ayers reminisced that "guys like my father" (Thomas Ayers, CEO of Commonwealth Edison) viewed Daley as a "modern politician . . . not a bad actor . . . not a patronage guy like his father." At that time there also was a national push to replace superintendents with lawyers, business leaders, and retired military. Ayers said, "Those business guys thought the one on top needed broad powers and accountability for results to run the system well." That would also make the new CEO "just like them."[85]

Koldyke volunteered to convince state senate leader Pate Philip to support an Amendatory Act that would return authority to the mayor. Philip and his Republican majority were mostly indifferent to what happened in Chicago and the CPS, since the city was democratic and the CPS served a population that they did not see as their constituency.[86] Koldyke assured Philip that an Amendatory Act was a chance to enact the Republican agenda by "damaging" organized labor, make the democratic mayor "suffer" under the problems of a dramatically underfunded system, and weaken the city's power structure overall. Philip whipped the votes.

In negotiations leading up to it, CTU bargaining rights were one point of contention. The role and authorities of LSCs were another. Reformers fought to sustain and strengthen LSCs, and they were opposed by those who wanted to reduce their authority or abolish them altogether.[87] Eventually, the 1995 Amendatory Act was layered on top of the 1988 School Reform Act such that some aspects of the old law were amended while others remained intact. Relative to the interests described above, it delivered in ways that would prove consequential and controversial in the future:

- To "damage the CTU," the Amendatory Act put an eighteen-month moratorium on strikes and limited collective bargaining to negotiations over salary and benefits. Class size, teacher evaluation processes, instructional time, seniority bumping rights, and much more were no longer negotiated.[88]
- To minimize budget oversight, the SFA was suspended until 1999. Less oversight meant more flexibility for the CEO.
- State Chapter 1 funds directed to schools were capped at current levels. LSCs retained control, but funds that exceeded the cap in future years would go into the central office budget.
- To increase mayoral control, the current Board of Education was vacated, and the mayor appointed all new members.[89] Additionally, the superintendent role was replaced with two positions—a chief executive officer (CEO) and a chief education officer (CEdO). The mayor appointed the CEO and approved other senior hires. These provisions strengthened the mayor's hand and increased his responsibility for a still failing system.
- LSC training around principal evaluation became mandatory.[90]
- Schools that posted low achievement scores could be put on "probation" and subject to district interventions that included vacating the LSC, replacing the principal, replacing the faculty, and school closure.[91]

In sum, these amendments rendered the district, and even schools within the district, a hybrid between top-down bureaucratic control of probation schools and bottom-up, local control of the rest. CPS was again navigating unchartered waters.

The Mayor Appoints an Unconventional CEO to Rebuild the Bureaucracy

Upon passage of the Amendatory Act, Mayor Daley appointed the city's budget director, Paul Vallas, to become the district's first CEO. Vallas was unconventional by old standards but fit the new executive profile. His public finance acumen and access to city hall proved invaluable in this role. With more fiscal flexibility and authority, and a close relationship with Daley, the two became a stealth team: Daley increased local real estate taxes, and the CPS began deferring payments into the teachers' pension fund. Vallas figured out ways to wrangle additional funding for CPS from extant state and federal programs. The Daley family's ties into the Clinton administration, and Chicago's importance to that administration as a Democratic stronghold, eased the way for additional federal grants. All of this brought much-needed fiscal stability to the system, helped to secure two multiyear contracts with the CTU, and assured a stretch of labor peace (that lasted through 2011 when Daley left city hall). The city's bond rating climbed too. Vallas also negotiated central office's move from the money pit that had become Pershing Road back into smaller, more suitable space in the Loop. (It also brought district leadership closer to city hall).

Vallas opened the capital expense coffers for massive school cleanups, repairs, and new school construction, and some of this occurred in schools serving African American communities that the CPS had neglected for decades. When the Latino community of Little Village lobbied for a new high school to relieve overcrowding, however, Vallas refused and never publicly stated why. His actions triggered community protest, hunger strikes by a mothers' group, and negative press.[92]

Internal to schools, Vallas embraced the higher academic standards of Goals 2000 and increased course requirements for high school graduation. He expanded International Baccalaureate from a pilot in Lincoln Park High (which served a gentrifying northside lakefront community), to fourteen more high schools spread across the city. In the elementary schools, promotion standards were introduced at grades 3, 6, and 8. The end of social promotion, discussed in chapter 2, retained thousands of students in grade, mostly in low performing schools in African American neighborhoods. As this reform played out over time, critics' worst fears proved true. Retention in grade did not help most students, and many retained students subsequently dropped out of school.

Vallas also put 109 low performing schools on probation—about 20 percent of the system.[93] Probation managers were assigned to supervise their principals, and faculty could choose an external partner from an approved list for support.[94] LSCs and their principals no longer determined the choice of curricula and pedagogy. Rather, central office staff quickly developed a "scripted" curriculum that was "fitted" to standardized tests. Teachers were required to use it during the academic year and mandatory summer school. This formulaic curriculum did little to improve student learning.

Families and communities also resisted these interventions because they usurped LSC authority and seemed punitive toward one student group, and few believed that they would be an improvement. A subsequent Consortium report in 2003 validated many of these concerns: "Current [probation] assistance efforts are simply not strong enough to overcome the deep problems in educator and organizational capacity necessary to fundamentally improve instruction."[95] Receiving less attention at the time, Vallas also initiated considerable efforts to turn around the failed bureaucracy that was still central office into a functional one that could reassert effective central control, and not just over low performing schools. Key here were multiple attempts to regain CEO authority over principal appointments.

Defending LSCs and Shifting Attention to Educational Improvement: The Chicago Annenberg Challenge (CAC)

Walter Annenberg announced the $500 million Annenberg Challenge in 1994. It was a matching grant that invited reform-minded districts to propose. Chicago's bid came about when the new presidents of MacArthur, Joyce, and Spencer committed their foundations to meet the match. They invited three reformers to develop Chicago's proposal: Bill Ayers, faculty in UIC's College of Education; Anne Hallett, head of the Wieboldt Foundation; and Warren Chapman at Joyce.[96] All three were champions of Chicago's decentralization reform and its LSCs. When they began drafting Chicago's proposal, the Amendatory Act was still being negotiated. They knew that LSCs were in the line of fire.

Chicago's proposal focused on solving problems of time, size, and isolation—three issues receiving national attention at the time. As Joseph McDonald and colleagues write in their analysis of the CAC,

> In most schools . . . time [was] too rigidly apportioned to support real learning, school size [was] too big for [educators] to know their students well, and isolation [meant there were] too many barriers to cooperation among people within and between schools, and between schools and their communities.[97]

The primary strategy was for schools, mostly elementary schools, to work in networks with a university partner to accelerate research-based improvement efforts. Local organizations that trained and otherwise supported LSCs could also apply for grants. This was timely because the philanthropic funding that had initially supported LSC elections and training had dried up, many of the organizations that supported LSCs were cash-strapped, and LSC participation overall was waning. When Vallas caught wind of their proposal, tensions flared, and Daley told Annenberg to keep the money unless he controlled its use in Chicago.[98] Regardless, the grant went ahead as initially proposed, and Chicago's award stipulated that the funds had to be expended on local schools and would not run through city hall or the central office.

Once funded, Graham (president of Spencer Foundation) was asked by the presidents of Joyce and MacArthur to organize the CAC board. Graham had "heard good things about a new guy who was teaching constitutional law at UChicago" and invited him to dinner. Barack Obama agreed to chair, but only if Graham was vice chair.[99] They hired Ken Rolling as CAC's director. Rolling had been director of the Woods Fund. He also was a youth minister whom Obama had gotten to know through community organizing.

Beyond the match, Chapman said that winning Chicago's grant had depended on a grassroots movement to bring it in, a "forward-looking" proposal, civic commitment, and capacity. The supplemental support it provided for the analytic capability at the Consortium, and media reporting by *Catalyst*, were icing on the cake. CAC pushed over $90 million into local schools and communities over the next six years—an unprecedented investment that has not been matched since. Chapman also credits the CAC with "saving" Chicago's LSCs by fortifying the citywide advocacy and local organizations that bolstered them.[100]

CAC's network structure created opportunities to bring the city's school of education faculty and cultural institutions more actively into reform. Discussed in chapter 3, individual education faculty had been doing discrete projects in the CPS prior to reform. That activity accelerated when the 1988 legislation passed and was transformed by CAC in Era 2.[101] Narrowly conceived projects, typically based in individual faculty members' own research interests, began to give way to sustained schoolwide instructional improvement efforts. Faculty groups from DePaul, Loyola, National Louis, and Roosevelt Universities and the Erikson Institute that had been "outside this story" or on its margins all came in through the CAC.[102] Importantly, they would stay involved, attract others, and grow and adapt their engagement in years to come and after CAC funding disappeared. Their commitment also paved the way for schools of education *as institutions* to engage reform—another topic taken up in chapter 3. Similarly, many of the city's cultural institutions, social service groups, and youth organizations that had been relegated to the periphery returned and partnered with schools again.[103] In short, CAC brought people, energy, a range of expertise, and diverse social networks in from the sidelines.[104] Embedded here was the beginning of an answer to how a governance reform could possibly catalyze a transformation in teaching and learning citywide. The capabilities first developing during Era 2 would prove to be a key resource for leveraging deeper instructional changes in Era 3.

Finally, when the CAC had spent down most of its funds, its board decided to use the last $2 million to start the Chicago Public Education Fund (the Fund). The aim was to continually raise unrestricted money from Chicago's civic leaders, deploy it nimbly to reform initiatives, and quickly evaluate these efforts through management reviews.[105] As Era 3 began, the Fund was another new and innovative organization in the exoskeleton, and it was poised to advance strategic investments in reform. Its contributions are discussed in subsequent chapters.

ERA 3: 2001–2009
IMPROVING DISTRICT SCHOOLS AND
CREATING NEW OPTIONS

In spring 2001 Daley asked Vallas to resign. Continued controversy around his accountability initiatives, his perceived dismissal of the Little Village Mexican community, and attempts to diminish the authorities of LSCs had generated upset and bad press and begun to overshadow the mayor's own public relations efforts.[106] While many business leaders and major media editorial boards initially had been enraptured with Vallas's energy, accessibility, and dynamism—not to mention the perennial hope that he was the charismatic leader who would finally fix the system—the harsh reality of the work eventually wore through. To his credit, Vallas had stabilized system finances and labor-management relations and begun to rebuild a more functional central bureaucracy. He had also raised academic standards for high school graduation. These were important steps, but actually improving the quality of teaching and learning was a different ball game. The Consortium studies funded by CAC, and discussed in chapter 2, brought attention to the need for more ambitious instruction in Chicago classrooms and the key levers toward that end: sustained professional development, school-based professional communities, and principals learning how to enact a new role as facilitative instructional leaders. While little of this had been embraced as yet by central office, seeds of these changes could now be seen in select Chicago schools associated with CAC. At CTU, Lynch was trying to move the union toward complementary professional efforts as well.

Daley seemed to sense that the winds were blowing in a new direction, as evidenced by his appointment of Arne Duncan as CEO. Duncan, in turn, asked Barbara Eason-Watkins to be CEdO. Their challenge was also their strategy: To honor and respect the expertise, values, and authorities of LSCs and the local stakeholders they represented, and simultaneously reconceptualize and reinvent CPS as a learning organization in service to a system of schools. This was a refutation of the old management idea that so far had refused to die: if you get the top of the system right, everything else will just follow.[107] While strong central administration is an important reform resource; meaningful improvement is the "everything else." The calculus in Era 3 was to focus on students, teachers, principals, classrooms, schools, families, and communities and make it the district's and the city's job to learn how better to support them. Some would later refer to this period as Chicago's "golden era."[108]

Another Unconventional CEO

Duncan grew up near UChicago, where his father was a professor. His mother had founded a children's center that served low-income African American children who lived in the neighborhood, although mostly on the "other side" of 47th Street. Duncan volunteered there throughout his childhood and even took a leave from Harvard his junior year to tutor full-time. After college and a stint playing basketball oversees, he was invited into the Ariel Foundation by John Rogers. (Rogers was a childhood friend who managed mutual funds and whose portfolio would later include the teachers' pension fund.) At Ariel, Duncan organized a program modeled after "I Have a Dream." It adopted a sixth-grade class at a local school that served the same children as his mother's center. In 1998 Vallas brought Duncan into central office, where he managed the implementation of a new community service program for high schoolers, an audit of the district's magnet school programming, and the launch of After School Matters. The latter was a favorite of Maggie Daley, the mayor's wife.[109]

When Vallas's departure was announced, *Catalyst* rounded up information about those rumored to replace him. In the blurb about Duncan, Rogers called him a "pied piper." A CPS colleague said he was "great, but a little green." His reported approach to improving schools was to "create new ones."[110] Duncan said he was as surprised as everyone else when he received "the call." At age 36 he was the district's youngest leader, and his lack of education, executive, policy, or political experience made him another unconventional appointment. When asked about his selection, Duncan replied that he "must have been a risk."[111]

The District's First Real Instructional Leader

Prior to becoming CEO, Duncan had never met Eason-Watkins. He recalled that she had "a tremendous reputation as an educator, and there was no plan B if she said no, except maybe to resign and have the shortest tenure ever."

Eason-Watkins had been a first-grade teacher in Detroit and principal of Chicago's Mollison Elementary School in the early 1980s. She then took on McCosh Elementary School, which was one of the south side's chronic low performers. Eight years later it won a citywide award for being "one of the city's most improved in reading and math." How this came about is elaborated in chapter 4.

When Eason-Watkins met Daley for the first time, he asked her "to do for the CPS what she had done for McCosh." She promised her best effort, and later she said that the mayor held her and Duncan accountable while always supporting their agenda. Eason-Watkins took the reins when the national conversation about the principal's role was transitioning—from that of a compliance manager, which was well defined, to that of an instructional leader—a role still under construction. At McCosh, Eason-Watkins gave that role definition. Chapman, the Joyce program officer, had first met Eason-Watkins when she invited him to a Real Men Read event at McCosh. He said it was her focus on building up what her teachers knew and could do and how they worked together that made her "unique" relative to other CPS principals he had worked with.[112] Eason-Watkins was the system's second CEdO, but its first real instructional leader.

Shared Aims, Different Portfolios

Duncan and Eason-Watkins decided at the outset to work as a team with shared aims and separate responsibilities. At a time when the mayor aspired for Chicago to become a "world class city," he also intended for CPS to become the nation's "premier urban district."[113] Duncan pledged to be its "moral leader"—a promise suggesting that he was, indeed, "a little green."[114] When Duncan and Eason-Watkins became the district's leaders, they generated the kind of energy that first flared in Chicago when the 1988 legislation passed—and myriad hopes and dreams were tied to it. This time it was their commitment to improve urban children's options and opportunities that enthused people.

Relative to their portfolios, Duncan served most of the performative and political functions expected of a CEO. He also focused on high school transformation and worked with the mayor and the business community to develop new school options, discussed below. When asked about the many interest groups pressing in on him, Duncan said a main strategy was to "just listen." For example, early in his tenure he met with the Little Village moms spurned by Vallas:

> We had the hunger strikers in Little Village—the moms striking for a high school. I remember going out . . . and really that one honestly moved me; that's a powerful thing to do—a hunger strike. . . . I felt they were right. They needed a high school in that community. Our capital budget was always difficult. We were always making trade-offs; there's never enough money. We did what we could with new schools and renovation and rehab. But one of the first things we did [when I became CEO] was approve that high school. . . . I wouldn't say that was [interest group] pressure. It was people showing real courage and real sacrifice for an issue that . . . made 100 percent sense.

Eason-Watkins's priority, in turn, was improving existing district schools, especially the elementary schools that she knew best. (CPS elementary schools were typically grades K–8.) She also joined with Duncan in the requisite political functions demanded of public leaders—town halls, school galas, Bud Billiken Parades, meetings with disgruntled aldermen at the mayor's request, and attending funerals for students felled by the city's relentless violence. As discussed in chapters 3 and 4, she and Duncan sought to rebuild central office as a learning organization in service to a system of schools. Partnering with individuals and organizations in the exoskeleton would be one of their main strategies to advance this aim.

Contributions of the Civic Exoskeleton

Media.   The *Sun-Times* continued to report on the launch of major district reform efforts. Early in Era 3 they also published two notable investigative exposés on the weak academic credentials of some CPS teachers and the very low college success rates among CPS graduates.[115] Duncan and Eason-Watkins were never implicated in any scandals—a fact that made CPS an outlier among city agencies at the time and gave the newspapers little to report in this regard.

Catalyst covered the start of new reform initiatives too, but it routinely went deeper by delving into the purpose, rationale, process, timetable, progress, and value proposition of each, and it regularly returned to these core topics. It was challenging to write about efforts to build capacity for ambitious instruction because the pedagogy is complex to learn and enact, few in the reading audience had experienced it as students, and so it was difficult to convey what it was or why it mattered. Helpful here was a *Sun-Times* article, published at the end of Era 2, that drew from a Consortium report, *The Quality of Intellectual Work in Chicago Schools*. The article included an example of the traditional math work sheets commonly found in CPS classrooms and an example of student work on a more ambitious math task occurring just down the hallway in the same school. Shortly thereafter *Catalyst* published an article titled "It's About Instruction, Stupid." The point raised in each of these publications was the same: Which would you want for your child?[116] Figure 1.2a and 1.2b afford a comparative example from the Consortium's original report of traditional and more ambitious student assignments.

Philanthropy.   The relationship between local foundations and the school system entered a new phase in Era 3. Some foundations had supported individual schools and organizations working with CPS schools in the past, but much like the CAC, they did not directly fund central office initiatives. In contrast, when Duncan and Eason-Watkins went downtown, program officers became partners helping them conceive, research, design, execute, and partially pay for new work.

From his perch as CEO, Duncan also successfully courted national foundations, including the Bill & Melinda Gates Foundation, the Michael & Susan Dell Foundation, and the Eli and Edythe Broad Foundation. CPS created the Children First Fund to serve as "fiscal sponsor" for these initiatives.[117] Albert Sanchez, its executive director, described how these three "new-economy, tech foundations" thought and worked differently:

> They were not interested in what was going on at the school level with teachers. They thought if you . . . develop a portfolio strategy and implement some metrics from central office, then everything else will fall in place.

In essence, this was the newest version of the mantra: if you get policies right at the top of the system, everything else follows. (Ron Huberman, a future CEO, was a believer too.) While good central policy is an assist, how to make any policy work reliably on the ground in varied classrooms, schools, and community contexts remained the largely unspecified work of improvement.

Duncan also collaborated closely with the Chicago Public Education Fund. Different in function from the national foundations, it became a local ally that supported district strategic planning, enabled key human capital initiatives, and incented national organizations to come to town.[118] At a time when central office capacity was very weak in these areas, the Fund positioned itself as a core professional resource around principal and teacher development. By doing so, it infused the city with new people, ideas,

Figure 1.2a Traditional assignment and student work: grade 3 writing

Assignment: "Use vocabulary words to fill in the blanks of the sentences, page 135. You may use definitions."

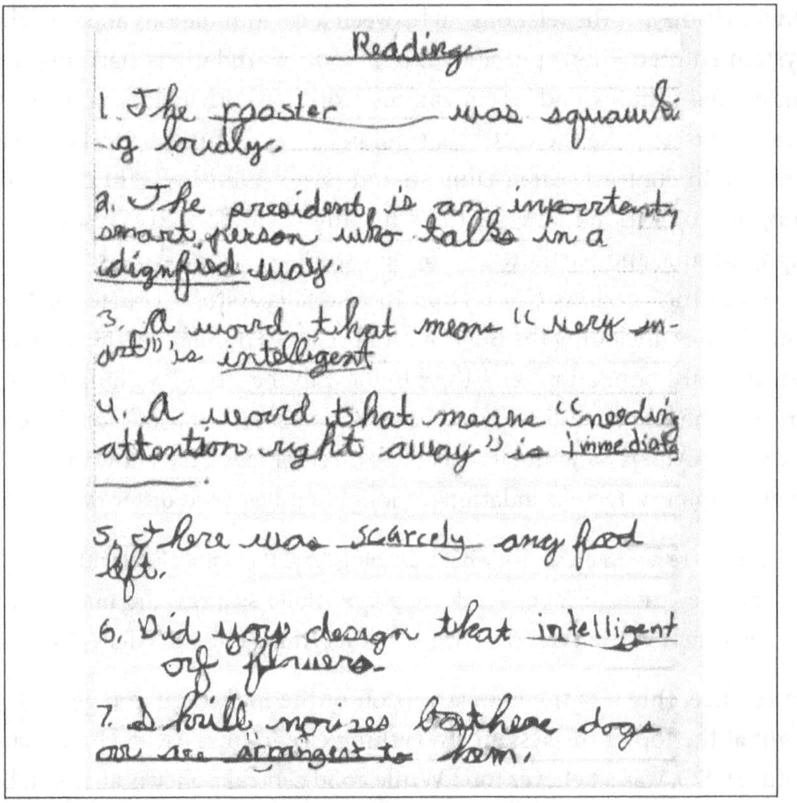
Reading

1. The rooster was squawking loudly.
2. The president is an important, smart person who talks in a dignified way.
3. A word that means "very smart" is intelligent
4. A word that means "needing attention right away" is immediate.
5. There was scarcely any food left.
6. Did you design that intelligent of flowers.
7. Shrill noises bother dogs are so strangest to them.

Source: Newmann, Lopez, and Bryk, *Quality of Intellectual Work in Chicago Schools*, 8.

Note: To complete this assignment correctly, students had to know the meaning of the words, but they did not have to interpret them or compose their own writing. This student made several errors.

leadership, and resources. As discussed in chapter 3, when individual Fund Board members connected with one or more specific CPS improvement initiatives, it also deepened civic leadership capacity.

Eason-Watkins was particularly strategic when it came to local foundations, big and small. She convened periodic meetings with them to share

Figure 1.2b   Ambitious assignment and student work: grade 3 writing

Assignment: Students were told to write four compositions: two persuasive, one expository, and one narrative, according to instructions for each. This example is the expository prompt.

"Your Mom has stated that you may have a pet. However, she wants you to be completely responsible for the pet you select. Your Mom has asked you to write a composition giving step by step details on how you plan on taking care of your particular pet. Write a composition using the following guidelines:

• Choose a pet

• In the beginning of your paper, name the pet you selected. Also, state in your introduction the steps that you will take in caring for your pet. Be sure and explain in detail the steps you will take on caring for your pet in the body paragraphs of your paper.

• Check points to remember:
Remember what you know about paragraphs.
Use correct language.
Check that your sentences have correct punctuation and spelling."

A dog would be a delightful pet to have. In order to take of a dog, a person would have to do the following: first, a person would have to feed a dog. Second, a person would have to bath a dog. Feeding and bathing a dog is very easy.

To begin with, a person would have to feed the dog. You would have to go to the store and buy dog dishes. Then buy some dog food. After that, you would have to put the dogs water in the water dish and use a can openner to open the dog food to put it in the food dish.

Also, a person would have to bath a dog. You get a clean washcloth and a dry off towel. Take off the dog's leash. Then let the water run and pour the dog's shampoo in the water. Then get a mop. After that put the dog in the tub. Scrub the dirt off the dog's back and rinse the shampoo off the dogs back. Finally, you take the dog out the tub and dry the dog's off.

In conclusion, feeding and bathing a dog is easy. First, a person would have to feed the dog. Second, a person would have to feed a dog.

Source: Newmann, Lopez, and Bryk, *Quality of Intellectual Work in Chicago Schools,* 25.

Note: This student organized the composition around feeding and bathing a dog and offered supportive details. Even though there are some mistakes, the writing shows interpretation and synthesis of knowledge, rather than mere reproduction of information.

her vision and plans, and asked funders to work in concert with her and support the external partners that she depended on.[119] These meetings were well attended, and her actions encouraged collaboration and coordination among program officers. This, in turn, assured that efforts were not duplicated or key needs ignored. Additionally, they enabled Chicago's many small and family foundations to find a niche in Eason-Watkins's plans that the big foundations chose not to fill, or to add onto what the bigger ones were doing, or begin work in an area before the district was able to.[120] Examples include an arts collaborative and a campaign to start community schools described in chapter 4.

Because Eason-Watkins could count on steady philanthropic support, she was able to mount long-term initiatives in core subject areas, starting with reading, math, and science and over time expanding to include social studies, middle school initiatives, and bilingual education. She regularly met with program officers and external partners to ensure the work stayed coordinated and did not drift. Like Duncan, she ceded to partners some functions that traditionally had resided in central office.

But focusing on CPS leaders tells only half the story. The evolution that was taking place at the Chicago Community Trust illustrates philanthropy's deepening role. When Don Stewart became its president in 2000, he asked his board for $50 million for education spending in Chicago over five years. He then launched the Trust's new initiative by publishing a compendium of articles by researchers and practitioners that "establish[ed] a baseline for what we know to be true about school reform in urban education." In its foreword Stewart noted that 2001 was a "propitious" time because there was new leadership and so new opportunity in both the CPS (Duncan and Eason-Watkins) and the CTU (Lynch).[121]

Terry Mazany followed Stewart at the Trust. Because he had been an assistant superintendent in Oakland, California, he had a sense of what might help Eason-Watkins. Peggy Mueller and Gudelia Lopez were the Trust's education program officers. Mueller's background was in research and practice. Her Trust portfolio focused on improving instruction in literacy, the social sciences, and art. Lopez had coauthored the Consortium reports on ambitious instruction referenced earlier, and at CPS she had worked in the Office of Postsecondary Education to strengthen CPS's internal analytic capacity around college enrollment planning.[122] Lopez was responsible for the Trust's initiatives in math and science. And because the Trust was one of the first local foundations to recognize the importance of language development, Mueller and Lopez brought this perspective to all of their CPS grants. This was critical to progressing English learners, but all students, and especially young children, stood to benefit if teachers learned to attend to their development in listening and speaking, spot learning lags, and intervene or seek support services. Mueller and Lopez also became knowledgeable about the research in the core subjects so that they could attract strong organizations to work with CPS, research concerns for district leaders that informed strategic planning, and assure that Trust-funded initiatives comported with best practice. And they were deliberate about building relationships with the mid-tier central office staff responsible for advancing this work. In short, they helped shape CPS initiatives and shared responsibility with district leaders and staff for results.[123]

In Era 3, philanthropy was again critical to reform—just as it had been an enabler of the mobilization and early implementation. But now the challenges and the leaders were different. Funders were now partners, strategists, catalyzers, idea generators, experts, investors, and colleagues. Their ties to mid-level central office staff would become especially important in Era 4 when the top of the system would revert to a revolving door.

Labor.   Perhaps most remarkable about Era 3 was that Duncan's and Eason-Watkins's reform efforts got minimal pushback from the CTU, even as they began to dig into core aspects of teachers' work. That absence of rancor, bordering on harmony, reduced distraction and created space and opportunity in both organizations for new ideas and activities to root and grow—and even when school closings, discussed below, were opposed by the union.[124]

This equanimity came about in part because Duncan was easy to reach and Eason-Watkins scheduled monthly, in-person meetings with CTU president Lynch. Their sustained conversation ensured that when problems came up, either could, and often did, just pick up the phone. For example, union delegates were unsettled when the Chicago Reading Initiative (discussed in chapter 4) began taking area instructional officers and reading coaches into classrooms for instructional rounds. Eason-Watkins recalled:

> Teachers did not feel that their work was public, so they complained to their union reps and Deb [Lynch] called me. Sharon [Greenberg, who was leading the rounds for me] and I went to meet with all the district-wide reps. We talked with them for almost two hours. Initially they were hostile, but as we talked and they saw that all we were trying to do was help teachers improve their practice, they were fine with it—as long as we did it respectfully.[125]

Duncan and Eason-Watkins had inherited the labor peace that began in Era 2. Freed from restrictive SFA oversight, Daley and Vallas had used a number of financial "tricks" to buy that peace—a strategy that would not come home to roost until Era 4. A bullish stock market was creating new philanthropic wealth, and up until the 2008 recession, federal dollars were flowing too.[126] The surplus ensured that Duncan had resources to negotiate two multiyear contracts and meet most union demands. He also encouraged a CTU priority to expand the Quest Center's influence and offerings and pushed for the Jacqueline B. Vaughn Graduate School of Education, named after the union's first African American president, to open in 2002. Additionally, and in a departure from the past, the district and CTU jointly supported National Board Certification, and they collaborated on efforts to introduce more rigorous and fair methods for evaluating teacher quality. As discussed in chapters 3 and 4, both efforts focused on a core system priority—improving the quality of teaching. Additionally, both received local foundation support, and this funding was one of the things that emboldened CTU's progressive wing to take on conflicts brewing inside the union.

Lynch's 2001 victory pitted her caucus, PACT, and its professionalization agenda, against the old guard. Lynch blamed herself for being "young, naïve and idealistic" when she left former president Tom Reese and his loyalists in leadership positions. Reflecting back, she blasted them for "trashing her personally and sabotaging her efforts every day, in the schools and within the leadership team" for two years. Their goal, she said, was to ensure that her presidency not exceed one term and that the union itself would never change.[127] Reese managed to defeat Lynch by a thin margin in the next election, but the progressive spirit that PACT had energized did not go away. A new group, the Caucus of Rank and File Educators (CORE), also was forming at that time. Its social justice mission challenged PACT from the left—another ripple of unknown strength in a choppy sea.[128]

Partnerships as Strategy

As evidenced above, Duncan and Eason-Watkins partnered with civic institutions (and national groups) on virtually everything they did. Given the base state of the system they inherited, there was no alternative. Partnering was a tacit acknowledgment that the district could not improve by itself, and Duncan saw strength in this. He said:

> I like your title "How a City Learned to Improve its Schools" [because] one of the biggest lessons [I learned] is that a district can't do it alone. Support from the business community . . . city agencies, the mayor's leadership, the Consortium, all the resources local organizations put in—they all played a really important role. They brought ideas, facts and sometimes tough truths, but important truths came from that. They were unbelievably helpful partners who challenged us. This was not just the Chicago Public Schools trying to improve the Chicago Public Schools.

Looking back, Duncan's and Eason-Watkins's willingness to build authentic partnerships and cede some control to third parties seems prescient. In large part because of the choices they made, Chicago's civic institutions grew smarter and more robust during and beyond their tenure, and that exoskeleton enabled the city to keep learning and the CPS to survive significant setbacks but still improve. Ironically, the mayor had a virtual lock on control of the city and CPS after 1995, yet the most striking advances in reform's thirty-year sweep were made under Duncan and Eason-Watkins:

Figure 1.3 The institutional reform map thirty years later

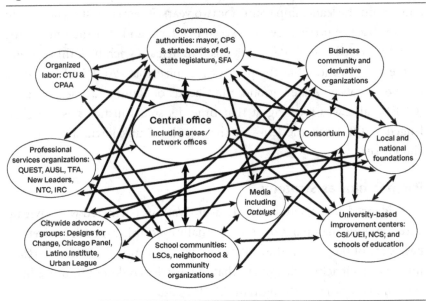

the team that used soft power wisely, resorted to top-down power sparingly, focused most on teaching and learning, and evolved the district to be centrally supportive but not centrally driven.[129]

The efforts by Duncan and Eason-Watkins to engage partners, and their openness to new ways of thinking about how a district might better support its system of schools, transformed the institutional map supporting Chicago school reform. Developments that had emerged in Eras 1 and 2 expanded and deepened such that by the end of Era 3, a very different infrastructure for school improvement existed. Figure 1.3, compared to Figure 1.1, depicts the scope of this transformation. The number of organizations involved had grown considerably, and the density of interactions among them was substantial. This innovative exoskeleton became the structural backbone for how Chicago learned to improve its schools.

In hindsight it is clear that important developments took root early in Era 3. But they were less obvious to Chicagoans at the time, and a couple years into Duncan's tenure, the mayor and many in the business community were growing restless. Student achievement and graduation rates had barely changed; the pace of improvement was slow. The 2001 No Child Left Behind Act mandated that districts intervene in their weakest schools, and policies promoting choice, charter schools, and the closing of underperforming ones were being touted as a quick fix in the national conversation about reform. Duncan knew that the profound district transformation he and Eason-Watkins were after would take time, but he also felt responsible to create "a high-quality seat for every student" as quickly as possible, and he was agnostic about where those seats came from. He continued to support Eason-Watkins's efforts to improve instruction, and his response to the "either/or proposition of opening new charters versus improving district schools" was "do both." In his view, letting market forces in was not a competing theory, nor would it upend internal capacity-building efforts. It was an additional, parallel strategy in a district "that just needed more good seats . . . more good schools."[130]

Market Forces Take Center Stage

The country's first charter school opened in Minnesota in 1991. A decade later a charter movement was growing nationwide. Charters were subject to the same student outcome accountabilities as district schools, but they could bypass certification requirements and ignore many district regulations, and teachers did not have to be unionized. Given these flexibilities, charters were promoted as engines of innovation that could solve the problems of chronically failing district schools. They also were a new and immediate way to offer more choices to families. Championed early on nationally by business groups and some politicians from both sides of the aisle, it was Chicago's business community that brought charters to Chicago.

Arnold Weber, president of Northwestern University, had been chair of the Civic Committee since 1995. His friend, Thomas Ayers, described him, and their generation of civic leaders including Koldyke, Steans, Perkins, and Bacon, as "civic-minded, generalists and humanitarians" who advanced social causes including civil rights and education reform.[131] Neither the 1988 School Reform Act nor the 1995 Amendatory Act would have passed without them. Power shifted when Eden Martin became chair of the Civic

Committee in 1999. He was senior partner at one of Chicago's most liti-
gious law firms, and he too wanted better schools and a functional system.
Martin, however, represented "the next generation [of] bean counters . . .
finance-focused CEOs . . . who mainly cared about the bottom line and was
vehemently opposed to labor."[132] While many might question the altruism
of the business elite, this changing of the guard foretold new challenges and
a shuffling of political coalitions.[133]

Local schools are an anchoring institution in their neighborhoods, and
their fate is inextricably linked to that of their community and its housing. In 2000 the Chicago Housing Authority (CHA) announced its *Plan
for Transformation* of public housing and a companion Mid-South Plan,
which focused on overhauling that area's "project" schools. These were
announced just after Martin took over the Civic Committee and Daley
regained control of Chicago's public housing from the US Department
of Housing and Urban Development (HUD).[134] The *Plan* was a $1.6 billion
effort to implode Chicago's thirty-six high-rise projects, and most of the
city's other subsidized housing as well. These areas were to be revitalized
as racially diverse, mixed-income communities with amenities that might
attract middle-class families back to the city, including new schools integrated by race and family income.[135] To achieve this diversity, one third of
the new units would be sold at market rates, a third under market, and a
third set aside for CHA residents. The plan called for the new housing to
be developed apace with the demolitions so that displaced families could
move right in, and the new schools would open quickly too. Duncan called
it "a once in a lifetime opportunity to link community revitalization
and school development."[136]

Many of the families that lived in the projects, however, were skeptical
about the promised housing transformation, since even in the best of circumstances, there is always a lag between demolition and moving in, and
hundreds were still waiting for apartments following rounds of demolition
in 1996 and 1997 under HUD. Moreover, the one third set aside was not
nearly enough to house the thousands losing their homes. Regardless, dy-
namited buildings started falling down.

The Mid-South Plan for school reform met with a different fate. It proposed closing twenty-two low performing schools in the Bronzeville and Grand Boulevard communities—where some of the first high-rises were imploded—and opening charters or new district schools. Families mistrusted this plan too, since historically the CPS mostly had bypassed them whenever it opened new schools or buildings, choice programs, or selective enrollment sites. Even though Vallas and Duncan recently had bucked this past trend, families still worried that the new schools would cater to a different clientele and if they managed to stay in their neighborhoods, their children would have to transfer elsewhere. Safety was a big concern too if their children had to breach gang boundaries to get to their new school. And there was no assurance that the school their children transferred to would be any better academically than the one they left. A coalition of local parents, teachers, and community groups formed in protest. With support from their alderwoman, the Mid-South Plan was defeated—but only temporarily.[137]

A year later, in 2003, the Civic Committee issued *Left Behind*, which reported on the failure of schools citywide. Fifteen years had transpired since the Worst in America article hit the newsstands, but *Left Behind* read like a cut and paste:[138]

> The school system lacks competitive pressures pushing it to achieve desired results. It responds more to politics and pressures from the school unions than to community or parental demands for quality. Schools, principals and teachers are largely insulated from accountability or responsibility for results. The system is largely decentralized, with limited ability or willingness on the part of the central administration to intervene in failing schools.[139]

This was not a balanced analysis. Rather, it was advocacy for a different approach to governing the operations of the school system. It followed on the heels of Vallas's accountability initiatives and interventions in over one hundred probation schools. He had mandated the curriculum in all of them, vacated some LSCs, and replaced a number of faculties and principals. These were among the most intensive and expansive interventions in

the country at that time. So, the problem was not a lack of authority or re-
luctance to intervene. It was knowing how to actually make a difference.

Martin was first author of *Left Behind*, and its 106 pages overflowed with
statistical analyses, charts, and graphs that were beautiful and easy to understand. However, Paul Zavitkovsky, who had done most of the analytic
work, refused to be listed as an author when he realized that the report
was drawing more negative conclusions than he felt the data warranted.[140]
Cloaked in the morality of defending parents and community members,
and seemingly unaware of the choice options that families had been exercis-
ing since the desegregation efforts of the 1960s, the report demanded one of
the most aggressive charter expansions anywhere in the country:

> What the Chicago system desperately needs to make fundamental im-
> provement is increasingly large doses of parental choice. It needs competi-
> tive alternatives that would give parents the right to vote with their feet. It
> needs more charter schools—publicly-funded but independent, innovative
> schools that operate with greater flexibility and give parents whose children
> attend failing schools an option they do not now have. Chicago should have
> at least 100 charter schools located predominantly in inner-city neighbor-
> hoods that are today served mostly by failing public schools.[141]

Because charters would not be governed by LSCs, parents whose children
attended them would gain the right to "vote with their feet" and leave district schools, but they would lose the ability to vote for their LSC members
and, with it, the democratic right to influence a key community institution—
their neighborhood school. Most charters were governed by charters boards,
whose members were often far removed from the families and communities the new schools would serve.

Additional to leading the Civic Committee, Martin directed its Financial Research and Advisory Committee (FRAC).[142] Following the release
of *Left Behind*, he contracted with its team of business consultants to turn
this policy proposal into an operational plan. Ten months later, in 2004,
Daley announced Renaissance 2010 (Ren10) at a Commercial Club event.[143]
Duncan stood beside him.

Ren10 was charged with creating one hundred new, high-quality schools in five years—an unprecedented launch. A board of trustees would provide oversight. Millions of dollars were raised quickly primarily from Chicago's business community, and a new organization, the Renaissance School Fund, was set up to manage it and continue fundraising. Ren10's fast start was enabled by a new and powerful alliance of the business community, the CEO, and mayor. Business leaders and the mayor had allied to pass the 1995 legislation, but back then there was more respect for the grassroots, and caution taken. Maintaining LSCs and most of their authorities, for example, had been a compromise pressed on Vallas and Daley by LSC advocates and members, with support from several of the senior business leaders mentioned above.[144] Those who promoted charters, in contrast, said little about LSCs and the role of parents and community members in new schools, even as they insisted that Ren10 was organized to serve the best interests of African American families on the south and west sides where most of the new schools would open. And in contrast to the long slog that was district renewal, Ren10 offered a promise—although one that lacked any empirical evidence and would prove largely specious over time—that charters would enable the city to finally address chronic, widespread failure in an innovative, ambitious, and immediate way.[145]

The Illinois state legislature had authorized fifteen Chicago charters in 1996. In 2003 the cap climbed to thirty, but this was far short of Ren10's ambition to open one hundred new schools. One work-around was to approve charters with the same name and administrative unit number but operating on multiple campuses. Another was to open Chicago's doors to performance, contract and alternative schools, military academies, and turnarounds. School operators sprang up locally, and some arrived from out of town. New schools began to open. All they needed were students.

Recruitment efforts pitched to students included radio ads, posters on city buses, and social media. Families were invited to citywide open houses, and regional CPS offices and community venues held school fairs.[146] There was no shortage of bravado. What was in limited supply were school operators whose knowledge extended beyond the belief that new schools, just by virtue of being new, would somehow solve the problems of the old ones. Few of them had managed successful schools before and especially ones intended to serve the mixed-income communities on the horizon or what Eason-Watkins called the "fragile" communities still hanging on. Referencing these fragile places, in a speech titled "Race in the Chicago School System," Charles Payne described the arrogance of those who enter a context with "one right way" and then fail to see the complications of the place, the complexities of the work, and the experience and thinking of those who would be most impacted by it.[147]

At base here is a powerful point about ideas that seem so compelling it becomes easy to believe that somehow their power will overcome not only the practical and ethical realities noted by Eason-Watkins and Payne, but also all that needs to be learned in response to these realities in order to execute them well, reliably, and over time. Unsurprising then are the results summarized in this book's introduction about charter schools. Some new, good schools opened. Families had more choices, and some benefited as a result. But overall the fate of these new charter schools more closely resembled the general improvement found systemwide rather than the renaissance they had promised. Their contribution was modest.

Buried in the small print when Ren10 was announced was that opening one hundred new schools would necessitate closing sixty to seventy existing schools. These would be chronic low performers that had proven impervious to interventions even reaching back before the 1988 reform.[148] Likewise, they had not improved under local community control in Era 1 or under the accountability and standards-raising efforts of Era 2. Moreover, the list of schools slated to close included many of the twenty-two in Bronzeville and Grand Boulevard that had been targeted by the Mid-South Plan. There was a logic and equity argument to closing such troubled places, but Ren10's champions had neglected to consider, or ask parents, teachers, and community members, whether they thought closing neighborhood schools en masse, while simultaneously opening so many new ones, was a good way forward, much less the only way.

A critical backdrop to all of this were shifts in CPS's enrollment. African American student enrollment had been declining gradually for years, as middle-class Black families moved out of the city and the African American birth rate overall declined. The demolition of public housing accelerated the enrollment decline as African American families were forced to leave their homes and the schools that served those communities emptied out. Some of these school buildings were beyond repair, but many, if closed and vacated, could be renovated and house charters. So just when Ren10 needed buildings to meet its commitment to open one hundred new schools, underutilization—which CPS defined at that time as below 50 percent enrollment—became another criterion for closing schools.[149] Yet another justification for Ren10 was the belief that low-income students would benefit from going to school and living in neighborhoods with higher-income peers.[150] Ren10's champions believed that they were serving a social justice mission and advancing much-needed economic development as well.

Still another background issue complicating Ren10 was that while African American enrollment was declining, Latino enrollment had been skyrocketing. In fact, the rising numbers of Latino students masked some of the decline in CPS enrollment overall. Latino neighborhoods desperately needed new schools—as witnessed by the protests that dogged Vallas when he chose not to build a high school in Little Village. However, few Ren10 schools were slated to open in Latino neighborhoods, because there were no buildings for them to go into. So instead of creating new seats in the neighborhoods that most needed them, Ren10 planned to open charters in the underutilized or vacated buildings in neighborhoods where few children remained. From a funding perspective this dearth of students would make operating the new schools even more challenging.

Between 2001 and 2006 some thirty-six schools were identified for transition primarily because of chronically poor academic performance.[151] Sixteen were closed outright, and twenty-two became home to one or more new schools. Families, teachers, and community members organized protests in many of them. Faculty members who were part of the CTU's CORE caucus often led these fights.[152] Their main concern was the threat to teachers who might be displaced or lose their jobs altogether if schools closed. It was mostly veteran African American teachers on the city's south and west sides who were in the line of fire.

As protests traveled from school to school, with a growing contingent of angry stakeholders attending each one, Duncan moved to calm the waters.[153] Throughout, Eason-Watkins had stayed focused on her efforts to improve the district's neighborhood schools. Now she pitched in to help Duncan right the ship. Eason-Watkins said:

> Personally, that was tough for me. My mother was a teacher. Growing up most of my teachers lived in our neighborhood; we were all familiar with our teachers. . . . My mother also came from a historically black college back in the day when African Americans didn't have an opportunity to get into more elite universities. That was their only mechanism for going into teaching. And many of them—we had two groups [in CPS]: We had some that we couldn't work with to improve. . . . We had others that had good relationships with the kids. They really wanted to do more, and they would participate in things. And that was one of the reasons why I really pushed to do a lot of professional development, and why my office had a few turnaround schools where we kept some of the teachers; we built the capacity of others. We didn't do it through a third party; I ran it out of my office. Part of that was my personal commitment to try to keep some of the neighborhood, African American teachers in the system, because for some of them it was systemic racism from back in the day that led to this, rather than them just not being quality teachers. I knew from a firsthand perspective.

The turnaround effort that Eason-Watkins managed from her office kept several schools from closing and kept some of the faculty in place.[154] Koldyke's Academy for Urban School Leadership (AUSL), which had also begun managing turnarounds, took on more schools and kept them open for their students too, but usually the principal and the faculty were replaced.[155] CTU's CORE leaders opposed every turnaround regardless of who orchestrated it.

To tamp down protest, Duncan and Eason-Watkins scheduled town halls in schools on the closing list. In these meetings, Duncan said, he and Eason-Watkins heard "hard truths" from parents and teachers about how racist and disrespectful CPS was. Duncan also shared with them "hard truths" about how their children were falling further behind academically every year.

By the end of Era 3, twenty-eight schools had been closed outright. All were underutilized and low performing.[156] This was not an immediate mass closing, but one that played out over eight years. In the same time period, ninety-eight new schools opened.[157] These were a combination of charters contracted to external groups, and new specialty schools and performance schools operated by CPS. Regardless of who managed the new schools, children's lives were disrupted, and the fabric of each neighborhood weakened because there was always a lag of a year or more between closing the old school and opening the new one. In the interim, students had to travel somewhere else. And even if their old school reopened, or a new one came into its building, it might have a different grade configuration than the old one, or have admissions criteria, or require an application. Each of these scenarios made it less likely, and in some cases impossible, for students to return.

The strategies that Duncan and Eason-Watkins deployed sought to minimize the number of outright closings, and their respectful, personal involvement was appreciated. Nevertheless, their efforts were insufficient to address the triple threat of Ren10's rush to open new schools, the CHA's decimation of public housing, and a shrinking school-age population that resulted in underutilized buildings. Adding onto that was the dearth of school operators who knew how to design and operate schools serving either the fragile communities reform had so far left behind, or the mixed-income ones that the *Plan for Transformation* and Ren10 intended. By pulling back on the number of school closings originally called for in Ren10, Duncan and Daley dodged some bullets. Kicked down the road and into the future, however, was an increasing number of underutilized schools. This would come to a head early in Era 4 as the aftermath of the 2008 recession instigated the next budget crisis.

Moreover, the initial promise of Ren10 had failed to materialize. The main rationale offered to the public for the Era 3 closings was to give students trapped in academically weak schools a pathway to stronger new ones. A 2009 Consortium report that analyzed this first wave of closings found that there was little academic gain for the vast majority of students whose schools closed. As discussed in chapter 2, most just moved from one low performing school to another one.[158]

ERA 4: 2009–2017
CONTINUING SYSTEM IMPROVEMENT IN A
TIME OF TURMOIL[159]

Leadership Corruption, Scandal, and Churn

In 2009 Duncan left CPS to become Obama's secretary of education. Eighteen months later Eason-Watkins left too. In her view, Daley's new CEO, Ron Huberman, was uninterested in the work she cared most about, which was building up what adults knew and could do together so that students' opportunities would grow.

Huberman, like Vallas and Duncan, had no education background. He had headed the Chicago Transit Authority and the Chicago Office of Emergency Management and Communications. Early on, Huberman introduced to CPS a performance management system modeled on a data-based crime-fighting method created by the New York City Police Department. Principals and central office staff subjected to its reviews described them as "shock and awe ... humiliating ... fearful ... traumatic."[160] Charles Payne, who would later become interim CEdO, called Huberman "a glorified bus driver ... a disaster. He used a set of really narrow quantifiable indicators to measure and then punish or reward. He cared about excellence, [which was good], and he cared about data [also good], but he was an absolute disaster."[161] Jesse Sharkey, who had just been elected CTU vice president, referred to Huberman as "the actual police."[162] A case study written a decade after Huberman left described educators still suffering aftershocks—a sort of CEO-induced PTSD.[163] Huberman resigned two months after Daley announced that he would not run for a seventh term. He had been CEO less than a year.

Daley appointed Terry Mazany interim CEO so that the next mayor could choose his own leader. Mazany, then president of the Chicago

Community Trust, asked Charles Payne to be CEdO. At that time Payne was a sociology professor at UChicago's school of social work, but his roots trace back to stints with the Comer and Algebra Projects, and work with westside high school youth. Even though this team did not expect to be in charge long, they engaged over one hundred educators, community activists, civic leaders, academics, and parents in a strategic planning process. Their plan attended to the development of "the whole child' (and her teachers) and so was a corrective to Huberman's performance management doctrine and its narrow measures. Payne said that their strategic plan, *Elevating Our Vision*, "had the priorities right in terms of how the system could move forward." He and Mazany hoped that the next CEO might be guided by it. But John-Claude Brizard, appointed CEO by Chicago's new mayor Rahm Emanuel, had other ideas.

Brizard had been superintendent in Rochester, New York. Its AFT local, which was among the most progressive in the country, gave him a vote of no confidence when he introduced charter schools, merit pay, and performance standards. The CTU opposed his appointment before his plane touched down.

Emanuel was elected mayor in 2011 after serving as Obama's chief of staff. Prior to that he had been in Congress and the Clinton administration. Once in office Emanuel learned that the second Mayor Daley, like his father before him, had been making clandestine financial deals throughout his tenure that put the city, the teachers' pension fund, and the CPS in dire financial straits. Moreover, the 2008 recession tumbled the economy, and much of the federal largesse that Vallas and Duncan enjoyed, through programs like 21st Century grants, were time-bound infusions that had run out. The state funding that the CPS received was comparable to other Illinois districts, but Illinois hovered near Mississippi in terms of least education funding of the fifty states. Consequently, Brizard had little to offer when he entered contract negotiations with CTU president Karen Lewis. (Her 2010 win capped a decade of internal organizing by CORE against both the moderate and regressive factions of the CTU.) By 2012 the CTU had a long list of grievances that had been building since the advent of reform. It included the union's loss of bargaining rights, the loss of seniority and bumping rights that would have protected veteran teachers if their schools closed, and the ascendance of nonunion schools. Changes to teacher evaluation made in Era 3 were also on the list, even though, as discussed in chapter 3, the union and the district had collaborated in developing this reform.[164]

The Amendatory Act in 1995 had limited the CTU's bargaining rights to salary and benefits. Regardless, the union issued several ultimatums under a threat to strike. These included a moratorium on more charters and turn-arounds, and a rollback of principal authorities, particularly those related to teacher hiring and evaluation. The CTU also rejected an effort by Brizard, with strong support from Emanuel, for a longer school day. Emanuel considered this particular fight some of the "unfinished business" of Era 3: Duncan had tried and failed to increase instructional time in both con-tracts he negotiated.[165] Now Emanuel framed it as an equity issue, and a wealth of recent research backed him up.[166] Relative to comparable urban districts, Chicago students were being shorted about three years of instruc-tional time across grades K–12, which greatly curtailed their opportunities to learn.[167] A parent survey conducted in Era 4 documented overwhelm-ing family support for a longer school day. When the CPS remained stead-fast on this issue, the CTU called a strike—its first in twenty-five years.

Emanuel entered directly into these negotiations. The contract that was ratified twelve days later included job protections and transfer supports for teachers if their schools closed. CTU was forced to accept a longer school day with commensurate pay.[168] Similarly, changes to teacher evaluation were now reformed within the contract—a more formal agreement than had been effected in Era 3. The CPS refused to discuss anything related to principals, since by then the Consortium had published numerous reports documenting that they were key to local improvement, and that fact was well accepted across the city. Everyone but Brizard came out a winner. He was gone before the ink on the contract dried.

Barbara Byrd-Bennett had been CEdO under Brizard. When Emanuel promoted her to CEO, she was highly regarded in Chicago and nationally as an instructional leader and thought to be politically savvy and strategic too. In 2015 Byrd-Bennett pled guilty to twenty-three counts of bribery and conspiracy in a kickback scheme to defraud CPS. She was sentenced to 4.5 years in federal prison.

Emanuel next asked Jesse Ruiz to be interim CEO. Ruiz was an accomplished lawyer who had devoted countless pro bono hours to education concerns in Illinois and Chicago, and he was vice-chair of the school board. As interim he was tasked with handling a $600 million budget shortfall. Once that was resolved, Emanuel appointed Forrest Claypool. Claypool had served as superintendent of the Chicago Parks Department, a Cook County commissioner, head of the Chicago Transit Authority, and Emanuel's chief of staff. Emanuel was counting on his steady hand to stabilize the system. Two years later Claypool resigned when the CPS inspector general accused him of covering up an ethics investigation in the general counsel's office.

In sum, CPS tore through seven CEOs in the six years after Duncan left. That the system continued to improve during Era 4 given the recession, the local budget crisis, and this level of corruption and CEO churn is remarkable; we return to that story shortly. But first there was Emanuel's decision, supported by the business community and informed by a school closing commission, to double down on school closures. It was a decision that reignited all that had engulfed and cleaved the city in Era 3. But this time, the rationale to close schools was different, the number of schools slated to close was larger, and so was the response.

Doubling Down: School Closings, Round Two

Still Left Behind (the sequel to *Left Behind*) was published by the Civic Committee in June 2009. It arrived a few months after Duncan's departure and a few weeks after the Illinois legislature raised the charter school cap from thirty to seventy and authorized thirty-five additional contract schools.[169] Daley was still mayor and Martin was still president of the Civic Committee. In the follow-up report no authors were listed, there were fewer pages, data was again cherry-picked so that the conclusions pointed in only one direction, and the message continued to be stated as a moral rendering: "We end where we began," the report concluded. "Until all of Chicago's families have school choices that include innovative charter or contract schools, equal opportunities for them will be only a slogan." *Still Left Behind* noted that over $70 million had been raised from the business community to support new schools.

Four schools were closed in 2012. In 2013, and following the teachers' strike, Emanuel announced that 120 more had to close. This number came from a school closing commission that had been formed, and it took into account the financial stress of CPS operating what by then was a vast number of severely underutilized schools.[170] By 2013 Chicago simply had too many schools, too few students in proximity to those schools, and too little revenue to keep them all afloat. Emanuel inherited all the problems that Daley and Duncan had kicked down the road.

In his memoir Emanuel devotes a paragraph to the closings. Reflecting back, and similar to the argument Martin had made in Era 3, Emanuel wrote that he was doing what was best for children and it was time to "finish the business" started a few years before.[171] In the moment, however, and in many of their public comments, he and CEO Byrd-Bennett justified the proposed closings in financial terms: "Children in certain parts of our city," Byrd-Bennett said, "are trapped in underutilized schools. These underutilized schools are also under-resourced . . . we can no longer embrace the status quo."[172] In contrast to Era 3 when more new schools opened than closed, the goal in Era 4 was just to close a lot of them.

The CTU, now dominated by CORE, helped an outraged public organize. Chicago parents and the union had been enemies in the run-up to reform in 1987. Now, the alliance between them that began to form in Era 3 with the first wave of closings grew that much stronger in Era 4.

Hoping again to tamp down the growing outcry, CPS organized community forums and school meetings to justify the planned closings. But Duncan and Eason-Watkins were no longer at the helm. Eve Ewing was a teacher in one of the Bronzeville schools first targeted to close in the Mid-South Plan, and she is now a professor at UChicago. In her book *Ghosts in the Schoolyard: Racism and School Closings on Chicago's South Side*, she takes aim at the scripted remarks offered by district representatives who led those meetings. They often were unknown to the communities they walked into and not even high in the CPS hierarchy. These individuals detailed an "alien . . . enrollment efficiency range" and other formulas used to determine underutilization and closings—formulas that were nonsensical on their face and that did not land well with families who were worried about their children's safety, their educational opportunities, and their futures.[173] The representatives also restricted questions and comments to the end of these meetings and then cut off microphones and ended the meetings if they did not like what they heard.

Following months of protest that was covered by the press, the school closing commission dropped the number of schools on the closing list from 120 to 49. It also recommended which ones to close. The schools that students would transfer to—called "welcoming schools"—were identified too. Board of Education members conducted their own "deep analysis" after that.[174] Several were CPS graduates and as a group had strong legal, academic, and financial backgrounds relevant to being decision-makers for the district. In this regard the Era 4 board differed from earlier boards. The second Mayor Daley had made appointments based largely on racial and community representation. Mayors before him, including his father, had sustained a patronage system. Emanuel, in contrast, had aimed for a more sophisticated professional board, and one that could actually do due diligence in a situation like this one.[175] That due diligence included visits to each of the forty-nine school communities by one or more board members. They also visited the welcoming schools and traveled the routes that would take students from their neighborhoods to the welcoming ones. The board then decided to close only elementary schools and only ones that were "dismal and largely vacant." They lobbied for unprecedented investments by multiple city agencies to strengthen the security of the welcoming schools, their neighborhoods, and the passage routes, and they requested and received a waiver from state law so that there might be more time for community input.[176]

Board members describe the personal toll this took as "immense."[177] Most of these activities were never shared with the public or the press, however, which left Chicagoans to surmise that a disengaged and distant bureaucracy had ruled without regard for the families and communities who depended on those schools. In May 2013, and over the protests of a "raucous" audience, the board voted to close all forty-nine a few weeks later when the academic year ended.[178]

In protest, thousands marched in the streets for three days straight, with the CTU in the lead. A closing of this magnitude had never happened anywhere before. The *Tribune* and the *Sun-Times* portrayed this largely as a brawl between two outsized personalities—CTU President Lewis and Mayor Emanuel. This characterization ill served a city whose real battle was figuring how to educate its children and resolve the problems created a decade before by the CHA's involvement and Ren10. *Catalyst* reporters tried to help the public understand the complexity of the issues involved and give voice to multiple perspectives. Its journalists also investigated and reported that the closures would make only a small dent in the district's massive budget problems.[179]

The Consortium eventually published two reports about the Era 4 closings. Discussed in chapter 2, their analyses showed that it was mostly low-income African American students and veteran African American teachers who were displaced; the displaced students suffered as relationships with teachers and friends were disrupted; families continued to express overwhelming concern about their children's safety when they had to leave their neighborhoods; and there was negligible achievement gain for the vast majority of students who traded one weak school for another one. Moreover, parents had difficulty building ties to their children's new schools, or even showing up for conferences and events, because many lived far away and lacked transportation. And communities that already were disinvested lost an anchoring institution.[180] The magnitude of this second wave of closings compounded the trauma of the first and piled on more. Ewing called it a "grieving process."[181]

Emanuel was blamed for this episode of Chicago's grief, which is likely one of the reasons Lewis started calling him the nation's "murder mayor."[182] She gave a speech at the City Club of Chicago shortly after her second election as CTU president and just after the closures. She welcomed the new alliance of parents and teachers. She then ridiculed the hubris and misguided thinking of those who believed that you could simply move the students, or swap educators, or close and open anew in a setting that had been neglected for decades and all would be well. Like Ewing, she situated the closures in the much bigger and more formidable context of the systemic racism and economic forces, attendant policies, and unholy alliances that had disadvantaged Chicago's low-income children of color, their families, and their public school system over generations and at every turn. Lewis wondered aloud why Chicago stayed faithful to the Cubs—why fans kept loving the players, coming to the ballpark and cheering them on, why owners kept investing in the team, and why the city never threatened to dismantle the roster or sell off Wrigley Field to a start-up—even though, in 2013, it had been 105 years since the Cubs had won a World Series. Lewis concluded by suggesting that even if Chicago had chosen a wrong path, there was always a way back to a better path, "a way back in."[183]

Sustained improvement is an unexpected outcome when there is leadership churn, corruption, scandal, trauma, and a fresh layer of policy that shocks the system and redraws political battle lines. But the story ahead documents that Chicago's public education system did stay the course in Era 4, and it did so despite continuing monetary shortfalls, shifting state politics and local alliances, a dramatic change in CTU leadership, and a revolving door of system leaders. The 2012 strike and the 2013 school closings dominated headlines, but behind the scenes, foundations and organizations in the exoskeleton continued to work with mid-level central office staff and school-based leaders. Board members were maligned when they voted to shutter forty-nine schools, and the repercussions of those events continued to reverberate, but they too stayed focused on district improvement. In short, the story ahead tells how Chicago's "collective us" managed to work together to defend and advance reforms that had been started in earlier eras, and especially those aimed at improving educator quality, instruction, and students' opportunities to learn.

2

An Analytic
Infrastructure Emerges

IT ALMOST NEVER HAPPENED

It started with a phone call. Maxey Bacchus had a problem he hoped Anthony Bryk could help him address. Bacchus was responsible for the Department of Research, Evaluation and Planning (DREP) at the Chicago Public Schools. He and Bryk had been working together for a couple of years on a project that the former CPS superintendent, Manford Byrd, had invited. It was now 1989. Chicago reformers wanted evidence about how their new reform law was being implemented. DREP carried out annual evaluation studies on the district's numerous state and federal programs so it was the natural place to turn for this. But Bacchus was in a no-win spot. He was being pressed to carry out studies that likely would be critical of his own bosses, and regardless of the results, the studies probably would not be trusted by the reform community. He had no reason to believe that he could succeed.

Bacchus asked if Bryk would help him convene the deans of the schools of education from around the city to evaluate the reform. Bryk and Sharon Greenberg, a colleague at the Center for School Improvement (the Center) at UChicago, agreed to organize a meeting but recommended a broader invitation list. In addition to the deans, they reached out to research staff from community advocacy organizations, including Designs for Change and the Chicago Panel, and from citywide organizations such as the Urban League and the Latino Institute. They also invited a small group of individual faculty members from around the city who were already active in research on reform. Program officers from the major Chicago foundations supporting reform—MacArthur, the Chicago Community Trust, Joyce, and Spencer—also were invited.

More than forty individuals participated in an initial meeting on neutral turf at UChicago. Bryk and Greenberg facilitated, and the conversation was tense at times. This was a rare occasion where senior CPS staff were sitting with the activists who had been mobilizing against them. Bryk's objectives for the meeting were modest: Could a civil conversation be sustained? Would there be interest in more conversations to follow?

The group continued to meet over the next several months and winnowed down to about twenty regular participants. A steering committee for a proposed new organization—the Consortium on Chicago School Research—had begun to form. Bryk encouraged an explicitly pluralist membership that would include individuals from four different sectors: (1) school system leaders—a group that would expand to include a representative from the Chicago Teachers Union and the Principals Association, (2) individual researchers and school of education deans committed to engaging Chicago's school reform, (3) activists from school reform organizations that connected with Chicago's African American and Latino communities, and (4) program officers from the city's major foundations. Subsequently, the foundation officers decided that they should not be formally recognized as steering committee members, but they would still regularly participate. Their sustained engagement proved critical as glue and lubricant for the work ahead.[1]

Across many conversations, questions were raised about how the Consortium would do its work. How would decisions be made about what got studied? How would studies be conducted? Where would it be housed? Who would be responsible for fundraising and managing finances? Who would have editorial control over reports? What would be its formal relationship to the CPS? The list seemed endless and especially so since no applied research group anywhere looked anything like what this group was trying to invent. Eventually, Larry Braskamp, dean of the College of Education at the University of Illinois Chicago (UIC), broke the logjam: why not just try collaborating on a project or two, and let the organization evolve through doing the work? This proved sage advice.

Fortuitously, Bryk and John Easton, then at the Chicago Panel, were just beginning a joint research project. Fred Hess, the Panel's executive director and an early participant in the Consortium's organizing meetings, had invited Bryk to help the Panel develop a survey of teachers' engagement with reform. Hess suggested that they expand this into a pilot effort under the new Consortium. The decision made sense since the Consortium had no funding of its own yet, this project already had resources, and the topic was relevant to concerns raised by some critics that the legislation was antiprofessional.[2] Since the Chicago Teachers Union (CTU) had done little to shape the reform, and if its members followed suit and were disengaged in their local schools, then the reform seemed unlikely to succeed. It was critical to know what teachers were actually thinking and doing. This first study came to mark out a genre of work that the Consortium would pursue going forward: to anticipate issues which might not be a focus of public attention yet, but likely would be key if Chicago's reform were to continue to evolve in productive ways.

Bryk recruited Penny Sebring to join the project. She had been leading the national High School and Beyond survey development at NORC at the University of Chicago. In turn, Easton, Sebring, and Bryk recruited a diverse study team including John Kotsakis from the CTU, Mary Driscoll, a faculty member at UIC, and Arie van der Ploeg, from DREP. The study team also reached out to twenty-five principals and teacher leaders from around the city to advise about what the survey should ask, how it should be administered, and how results should be shared. This practitioner group later reviewed a draft of the report and advised on the presentation of findings and interpretation of results.

In a city as fractious as Chicago, Bryk believed that a pluralist orientation needed to ground the Consortium's work. This was especially so given the distinctive democratic character of Chicago's 1988 reform. Its evaluation should not be captured inside any one institution. A Consortium of applied researchers externally funded and with a shared focus on improving public education was a better match to the character of the reform that had emerged. The organization of this first study concretized this guiding principle.[3]

The study also established a commitment to stakeholder engagement in shaping how the Consortium shared results with local school communities. The study team on *Charting Reform: The Teachers' Turn* prepared individual reports for each participating school. The North Central Regional Lab, an institutional member of the steering committee, produced a support video that summarized overall study findings, highlighted the major sections in individual school reports, and suggested meeting structures and discussion questions to help school teams lift the hood on their own data. This activity set the direction for another regular Consortium practice going forward: preparing individual school reports to complement its citywide report and collaborating with other organizations in Chicago's exoskeleton to support schools' considerations of these data.

Further extending this public outreach, the citywide report was included as an addendum to an issue of *Catalyst*—a distribution that assured that every LSC member in the city had direct access to the report, since each had a *Catalyst* subscription. This also marked the first time the Consortium and *Catalyst* worked together. The Consortium would go on to distribute its second report, *Charting Reform: The Principals' Perspective* through *Catalyst* as well. Results from subsequent studies would become a regular topic covered by *Catalyst* in the years ahead.[4] The interconnections between these two new, independent, and innovative organizations would deepen over time as they shared a common aspiration to inform the city about efforts to improve its schools.

The Teachers' Turn reported that teachers were generally positive about the early implementation of the 1988 School Reform Act and especially in smaller schools. This finding shed light on what subsequently emerged as an important improvement driver over the next three decades. It gave impetus to the formation of the Small Schools Workshop at UIC in Era 1 and became one of the organizing pillars for the Chicago Annenberg Challenge in Era 2. A decade later it would operate as an enabling condition for the high school transformation initiative that sought to strengthen the personal connections among adults with students to improve students' school engagement and successful transition to college.[5]

As work progressed on *The Teachers' Turn*, Greenberg, Sebring, and Bryk started writing proposals for Consortium support to several local foundations. Even though the opening to form the Consortium had come from the CPS, it needed to be financially independent to avoid any perception of bias. Moreover, mindful of the adage that "he who pays the piper gets to call the tune," a diverse funding portfolio seemed essential to vitalizing the Consortium's ambitions to serve a broad public. While the Chicago philanthropic community was increasing its commitments to support school reform, convincing them that research could productively contribute was a challenge: Researchers typically went into communities and collected data on "subjects," studied them, and then disappeared. This perception was especially salient with regard to UChicago, which from the 1950s had walled itself off from the racially isolated and impoverished neighborhoods that surrounded it.[6]

Program officers at the Joyce and Spencer Foundations and the Chicago Community Trust, who participated in steering committee conversations, came to see a new role for local university faculty but were unable to provide immediate support, for a variety of reasons. Moreover, given the scope of the efforts envisioned, it was clear that engaging the MacArthur Foundation would be key, but it was in the midst of a leadership transition and could not entertain the idea just then either. So there the Consortium sat— an innovative idea with broad interest expressed, but no money. Early in the summer of 1990, prospects seemed dim.

Then the phone rang again. It was the end of their fiscal year at the Joyce Foundation, and program officer Bill McKersie had $40,000 left to spend. He wanted to know what Bryk and Sebring could do with it. They shared their idea for a research-agenda-setting task that would engage stakeholders from across the city to help articulate research priorities. Joyce funded this, and the Consortium's organizing efforts had another six months to live.[7]

AN INITIAL RESEARCH AGENDA:
SETTING THE COURSE

Developing the Consortium's research agenda involved interviews with key system and civic leaders, and focus groups with students, teachers, principals, and LSC members. The goal was to chart the information needs of this diverse group. But "What are your information needs?" is not a question people can respond to easily. So, the interview and focus group protocols opened up conversations about current challenges and the issues that respondents saw lying ahead for Chicago's schools. The transcribed texts from these interviews and focus groups were voluminous; yet, embedded within them were likely important insights that needed to be gleaned about what Chicago would need to know to improve its schools.

Bryk and Sebring were aiming for a reform-informing agenda built from the concerns of Chicago educators, system leaders, local community, and civic actors and undergirded by expert educational research. With the transcribed field commentaries in hand, it was time to engage a larger research community.[8] Bryk and Sebring organized a full-day meeting downtown that brought national and local researchers together to analyze the interview and focus group commentary. A jigsaw process assigned different sections of these field commentaries to small groups. Each was asked to summarize what they read, consider how and where it connected to extant educational research, and then reflect on the implications for reform.

The Consortium's final *Research Agenda* emerged out of this process. It was a substantive product that identified *what* to study. Importantly, the process for developing the agenda also reframed *how* this applied research should be carried out.[9] It would take researchers out of ivory towers like UChicago and involve them in dynamic, place-based social networks with practitioners and local school leaders, with policy advocates and interest groups, and more generally, with a diverse cross section of civic actors and institutions, all of whom wanted the city's schools to improve. This process of engaging stakeholders became another staple for how the Consortium operated, as it periodically revisited and reset its research agenda in the years ahead. A novel and distinctive social organization for applied research was forming.

Something else happened at the research-agenda event. Peter Martinez (who had helped warring factions reach consensus on the 1988 School Reform Act) had just been appointed senior program officer at the MacArthur Foundation. The stakeholder process used to create the agenda aligned with his community organizing orientation, and he also recognized how important it would be for reformers to have access to trustworthy evidence.[10] Martinez had become an advocate for the Consortium inside the MacArthur Foundation, even though Bryk and Sebring were unaware of it at the time.

Also fortuitous, Patricia Graham had just become president of the Spencer Foundation. She had known Bryk when they were both on the faculty at Harvard, and she reached out to learn more about his work on Chicago's reform. Even though Spencer is a national education research foundation, some of its board members wanted the foundation more involved in Chicago, and the Consortium seemed like a promising route.[11] In a two-month span the Consortium went from a good idea barely hanging on, to a start-up organization aiming to inform reform.

An Innovative Vision

The 1988 legislation was a governance reform. Consequently, the Consortium's initial *Research Agenda* placed issues embedded in the newly implemented local community control of schools at the top of the agenda and closed with a consideration of central district-level changes needed to support this. Efforts to improve the technical core of schooling composed its core. This included the quality of the district's human resources and efforts to enhance teaching and learning (discussed in chapters 3 and 4). This general framework would shape the Consortium's work over the next three decades.

Key Standpoints Organizing the Inquiries.   The *Research Agenda* also established guidance for how it would approach subsequent inquiries. First, the problems in Chicago schools did not arise overnight, nor would they be resolved overnight. Bryk reasoned that the city would be best served if the Consortium did not jump from issue to issue, but sustained its focus on the enduring concerns that Chicago would need to solve for genuine improvements to occur. This meant ongoing conversations among the Consortium directors, within the steering committee, and with other key civic actors to *prioritize major concerns on the horizon*. Some of these were already obvious, others less so, and in these instances focusing more attention there was critical. Consortium studies early in Era 1, for example, examined the role of principal leadership in advancing local school improvement well before this concern received system-level attention in Era 2. Similarly, an integrated set of studies on professional development, instruction, and students' engagement in schooling, which were initiated in Era 2, helped frame district priorities for Era 3.

The challenge was to step back from the overwhelming number of issues that had been raised through the research-agenda-setting process and ask: What are the big, overarching considerations that tied many of these more specific concerns together? This brought forward a second demand to *embrace systems thinking*: to see how these various elements fit together to create the unsatisfactory outcomes that the CPS continued to produce. Specifically, since Chicago's governance reform had placed primacy on the school site as the unit for change, this encouraged thinking about the organization of a productive school community, its core elements, and their functional interconnections. The "five essential supports for school improvement (5Es)," discussed later in this chapter, eventually emerged from these discussions. Similarly, a deepened understanding of the operational dynamics affecting students as they moved from elementary schools into high schools led to the invention of the concept of Freshman OnTrack that fueled the measurable improvements in high school graduation noted in the introduction.[12]

Third, while the *Research Agenda* was anchored in student outcomes, its authors posited that improving these outcomes meant *articulating the causal connections* assumed in each reform initiative and then examining these assumptions against data. This way of thinking opened for scrutiny the logic of proposed change efforts, which often have embedded within them zones of wishful thinking. Reformers embrace an idea that feels so compelling that they come to believe "something good is sure to happen." In contrast, interrogating these beliefs meant asking, What specifically needs to happen for this reform idea to produce the outcomes desired? During Era 1, for example, this meant asking several questions: How would the introduction of LSCs, which were at the heart of the 1988 reform, possibly lead to improved student outcomes? How would the LSCs need to operate, what would they need to focus attention on, and through what mechanisms would their improvement intentions get transformed into actions that advanced student learning? Similarly, when system-level policy initiatives came forward in Era 2, such as ending social promotion, it was critical to ask, What would have to happen for retained-in-grade students to actually improve their outcomes? And what else might happen that could well be problematic? The last is a basic characteristic of interventions in a complex system. A change often casts a wider net than intended.

A Methodological Pluralism.[13]   At the outset the specific expertise required to attack the research agenda was not fully obvious, but the overall contours were. Bryk reasoned that multisite case studies would help researchers understand the root causes of problems in local schools and initial efforts to improve on them. Moreover, because these problems were conceptually varied and interconnected, carrying out studies on them would likely require bringing together inquiry teams crossing bodies of research and professional knowledge. Additionally, the ability to address questions about the prevalence of a phenomenon and how it was distributed across varied school communities and subpopulations of students would press the Consortium toward sophisticated analyses of extant student data along with information drawn from new surveys. And since the Consortium's focus was on improvement, and improvement involves processes of change occurring over time, a development focus was needed to understand how schools might be changing relative to their baseline results. Doing this, in turn, meant building and sustaining an integrated longitudinal data system at the student, teacher, and school-community levels. And finally, some of the deepest insights were likely to emerge as researchers learned how to partner with school-based educators and local community leaders to solve specific problems. In this regard, the Consortium was informed by the wisdom of Kurt Lewin: if you want to really understand a system, try to change it.[14]

An Explicit Public Philosophy.   Bryk maintained that the relationship of applied social science to social problem-solving in a democratic society is best viewed as an educative one.[15] Because democratic decision-making involves a competition of ideas, it was the Consortium's role to bring the best empirical evidence into those discussions wherever they were occurring—in local school communities, among citywide organizations, as well as among formal leaders in the school system, the city, and the state. While direct instrumental use of research findings might happen on occasion—where the Consortium documented some result and a policy or practice change followed—over the long haul, many important contributions would likely arise from providing coherent, empirically grounded accounts of actions and their consequences.[16]

Moreover, those involved in this applied research shared an ethical responsibility to engage the voices of the individuals doing the work and those most directly affected by it. This meant assuring that a wide range of questions, emanating from different stakeholders, be addressed in each study. Assuring this, in turn, demanded a multipartisan steering committee and ongoing processes to revisit research priorities. It required project leaders to regularly engage with these diverse perspectives as they designed their studies, and as they carried out analyses and considered alternative explanations for emergent results. And it required broadly engaging actors across the city as reports came forward. Each new report offered a context for conversations about what was being learned and what that learning implied for ongoing work. Since the focus was on informing stakeholders' future actions, the *Consortium* also decided to *assiduously avoid making specific policy recommendations.* Its aim was to focus sustained attention on critical processes and systems needing attention and anchor these discussions with the best evidence that could be assembled. While different interest groups might disagree about what should be done, the Consortium's

aspiration was to locate this debate within a core set of concepts, linked together with explicit causal reasoning and grounded in evidence about
what was currently happening.

Counterbalancing this active local democratic engagement was the Consortium's commitment to scientific rigor in the execution of its various
studies and to transparency with the steering committee, funders, and independent researchers as work developed. Project investigators agreed to
report regularly to the steering committee, which met every six to eight
weeks, and subject their study designs and emergent observations to in-
terrogation. These meetings earned the name "going into the pit." They were
typically held in a large mahogany-paneled conference room on the UChicago campus, with furniture arranged in a U shape and presenters at the
open center. Feedback felt brutal at times. But realistically, if you could not
make your case in front of twenty people, a better reception from a broader
public seemed unlikely. Put simply, it was better to lose an argument in this
small environment where you had an opportunity to ask questions, revise,
and retry, rather than release a report still needing more attention into the
contentious politics operating citywide.

Summing up, the Consortium's work was consciously guided by a democratic charter as to *how applied research should "speak truth to power."*[17]
Power would continue to be exercised in plural spaces around the city even
as its distribution among groups and interests would shift substantially over
the next thirty years. The Consortium's public philosophy was a response
to a concern set out by John Dewey over a century ago in *The Public and
Its Problems:* How is it that scientific knowledge properly enters social
problem-solving in a democratic society? The Consortium's answer was
rooted in a belief that such social problem-solving was the work of a city.
The issues and specific questions to be investigated were shaped by the diverse constituents engaged in school reform, and multiple contexts were
organized to discuss broadly the findings that emerged. These processes,
in turn, created potential for shared understandings to evolve that could
ground subsequent actions.

The end result was innovative work of high technical quality, anchored
in conceptually important yet also practical insights about the actual

dynamics of school improvement. And all of this was carried out under a unique set of social arrangements where community education about the improvement of public education was the organizing mission.

ERA 1: 1988–1995
A FOCUS ON LOCAL SCHOOL GOVERNANCE, BUILDING RESEARCH CAPACITIES, AND FORGING RELATIONSHIPS

Most of the Consortium's efforts in Era 1 focused on the early implementation of local school governance and how teachers, principals, parents, and community leaders engaged in it.

Principals Play a Vital Role

Two independent case study projects on the early implementation of LSCs began prior to the Consortium's formation: one at the Chicago Panel on Public School Policy and Finance, led by Easton; and a second at the Center carried out by Greenberg, Bryk, and Barbara Schneider.[18] Both teams recognized early in their field studies how central principals were in vitalizing local school governance. LSCs were highly dependent on their schools' principals to turn the concerns they raised into constructive action. The 1988 reform was a huge change for school principals. In the past they were hired and assigned by central office and accountable to district superintendents. Now they were hired by and accountable to their LSCs and worked under four-year performance contracts. They also had new authorities over discretionary resources and teacher hiring. Little attention, however, had focused on the challenges that these changes would pose to individuals taking on what was essentially a new role. Identifying this as a significant issue "on the horizon" to be addressed created the impetus for the second Consortium project, *The Principals' Perspective.*

This study allowed the Consortium to expand its connections into the city. To lead it, Bryk recruited Albert Bennett, a former DREP staff member who was then on the faculty of Roosevelt University. Bennett in turn recruited university faculty from Northeastern Illinois and National Louis Universities and UIC to the study team. The project was also the Consortium's first opportunity to work directly with the Principals Association.[19] Bennett would subsequently join Bryk, Sebring, and Easton as a Consortium codirector.

Two years in, by 1992, the Consortium had taken steps toward building working relationships with both the CTU, through *The Teachers' Turn*, and the Principals Association through *The Principals' Perspective*. These were the two largest and most significant organizations for educational professionals in the city. Both had been on the sidelines in the city's mobilization for reform and remained there as reform began. In the near term, their support for teacher and principal studies, and especially ones that relied on achieving good survey participation, was essential. Longer term, their engagement in the steering committee and in various public convenings around specific reports would prove integral to the broad-based social learning about school improvement that the Consortium aimed to effect.

Charting Reform: The Principals' Perspective complemented the views expressed the year before by teachers. Like teachers, principals offered generally positive reports about how the 1988 reform was working in their school communities, although they also emphasized the exhausting new demands they faced. The survey also inquired about principals' perceptions of the quality of their staff, their teachers' capacities to work collegially toward improving their school, and initial efforts to strengthen the quality of teaching and learning in their buildings. Principals were positive about how the reform had given them authority to hire teachers, and how this authority, coupled with the discretionary resources now available for school site budgeting, was allowing them to bring in "new blood" who really wanted to teach in their buildings and engage students and families. A third of the principals reported that they had hired 20 percent or more new staff in those first two years. The survey also documented a major demographic shift in the principalship: principals were now younger, there were more women, and more educators of color "matched" their communities. Schools that had been criticized as "shutting out parents" in the parent community forums just two years before were now open to their local communities.

Aiming to deepen understandings about principals' key role in leading change, the Consortium sustained attention to their experiences going forward. By doing so, it informed subsequent reform efforts on what arguably proved to be the single strongest lever for improving schools—the quality of school leadership.

Early Relationships with CPS

As noted in chapter 1, the senior leadership of the school system (and the mayor after 1995) are major sources of power in any political analysis of reform. Through 1993, annual budget shortfalls and labor stoppages dominated their attention. The district's legitimacy had been called into question in the run-up to reform, and the 1988 legislation deliberately gutted the "bloated bureaucracy." There were four different superintendents over the six years of Era 1, and none acted on the truly profound implications of the 1988 reform: that Chicago aspired to become a system of locally controlled schools with a smaller and very different central support capacity. In these early years, senior CPS leaders showed minimal interest in what Consortium researchers were doing and learning, and the Consortium was left alone to do its work.

An exception was DREP. Several DREP staff participated in select Era 1 studies. Bacchus was also a steering committee member. He regularly attended meetings, and through that venue he offered a CPS perspective about what should get studied. Importantly, during Era 1 through Era 3, the district did not exercise independent approval authority on individual projects. This assured that the Consortium's work remained responsive to issues raised by the steering committee and the stakeholders that the Consortium brought together for targeted convenings. No topic was ever judged too politically sensitive to investigate. While guidance from the steering committee was often extensive, it was counterbalanced by a second principle: The staff for each study held broad authority over the technical execution of each project and maintained final editorial control over the content of its reports.

The State of Reform Circa 1993

The reform legislation had been passed in 1988, and by 1992, questioning whether it was working or not had become a new civic sport. At that point, half of the schools were about two years into the process—those that had selected their principals in the spring of 1990; the other half were just one year in, having contracted with their principals the following spring. Regardless of this short time frame, the legislation called for every school to be at national norms on standardized tests by 1994. As a serious expression of aspirations, this was laudable. As a realistic timeline, it was indefensible. No district anywhere had produced anything close to the magnitude of change set out in the legislation in a few years.[20] Simply looking at short-term test score trends would be grossly uninformative.

But this just begged the question: What was an appropriate standpoint for assessing such a novel reform early on? The Consortium's task was to deepen understandings about how reform was supposed to work and gather evidence about whether (and where and how) this was happening. Specifically, what did local school governance look like in actual operation, what were local leaders attending to, and how might their actions result in improved student outcomes? Articulating the logic in action assumed in the law and developing evidence for assessing it grounded the study. Learning how to conduct research in this fashion became core design for much of the Consortium over the next three decades.

Specifically, the *State of School Reform* study, published in 1993, was informed by observations from the two large ongoing case study projects mentioned earlier; an in-depth look at six additional Chicago schools that had been identified by multiple informants as engaging reform well; and relied heavily on firsthand experiences of Center staff who, by that time, had been supporting a network of schools for three years. Drawing on these observations, the team explicated a theory about the workings of democratic localism inside school communities and coupled this to a second theory on the core processes involved in restructuring schools toward more ambitious student outcomes.[21] The study team developed a classification scheme for local school community politics. At the positive end were "strong democracy schools" where all three local sites of power—parents and community, the school principal, and the faculty—were working constructively together.[22] At the negative end were school communities where "consolidated principal power" had emerged. LSCs were not functioning, faculty were not engaged, and by default an autocratic principal prevailed. Complementing this political analysis, study staff also characterized the nature of improvement efforts underway. The case studies had identified a group of "Christmas tree" schools where many new initiatives had sprung forward, but they were incoherent, and implementation was weak. These schools might look good at first glance—like a tree with lots of ornaments— but absent cultivation, little of significance was taking root. At the other end of this typology were schools where a systemic focus on students' experiences and improving instruction was prioritized. Extant research suggested that these places were doing things that would eventually move student outcomes.[23] The study team used citywide data from both the 1991 teacher survey and the 1992 principal surveys to categorize each school's local politics and the nature of their improvement efforts. The validity of these statistical classifications was then cross-checked and confirmed for the sample of schools where extensive field study had been carried out.[24]

The Consortium's report came to be characterized across the city as a "story of three thirds."[25] The major finding was that systemic restructuring efforts were more likely to be found in school communities where a strong democratic polity had taken hold. Approximately a third of the elementary school communities looked like this. Another third shared some of these characteristics but also were struggling in some regards. Absent an external support system, these schools seemed less likely to succeed. As for the remaining schools, local school governance had defaulted to consolidated principal control and no significant change efforts appeared underway. Left to their own devices, there was little reason to believe that improvements would be forthcoming in these schools. The study suggested that the 1988 reform had come up short in two regards: no external system had been created to support struggling schools, and no accountability mechanism functioned to identify and intervene in the schools left behind.[26]

A distinctive geographic phenomenon had also become visible: Improving schools could be found in virtually every neighborhood in the city, but stagnant schools were concentrated in low-income African American communities on the south and west sides. Although unknown at the time, this would prove a stubborn problem to solve. It would continue to challenge Chicago over the decades as several different strategies were tried and failed.

A general improvement lesson also came visible. Regardless of the nature of the specific educational reform attempted, performance variation is the natural state of affairs. This observation meant that studies needed to move beyond a simple account of "on average *what* was happening" to discern the contours of variation in reform processes and outcomes and then ask *why and how* this variation was occurring.[27] Advancing more equitable educational outcomes demanded this analytic orientation.

Engaging the City Around the Findings. The Consortium held a citywide convening to bring the findings in the *State of School Reform* report to a broad swath of school and civic actors. Individual presentations were made to targeted groups, including the CTU, the Principals Association, and Leadership for Quality Education (LQE). The results were considered good news among those who had championed community control: democratic localism was fueling constructive improvements in many school communities, and the changes being enacted there could plausibly be linked to making future progress on the student outcomes goals set out in the 1988 reform. (Evidence documenting this link would come forward two years later.) In this regard, the Consortium's findings moderated an argument that had been simmering since 1988: that Chicago's reform was all about governance and not student learning. Indeed, Chicago's was a governance reform, but it was proving to be one that was enabling new possibilities for strengthening school communities to advance student learning. And this was occurring in many schools across the city.

While the report did not recommend specific policies, it did advocate for more time to implement reform and to identify key areas where more attention was needed. Two areas have already been mentioned: the need for a support system for struggling schools, and an external accountability system to identify and intervene in schools left behind under local control.[28] The report also directed attention to further investments that were needed to develop the capacities of LSC members, and it echoed the *Principals' Perspective* report: Chicago needed a deeper bench of better-prepared new school leaders. Theirs was a challenging new role, and unlike any other in the country. It also was one for which there was no professional preparation. Principals were key to the success of decentralization, but they needed help. Last, the *State of School Reform* called attention to the fragility of school reform more generally amid the enduring fiscal crises plaguing the CPS. It asserted:

> Much of the first phase of reform has focused on rebuilding a sense of agency among both parents and professionals with regard to neighborhood schools. It is their willingness to commit personal effort, and the growing collective enablement of school communities that are most at risk now in the current fiscal crisis. All that has been accomplished in schools over the last four years could easily come unraveled in a few short months. . . .
>
> There is only a limited number of issues that top leadership in an organization can entertain at any one point in time. Unless fiscal issues are moved to the back burner, the school system may never devote sufficient attention to how it might best support the work of schools.

The report's release and the discussion of its findings catapulted the Consortium into the public eye. A set of priorities for reinventing the system center had come into focus, and it subsequently informed the Amendatory Act of 1995. Chicago needed to build a support infrastructure for local schools and vitalize an external accountability function that would complement local responsibility for improvement. And for this to happen in a sustainable way, the chronic financial crises and attendant labor-management conflicts had to be ameliorated. Realizing these priorities would also take time.

Transitional Leadership for Change. Coinciding with the release of the report, Argie Johnson, a highly regarded African American community district superintendent in New York City, was appointed superintendent. Johnson immediately focused on the support and accountability needs identified in the *State of School Reform* report. Reformers, however, criticized her proposed responses for being inconsistent with the spirit of Chicago's decentralization. To her credit, Johnson put her initial ideas on hold and invited a cross section of activists to dialogue with her. Consortium staff participated in these conversations and drafted the final report of the committee. It was called *Pathways to Achievement* and was subsequently published by the CPS as the district's self-study guide for schools. Much of what would eventually crystallize as the Consortium's 5Es, detailed later in this chapter, evolved from these conversations and closely related discussions occurring simultaneously inside the Consortium's steering committee. The participants in these various meetings were key to subsequently moving this early framing of the 5Es out into the city through their own organizations and the social networks of which they were a part.

The business community had taken note of the *State of School Reform* report. John Ayers, executive director of LQE, had been in communication with Johnson about the business community's interest in improving the district's central office operations. LQE offered to bring in a consultant team associated with Hammer and Champy, authors of *Reengineering the Corporation*, to work on a wide range of problems, many of which dated back to the 1981 Chicago United report. It was also clear to business leaders that DREP needed to be strengthened to better support data needs in schools and the central office. Late in 1993 Ayers asked Bryk if he would consider taking a leave from UChicago to work inside the central office on rebuilding DREP and to advise Johnson on the system-level restructuring efforts that LQE would support.[29] Bryk agreed to go into CPS half-time if Ayers could also arrange for John Easton to join him full-time.[30] The two were active collaborators through the Consortium, and Easton had worked previously inside the central office. This was a most unusual arrangement for CPS at the time, but Ayers made it happen. Easton took day-to-day responsibility for strengthening DREP capacity. Bryk supported this and advised on the larger, system-level restructuring effort.

One of Easton's first projects at DREP was to reduce the time that it took to report standardized test scores back to schools. Testing occurred in late April, but schools did not receive their reports until October. The system had worked this way for years; no one had ever questioned it. The challenge came from the 1988 reform. Schools were required to submit annual school improvement plans (SIPs) in June, but their planning was uninformed by current test results. Easton guided DREP staff to map every step of the process and suggest efficiencies in each: How and when test forms were sent into DREP; how long they sat on the delivery docks; how they were scanned and then examined for cheating; how school reports were generated, reviewed, and how systemwide results were shared with CPS leaders and their public communications staff—to name a few. Working as a team, DREP staff reduced the time from five months to three weeks. Schools now had data in time to inform their SIPs.

Regarding central office restructuring, Bryk was tasked to design a new school accountability system that addressed the weaknesses identified in the *State of School Reform* report while remaining consistent with the spirit of Chicago's decentralization reform. He recommended the creation of an accountability council that would develop and maintain a broad-based indicator system for each school and conduct professional-quality school reviews. The intent was to capture a breadth of information about life in schools to inform subsequent improvement efforts. A combination of quantitative indicators and quality reviews would help to identify where bright spots had developed around the city and create opportunities for other schools to learn from them. Up to that point, both school successes and failures had been largely invisible. From a design perspective, the accountability system that Bryk conceptualized had three primary aims: to inform individual schools' improvement efforts, to identify contexts in need of external intervention, and to raise up more pervasive problems that demanded district-wide attention. The proposal embraced a separation of powers concept: an accountability council would generate the quality reviews and data reports; the school board, working through their designated officials, would decide where and when interventions were needed. A separate accountability council board, composed of appointments made by both the mayor and the governor, would oversee the operations of the council's permanent professional staff and rotating teachers on leave who would join in the school quality reviews. The proposal had been specifically crafted cognizant of the fact that trust in the central office remained weak and its professional capacities limited.[31]

The design for the accountability council was another innovative idea emerging from Chicago's context. It sought to craft a form of external accountability compatible with decentralization that was both rigorous and professionally educative—one that might expand improvement learning among schools across the city. Ayers brokered a connection to the Civic Committee on Bryk's proposal. Although it was not the simple report card that some Civic Committee members expected, they came to see value in it and included it in their lobbying efforts for the Amendatory Act in spring 1995. Even though the provision for an accountability council was enacted into law, Mayor Daley was not a fan of a council that he did not fully control. He dragged his feet on its implementation, and most significant, he blocked funding for the quality reviews. In the end, a simplistic test-based form of accountability was put in place during Era 2 instead. Relying just on these numbers obscured much about the actual challenges confronting different school communities and how these places were experienced by their students and families. These differences in perspective would rear up again in the school closing controversies of Era 3 and Era 4.

ERA 2: 1995–2001
THE CONSORTIUM STRUGGLES TO SURVIVE

The beginning of Era 2 was marked by an increase in the Consortium's visibility in the city and continued connections with the central office. When Vallas replaced Johnson as CEO in 1995, Bryk returned to UChicago as originally planned, but Easton stayed on in the central office for another two years.[32] Two principals whose work the Consortium had highlighted in the *State of School Reform,* Pat Harvey and Carlos Azcoitia, assumed leadership roles in the new administration. They were at the vanguard of a new generation of CPS school principals leading change in their schools and among the first to move up into key central office positions.

Unfortunately, the Consortium's relationship to Vallas quickly proved challenging.

His vision was to rebuild the traditional form of a functional public bureaucracy, one capable of driving change from central office down to schools and across the city. As such, his aims and methods ran counter to the spirit of Chicago's decentralization. To build agency for his agenda, Vallas also sought to control the narrative—to literally make the news that local media would report each day about CPS. Prior to social media and a 24-7 news cycle, this was an attainable goal. Unsurprisingly, the reform community opposed him, and the Consortium often found itself in the middle. As noted by *Catalyst* editors, Vallas [was] "a hot-tempered overseer who brokered no criticism." As Charles Payne summarized it, "he made fear the primary motivational tool inside the system, squelched debate of complex issues, and failed to understand the importance of building a stronger teaching staff."[33] These were difficult conditions for carrying out the Consortium's public-informing agenda.

Looking back, the conflict between reformers and Vallas, with the Consortium caught in between, was inevitable. In an attempt to mitigate this contentious space, the Consortium invited Vallas to join the steering committee. (He rarely attended but would sometimes send a surrogate.) Tariq Butts, a member of the new reform board of trustees, was also invited.[34] Additionally, the Consortium had established a "no surprises rule" early on. District and board leaders were briefed about each report prior to its release to assure that they were never caught flat-footed by the press. Even so, there was no way to control how other civic actors, including members of the steering committee, might use Consortium findings to take issue with CPS initiatives and advance their own arguments about what should happen next. Worrying about how citywide media reported on the Consortium's work became an ongoing concern. The context was ripe for conflict, and conflict sold newspapers then in the same way that it fuels much of social media today.

At times the continued existence of the Consortium seemed in doubt. Regular access to student data had been negotiated with DREP years before. Now there were unexpected and unexplained delays. School community leaders were cautioned by the district about engaging in Consortium-related field studies. Vallas urged foundation program officers to redirect Consortium funds to the CPS instead.

Fortunately, by the start of Era 2, the Consortium had earned respect in the foundation and business communities and was publicly endorsed by the Citywide Association of Local School Councils.[35] Positive connections had also been forged with numerous faculty members in local colleges of education and with staff at the Illinois State Board of Education. Leaders from many of these institutions were on the steering committee. Although any one of them might take issue with a specific finding, they valued the Consortium's independent analyses and reporting, and none was inclined to abandon it. With this broad base of civic support, the Consortium survived.[36]

Bringing Evidence amid Public Controversies

As Era 2 began, changes emanating quickly from the top down had a major impact on the Consortium's work and its relationships across the city. In an era of conflict between reformers and Vallas, Consortium research now functioned as a mediating resource.

Ending Social Promotion. Chief among Vallas's initiatives was a plan to end "social promotion." To do so, the CPS introduced promotional gates at grades 3, 6, and 8. Students who failed to achieve adequate end-of-year test scores were required to attend summer school and then retained in grade if their performance on an end-of-summer test remained unsatisfactory. The initiative aimed to incent greater effort from both students and teachers. For students, the incentive to work harder was to avoid the stigma of retention and not moving forward with classmates. Teachers were targeted as well because continued low scores could result in their school being put on probation, and all the consequences attendant to that.[37]

Opinions divided sharply on this policy. In a State of the Union address, President Clinton applauded Chicago's initiative, and it resonated with much of the local public as well. Within the steering committee, Barbara Sizemore, then dean of the school of education at DePaul University, argued that the policy promoted much-needed higher standards. Don Moore, in contrast, maintained that grade retention did not improve student learning and would push more students to drop out and that these effects would disproportionately impact low-income students of color. For the Consortium staff, the project posed a professional dilemma. Moore's summary of extant research findings on grade retention was accurate. Even so, results from these prior studies did not mean that such a policy *could not work* under different circumstances: Chicago's initiative included funding for mandatory summer school, development of a scripted curriculum aligned to the test, increased support through after-school programming during the academic year, and the possibility of a midyear promotion for retained students who were showing good progress. This was another instance where the Consortium's role was not to judge the policy, but to assemble evidence that would deepen understandings about its actual operational dynamics.

Steering committee discussions about social promotion were fractious at times, and the differing views expressed by members shaped what the Consortium investigated. Its researchers embraced an improvement science orientation. You have to see how the new system operates—how students flow through it—to produce the end results. Did the incentives introduced in grades 3, 6, and 8, for example, lead to increased student effort? How were students targeted for mandated summer school, and who actually attended? What was the quality of their summer school experiences and their immediate impact? What happened in the next academic year to students who were promoted, compared to those that were retained? And what happened to these students in the longer term? A five-year research program, led by Melissa Roderick, ensured that this logic was assessed, and evidence gathered on each component. Seven reports were published during this time.[38]

Initial results seemed encouraging: On average, a bump up in test scores was reported after the first year in grades 6 and 8 (but not grade 3) from the introduction of the promotional gate. This supported the argument about positive effects accruing from the introduction of incentives for students to work harder and test better. Likewise, relatively large on-average effects were found for students who attended summer school. So, some of the new program components seemed effective. However, some troubling patterns emerged as researchers followed students over time and began to disaggregate results. The absolute achievement of the students who had recorded large gains during the promotional gate year and summer school, and consequently were promoted to the next grade, remained low. And as Moore had predicted, students who were retained in grade began dropping out a few years later at a higher rate than comparable students in previous years. Moreover, while some students appeared to benefit, those with the weakest prior achievement were the least likely to do so. And the effects of the policy were not uniform; the most damaging outcomes were experienced by African American students. By paying explicit attention to the variability in students' progress over time, the Consortium surfaced important evidence about inequitable impacts—results that likely would have gone unrecognized in the district's annual overall test score reporting to the city.

Retention in grade also impacted school operations in unanticipated ways.[39] As more students were held back in grades 3, 6, and 8, correspondingly fewer were enrolled in the next grade. This affected the composition of elementary classes, with some now having large enrollments of retained students. In subsequent years an increasing number of previously retained students were reclassified as special education students and allowed to pass through the next promotional gate. However, as they moved into high schools, these students disproportionately enrolled in already challenged neighborhood schools. Many of these schools suddenly had more than 30 percent of their students in special education—a phenomenon that never existed before and for which the schools, and especially this group of schools, was unprepared.

Reformers, including Moore, continued to press on Vallas to reverse direction, and they drew selectively on Consortium findings to advance their arguments. Consortium researchers saw their work weaponized as these arguments played out in the pages of the *Tribune, Sun-Times,* and *Crain's Chicago Business.* The school system continued to tinker with its policy; behind closed doors, senior staff read the Consortium's reports and occasionally asked Roderick for advice. The policy was never formally abandoned, but student retention rates declined substantially over time, and the policy, as a major reform initiative, largely faded from the scene.[40]

The social promotion story offered a vibrant example of the steering committee as a "room" where significant social learning was happening. Conversations continued to evolve as the full scope of results accumulated over time and discussions about their implications crystallized.[41] At one point Barbara Sizemore said, "I know that just socially promoting kids, where they are not really developing the skills they need, is bad. But I also now see that retaining them in grade doesn't work either." No longer a debate about the pros and cons of grade retention, the dialogue had shifted to, "Well, what do we do instead?"[42] Shortly thereafter, *Catalyst's* editorial board came to a similar conclusion.[43] The "end of social promotion" was an ambitious initiative in response to a serious problem, and parts of the initiative could reasonably be seen as constructive. And yet, when the full array of evidence was assembled, the conclusion was obvious: a new direction was needed.

The Chicago Annenberg Challenge (CAC).　As noted in chapter 1, CAC funded its first set of improvement networks in January 1996. Shortly thereafter, the Consortium became its developmental evaluation partner, producing ten reports over a six-year period. The Challenge was premised on the belief that educators, parents, and community members could and should identify their own ways to solve local problems and improve their schools. CAC funding aimed to catalyze the development of an infrastructure around the city to support local schools' efforts to enhance teaching, student engagement, and learning.[44] Philosophically, it ran opposite to the central-directed initiatives that emerged in Era 2. Thus, the Consortium was again caught in the middle between the Vallas administration and a reform community that remained committed to local community control.

Unlike his predecessors, Vallas brought considerable political acumen to the CEO role. Noted earlier, he operated as his own communications machine touting his accountability initiatives and high school interventions. The community that formed around CAC often pressed back, drawing on Consortium research findings, to take issue especially with Vallas's lack of attention to improving classroom instruction.[45] Activists also drew on other Consortium reports that questioned the student outcome data being released by central office. The Consortium had identified several new system policies affecting the tabulation of annual test score reports that made these new numbers less comparable to those reported in previous years. This raised questions about how much, if any, improvement was occurring in Era 2.[46] Here again Consortium staff found themselves in the middle of political controversy. They had all been trained as researchers but were now forced to learn how to navigate public media and big-city politics.

As for the Consortium's summative findings about the Chicago Annenberg Challenge, its aims were ambitious, and the Annenberg gift was the largest of its time. However, it added only about $100 per year per student to improve outcomes in the district that was still reputed to be "worst in the nation." In short, its aspirations far exceeded any realistic assessment as to what it would take in terms of time, money, and capacities to achieve them. Change efforts motivated by CAC were spotty at best, and overall improvements were hard to discern.[47]

Even so, CAC staff, and the network of reformers that they were connected to, were learning important lessons about the actual work of improving schools. Initially, CAC had embraced the idea of local schools developing their own improvement initiatives with support from an external partner. As these efforts proceeded, however, it became clear that for more progress to occur, these efforts needed to be guided by well-researched frameworks. By the time the CAC spent down most of its funds and closed operations after six years, there was broad acknowledgment that instructional improvement would require intensive support for teacher professional development, the formation of school-based professional learning communities organized around this, and a transformation in the work of school leaders to support it.[48] While the Challenge had not achieved the changes it sought, it helped set priorities for the next decade. This was captured succinctly in a *Catalyst* story published at this key juncture, titled "It's About Instruction, Stupid."[49]

In sum, CAC initiated what became a long-term process of developing human capabilities and organizational capacities to support school improvement in Chicago. As taken up in chapters 3 and 4, the early roots developed by CAC became a significant resource for the forthcoming Duncan administration. And the 5Es framework that centered the CAC evaluation would function as a coherent guide for these next new efforts.

The Five Essential Supports: A Framework to Inform Improvement

As noted earlier, the idea of the 5Es emerged at the end of Era 1. It was grounded in the learning from the Center's direct work in schools, multiple case study projects on the early implementation of reform, analyses of bright spots where the decentralization reform was working well, and extensive conversations occurring in the Consortium steering committee. CAC evaluation funding allowed the Consortium to engage a large external research community to further detail the framework and develop and validate the systems of measures that operationalized it. (For a brief description of the 5Es, see Five Essential Supports for School Improvement).

Anchoring Concepts and Measures. During Era 1, Bryk was a co-principal investigator in National Center for School Restructuring at the University of Wisconsin, led by Fred Newmann. Newmann had assembled researchers from multiple universities to study early efforts nationally to restructure schools toward more ambitious educational outcomes. Bryk recruited several colleagues from this group to join in the Consortium's work.

The development of the concept of a *school-based professional community* and a survey measure to capture this was one product.[50] It subsequently became a core element within the professional capacity domain in the 5E framework. The concept *of instructional program coherence* was another. It was the antidote to the problematic "Christmas tree school" phenomenon previously identified in Chicago and mentioned earlier.[51] Its associated measure became part of the leadership driver within the 5Es.[52] Consortium staff also collaborated with Newmann to examine the *intellectual demand* of the curricular tasks that Chicago students were given.[53] This work informed survey measure development and advanced conversations about the need for more ambitious academic standards for all students. This concept and related measures lie at the heart of one of the 5Es—the quality of instruction driver.[54] Innovative work on *instructional pacing* also found a home there. A program of research on *academic press and personalism* came to anchor the Consortium's framing of a student-centered learning climate.[55] This work continued to evolve over the next fifteen years and eventually undergirded a program of research on the nature of students' social-emotional learning and the school factors influencing it.

Last, researchers identified how *relational trust*, not originally part of the 5Es, was central to the sustained cooperative action necessary to improve schools.[56] This research empirically demonstrated that the quality of parent-teacher, teacher-teacher, teacher-student, and teacher-principal relationships enabled (or impeded) the emergence of a school-based professional community, the vitality of a student-centered learning climate, and the nature of school-parent-community ties. An intuitively powerful but seemingly "soft idea" had been specified in sufficient detail that it could be reliably measured as a property of a school community.

Accompanying this, a key field-based validation of the 5Es was carried out by a steering committee member, Charles Payne, who was then a professor at Northwestern University. Payne had questioned how well the survey indicators actually aligned with what others, more embedded in those school communities, saw. To find out, the Consortium gave him a list of schools that represented a range of rankings on the 5E measures. However, his team was blind to the survey results when they conducted their own interviews and observations. Based on their field work, Payne's group developed their own ratings of these schools relative to the 5Es. Strong agreement was found between these two sources of evidence. Payne's in-depth field study reports contained more detail and nuance than possible with a short survey instrument, but overall, the accounts aligned.[57] The Consortium surveys had passed a key validity test: Do you see what I see?

Five Essential Supports for School Improvement

Over the last three decades, the Consortium has sustained a longitudinal study of the internal workings and external community conditions that distinguished schools that improved from those that failed to do so.[58] These data open an extraordinary window to examine the complex interplay of how schools are organized and interact with local context to affect student outcomes.

Five essential features in the organization of a school shape the work lives of its students and teachers, as set out in *Organizing Schools for Improvement: Lessons from Chicago.* (See figure 2.1.) First is the coherence of the *instructional guidance system* that articulates the "what and how" of teaching and learning. Key here are the learning tasks posed for students, the assessments that make manifest what students know and provide feedback to inform ongoing learning, and the curricular materials and instructional routines that scaffold all of this. Although substantial discretion may exist in how individual teachers use these resources, the efficacy of teachers'

Figure 2.1 Organizational features of schools that interact to advance student achievement

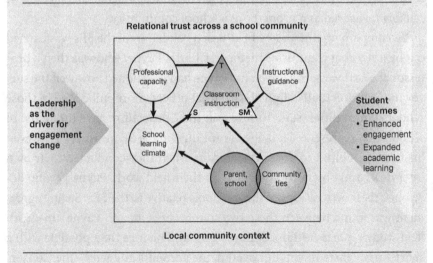

Relational trust across a school community

Leadership as the driver for engagement change

Professional capacity

Instructional guidance

Classroom instruction

School learning climate

Parent, school

Community ties

Student outcomes
• Enhanced engagement
• Expanded academic learning

Local community context

efforts depends on the nature and quality of the artifacts assembled here.

Second, schooling is a human-resource-intensive enterprise. Schools are only as good as the quality of faculty, the professional development in place to support their learning, and their capacity to work together to improve instruction. This support, called *professional capacity*, directs attention to a school's ability to recruit and retain capable staff, the efficacy of its performance feedback and professional development programs, and the capability of a staff to work together to solve local problems.

The third organizational support focuses on *parent-community-school ties*. These relationships can be very challenging, especially in urban communities. The quality of these ties links directly to students' motivation and school participation and can extend the resources in a school community available to support different students' needs. An absence of vital ties is a problem; their presence is a multifaceted resource for improvement.

Fourth is a *student-centered learning climate*. At a minimum, improving schools establish a safe and orderly environment—the most basic prerequisite for learning. They also press toward encouraging ambitious academic work and provide the necessary personal support for all students to believe in themselves, to persist, and ultimately to achieve. A supportive climate sustains students' engagement with schooling and develops their sense of individual competence and identities as learners.

The fifth and final support focuses on *leadership as the driver* for change. School leaders influence local activity around core instructional programs, supplemental academic and social supports, and the hiring and development of staff. They establish strategic priorities for where and how marginal resources (including time) are to be spent, and they buffer externalities that might distract from coherent actions. Throughout all of this, school leaders also constantly attend to building relationships within the school community. Moving a coherent improvement plan across the other four essential supports depends upon school leaders' ability to cultivate teacher, student, and parent engagement around the deep cultural changes entailed. Consequently, attention to building relational trust comes forcefully into play.[59]

Using data collected from teachers, principals, and students, the Consortium developed school indicators for each of the essential supports, charted changes in these indicators over time, and then related these organizational conditions to subsequent changes in student attendance and learning gains in reading and mathematics. Elementary schools with strong indicators on most supports were ten times more likely to improve than schools with weak reports. Half of the schools strong on most supports improved substantially in reading. Not a single school weak on most supports improved in mathematics. More recent studies have further validated these findings and extended them to high schools as well: Strengths on the 5Es are linked to improvements in Freshman OnTrack, students' grade point averages, and college enrollment.[60]

Some of the most powerful relationships found in these data are associated with how relational trust among the school principal, teachers, students, and parents operates as both a lubricant for organizational change and a moral resource for sustaining the hard work of local improvement. Absent such trust, it is nearly impossible to strengthen parent-community ties, build professional capacity, and enable a student-centered learning climate.

In sum, schools are complex organizations consisting of multiple interacting subsystems (i.e., the five essential supports). Only if mutually reinforcing developments occur across these five domains is student learning likely to improve. Correspondingly, student outcomes stagnate if a material weakness persists in any of the supports. Taken together, these five subsystems constitute the core organizational elements for advancing student engagement and learning.

In sum, by the end of Era 2, the research underpinning the 5Es framework had been firmly established, and its associated measures had been refined over the course of four administrations between 1994 and 2001. As the 5Es moved into school communities, educators were increasingly able to "see" the concepts in their contexts and use 5E measures to guide local improvement efforts. In short, the 5Es both met rigorous research standards and had practical validity in the field. In the years ahead, 5Es' core concepts were absorbed by CPS and multiple organizations citywide. They began to function as an anchoring set of ideas and evidence for how Chicago could improve its schools. Figure 2.2 displays some of the multifaceted representations of the 5Es in Chicago, beginning in Era 2 and then evolving over the next two decades of reform.

Stimulating Social Learning.   In Era 2 and into Era 3, Consortium directors took the 5Es into the city. Elaine Allensworth, Bryk, Easton, and Sebring introduced principals and teachers to the framework and suggested how each school's survey reports might help them see their strengths and weaknesses and possible implications for improvement. Some of these events were facilitated by intermediary organizations working with school networks including the Comer Project and North Central Regional Lab. Both the Chicago Principals and Administrators Association (CPAA) and the CTU's Quest Center organized workshops for their members. The Consortium also hosted civic leadership events so that these groups might join the conversation as well.

To support these public-informing efforts, the Consortium developed an accessible writing style and distinct ways to display data in its reports. Early on, it broke from conventional academic writing that begins with a literature review, followed by the core study questions and hypotheses, then a section on methods, data sources and measures, and finally the results, limitations, and interpretative conclusions. While these were all still covered, each report was written as a narrative that invited readers into a deeper understanding of the topic. Key concepts, inquiry methods (i.e., How did we look at this issue?) and results were introduced as the accounts unfolded. The writing also encouraged systems thinking by describing how different

Figure 2.2a   Manifestations of the five essential supports for improving schools over a twenty-five-year history

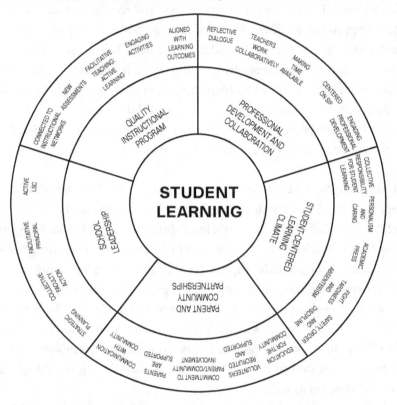

PATHWAYS TO ACHIEVEMENT

As it first appeared in the CPS's *Pathways to Achievement Report* (1994).

Source: Pathways to Achievement: Self-Analysis Guide (Chicago: Chicago Public Schools, Department of Research, Evaluation, and Planning, 1994), 2.

Figure 2.2b   Manifestations of the five essential supports for improving schools over a twenty-five-year history

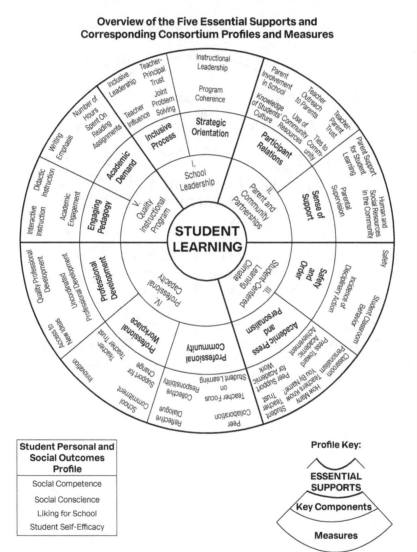

Source: Stuart Luppescu, Holly Hart, Jenny Nagaoka, John Q. Easton, and Rose E. Sweeney, *Zora Neale Hurston Academy: Details of Student and Teacher Responses* (Sample School Report) (Chicago: University of Chicago Consortium on School Research, 2001), 8.

Figure 2.2c Manifestations of the five essential supports for improving schools over a twenty-five-year history

As it appeared in the evaluation of the Annenberg Challenge final report (2003).

Model of Essential Supports for Student Learning

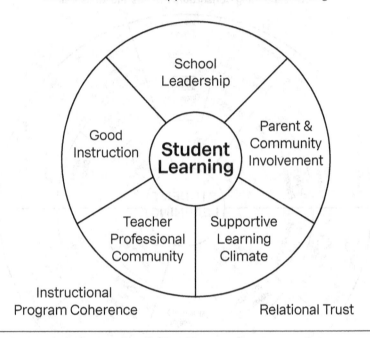

Source: Smylie et al., *Chicago Annenberg Challenge,* 27.

Figure 2.2d   Manifestations of the five essential supports for improving schools over a twenty-five-year history

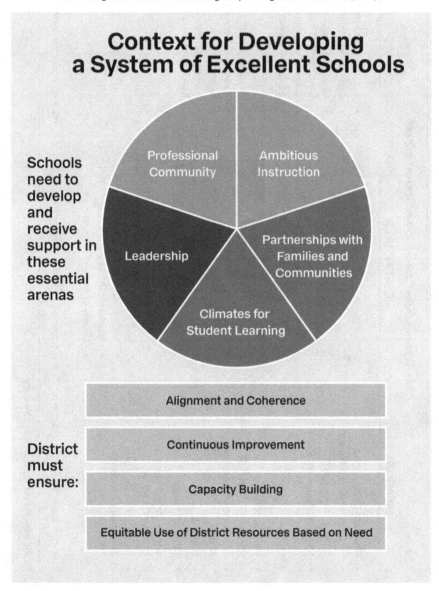

As it appeared in CPS report:
Elevating Our Vision for Learning: Improving Schools for All (2011).

Context for Developing a System of Excellent Schools

Schools need to develop and receive support in these essential arenas

Professional Community

Ambitious Instruction

Leadership

Partnerships with Families and Communities

Climates for Student Learning

District must ensure:

Alignment and Coherence

Continuous Improvement

Capacity Building

Equitable Use of District Resources Based on Need

Source: Elevating Our Vision for Learning: Improving Schools for All (Chicago: Chicago Public Schools, 2011), 6.

Figure 2.2e Manifestations of the five essential supports for improving schools over a twenty-five-year history

As it appears in the Consortium's online portal (2020).

MEASURES

- Program Coherence *T*
- Teacher-Principal Trust *T*
- Teacher Influence *T*
- Instructional Leadership *T*

- Peer Support for Academic Work *K-8, S*
- Academic Personalism *K-8, S*
- Safety *S*
- Student-Teacher Trust *S*
- School-Wide Future Orientation *HS, S*
- Expectations for Post-Secondary Education *HS, T*

ESSENTIALS

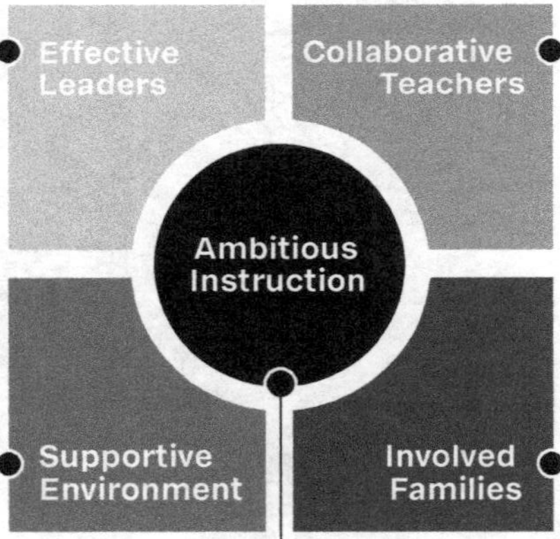

Effective Leaders

Collaborative Teachers

Ambitious Instruction

Supportive Environment

Involved Families

- English Instruction *S*
- Math Instruction *S*
- Academic Press *T*
- Quality of Student Discussion *T*

MEASURES

- Collaborative Practices *T*
- Collective Responsibility *T*
- Quality Professional Development *T*
- School Commitment *T*
- Teacher-Teacher Trust *T*

- Teacher-Parent Trust *T*
- Parent Involvement in School *T*
- Parent Influence on Decision Making in Schools *T*

T Teacher Survey Measure *S* Student Survey Measure *K-8* K-8 Survey Measure Only *HS* High School Survey Measure Only

Source: Holly Hart et al., *Supporting School Improvement,* 2.

Note: Measures that comprise the supportive environment essential are different for elementary schools (safety, student-teacher trust, peer support for academic work, academic personalism) and high schools (safety, student-teacher trust, school-wide future orientation, expectations for post-secondary education). Thus, each *5Essentials* survey includes twenty measures, but there are twenty-two unique measures.

pieces interconnected, and how a change in one area might produce unintended consequences somewhere else. Similarly, each data display was crafted to "stand on its own" so that readers would be able to understand the core finding(s) represented in a visualization without having to read the accompanying text. Consortium staff also considered ways that a data display might be misinterpreted and deliberately tried to head off such problems.

All of this contributed to a broad take-up of the 5Es in Chicago. As already noted, the framework was first integrated into a CPS template for annual school improvement plans in 1995. Three years later, it had been woven into the CPAA's professional development initiatives, discussed in chapter 3.[61] CPS subsequently encouraged schools to use evidence from their individual reports as the basis for creating these plans. The 5Es also helped structure the first school leadership standards for Chicago schools established in 1998.[62] In the 2000s, it functioned as an anchoring framework for funding decisions by several Chicago foundations, including the Chicago Community Trust and Polk Bros. And as it was taken up by local schools of education in the professional preparation of teachers and principals, it helped shape the "thinking and doing" of a next generation of educators. By the middle 2000s, the 5Es were fully baked into CPS and its exoskeleton and remain so today.

Social learning theorists draw attention to how select frameworks can bring individuals from different backgrounds, who may hold different understandings and interests, into cooperative actions on complex problems.[63] Artifacts that function in this way are called *boundary objects*. Coherent systems of action can emerge from their use even when individuals and organizations operate independently and within separate domains of influence.[64] The 5Es, in conjunction with the Consortium's public-informing efforts, became a boundary object in Chicago. The framework offered a coherent account about the core elements, and interconnections among them, in improving a school to generate better student outcomes. By framing the descriptive reports that the Consortium shared with each school community around the 5Es, and also organizing its analytic accounts to civic actors around them, the Consortium created opportunities for shared learnings to emerge across school communities, inside a still balkanized central office, in the CTU and CPAA, and among foundation officers and their civic leadership boards. With so many possible things that people could talk about and attempt to work on, the framework, and the regular reporting of evidence anchored around it, encouraged sustained attention to the core five essential supports.

An Analytic Complement: A Focus on Learning Gains

Contemporaneous with developing the 5Es framework, another Consortium project was figuring out how best to utilize the CPS's annual test data to evaluate how much students were learning and whether these learning rates were improving over time.[65] This work took longer than expected, as the task was akin to building an infrastructure out of stale marshmallows. On first touch, the marshmallows seemed firm, but when poked—which in this case meant looking more closely at how these data linked together over grade levels and years—it became a sticky mess. Nothing quite lined up as expected and anomalies abounded. This called into question the accuracy of judgments typically offered about the progress of reform based on year-to-year changes in annual test scores.

These concerns led to an effort to develop a more defensible measure of a school's academic productivity.[66] Basically, we needed a better answer to two questions: How much learning is occurring while children are enrolled in a school? Are these learning gains improving over time? Earlier statistical work had revealed that much more variability was found among schools when the focus shifted to learning gains rather than average annual scores.[67] Moreover, conceptually trends in learning gains were a better indicator for judging schools' changing productivity over time.

While it would take several years to sort through the "sticky mess" that was Chicago's test score data, a usable indicator of schools' changing productivity, anchored in student learning gains, finally emerged. This was the last technical problem to solve en route to connecting the 5Es to Chicago's reform aims. At last, the Consortium had hard empirical evidence that a school's data on the 5Es was strongly linked to whether that school showed improving learning gains over time. Moreover, subsequent research would find that these results held up across the system decentralization of Era 1, the centralized accountability-driven reforms of Era 2, and a period of expanded choice that began in Era 3 and continued into Era 4. Regardless of these major policy shifts, the difference between improving and non-improving schools remained characterized by their progress on strengthening the 5Es.[68]

Within a five-year period that began at the end of Era 1 and continued to the end of Era 2, Chicago had moved to the forefront on research informing school improvement. The evaluation of the CAC had created the opportunity for much of this to happen. Its final report, published early in Era 3, described the quality of the classroom instruction and coherence of instructional programs across grades and supplemental services. It examined the quality of the professional development efforts to support instructional improvement and the capacity of a school faculty to work collaboratively toward this. Undergirding this was attention to the social relational aspect of schooling—a student-centered learning climate and connections to parents and community. Last, it focused on how school leadership could advance (or sometimes undermine) all of this. Although parts of the 5E framework had been in use since 1995, the CAC evaluation was the first time that longitudinal data on how individual school communities were changing was directly connected to improved student learning gains and attendance.[69] An integrated evidentiary system showing how schools generated improved outcomes finally existed.[70] Looking back now, the timing proved propitious because it coincided with the arrival of new system leaders who were ready and willing to engage it.

ERA 3: 2001–2009
DIRECT PARTNERSHIPS WITH THE CPS:
A GOLDEN ERA

As noted in chapter 1, a near unitary politics operated in Chicago under the second Mayor Daley. The Amendatory Act gave him unprecedented control over the school system. He also held a strong majority across the voting public and maintained a stranglehold over the city council.[71] Consequently, any CEO the mayor appointed had extensive power and Vallas had wielded this authority during Era 2. In contrast, CEO Duncan brought a different orientation into Era 3. Humble about what he could directly affect, he listened to others about what they thought the CPS needed. This openness sometimes gave the impression that the system was rudderless, but it also reflected a realistic appraisal of the complexity of the challenges confronting the district and the limited capabilities in the central office that Duncan had inherited, especially around improving teaching and learning. As detailed in chapters 3 and 4, utilizing partnerships with external organizations that had capabilities that the district lacked became a major strategy for filling the gaps. This put the Consortium in position to work in new ways with the district and represented a seismic shift for the Consortium relative to the Vallas era. During Era 2, Duncan had been reading Consortium reports and trusting them as the best source of evidence about what was and was not happening in the district. Moreover, Easton had been helpful to him on numerous occasions both before and after he began working for Vallas; a positive relationship had developed between them.[72] Duncan invited both Easton and Roderick to help him in the central office to get his new administration off the ground.[73]

The Consortium's Era 3 research agenda had multiple strands. The 5Es remained a major organizing framework for in-depth looks at school leadership, the quality of teaching resources, and emerging district efforts to improve instruction.[74] It was now deeply embraced by the CPS.[75] *Catalyst* continued to direct attention to the 5Es as a framework for improving practice in schools. The lead story in the November 2006 issue—"How the Good Schools Do It"—used the 5Es as an organizer for their in-depth accounts of transformation efforts in three schools. Likewise, with Easton back inside the CPS, the metric of schools' learning gains quickly became part of CPS's annual school report cards, alongside average test scores, and well before any national attention focused there. (The power of this development would surface some ten years later in the learning rate results reported by Sean Reardon and colleagues and summarized in this book's introduction.)

Consortium researchers also targeted inquiries on variation in outcomes for specific subgroups of students, including those who were English learners, mobile, or special education students and those living in challenging circumstances such as homelessness, foster care, domestic violence, and abuse. While the agenda in Era 1 had focused almost exclusively on elementary schools, with attention to high schools added during Era 2, improving high schools moved to the forefront of the Consortium's work in Era 3. This led to the development of a second major framework: keeping students on track to succeed in high school, to graduate, and to move onto college. Although its full impact was not apparent until Era 4, high school graduation rates, which had been stagnant for decades, now began to improve. Here again an initiating force for productive change came from the exoskeleton into CPS, but now system leaders were open to these changes and put their resources and authorities behind scaling them.

On Track Through High School

In 1989, Yeow Meng Thum and Bryk used national data to explore high schools' effects on students' dropping out. Almost all prior research had focused on student characteristics—how students of color, those with weak academic backgrounds, and those from low-income families or where neither parent had gone to college were more likely to drop out. There had been little examination, however, of the role that the schools themselves played.[76] The tacit assumption was that by the time these students got to the more rigorous academic demands of high school, they just couldn't keep up and dropping out was inevitable. In contrast, Bryk and Thum's study, which controlled for student characteristics, found significant variation in dropout rates among high schools, linked to how these places were organized and operated.

Melissa Roderick's recruitment to UChicago created an opportunity for the Consortium to pursue this further. Her dissertation had focused on how students' experiences in high schools led many to drop out. Bryk recruited her to extend this work in Chicago by securing funding for a study that followed ninety-eight students as they moved from eighth grade through their freshman year of high school.[77] Much as the Center took direct efforts in elementary schools, Roderick also embedded herself in high schools in North Lawndale, a westside, economically depressed African

American neighborhood. She, like her colleagues in the Center for School Improvement, was proximate to the real challenges confronting neighborhood schools seeking to improve.

In tandem with these case study accounts, Eric Camburn, then on the Consortium's staff, began to access the district's high school transcript files. He analyzed the courses that students were taking and the grades they earned. He also looked at absenteeism over time and course by course. No one had done this before. The evidence was overwhelming; high schools in Chicago were organized for failure.[78] Even students who had been successful in elementary school ran a substantial risk of failing one or more academic courses in their first high school semester. The pass rate for these students typically worsened over the next few semesters, culminating in their dropping out. The full depth and contours of these findings would take considerably more analysis over the next several years, but the general pattern was clear. The concept of a student being on track for high school success was first introduced in individual reports to elementary and high schools in 1999, formalized as "OnTrack" in a 2002 citywide report and then validated as a key predictor for high school graduation in 2005 by Allensworth and Easton.[79] A robust theoretical-analytic foundation was taking shape to attack this problem early in Era 3, and the relationship between the Consortium and CPS's new leaders eased the way.

Soon after the release of the 2002 study, Duncan added the OnTrack indicator to high school accountability reports. He told his senior leadership team that "this is what we should be working on," and principals soon realized that their area instructional officers (AIOs) would be asking how their freshman were doing.[80] To support this, Allensworth and Easton visited high schools regularly to share findings and answer questions, and Duncan invited Easton to update his senior cabinet about the work many times. From the start, Duncan's embrace signaled districtwide the importance of getting and keeping students on track. Nevertheless, the district's OnTrack rate barely moved the next four years. (See figure 2.3.) The indicator itself, even when championed by the CEO, was insufficient.

The tide started to turn when Roderick invited a select group of high school principals—whom she knew were frustrated about the pace of change in their schools—to work with her on the OnTrack problem. Sarah

Figure 2.3   Trends in Freshman OnTrack rates and high school graduation rates four years later

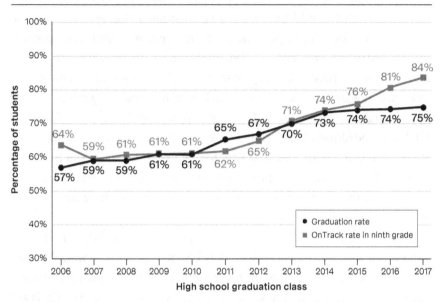

Source: Jenny Nagaoka, Alex Seeskin, and Vanessa M. Coca, *The Educational Attainment of Chicago Public Schools Students: 2016* (Chicago: University of Chicago Consortium on School Research, 2017), 5, 10.

Note: A more restrictive definition of the graduation rate was used in this study as compared to the rates reported in figure 1.2. See note in that figure for a further explanation.

Duncan, a colleague at UChicago, joined the effort. The Network for College Success (NCS) grew from this small group of reform-oriented educators. Some of them would eventually start new charter schools, a few became core staff at NCS, and others would continue to work directly on improving CPS high schools. Future CEO Janice Jackson was in that last group.[81]

Facilitating the subsequent growth of NCS was a rapid turnover among high school principals that had been precipitated by the opening of new high schools and the large numbers of schools placed on probation, which often meant a new principal was assigned. Roderick recruited from among these new leaders, looking for colleagues who shared an improvement mindset.[82] This meant committing to keeping students on track for success, supporting teacher development and pluralizing leadership around this specific challenge, using data as a resource to inform improvement efforts, and engaging as a network learning community.[83]

NCS was an important addition to Chicago's exoskeleton. Internal to the district and in tandem with NCS's emergence, Duncan hired Paige Ponder to take on what would become his Graduation Pathways Department. "How the district might pull the lever on Freshman OnTrack" became Ponder's driving concern. While numerous CPS dropout prevention and recovery initiatives already existed, little impact was apparent. Rather than rush out still another systemwide initiative, Ponder organized a small improvement network consisting of six high schools with two full-time OnTrack coordinators embedded in each. The coordinators reported to their principals, with a dotted line to Ponder. Like NCS, the initiative embraced a continuous improvement orientation: Local educators were encouraged to try things, learn by trial and error, and share information about what they were learning.

Ponder's central office team developed an information infrastructure to support these improvement efforts. They began by piloting a "watchlist data report" for each high school on their incoming ninth graders, including age on entry, prior grades, and attendance.[84] Based on what her OnTrack coordinators were learning through their work in schools, Ponder and her colleagues continually modified the reports to improve their clarity and usefulness. By 2008, their efforts had expanded into an integrated system of reports to assist high schools: The watchlist identified which students might be at risk for failure as they started high school, a success report captured each student's grades and attendance every five weeks and identified anyone falling off track, and a credit recovery report listed freshmen who had failed courses and needed to enroll in summer school or another credit recovery program. These reports kept a stream of timely information in front of the educators who were working directly with students.

Complementing this, the Consortium also produced individualized reports for every high school based on end-of-year data. It plotted OnTrack rates, attendance, and grades for different subgroups of students and whether these trend lines were improving or declining over time. These reports were especially useful to principals and instructional leadership teams because they provided an actionable view of where the school was succeeding and where more attention was needed.

Taken together, these efforts signaled a normative shift about data: From data "about them" aiming to hold them accountable, to information to "for them" to assist their local change efforts. Schools became more aware of what was and was not happening in their buildings and began to see patterns in their individual school results. This system of reports provided an essential feedback loop. Staff could readily see in these data whether the changes they were attempting were paying off in improvements for students.

Along the way, Consortium researchers had continued to study the factors affecting the flows of students through high school. Ponder viewed their 2007 report, *What Matters for Staying On-Track and Graduating in Chicago Public High Schools*, as her bible.[85] Consortium research had finally traced the dropout problem back to primary sources.[86] The initial studies had focused on whether students were OnTrack in ninth grade, based on the number of courses passed during their freshman year. But a final course grade, including an F for failing a course, is a lagging indicator. Like dropping out, the information is only available after the process is concluded. The 2007 study sharpened attention to how student attendance was key to attaining the passing grades necessary to achieve course credit. And researchers went one step further upstream in recognizing that a final course grade is the cumulative result of a set of processes that occur day by day in schools. They found that one of the 5Es, the presence of a student-centered learning climate, proved especially significant in shaping how these processes played out. A working improvement theory had formed: students were more likely to attend regularly, and thereby achieve passing grades, in schools where they felt safe, had supportive relationships with their teachers, and believed that the academic work they were doing was important for their future.[87]

Drawing on the data reports from the Graduation Pathways Department, high schools began developing new structures and processes for reaching out to students at the first sign that they might be falling behind in a class or slipping in attendance. Drawing on lessons from the Consortium studies, school staff were now focused on strengthening their personal ties to students. If they were more aware of what might be going on for a given student, they could more readily address concerns that might arise.

The CPS and Consortium teams became an intense problem-solving partnership. Ponder commented, "[We all] shared a mission, and we coached each other. It was gritty, challenging work about putting research into practice, and we were a team."[88]

In close connection to these informing-improvement efforts, NCS continued to expand the human capabilities and professional communities needed to use this information well. Roderick managed to have the NCS-affiliated schools formally designated as one of the district's support "areas." (*Areas* was Era 2's term for what had formerly been subdistricts or regions and would later be called networks.) Geographically, NCS schools were sprinkled across the city, but as an affinity group they were called Area 21. This arrangement freed principals and teacher leaders from required Area meetings and created time for them to team on this targeted concern. Area 21 had been consciously designed as a supportive space, where principals explored each other's data and where it was safe to ask, "Your students are a lot like mine, but your outcomes are better. What are you doing to get those results?"[89]

In 2012 the district reorganized its area offices, and Area 21 schools were folded back into the general system. Regardless, much had been learned while Area 21 had functioned as an affinity group. Numerous school staff had gained experience attacking the OnTrack problem, an improvement-oriented colleagueship had formed, and evangelizing leaders emerged to spread this work. Moreover, while the inspiration for Area 21 had been to keep freshmen on track, an overall strategy for school improvement had emerged: educators joined as communities within and across schools, focused on a specific problem with a measurable aim, experimented with different interventions, regularly used evidence to evaluate progress, and continued to revise and retry iterating toward better results.[90] A broad-based networked improvement community had dynamically evolved in Chicago.

As is often noted, distinctive aspects of a culture are most salient to the stranger who is new to the scene. As Krone Phillips recounts in her book *The Make-or-Break Year*, it was the OnTrack movement that stood out to Jean-Claude Brizard when he was recruited from Rochester to take on the CEO role in Chicago. He said:

The CPS was not short on strategy. It was short on execution. I called the system Frankenstein's monster because I saw a lot of amazing parts, but the whole was incoherent. Freshman OnTrack [however] was the clear outlier. When I talked to principals, they all talked about the ninth-grade metric. Principals just didn't care about it, they believed in it, and they believed in the results they were getting. . . . It was everywhere. I had never seen that before. Ever.[91]

By the end of Era 3 a district-wide OnTrack improvement movement had been launched, and it persisted through Era 4. As seen in figure 2.3, OnTrack rates in ninth grade began to steadily rise and improved graduation rates followed four years later. Corroborating evidence about the core mechanisms for these improvements are found in trend data from the Consortium's high school students' surveys. (See figure 2.4.) Increasingly, students reported more positive relationships with their teachers and peers, and a deepening engagement with academic work. Strengthening a more personalized environment that both pressed and supported students to work hard academically, while simultaneously fostering a schoolwide climate of academic success, were at the heart of efforts to keep students on track.

To and Through to College Success

OnTrack had brought attention to the transition of students from elementary into high schools. Beginning in 2003, Roderick's research began to shift to their transition from high school to postsecondary and beyond. Big urban school systems are akin to "leaky pipelines" where, at multiple junctures, a student's progress easily can be sidetracked.[92] These leaks persist because in the traditional organization of school systems, no one typically owns these transitions as their problem to solve.[93]

Joining Roderick in this work on the CPS side was Gudelia Lopez. Lopez had been at the Consortium on the CAC evaluation team investigating the quality of classroom instruction. She had seen firsthand the weak quality of the lessons in many Chicago classrooms, but also that when more ambitious tasks were offered with support to succeed, students rose to the

Figure 2.4 Improving high school student reports about supportive relationships with teachers and peers, and increased press toward academic work

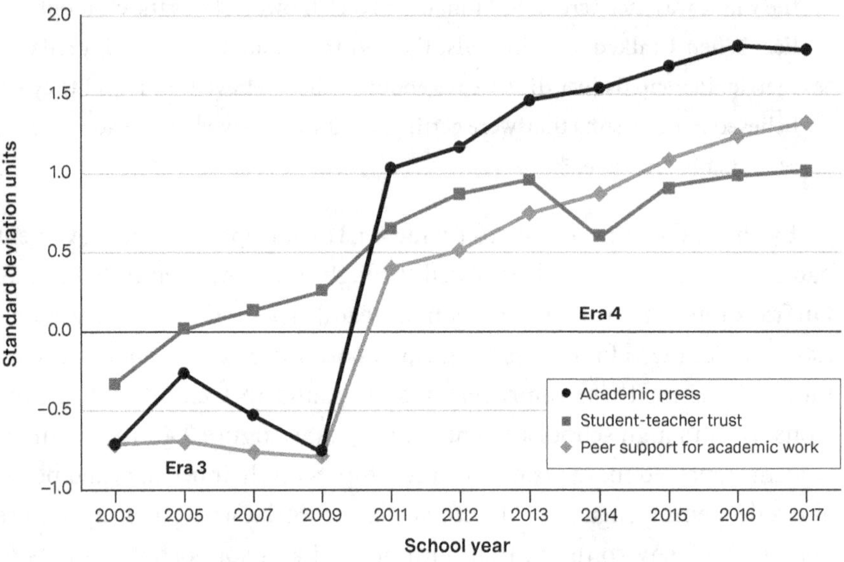

Source: UChicago Consortium on School Research, 2021.

Note: Trends are based on Rasch measures constructed from survey items collected by the Consortium in repeated 5E surveys. Academic press consists of student reports about their teachers' academic expectations. Student-teacher trust gauges student reports about the quality of the relationships themselves and their teachers. Peer support for academic work measures student reports on their peers' behaviors.

challenge. She had moved over to CPS in 1998, as part of Easton's effort to strengthen the district's internal research capacity. She was subsequently recruited into a new CPS Department on Postsecondary Education that Greg Darnieder had been hired to launch. Darnieder and Roderick had previously partnered to develop a charter high school in North Lawndale when Darnieder was CEO for the Steans Family Foundation. Leading the research side for this new department was especially salient to Lopez, who was a first-generation Latina college-goer.[94]

Roderick, Lopez, Allensworth, and Jenny Nagaoka, a Consortium deputy director, collaborated on a breakthrough contribution by linking CPS student data to information from the National Student Clearinghouse on individual students' enrollment and progress through college. This was the first time that any district had detailed evidence about what happened to its graduates. It also signaled the emergence of a productive division of labor between the CPS and Consortium, with the more rapid formative evaluation work and reporting to schools occurring under Lopez at CPS, and the longer-term and more complex measure development and predictive analytic studies to inform those efforts conducted by the Consortium.

Critical conversation characterized the dialogue between this research partnership and Darnieder program staff as they met every five to six weeks. According to Darnieder, Roderick would present new analyses and then ask her CPS colleagues, "What are you going to do about this? . . . We did not take it personally. She never told us what to do. She just presented the data and challenged us to do something about it. This continued for seven years! . . . Data was the truth teller. It is about being smart about the work that needs to be done."[95]

It quickly became apparent in the course of these deliberations that the system needed to build capacity to better support students' postsecondary pursuits.[96] High schools were generally understaffed for college counseling, and no extant professional preparation existed for this specialized role. The CPS team confronted a human resource development problem. The effort to resolve it started small, initially in twelve high schools. Darnieder recruited six "postsecondary specialists" to lead this work; most came from local nonprofit organizations focused on college access. These individuals in turn supported twelve "college coaches" who were recent college graduates, had been educated in the CPS, and were often assigned back to their original high schools. They knew both the school communities and the journey ahead for the students they were coaching. In addition, Darnieder tasked the CPS head of high school counseling to design a specialized professional education program to build counselors' capabilities for this new CPS role. By redeploying federal Perkins funding and obtaining resources from other governmental programs and local foundation support, some ninety coaching positions were eventually created.

One early discovery on the data side was how critical students' completion of the Free Application for Federal Student Aid (FAFSA) was for enrolling in college. These data previously had not been accessible, and this was still one more problem that had been hiding in plain sight. The team was the first in a major district to create a FAFSA data system that notified high schools about their students' progress submitting the form.

Another early discovery came to be called "summer melt." Numerous students were seemingly leaking from the pipeline: they completed the application and financial aid processes, were accepted by a postsecondary institution, indicated in late spring that they planned to enroll, but then failed to do so in the fall. So, the CPS again moved in an innovative direction when it began to "own the transition" into postsecondary. This spawned efforts to strengthen partnerships with local colleges around assuring student progress.

The working relationship between the Consortium and CPS, however, took a hit in 2006 when the Consortium published *From High School to the Future: A First Look at Chicago Public School Graduates' College Enrollment, College Preparation, and Graduation from Four-Year Colleges.* This was its first public report from this research program. The problem arose when the *Chicago Tribune* drew on select results from the report to assemble an unsettling data visualization. It depicted one hundred freshman students as stickpins and showed that only six would receive a bachelor's degree within ten years. (See figure 2.5.) The headline surprised both CPS and Consortium staff, as this particular result was not called out explicitly

Figure 2.5   How the *Chicago Tribune* reported on *From High School to the Future*

in the report summary nor in the "no surprises" prebriefing. The story appeared at the top of *Tribune*'s front page and garnered immediate public attention. Duncan told Easton it was "the worst publicity I've ever gotten. . . . People ask me why I bother with you guys when you can cause so much trouble."[97] This was déjà vu for the Consortium, but now it was Duncan, rather than Vallas, who was upset. On balance, the *Tribune* was just doing its journalists' job as a public watchdog, bringing attention to this important problem. Easton apologized for not foreseeing how the *Tribune* would report this, but he also pointed out how findings from the report suggested productive next steps that Duncan might take.[98] Inside the politics of a research-practice partnership, this media ambush represented an existential threat. The partnership survived this attack because of the past reservoir of trust that had built up between Duncan and Easton.

Darnieder, Lopez, Roderick, and Nagaoka continued to identify more leaks in the pipeline that derailed students from their postsecondary aspirations.[99] One was the "undermatching problem." Many CPS graduates were enrolling in colleges that were less selective than they were actually qualified to attend, and where completion rates were often lower. When students enrolled in these colleges, their likelihood of success diminished.[100] Another new target for improvement had been identified.

Along the way, and as news of this work spread locally and nationally, requests for advice from Consortium staff escalated. The Consortium now needed a standing communications capacity to support this expanding public-informing mission. By 2013 this grew to represent about 10 percent of the Consortium's staffing.[101] In addition to this was the time spent by study researchers with the steering committee and in maintaining relationships with the district's central office, the mayor's office, CTU, nonprofits, foundation and business groups, *Catalyst*, and principals and teachers in schools. Being present and proximate to these various Chicago's constituents was an essential complement to the academic rigor that Consortium staff brought to their research activities.

By the end of Era 3, both OnTrack (including attention through to postsecondary success) and the 5Es were deeply established in the Chicago context. Each offered a compelling framework coupled with regular data feedback. Both were grounded in basic educational research findings, and their detailed specification benefitted from collaborations among researchers, school-based educators, and reform advocates—all trying, from their own vantage points, to improve schools. Both functioned as well-crafted boundary objects that brought people together to reflect and initiate new forms of collective action. And this improvement learning was spread, in turn, citywide through an expanded set of boundary spanners who worked across different institutions over time—in schools, in central office, in local foundations, and in the other key institutions identified in chapter 1. These individuals brought what they were learning into the work life of these many varied organizations. The DNA of decentralization, which had grown out of a citywide mobilization for reform in the mid-1980s, birthed this dynamic. It matured in form and expanded in size under supportive system leadership in Era 3 and constituted a formidable resource as Era 4 began.

ERA 4: 2010–2017
NEW CHALLENGES EMERGE

New Year's 2009 heralded the first of many changes in leadership in CPS and its exoskeleton. Duncan left to become Obama's secretary of education. The following year, Eason-Watkins left to become a superintendent in a neighboring district. Daley chose not to stand for reelection in 2011 and was succeeded by Rahm Emanuel. And so started an eight-year period of CPS leadership churn. Responding to these rapid changes proved challenging for the Consortium. Until the appointment of Janice Jackson in 2017, most of the new CEOs were from outside the system, and Huberman (2009) and Claypool (2015) were not educators. Bringing these new leaders up to speed in terms of the Consortium's mission, the distinctive way it did its work, and most importantly, the significance of its major frameworks—the 5Es, OnTrack, and To&Through—was critical. This charge fell to Allensworth, Roderick, Sebring, and Nagaoka. (Easton followed Duncan to Washington to lead the Institute of Education Sciences.) Allensworth became Consortium executive director in 2013.

Throughout this period Consortium directors had no choice but to spent considerable time building relationships with each new CEO, articulating how existing research plans connected to their expressed concerns, and starting new projects responsive to their priorities. Relational trust had to be built with each, and the Consortium had to prove itself again and again. In each transition the Consortium's continued access to data was subject to question. On one occasion its ability to continue to produce Freshman OnTrack reports was placed in doubt. Fortunately, the Consortium's relationships with stakeholders in the exoskeleton and with middle managers in CPS provided crucial support. In one key meeting, network chiefs and principals pleaded with the CEO for the continuation of the Consortium trend reports for Freshman OnTrack, as they were using these to guide their improvement efforts.[102] All new studies were now subject to extensive review and preapproval by CPS. Bureaucratic processes overlaid what previously was a more collegial undertaking. Although most proposed studies were allowed to go forward, new hurdles and time delays accrued.

Nevertheless, the productive relationships built up during Era 3 between individual department heads and Consortium staff enabled good work to continue. When Chicago embraced universal preschool and full-day kindergarten, a strong collaboration developed among the Consortium, the CPS Office of Early Childhood Education, the Chicago Department of Family and Support Services and the Ounce of Prevention (a local nonprofit focused on early childhood that was subsequently renamed Start Early).[103] The Consortium also partnered with the CPS talent office on a series of studies to inform their effort to implement a new teacher evaluation system, discussed in chapter 3. In addition, targeted studies focused on new CPS initiatives, including the introduction of the Common Core State Standards, efforts to improve student success in algebra classes, and better integration of technology into teaching and learning.

Shifting priorities with each new CEO and then a state budget crisis partway through Era 4, however, eventually caused significant churn among key CPS departmental leaders.[104] Some of the Consortium's strongest partners from Era 3 left, and a few projects lost their CPS connection.

Consortium researchers finished them, but there was literally no one at CPS to talk with about the findings.[105] Even when staff were replaced, the generative quality of the learning, which had characterized the CPS-Consortium relationship during Era 3, weakened. For example, when Darnieder left CPS to join Duncan in DC, Huberman brought in a staffer from the Chicago Transit Authority to take over. She had no education background and never got close to the improvement work occurring in schools.[106] Conversations about new studies and the implications of previous findings became more transactional.

Even so, Consortium staff continued their outreach to the central office, individual schools, networks of schools, and community-based organizations in the city. Consortium and Urban Education Institute (UEI) leaders also now regularly engaged Chicago's civic leadership. (UEI evolved out of the Center and became the home for the Consortium within the University of Chicago.) Timothy Knowles, who led UEI, served on several boards, including those of Renaissance 2010, After School Matters (an organization founded by Mayor Daley's wife), and A Better Chicago, which worked to build the capacity of nonprofits to reduce poverty. Emanuel frequently turned to Knowles for advice as well. Allensworth was cochair of the Illinois Commission on High School Graduation Achievement and Success and served on the academic advisory committee for Archdiocese of Chicago Catholic Schools. Sebring was a board member for the Chicago Public Education Fund and the School of Education and Social Policy at Northwestern University. Joining Sebring in these efforts was her husband, Chuck Lewis. They had launched the Lewis-Sebring Family Foundation focused on education and equity, and Lewis served on the UChicago board of trustees. Meetings of these various boards, and other social occasions derivative of them, created opportunities for Knowles, Sebring, Allensworth, and Lewis to share study findings. The Consortium's core frameworks and measures and the analyses based on them continued to spread across the city, moved statewide, and increasingly drew national attention as well.

Choice, Charters, Contracting, and Closing Schools

As noted in chapter 1, Ren10 began under Duncan and Daley in Era 3, but it exploded in Era 4 when Emanuel became mayor. This was another instance where the Consortium had to wade into a highly controversial space initiated by district-level policy actions. As detailed in chapter 1, the original Ren10 plan from 2004 called for the closing of many neighborhood schools and the opening of new charter and contract schools. While the opening of new schools had rapidly moved forward in Era 3, the complementary closing of neighborhood schools proceeded at a slower pace. By 2013, CPS leaders had to confront the true cost of Ren10. Over the previous decade, the number of schools had grown substantially while overall enrollment had declined. Many facilities were substantially underutilized, and after 2010, revenues were more constrained, precipitated first by the Great Recession and then the State of Illinois's own fiscal issues. The consequences played out mostly in African American communities on the south and west sides.

The Consortium had published a report in 2009 focused on the first group of eighteen elementary schools closed during Era 3. Some of these schools were subsequently reopened as focused themed schools directly operated by the CPS; other closures created space for new charter and contract schools run by a variety of nonprofit organizations. While new schools opened in over half of the old facilities, others were permanently shuttered, primarily in the areas adjacent to demolished high-rise public housing.

As noted in chapter 1, the explicit rationale for this first round of school closures, and for Ren10 more generally, was to improve children's learning opportunities, but this first Consortium study found that this proved not to be the case.[107] The lives of many students and their families were disrupted by this process, and most displaced students just moved from one low performing school to another. A small number, about 6 percent of students, did manage to transfer to a substantially higher performing school and did benefit, but the vast majority did not. While the promise of students moving to opportunity was a compelling idea, the district's ability to execute on this, equitably and reliably, proved elusive.[108]

Come 2013, CPS leaders were aware of these challenges, but they now confronted what had taken shape as an "impossible problem to solve."[109] The system simply had too many schools, and some forty-nine more were closed in one sweep.

The Consortium set out to analyze the impact of this new wave of closings in what was then a fraught civic context. Even initiating the project proved challenging. In contrast to earlier eras when general operating support from local foundations funded much of the Consortium's work, by Era 4 every major project needed separate funding. Some funders, however, viewed further inquiries about school closures too sensitive and chose not to support the study. Consortium leaders did not give up; they knew that this issue had to be investigated. The search for funding delayed the project, but staff were eventually able to cobble resources together to move it forward.[110]

A first report, focused on parental choices and experiences, was released in 2015. The findings showed that for many families, a school's quality rating was often less important than basic logistical considerations of proximity to home and getting their child safely to and from school.[111] Significantly, all of the closings were elementary schools, and attending a neighborhood elementary school remained a strong parental preference, even within a district now committed to choice. About 20 percent of students had transferred to a substantially better school, and their outcomes looked improved. For most students, however, either neutral or negative impacts occurred across an array of indicators.

The convening organized by the Consortium for the report's public release was packed with angry parents, teachers, and community leaders who interrupted the panel discussion that followed the presentation of findings.[112] Widespread upset was expressed about the chaotic processes they had experienced as so many schools were closed all at once. A second report, which examined students' outcomes and impact on teachers, was ready for release in 2017, but it was delayed because of multiple requests for prerelease briefings. Several rounds occurred at CPS and the mayor's office.[113] The Consortium Investor Council, which had provided some financial support, also requested its own prerelease briefing, as did UChicago's

Information Office and its Office of Civic Engagement. And although the school closings had unfolded back in the summer of 2013, the visceral reactions among parents and teachers had not been forgotten even as the final report was released five years later in 2018.

Zooming out from the specific impacts of the school closures, assessments of Ren10 reflect two very different evaluative standpoints. Advocates for the strategy, while recognizing the many issues raised, still saw much to praise.[114] The schools closed were extremely low achieving and had a long history of dysfunction.[115] Parents and communities had been empowered during Era 1, and these schools had received a substantial influx of discretionary dollars, but the schools did not improve. Vallas had targeted these same schools with both extended programming and strong accountability efforts, and this too had failed. Corporate leaders, and some community and civil rights advocates, saw a need for a more radical turn. Extending parents' choice through the opening of new schools seemed a plausible answer.

As noted in the introduction, the overall distribution on student outcomes did improve in charter high schools, especially in terms of graduates moving on to postsecondary institutions. So, "more good seats" existed than had been the case a decade earlier, and choice among high schools had expanded. That was Duncan's original aspiration, and from this point of view, advocates could claim some success.

A very different story unfolded in terms of the students and communities affected by the elementary school closings.[116] In contrast to charter high schools, there is no evidence of superior outcomes in Chicago's charter elementary schools, and this is significant in that all of the closings were elementary schools.[117] So even as these new schools opened, often on the south and west sides of the city, they did not fundamentally change students' educational opportunities. Moreover, neighborhood children were not even assured of admission to these new schools, and many families were challenged with getting their children to more distant schools where concerns about their children's safety were heightened. And for the affected communities, long-standing relationships of residents to the people and places of their neighborhood schools had been ruptured. Their closing was one more insult, one more reminder of a long history of discrimination they had experienced. The trauma this caused would not ease any time soon.

Pressing Ahead

While the Consortium was navigating its way through this political maelstrom, work continued on other fronts.

Evolution of the 5Es Survey.   In 2011, the 5Es survey system went online and was administered annually.[118] Consonant with the spirit of the original decentralization reform, the 5E surveys had been designed and operated for two decades as a support to inform local school improvement efforts. Survey reports were made available to the principal, the chairs of the LSC and the teachers' professional advisory committee. The Consortium treated the reports as the property of each local school community and encouraged local school leaders to share them broadly within their communities. No individual school-by-school comparative results were ever released. This policy was thought essential to assure participation and preserve the integrity of the data system.

But Chicago's institutional reform logic had now evolved and become multifaceted. While local control persisted, Chicago was now also a "choice district," and CPS leaders argued that families should have access to information on all schools, to inform their enrollment decisions. Also, Huberman had ushered in a performance management system and district leaders wanted to own and use this data accordingly.[119] This set off a difficult round of conversations, in which it remained unclear for a while whether the 5E surveys would continue or be replaced by some district alternative. Gradually a set of compromises was struck. In 2013, Consortium leaders agreed to make the results from all schools publicly available to everyone in the city, and all 5E school reports became accessible online. As part of the compromise, and consistent with the Consortium's "no surprises rule," CPS agreed that school leaders could receive the results during the summer (after a spring administration) and have time to examine them and engage their communities around them before a public release in the fall.

Also in 2013, the 5Es surveys went statewide in Illinois. From a historical perspective, this was an extraordinary development. An initiative that
had developed in the "worst system in the nation" was being adopted by
districts well outside its boundaries. This state-level initiative, fueled by developments in Chicago, was also consonant with a national press to expand the evidence available to the public about their schools.[120]

In a complementary fashion, CPS moved in 2014 to incorporate 5Es
results as a component of a school's overall accountability rating. Consortium staff understood that the incentives embedded in high-stakes
accountability systems—to maximize what is measured—can distort future
individual and organizational performance and ultimately the validity
of the evidence itself. Counterbalancing this was an argument that
making this data a small component in a school's accountability rating
would deepen school leaders' attention to the framework as a guide for
improvement.[121] In the end, CPS leaders insisted, and the Consortium
acquiesced.

As these extensive changes played out, the Consortium proceeded to examine what was happening on the ground. A field study reported that
some teachers in some schools had become skeptical of the results and were
now doubtful about their usefulness for informing improvement plans.[122]
The Consortium also replicated earlier validation studies that had previously linked improvements in the 5Es measures to gains in student learning, attendance, and grades. A quick jump districtwide in some survey
measures had occurred once 5Es data became part of the accountability
system. Even so, the 5Es continued to function as strong predictors dis-
criminating between improving and non-improving schools.[123] Data corruption may have occurred in some schools, but it was not so widespread
as to undermine the overall utility of the system.

Freshman OnTrack and To&Through to College Success.[124]   Collaboration between the Network for College Success (NCS), the CPS office of
graduation pathways, and the Consortium was sustained in Era 4.[125] Eventually the Graduation Pathways Department closed, but the momentum
around keeping freshman on track to high school graduation persisted, as

the work now had strong footing in schools. By 2017, the networked improvement community launched by NCS had reached thirty-four high schools. Hundreds of teachers and dozens of counselors and principals were working together on this problem. Other school-support organizations in the exoskeleton had also stepped up, and the real-time CPS data system to inform these efforts remained in place.[126] Despite district cutbacks, improvements continued to spread.

The Consortium also was able to continue a strong relationship with the Office of Postsecondary Education.[127] Almost every year, the Consortium released a new study, and its researchers, along with NCS leaders, met regularly with district staff to tease out the practical implications of emerging results.[128] NCS in turn brought these findings into their ongoing meetings with high school staff and the professional learning community that had formed among college counselors. Along the way, the district added college enrollment and persistence data to its accountability scorecard for high schools and developed an information system for real-time tracking of students' college applications and financial aid applications for college. Families also had access to these data. Improvement learning continued to deepen and expand here too.

A New Program Develops.   Beginning in 2012, a research program that was initially referred to as "noncognitive development," and is now described as social-emotional development, emerged.[129] It was led by Camille Farrington collaborating with Allensworth, Roderick, and Nagaoka.[130] Past Consortium projects typically involved field studies, the design of new survey instruments, and analyses of extant data resources. In contrast, this initiative consisted primarily of literature reviews. Articles were published in national academic journals and policy outlets, and this too was a departure from the Consortium's long-standing priority of first reporting out to district and citywide leadership groups and individual schools. A reliance on non-Chicago-based funding sources caused this shift in how the Consortium did its work.[131]

The program focused attention on an array of student outcomes, beyond test scores, grades, and attendance.[132] Experimental studies in social psychology had drawn attention to how students' educational success depends on their sense of belonging at school; maintaining a growth mindset to persist when confronting new challenges; and seeing the relevance, purpose, and value of what they were being asked to learn. This line of research directed still more attention to the salience of a student-centered learning environment—one of the 5Es. Order and safety in schools, and personal support for students from both teachers and other students, came forward in this literature as key levers for change. In this regard, the project's articles had a ready audience in NCS, as they spoke directly to its own efforts to reform relationships in high schools in ways that better engaged students. New change ideas were being tested and refined in NCS schools that aimed to assure that every student was known well by at least one adult. By strengthening these connections, teachers better understood the many day-to-day issues affecting students and could respond better. In addition, teachers could now see how their efforts were making a real difference. A virtuous cycle of reciprocal benefits manifested with teachers achieving psychic rewards from the very tangible impacts they were having on students' lives.

A residual from prior reforms assisted in this regard. Beginning in the mid-1990s numerous efforts resulted in the creation of substantially smaller schools in Chicago. Some of this was deliberate, such as the small-high school movement of the early 2000s. In other instances, it was a by-product of Ren10, which had created many new schools. A long stream of Consortium studies had documented that smaller school size was a supportive condition for sustaining more intimate social connections. This favorable structural condition became an enabling resource for the efforts of NCS and others working with Chicago high schools.

The program on students' social-emotional development continued to build as Era 4 ended and offered promise for further impact. Attending to students' social-emotional development had achieved status as a valued educational goal in its own right. In addition, extant research suggested that it played an important role in advancing the deeper academic learning goals that CPS began to embrace in Era 3, deepened commitment to in Era 4, and was poised to deepen further going forward. Research from the 1990s had documented that efforts to increase the academic press on students needed to be accompanied by strong personal connections with students, and that this was especially salient for students with weaker academic backgrounds and more-challenging family circumstances.[133] So findings from this research program were also a key informing resource for teachers' efforts, detailed in chapter 4, to engage students around more ambitious subject matter.

TAKING STOCK

In 1987, Chicago had no access to trustworthy data on even such basic questions as the size of the dropout rate and the inequities in student outcomes along race and class lines and across different neighborhoods. In response, the Consortium came into existence. Early on, the Consortium became a core resource to many individuals and organizations in the exoskeleton; in turn, it was supported by them, and especially so when relations with the system center became contentious. By the end of Era 3, the Consortium established itself as a central node in what had become a very dense and interconnected set of learning networks in schools, inside the system managerial hierarchy, among key policy leaders, and across numerous organizations in the civic architecture. This allowed much of the improvement learning initiated in Era 3 to continue to evolve, deepen, and spread, and to do so even under the less favorable system-level circumstances of Era 4. With the passing of each era, greater knowledge, clarity, and vision came into focus about what was needed to promote growth in student learning and attainments. As Era 4 closed, educators, civic and community leaders, and the media had become well versed in and sophisticated about the core aspects of school improvement in Chicago. This shared intelligence boded well for the continued development of public education in the city.

It was the challenge to a dysfunctional central bureaucracy in 1987, and the subsequent decentralization of the system, that opened space for the Consortium to emerge as an innovative organizational form. Up to then, serious researchers had not engaged much in place-based studies on improving public education systems. Even the term *research-practice partnership* did not exist. The Consortium and the Center at UChicago broke new ground. Once this path was opened, numerous others entered. Some were highly complementary in extending this improvement-learning ecosystem. Work led by Paul Zavitkovsky at UIC, for example, became the go-to place for in-depth analysis of student test score trends, using local, state, and national data. The Chicago Public Education Fund has built a professional database on school principals, their work histories in the system, and changing outcomes in their respective school communities. Both enterprises are deeply invested in Chicago, in improving its city's schools, and in broadly informing efforts toward this end.

However, some worrisome signs also emerged. The Consortium's access to data became more constrained. While the Consortium continued its stakeholder-based research agenda-setting process, by Era 4 each study, and even their specific research questions, had to be independently approved by the CPS. And new questions that arose during a study could not be investigated without formal CPS approval, even if the data already existed. The Consortium's public-informing mission was now controlled in new ways.

The city also had taken on the trappings of a research marketplace with multiple groups competing for access to data and schools. In principle this brought more research talent to bear on improving schooling. At the same time, it strengthened the CPS as the broker in control of what gets studied, whether report findings are publicly released, and whether opportunities are created for public engagement around them. The civic mission of public informing about efforts to improve schooling, which has been central to the social learning among diverse civic actors, hung in the balance. To date, the balance has remained constructive, but the altered power arrangements that existed as Era 4 closed have created potential for constricting these activities down the road.[134]

Funding for the Consortium had changed too. The general operating support it received during the first two decades allowed it to quickly launch new investigations and supported its public engagement agenda. These grants also covered the costs of the extensive staff involvement in local schools, with CPS department heads and key civic leaders in the exoskeleton. All of this was essential fuel that sustained how the city learned to improve its schools. By Era 4, the Consortium was mostly dependent on project-based funding. While the Consortium's engagement activities remained highly valued, sustaining this aspect of its public-serving mission became more difficult because no grants fully supported it. In response, a Consortium Investment Council came into existence through the leadership efforts of Sebring, Lewis, and Allensworth. It launched an annual giving campaign, targeting individuals and philanthropic organizations, to support the Consortium's outreach efforts, continue to refresh its core data archive, seed new studies, and update core findings over time. The emergence of the investment council is one more instance of the continued evolution in Chicago's exoskeleton as a new issue is identified and an innovation brought forward.

3

Developing the Educator Workforce

In 1988 weaknesses existed at every level of the school system—classroom teaching, school leadership, and basic central office functioning. When the centralized bureaucracy was responsible for hiring teachers and principals, local school and community needs typically were ignored. Teachers were assigned to vacancies without much attention to subject matter certification or prior experience, and new teachers were regularly placed in schools facing the most challenges. Principals often were appointed based on who they knew or how much they contributed to someone's election campaign. The "bloated bureaucracy" was a barrier to improvement.

When the School Reform Act first was enacted, about 85 percent of the city's schools fell well below the student learning targets set out in the legislation. The need for change was enormous, but the overall base of human resources was not up to the task. The decentralization reform had devolved extensive hiring and professional development decisions to local school communities. This was unprecedented for large school districts, and, as noted earlier, school and district leadership churn characterized much of the next thirty years. These were extraordinary conditions and not ones that inspired confidence. Yet the quality of the system's human resources substantially improved over these three decades. How this happened, absent an obvious mechanism for doing so, is the story told here.

ERA 1
BEGINNINGS

Improving the quality of the school system's human resources was not an explicit focus when reform began. Chicago had embraced a governance initiative aiming to shift power from a centralized bureaucracy to parents and community leaders. It was argued that they would be able to make better decisions about how to educate their children and renew schools in ways more attuned to the diverse needs of Chicago's neighborhoods. The 1988 law explicitly reduced central office administrative personnel, and the remaining staff did not see themselves as advocates for the effective implementation of the law and did little to support it. As noted in chapter 1, it was primarily the city's business and philanthropic communities that funded the initiation of Chicago's governance reform. At the same time, Chicago foundations began to seed efforts aimed more broadly at improving how schools worked and the capabilities of the people working in them.[1] A small number of grants made in Era 1 catalyzed early efforts toward whole school transformation, as well as professional development for teachers and principals.[2] While the 1988 governance reform opened up the system to change, achieving better student outcomes depended on educators learning how to use this "opening up" to improve teaching and leading at the school site. Supporting this evolution of understandings were ongoing research studies from the Consortium and *Catalyst* articles that probed into the black box of school improvement. They helped to inform the extensive capacity building that emerged in the exoskeleton in response to these needs across the years of reform. Virtually all of this began outside the system in Eras 1 and 2, with many of the individuals and organizations shifting to work in partnership with the central office beginning in Era 3. This in turn catalyzed efforts at rebuilding the central office's capacity. Most importantly it would change its purpose from compliance management to support for a system of schools.

Early Efforts to Develop Principal Capacities

The 1988 reform had an immediate impact on the principalship in Chicago. LSCs first appointed principals in 1990 and 1991, and by 1992, some 43 percent of principals were new to their schools and 94 percent of the new hires were new principals. In a 1992 Consortium survey almost two-thirds of them agreed with the statement that "school reform created the opportunity for me to become a principal." The new principals were younger and included more women—up from 45 percent pre-reform to 57 percent in 1992. Additionally, reform had created a path for many more African American and Latino educators to be hired into these roles, and they now had authority to reshape their school faculties too.[3] In schools that enrolled predominantly African American or Latino students, over 90 percent of the new principals "matched" their community's race-ethnic composition. A multidecade effort to renew Chicago's human resources had begun.

Historically, CPS principals had looked up into the system for direction. "Good principals" enforced compliance with central office initiatives, controlled their buildings, and were loyal to their immediate supervisors. Decentralization transformed the role and made principals responsible for developing an annual school improvement plan, strategically allocating discretionary resources upward of a half million dollars a year, hiring teachers, revitalizing connections with families and community, and enabling school-based efforts to improve instruction. No longer primarily looking up into the bureaucracy, principals were now looking out into their own school communities. All of this was new, how to do it uncertain, and little in their professional training and prior experience had prepared them for it.

Moreover, support for principals to enact their new roles was largely ignored initially across the city. Unlike with teacher professional development (discussed below), minimal district resources were directed to supporting principals, and the importance of the principalship had only minimally registered within the foundation community.[4] An exception was 1990 funding from the Joyce Foundation and Chicago Community Trust to UChicago to establish a Center for School Improvement supporting comprehensive improvement in a network of southside and westside schools.[5]

As a starting point for a broader program of activity aimed at advancing more ambitious student learning, the Center assisted the implementation of the new governance reform in these school communities. A central strand of its work was direct support for their principals and, extending out from this, engaging a larger group of principals citywide in how they might use their new resources and authorities to achieve meaningful school change. Informed by his mentoring work in Center schools, Al Bertani joined with UChicago professor Dan Lortie to develop a summer institute called Leading Change. Lortie had been studying the principalship and working with an innovative summer residency program for new school superintendents in Minnesota. He brought those experiences to the program's design. Leading Change was a two-week residential program that contrasted sharply with the "sit and git" professional development sessions that the CPS had historically mandated for principals. Instead, an annual cohort of approximately twenty-five principals engaged in sustained conversations in a safe, small group. Local and national scholars, researchers, and practitioners served as their faculty.[6]

Viewed from a contemporary design perspective, Leading Change and the Center's efforts with its network of schools were small-scale innovations. Through direct engagement with principals and their school communities, Bertani, Lortie, and Center colleagues were deepening their own understandings about the varied problems that educators confronted in these settings and were learning about the efficacy of their own efforts to be supportive, effective partners. This kind of practice-improvement partnership differed significantly from the dominant paradigm where university faculty developed programs that schools were supposed to "implement with fidelity." Such programs regularly fell short of the mark. In contrast, the Center embraced a learning-by-doing orientation around one central question: What would it really take to support improvements in neighborhood schools? This innovation space was foundational for Bertani, who would subsequently move to Chicago Principals and Administrators Association (CPAA) and then into the central office, where he would shape larger systemwide efforts for principals and teachers. Important developments that sprouted in Era 2 were seeded here.

Efforts to Develop Teacher Capabilities

Even though the principalship was largely ignored by Chicago foundations during Era 1, significant resources were committed to teacher development.[7] This support was in addition to the new, discretionary dollars that individual schools could target to professional development if they chose to. Under the 1988 reform, schools could contract directly with individual providers and bypass a central office bureaucracy that had created bottlenecks and controlled access in the past. This gave rise to a new professional development marketplace, and individual faculty in colleges of education responded by creating a diverse array of teacher workshops. These tended to be one-shot or short-term, organized around discrete topics, and mostly focused on the interests and knowledge of the academic providers. One notable exception was the launch of the Teachers Academy for Math and Science (TAMS), which began to offer comprehensive integrated professional development programs in a small number of schools in Chicago and surrounding districts.[8] TAMS was another innovation organization that started small, but as seen in chapter 4, the organizational learning and the relationship building that developed through it became a resource in Era 3 when district attention began to focus explicitly on improving instruction. Another seed was sown.

Although the overall environment remained entropic, some principals and teacher teams were making reasonable professional development choices in this wide-open and uncoordinated new marketplace. They were figuring out how to piece things together to move their schools forward. By the end of Era 1, a quarter of Chicago's elementary schools showed substantially improved student learning gains in both reading and math. Consortium research subsequently documented that a core driver for these better outcomes was the priority schools placed on strengthening their professional capacities.[9] Improvements in these schools, in turn, undergirded the average systemwide gains in learning rates (years of learning for each year of instruction) documented in the introduction— moving from 0.85 in 1988 to 0.94 as Era 1 ended. No similar improvements, however, were found in CPS high schools. The scope and severity of the problems confronting them seemed beyond what decentralization alone could bring to the task.

ERA 2
INITIAL SYSTEM-LEVEL EFFORTS TO IMPROVE TEACHER QUALITY

Concerns about the quality of teaching moved to center stage in Era 2. Noted in chapter 2, this was enabled by a newly empowered central office and investments flowing from the Chicago Annenberg Challenge (CAC). Conceptually these two loci for improvement could have melded productively, but that is not how this story unfolded. College and university faculty hosted multiple CAC networks, and their institutions sought ways to address teacher shortages in specific areas. While efforts remained unaligned, these developments laid a foundation for more systemic initiatives to follow.

Responding to Teacher Shortages

The demography of the CPS workforce had started to shift in Era 1. Educators who had been hired in response to the post–World War II baby boom were retiring. Additionally, many principals were using their discretionary funds to create new positions and hire more teachers. The district focused mainly on alternative certification routes to bring new teachers in quickly. One was Teachers for Chicago, which brought together the CTU, the CPS, and eight local universities. Another was the Golden Apple Teacher Education Program. It was an alternative, postbaccalaureate model that operated as a partnership with Northwestern University and University of Illinois Chicago (UIC).[10] Alternative certification programs for bilingual teachers were also created in local colleges of education, and these certified hundreds of bilingual teachers for CPS.[11] A short-lived CPS program called GEO recruited teachers from other countries, mainly in Africa, to fill high school math and science openings.

These new routes into teaching filled vacant classrooms. They stood in tension, however, with a growing national professional standards movement that argued for more rigorous teacher preparation for all teachers and especially urban teachers.[12] Moreover, the standards movement itself was responding to a long history of districts ignoring certification standards whenever there was urgency to fill slots. Resolving this tension was not a district priority under Vallas, but momentum to attack this problem was building elsewhere in the city.

With encouragement from Mayor Daley, the business community stepped up to help CPS begin to address candidate quality concerns. The Financial Research and Advisory Committee (FRAC) of the Commercial Club organized an effort to improve marketing to new teachers and ramp up the number of applicants.[13] Strategies included outreach beyond local colleges and universities. FRAC also established a call center that reached out to candidates, responded to inquiries, and conducted screening interviews.

The most significant press on teacher quality came when Illinois passed a new teacher licensure law in 1997. To earn the state's Standard Teaching Certificate, novice teachers now had to demonstrate satisfactory classroom performance within their first three years. This initiative, however, posed a potential new problem for Chicago: if a significant number of new teachers failed to achieve standard licensure, Chicago's teacher shortages would worsen. To head off this concern, Martinez, at the MacArthur Foundation, encouraged a collaboration among the school system, UIC, and the Quest Center at the Chicago Teachers Union (CTU) to create the Mentoring and Induction of New Teachers (MINT) program. In addition to the thirty-hour in-service series then mandated for new teachers, MINT added classroom-embedded mentoring from a trained senior teacher. MacArthur and the McDougal Family Foundation funded MINT through most of Era 2. Unsurprisingly, an early learning was that the principals' actions largely determined whether new teacher mentoring was successful or not.

A Focus on Teacher Professional Development: The Chicago Annenberg Challenge

Vallas held the extant CPS workforce in low regard and did not see their professional development as a core strategy for district improvement.[14] He pressed instead on educator accountability. As discussed in chapter 1, he mandated a hastily conceived, scripted curriculum, accompanied by a test-driven accountability system in the system's 109 probation schools.[15] A small number of those schools were reconstituted, with principals replaced and the entire faculty or substantial numbers of teachers removed. Additional schools were threatened with reconstitution if they did not improve. University-based probation partners were provided to assure the implementation of these centrally driven initiatives, but overall, these efforts felt punitive to those on the receiving end. Little was accomplished in most places, and quietly, the scripted curriculum just disappeared.[16]

In contrast, the Chicago Annenberg Challenge (CAC) put educators' development at the center of its work. Over its five years, CAC reframed professional development from what had been mainly the eclectic initiatives of individual teachers, to professional learning as a collective, schoolwide concern. The interconnections among principal and teacher development became visible through this work. CAC also brought attention to the importance of instructional coherence across classrooms and grade levels, the value of collaboration among school faculty around instructional improvement, and how educators might more productively engage students, parents, and their local community. Through CAC, local colleges and universities became more directly integrated into the school reform landscape as well. The school, as the unit for change, came sharply into focus, as did the key role principals played in enabling and shepherding these efforts.[17]

Unfortunately, CAC suffered from two core constraints. From a philanthropic perspective its resources were substantial, but they paled in comparison to the scope of CAC's ambition—transforming the third-largest public school system in America. The Consortium's evaluation of CAC, discussed in chapter 2, found little overall effect on student outcomes. Importantly, however, positive outcomes did occur in a subset of schools where resource commitments were greater and local conditions enabled a more intensive take-up. So, a key piece of evidence had come into view: investing in educators' development and their capacities to work together *could* lead to improved student outcomes.

CAC had banked on the formation of networks of schools working together with external partners, many of whom were faculty in the city's colleges of education. This was, however, largely new and uncertain activity. Enduring relationships did form through these networks, and much was learned about the work of improving schools, by both the educators directly involved and the external partners who supported them. At base here is a fundament in improvement science: more is often learned from a failure, or when something doesn't quite work as hoped, than from some seeming success. Practical knowledge about improvement was developing, and strong roots were growing through CAC, even if aboveground very little was visible yet. As seen in chapter 4, this early capacity building became an important resource to Duncan and Eason-Watkins when they began to bring a systems focus to professional learning aimed at improving instruction.

CAC also brought to light a hard reality about Chicago's first two eras of reform: while expertise was developing among educators in schools about how to improve them, and among select college- and university-based faculty and staff about how to mentor such change, this expertise remained in short supply.[18] Similarly, central office staff had no prior experience supporting schools in a decentralized system, and they did not even see it as their job initially. They too struggled as their roles and responsibilities changed. As Chicago moved into the new millennium, a general organizational development lesson was manifest: the extent of available expertise functions as a core constraint on the speed and scope with which large-scale changes can be pushed forward effectively. Little improvement capacity existed when Era 2 began, and while some positive developments had occurred by the end, much more still was needed. This capabilities constraint appeared repeatedly in efforts that aimed to scale improvements quickly across the city.

INITIAL SYSTEM-LEVEL ATTENTION TO THE PRINCIPALSHIP

An External Organization Takes a Lead Role

The need to strengthen the principalship had been clearly staked out by the end of Era 1. Significant system resources began flowing in this direction during Era 2, but the locus for this new activity was again situated outside the system in a newly invigorated CPAA.

Historically the CPAA advocated for principals around work conditions and bread-and-butter salary issues. While it was never formally recognized as a collective bargaining unit, it had functioned akin to a public-sector union. When the 1988 School Reform Act did away with principals' tenure, the CPAA sued to vacate the law and lost in court. That loss, coupled with the extensive principal turnover early in Era 1, depleted its membership and called its future into question. The organization was granted a second life when Beverly Tunney was elected president in 1993. Recognizing that the principalship had changed dramatically under reform, she advocated for CPAA to become a professional association that would support principals as they learned how to improve schools in Chicago's newly decentralized system. Prior to becoming CPAA president, Tunney had been a respected principal at Healey Elementary School, which was near where Mayor Daley and much of his inner circle lived.

Around the same time that Tunney took over CPAA, Bertani's and Lortie's work at the Center had developed a reputation as a high-quality, small-scale principal center. A key consideration was how to extend its reach. Because the Center had been designed as a research and innovation "skunk works" and never intended to operate at scale, Bertani pursued a partnership between the Center and CPAA to expand impact. Tunney was suspicious when these conversations began. In her view, universities were part of the problem. Places like UChicago were more interested in research than practice, and most other colleges of education were focused on tuition dollars more than program quality. Moreover, they held a generalist orientation to leadership preparation that gave little attention to the practical issues of effectively leading schools in Chicago's decentralized system. Eventually, Tunney agreed to work with Bertani on what had become her most pressing problem—a daily inbox filled with concerns "about" and "from" new principals. These new principals, and there were hundreds of them, now composed CPAA's core membership.[19]

Conditions also were changing at the top. Because Vallas viewed strong principals as central to his accountability strategy, Tunney had no difficulty convincing him to invest in them, and she quickly became his confidant and advisor. Investing in principals also made sense to business leaders in the Civic Committee, who continued to advocate for improving the overall managerial capacities in CPS through Leadership for Quality Education (LQE)—their educational reform organization. Tunney convinced Vallas to send CPS funds in her direction to design and operate an expansive set of new programs. Tactically, this made sense to Vallas, as there was little internal professional capacity at Pershing Road to do so.

Working together, Tunney and Bertani created an induction program to support CPS's new principals in 1995 called LIFT. Its initial design drew heavily on lessons from the Center's early work. Faculty from Northwestern University joined this effort along with LQE and CPAA staff. CPS funded the program.[20] Over the next few years, CPAA targeted other career stages for principal development. Chicago Academy for School Leadership (CASL) debuted in 1996 and offered advanced professional development and support for practicing principals and their school leadership teams.[21] Its design borrowed from the California School Leadership Academy. This was a group that Terry Mazany had worked with while he was associate superintendent in the Oakland Public Schools. In 1998, CPAA added LAUNCH to its programmatic lineup to strengthen the preparation of new principals. While a large reservoir of candidates already held the necessary state type 75 certification, most were not qualified in terms of newly promulgated Chicago-specific standards for leading a school (discussed below). So CPAA filled yet another gap.[22] By the end of Era 2, CPAA was operating a full portfolio of career-stage programs, and Bertani crossed over from the Center to CPAA to lead these initiatives full-time.

CPAA's efforts in Era 2 marked the beginnings of an integrated professional development pipeline for Chicago's principals. Principal candidates began in LAUNCH, then moved into LIFT, with CASL providing follow-up support. All three programs would transfer to CPS early in Era 3 when the district opened an Office of Principal Preparation and Development (OPPD) and assumed responsibility for principal quality efforts. Many of the coaching and support functions in LIFT and CASL were gradually absorbed into the newly created "area instructional officers" role. (As discussed below, this role was introduced in Era 3 and further refined and renamed "network chiefs" in Era 4.) LAUNCH, in contrast, would phase out as the district shifted to supporting a small set of external organizations that had comprehensively redesigned their initial administrative certification programs tailored to new and more-detailed Chicago-specific standards.

Tunney's contribution to improving the public education landscape in Chicago was considerable throughout Era 2 and into Era 3. As she rebuilt CPAA, she drew together some senior CPS principals from earlier times with a large number of new principals hired in the 1990s. She was well respected by senior system leaders and members of Chicago's business community. She was also a frequent contributor to *Catalyst* and active on the Consortium's steering committee where she helped to shape its research agenda and regularly shared what was being learned there with CPAA members. By linking across these people and institutions, Tunney functioned as key connector in the ongoing social enterprise of how Chicago was learning to improve its schools.[23]

Ensuring Principal Quality in a Decentralized System

Era 2 was not without conflict in the human capital sphere. A battle emerged shortly after the 1995 Amendatory Act was passed that threatened the future of the district's decentralization reform. Noted in chapter 1, the LSCs' most significant authority was principal appointment, but once the Amendatory Act passed, Vallas and Daley encouraged the legislature to return control of principal appointments to them.[24] They maintained that the principalship was too important to be left to an elected body of nonexpert community people (including two teachers) in each school. Unsurprisingly, the reform community saw this as a power grab: testimony from the 1987 parent community council forums bore witness to how poorly the old system had served local school communities. LSC members, and those they represented, did not want to return to a patronage system where the principalship was a plum job that the CEO and mayor could dole out.[25] The reform community maintained that the LSCs' power to hire and fire principals was essential to sustaining meaningful reform. LQE and CAC pooled resources to start a new organization, the Chicago School Leadership Cooperative (CSLC), to protect LSCs from efforts to diminish their roles.

By the mid-1990s, wide variability in the capabilities of Chicago's principals was visible. LSCs varied in the processes they used to hire their principals too. While many LSCs were deliberative and made good choices when it came time to hire a principal, others were simply promoting their current assistant principal and not considering external candidates who might be stronger.[26] This was especially problematic for schools where there was little evidence that any productive change had begun. Rather than simply shifting appointment authority from LSCs back to the central office, and with leadership from CSLC, an alternative policy solution was eventually hammered out. System leaders and LSC advocates agreed that LSCs needed better information and direct support around principal hiring, and LSC training for this process was instituted. Most significant, it was acknowledged that the overall pool of qualified principal candidates needed to be stronger. This, in turn, necessitated a strengthening of the professional preparation and certification of leadership candidates, and this became the basis for Senate Bill 1019 (SB1019), a political compromise legislated in 1996.

SB1019 authorized CPS to impose requirements on principal eligibility in addition to the state administrative endorsement, the type 75 certificate. This set a course going forward for innovative programming to emerge in Chicago that would ultimately transform its principalship over the next twenty years, and influence all of Illinois along the way. Reflecting back, this was a clear fork in Chicago's reform road. Rather than just shifting power back to the central office, the conflict's resolution came down on the side of a reframed district role: how a newly empowered central office could better support principal preparation, selection, and development in a decentralized system. That this happened was a direct "mutation" evolving out of the DNA of decentralization. It was also an instance of the exoskeleton at work; in this case, mounting a defense of LSCs as a core educational institution of the city.

To implement SB1019, the district partnered with a broad base of actors in civic institutions, including FRAC and CPAA, to establish an initial set of principal competencies that candidates would need to demonstrate prior to taking on this role. Standards developed that same year by the Interstate School Leaders Licensure Consortium (ISLLC) informed this effort.[27] These standards were a first attempt nationally to describe what was then emerging as a substantially changed landscape for school leadership practice.[28] Aiming to assure broad endorsement, the language embedded in the ISLLC standards was fairly general, so they lacked the specificity needed to truly guide school improvement. Chicago built on these standards and operationalized them in more detail. This led to a related shift in how a candidate would demonstrate these competencies. In the past a "demonstration of competency" meant completing some prescribed hours of coursework. Now, a Principal Assessment Center came into existence to develop a set of competency-based assessments and processes for their use. This was another instance where external organizations, in this instance LQE, FRAC, and its parent organization the Civic Committee, brought an innovation into play.[29] Efforts to refine the list of competencies and how they might be assessed would evolve in Era 3 as CPS continued to collaborate with CPAA, and as two new initiatives began operating in this space—New Leaders for New Schools (subsequently called New Leaders) and the Urban Education Leadership Program at UIC, discussed below.

Undergirding these developments were ongoing research efforts both local and national. In 2000 Sebring and Bryk published a short article in *The Kappan* titled "School Leadership and the Bottom Line in Chicago." Drawing on the corpus of past and ongoing Consortium studies, they identified key elements in *how* effective principals were leading school improvement. Chicago's educators were navigating a dynamic interplay among four focal concerns: the efficient management of day-to-day school operations; engaging teachers, parents, and the local community in ongoing change efforts and facilitating their work together; sustaining long-term attention to improving students' school experiences and instruction; and using a combination of pressure and supports to catalyze change efforts. Productive principals recognized the importance of early "quick hits" to demonstrate that improvements were possible. This helped them build agency for change in their communities. They balanced this with a strategic orientation to the longer-term efforts needed to improve instruction. In a big, decentralized district, this often included buffering out sources of incoherence that pressed in from many sides.

In tandem with this focus on *how* effective principals worked, there was ongoing Consortium reporting on the 5Es that detailed *what* school leaders needed to attend to. Discussed in chapter 2, the 5Es framework had been routinely used by the Consortium since its development in the mid-1990s to describe challenges and changes in Chicago schools.[30] These reports brought attention to the importance of strong school-based professional learning communities, continued investments in teachers' professional development, and a press to create opportunity for students to engage more ambitious, coherent, and aligned instruction. Consortium researchers subsequently linked improvements in the 5Es to improvements in students' attendance and their learning gains in reading and math. As this research progressed, the steering committee continued to discuss what was being learned and its implications. Those conversations, in turn, informed efforts to further strengthen principal preparation and development programs offered by CPAA, New Leaders, and at UIC. When the area instructional officer (AIO) role was created in Era 3, these lessons informed the AIOs' work too.[31]

Complementary research accounts emerged nationally as well. In 1999, Richard Elmore published "Building a New Structure for School Leadership." He argued that the new student learning and professional standards would never make a difference if principals were not working with teachers to improve instructional practice.[32] Elmore was a founder of Harvard's Public Education Leadership Program. He also mentored Eason-Watkins and connected her and Duncan to a national network of district leaders working to improve schools. The parochialism that had characterized Chicago was becoming a thing of the past.

As Era 2 drew to a close, policy development and research were converging around the centrality of the school as the unit of change and the principalship as key to leading that change. A fundamental reconceptualization of their work had emerged. For those in the maelstrom of reform, it felt like an ever-expanding list of urgent problems to solve. Looking back now at the totality of the changes that were occurring, we can see that an integrated human capital pipeline was actually forming.

Figure 3.1 highlights the work focused on principal preparation and support that was accomplished by the end of Era 2 and how it would continue to evolve in Eras 3 and 4 as discussed further below. Two additional pipelines, on teacher development and district-level capabilities, materialized subsequently. Taken together, by the end of Era 4, an integrated human resource system, aligned to the three major organizational levels that constitute the operations of a school system—the classroom, the school, and a district support infrastructure—would come into existence.

ERA 3
AN EXPANDING INSTITUTIONAL BASE

By 2001, human capital development had become a priority in the city. CAC had expanded faculty engagement from local schools of education. The Chicago Public Education Fund (the Fund), which had emerged from CAC, was investing in strengthening teacher and principal quality and positioning itself as a strategic partner to CPS. The Joyce Foundation and the Chicago Community Trust were making substantial targeted grants here as well.

The Quest Center at the CTU, which opened in Era 1, also expanded its scope. Under its newly elected president, Deborah Lynch, and with support from the Fund, the CTU advanced a professionalization agenda for Chicago's teachers. Some of its initiatives had mixed results, such as the launch of a graduate school of education and partnering with CPS to create a National Teachers Academy. More successful were the extensive learning opportunities for future teacher leaders that Quest developed, as well as a program to prepare teachers for National Board Certification. These efforts aligned well with new district initiatives, detailed in chapter 4, to introduce school-based instructional coaches. From the district's perspective,

Figure 3.1   Select major initiatives in the evolution of a principal development pipeline

Core pipeline elements	Era 1: 1988–1995	Era 2: 1995–2001	Era 3: 2001–2009	Era 4: 2009–2017
Initial professional preparation		SB1019 results in new principal competencies and additional prep → requirements 1996 CPAA LAUNCH 1998 →	New Office of Principal Preparation and Development → (OPPD) 2003 New Leaders and UIC start 2002–2003 → The Chicago Public Education Fund (the Fund) begins to support principal preparation 2001 →	Chicago Leadership Collaborative (CLC) 2012
New principal support		CPAA LIFT 1995 →	CPS hires cadre of new principal → coaches	Network chiefs charged with new principal support
Ongoing professional development and evaluation for practicing leaders	CSI introduces Leading Change, → Principals' Institute	CPAA CASL 1997 → LSCs trained for principal evaluation 1996 → Principal Assessment Center created 1998–2000 →	New area instructional → officers support and evaluate principals	Network chiefs replace AIOs & use performance management metrics 2012 Performance management evolves into continuous improvement strategy 2016
Principal retention				The Fund starts Principal Fellows Program, 2014 The Fund partners with CPS to establish Independent School Principals, 2015

Note: The → in this figure indicates the evolution of programmatic efforts across eras and in a few instances within eras. In cases where no text follows in the next era, the → means that the initiative continued forward in that era.

QUEST was enlarging capabilities in a space where not much had existed previously. The CTU valued the enhanced teacher status and increased income that accompanied it. In addition, as the district partnered with CTU, the relationship between its leaders expanded beyond the traditional labor-management issues conflicts that had dominated their history. CPS's willingness to bring resources to the table helped to sustain the peace that had emerged during Era 2 and continued through Era 3. While Lynch was president for only two years, her professionalism agenda persisted into Era 4.

Seeds for change also were sprouting among the twenty higher education institutions, who prepare the lion's share of CPS teachers and principals and call Chicago and its suburbs home. Of special significance here was what happened at UIC, Chicago's largest public research university. Opened in 1965, UIC served a predominantly commuter student population and so was unlike the main campus at Urbana-Champaign, which drew students nationally. However, it shared the same status aspirations as its flagship campus, and by the mid-1980s it had achieved a Carnegie Classification designation as a "Research 1" institution. As was generally the case in such institutions, professional preparation and direct work with schools took a back seat to research. Moreover, many of the new teachers that UIC prepared each year did their student teaching in suburban schools where they stayed. The college also operated an undistinguished master's program that awarded a type 75 general administrative certificate. A type 75 was necessary to become a principal, but as noted earlier, little in this program specifically prepared participants to lead school improvement. This was all about to change.

A Great Cities Initiative led by then UIC chancellor James Stukel pressed on how the university's teaching and research efforts might better tackle the challenges of improving urban life.[33] Stukel advanced a distinctive vision aiming to set UIC apart from its downstate flagship. He coupled it with a willingness to spend internal resources to bring that mission to life. Leaders in the school of education would soon step up to the challenge of turning Stukel's aspiration into constructive action.

Bringing vitality to all of this, Duncan and Eason-Watkins both priori-tized human capital development and valued partnerships with external organizations. Eason-Watkins had lived this work as a principal during Eras 1 and 2. As CEdO she was taking these lessons into central office. She understood the centrality of both teacher professional development and principal leadership for improving student outcomes. As detailed in chap-ter 4, she reached out to the individuals and organizations in Chicago that had worked with her when she was a principal to help her now build these same capabilities for the whole system. Complementing these local rela-tionships, Duncan took the lead on the national front and welcomed into Chicago two new organizations explicitly focused on human capi-tal development—Teach For America and New Leaders for New Schools. The Fund had helped to attract both to Chicago and financially supported that work. Duncan was also on point for increasing the number of charter schools during his tenure. This expanse of new organizations brought new talent into Chicago. Many of these newcomers had been educated in highly selective undergraduate institutions. They were committed to social justice and brought an entrepreneurial spirit to their start-up efforts. They also disdained the plodding pace of schools of education and their past failures to serve urban students.

In sum, the impetus for change in human capital development was broad-based at the start of Era 3: system leaders were taking action, pres-sures were building both internally and externally on local schools of edu-cation, and an entrepreneurial energy had been unleashed citywide.

RENEWING THE SYSTEM CENTER'S CAPACITY TO RECRUIT AND DEVELOP PEOPLE

The 1988 reform legislation severed much of the command-and-control authorities of the central office, and by directing state funds to local schools, it forced extensive budget cuts in the central office as well. While the 1995 Amendatory Act returned authorities over low performing schools to the central office, the bulk of the district remained largely decentralized. How a newly invigorated system center might best support local improvements efforts became a primary challenge for Duncan and Eason-Watkins. As Duncan commented:

> You can't have 50 different priorities. So, trying to do a few things over time in a world-class way—for us, focusing on reading in the early grades, teacher quality, and the Consortium's work on freshmen on track and high school graduation rates—was really important. Your priorities may change over time, but you can only have only a handful, three, maybe four, where you really push yourself to spend the time needed to execute against those as best you can before you move onto anything else.[34]

To advance their priorities, Duncan and Eason-Watkins directed their attention to select central office departments. As noted in chapter 2, two new departments had opened to improve students' success in high school and move onto college. In addition, two extant departments were reconceived to focus explicit attention on improving teaching—the Office of Human Resources and the Office of Professional Development.

Building Capacity in the Office of Human Resources

Early in Era 3, Ascensión Juarez accepted the challenge of directing the Office of Human Resources. His prior experience as a teacher, curriculum writer, principal, and human resources administrator gave him both a practitioner and systems perspective about CPS's successes and failures. Juarez inherited an office that had a terrible reputation with teachers and principals. Trust had to be rebuilt, and he thought the best way to do this was to deliver on things that mattered to both groups.[35] His orientation was collaborative—with central office and school colleagues and organizations around the city. He later observed, "Part of changing the culture of a system is understanding that you (central office) are not the end-all be-all; it is really all about bringing people around—bringing them in."[36] Juarez's team overhauled extant HR processes and invented a host of new ones to better support a decentralized system. Several are described below.

Improving Subcenter Operations.   Juarez insists that the smartest thing he ever did was ask Nancy Slavin to direct the CPS's subcenter.[37] It had a long history of dysfunction: good principals had figured out how to work around it; schools with less savvy principals just suffered. When Slavin stepped into her new role, about half of the classrooms that needed a substitute on any given day did not have one, and the substitutes who did show up were often neither prepared nor certified to teach the assigned subject and grade level.

Slavin began by engaging school principals, as well as her own staff, in a top-to-bottom review to identify specific problems in the subcenter's operations. Their list included outdated equipment such as phones, computers, and copiers; antiquated manual processes such as using 3 × 5 note cards to make placements; and no data system to track daily placements and the quality of the service provided. Several of the staff Slavin inherited were longtimers, resistant to change. Perhaps most significant, principals did not hesitate to say that they mistrusted the whole operation. Over the next 18 months, Slavin tackled each of these problems. Her transformation of subcenter operations earned praise from school principals, substitute teachers, and her central office colleagues.[38] Juarez promoted her to become the director of teacher recruitment—another thorny challenge.

Opening Up Teacher Recruitment.   Concerns about teacher qualifications had been percolating in Chicago forever. In 1985, Gary Orfield and colleagues reported that many Chicago teachers had been educated in Chicago's weak K–12 system, then matriculated from teacher preparation in under-resourced colleges of education, and then cycled back to teach the next generation of CPS students.[39] This intergenerational form of institutional racism had been operant for decades. It meant that students who needed the strongest teachers often were least likely to have one.

Rosalind Rossi, a *Sun-Times* education reporter, returned attention to this issue just as Era 3 began. In 1988 Illinois had instituted a basic skills test for new teachers; passing it was a requirement for state certification. The test was pegged to that era's eighth-grade standards—and so was very basic.

Rossi doggedly pursued a Freedom of Information request to access state data on teacher pass rates. When she finally got it, she identified a huge gap between Chicago and suburban teachers. Nearly a fifth of all Chicago teachers flunked at least one basic skills test. That was more than three times the suburban rate. Moreover, hundreds of Chicago teachers took and failed these tests multiple times. Rossi and her newspaper had shined a light on another clear weakness and need: how to recruit new teachers who were better prepared academically.[40]

Rossi's exposé occurred just as the school board was enlisting the pro bono assistance of McKinsey and Company, a business consulting firm, to inform what subsequently emerged as CPS's Human Capital Initiative. The McKinsey team brought together CPS personnel with higher education, foundation, and community leaders for a series of meetings organized around one question: How could CPS improve its teacher and leader workforce? Bertani and Steven Tozer, a UIC professor, led the teacher workforce development committee. Juarez led the principal development committee, which included Peter Martinez as he was transitioning from the MacArthur Foundation to a new role at UIC.

To improve the number and academic preparation of its teacher candidates, McKinsey recommended that CPS actively recruit new teachers beyond Chicago and the state. With support from Juarez, Duncan and Eason-Watkins began visiting colleges, including Big 10 universities across the Midwest. Over time, the system drew increased numbers of new teachers from a wider pool of institutions with both bachelor's and master's degrees.[41]

In another effort to open up the district, Duncan recruited new teachers from alternative sources, principally Teach For America and similar local initiatives, including the Academy for Urban School Leadership (AUSL), and the Golden Apple Teacher Education Program at Northwestern and UIC.[42] By addressing its teacher quality problem, CPS assumed a pragmatic stance amid a national policy debate that pitted advocates for alternative certification routes against an emerging teacher-professional-standards movement embraced by colleges of education. Rather than pick a side, CPS ultimately engaged both camps to address its needs for more and better-qualified teachers.

The partnership with Teach For America (TFA) began in 2003. Over the next decade it placed hundreds of candidates from the nation's more selective colleges and universities in high-need CPS schools.[43] By 2017, the year Reardon published his study, TFA had 811 core members or alumni in teaching positions, 84 principals (many prepared through UIC and New Leaders), and 163 deans, assistant principals, and other school leaders additional to principals. Virtually every school in the system had a TFA candidate or alum teaching or leading or both.[44] Several TFA alums also moved into senior leadership positions in exoskeleton organizations, including the Fund and the Urban Education Institute. While the overall numbers of TFA members in Chicago remained modest in comparison to the overall size of the district, their influence grew over time.

Improving Processes for Teacher Hiring.   Historically, CPS was always among the last to make hiring decisions in metropolitan Chicago. But waiting until summer's end meant that most of the best candidates had already been hired by other districts in the spring. A disconnect between the Office of Demographic Enrollment Planning and the Office of Budget kept this dysfunction locked in place. With support from Duncan and Eason-Watkins, Juarez brokered a policy change that placed CPS in a "first-movers" position for hiring new staff.

Then the district went one step further. A 1998 Consortium study entitled *It's About Time* documented multiple processes that substantially reduced the amount of instructional time and its effective use in Chicago classrooms. One major contributor was a process called "leveling." Historically, each school's staffing was not finalized until early October, with the twentieth-day count of the number of students enrolled in the school. Leveling created a chaotic start to the year: a new teacher might begin with a class in early September and be let go in October. Others might be working with a specific class or grade but be reassigned on the twentieth day. Leveling disrupted six weeks of what should have been sustained instructional time. Solving this problem would make a modest incremental demand on the school system's budget, but the return on investment in terms of lost instructional time and emotional burden was huge. Beginning in

2009, the system introduced a new policy that established next year's budget for each school in late spring based on its current year's enrollment. This assured schools that they could hire new teachers in the spring and promise specific assignments for the next school year regardless of the count on the twentieth day.

At a more micro level, Slavin also turned the pencil-and-paper teacher application into an online system. Prior to her arrival, principals were largely on their own to find good staff. The online system both improved the processing of thousands of applications and assured that principals across the system had access to the widest pool possible. Complementing this, the Office of Human Resources introduced citywide job fairs in 2003–2004. The fairs created a context for interviews between principals who had vacancies and individuals who were about to graduate from teacher education programs. Some 100 schools participated in the fairs in year one; by year three, the number was over 450. These job fairs made it easier for candidates interested in teaching in Chicago to connect to possible school sites, made the overall process more transparent, and expanded the quantity and quality of candidates.[45] Simultaneously, the fairs helped convince teacher candidates that CPS was a good place to work and Chicago a welcoming place to live.

In sum, Juarez and Slavin sustained attention to how the CPS's HR system was failing its schools and then relentlessly overhauled how these processes worked. The end result was major improvement in recruitment and hiring. These efforts had impact too. A 2006 study by the Illinois Educational Research Council reported that the undergraduate ACT scores for new Chicago teachers now closely approximated those of teachers hired by other districts across the state. (See figure 3.2.) The hiring gap that had existed between Chicago and the rest of the state, in terms of new teachers' academic background as Era 3 began, had all but disappeared.

Simultaneous with all of this, the demographics of the teaching force continued to shift. The proportion of white teachers increased from 45 percent in 2001 to 51 percent in 2010. The proportion of African American teachers declined from 40 percent to 30 percent in the same time period, and that of Latino teachers increased slightly from 12 to 15 percent.[46]

Figure 3.2 Rapidly improving ACT scores among new Chicago teachers

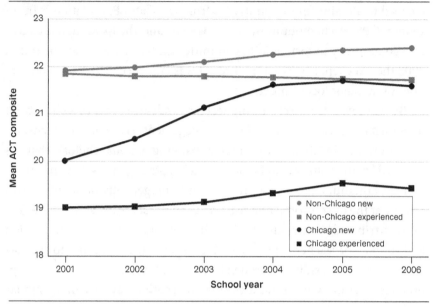

Source: Bradford R. White, Jennifer B. Presley, and Karen J. DeAngelis, *Leveling Up: Narrowing the Teacher Academic Capital Gap in Illinois* (Edwardsville, IL: Illinois Educational Research Council, Southern Illinois University, 2008), 9.

While new teacher recruitment initiatives during this period skewed the candidate pool toward an increasing number of white teachers joining CPS, the trend in this direction had actually started back in Era 1. Interestingly, even though CPS had more principals of color beginning in 1990, and they made the new teacher hiring decisions, the changing composition of the teacher workforce did not follow simply from this. Unfortunately, no systematic research has ever been carried out that explains why and how this came about.

Reforming Teacher Evaluation to Improve Teaching.   Dating back decades, Chicago principals had used a perfunctory checklist to evaluate annually their faculty. It was another instance of life at Lake Wobegon—year after year virtually all teachers were rated "excellent" or "superior," yet many of their students were struggling.[47] The impetus for improving this process was again external, in this case a report by the National Teacher Project coupled to a major funding initiative from the Gates Foundation.[48] In response, CPS reached out to the CTU, CPAA, and the local higher education community to form a joint committee on teacher evaluation, and in 2008 the Excellence in Teaching Project was launched. The Joyce Foundation was a major local funder.

By its very nature, rethinking teacher evaluation is a prickly subject because it resides at the apex of labor-management relations. These tensions were amplified in Chicago by an accompanying national rhetoric that envisioned "firing your way to Finland" as a key strategy for school improvement.[49] Finland, a small country with a homogeneous population, was scoring at the top on comparative international test results at that time. The Finns attributed their results to their deep investments in the preparation and support of teachers and in a social services infrastructure to support families. In contrast, it was argued by policy advocates in the US that vigorous teacher evaluation was a cheaper alternative way to achieve similar outcomes.

The Excellence in Teaching Project started small in forty-four elementary schools and expanded a year later to one hundred schools, including high schools. Then it scaled citywide. The Consortium was recruited to serve as an analytic partner that would inform the initiative's evolution. It developed some twelve reports and briefs on this topic over the next decade, and the authors actively engaged with committee leaders throughout this period. In addition, senior Consortium staff often presented separately to CTU leaders, who, prior to that, had mostly heard about evaluation from teachers filing grievances. The new research showed them that a majority of their members were having positive experiences with the new system. At the same time, Consortium studies validated some of CTU's concerns by identifying key process weaknesses that needed redress. This was one more instance where the Consortium functioned as a constructive mediating influence amid a conflictual local policy terrain.[50]

By the end of Era 3, major transformations in the district's management and support for its human resources had occurred. Satisfaction ratings from principals about the Office of Human Resources climbed over time from 9 percent to 96 percent.[51] Moreover, the improvements discussed above built upon each other into a coherent strategy in support of a decentralized system. Improvements in teaching and learning had to happen in each local school, and the Office of Human Resources had to provide reliable service to those schools. While much of the office's work took place behind the scenes, it nonetheless made a major contribution to the quality of the system's human capital.

Rebuilding an Office of Professional Development

The 1988 reform was largely silent about how teachers and principals would improve their practice. The law had devolved authority for hiring decisions to local schools, and LSCs had resources that they could allocate for professional development. While modest improvements in student learning were noticeable by the mid-1990s, there was still a very steep hill to climb when Duncan and Eason-Watkins took over in 2001.

Bertani was now asked to lead the professional development work inside CPS. His challenge was formidable: a modest set of programs had been initiated in Era 2 through Annenberg, the Quest Center, and the Teachers Academy, but central office lacked a functional professional development department. Bertani's background was in staff development. He was another boundary spanner connecting learnings from his direct work in Chicago schools through the Center, with his teaching in local colleges of education, to involvements with national professional and research organizations. Using his newly created cabinet-level position, he began assembling staff, identifying resources, and establishing the commitments needed to advance a coherent vision for improving the learning of principals and teachers.

To launch the initiative and assess the current state of professional development across the system, Bertani secured support from multiple local foundations. The project was guided by a steering committee that included representatives from CPS, CPAA, CTU, universities, foundation program officers, and the wider school reform community. For technical assistance, he engaged Education Resource Strategies (ERS), a national organization with experience conducting professional development audits. ERS asked two basic questions: How was CPS currently spending its professional development monies, and what strategic shifts might be needed to improve services to schools?

ERS identified several problems. There was no career development strategy for teachers, no coordination of professional development spending, and no coherent framework to help schools improve instruction. Substantial professional development budget lines were uncovered, but they were allocated across forty-four different departments and lacked an overall strategy to guide their use. ERS's recommendations motivated the district to act, guided subsequent philanthropic and civic efforts, and focused attention in local school communities too. To jumpstart these priorities, Eason-Watkins and Bertani reallocated the budget lines that ERS had identified.

Developing Educators for New Roles.   To support Eason-Watkins's instructional improvement efforts, the Office of Professional Development began to chart a new course. As detailed in chapter 4, new roles for instructional coaches in reading, math, and science were central to her strategy. Similar to principals who needed preparation and professional support for their new work, these coaches did too, and for the same reasons: the work was new and none of the programs offered at that time by schools of education were preparing educators to do it.[52]

Eason-Watkins also invested in a new intermediate organizational structure—area instructional offices—that sat between schools and central office. In the past, this middle level enforced schools' compliance with central mandates. Now, the primary mission was supporting local instructional improvements. New roles emerged here too for area instructional officers (AIOs) and area-based instructional coaches; professional development supports had to be invented for them as well. By 2004, a comprehensive strategy for human resource capacity building had emerged in CPS. (See figure 3.3.)

Expanding Mentoring for New Teachers.   The Office of Professional Development also stepped up to directly support new teacher development.

Figure 3.3   CPS Office of Professional Development's capacity building programs, 2002–2003

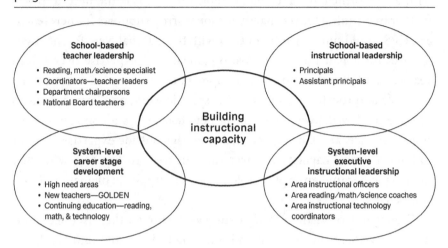

Source: Al Bertani, "Senior Administrative Retreat Presentation" (Summer, 2004), Chicago Public Schools, Chicago Illinois.

The Mentoring and Induction of New Teachers (MINT) program that had started in Era 2 was transformed into a system-supported program called GOLDEN. GOLDEN placed increased emphasis on mentoring support for new teachers, and online courses replaced classroom-based workshops. Overall resources for the program, however, were limited, including the supply of school-based mentors who knew how to do this work.

A subsequent Consortium evaluation found that support for new teachers was highly variable across schools with no discernable average effect on teacher retention.[53] Positive outcomes did occur, however, in a subset of schools where there was a welcoming faculty, strong principal involvement, and intensive one-on-one mentoring. Counterbalancing this good news, about a quarter of new teachers in other sites reported that no one had ever observed their teaching or offered feedback that year.

These findings pushed simultaneously in two directions. First and resonating with a core lesson from the 5Es, the report documented the centrality of building strong school-based professional communities with active principal leadership. Coupled to this was the need to invest further in building local capacity for mentoring supports for new teachers. CPS would subsequently contract with the national New Teacher Center because it had built extensive organizational expertise over fifteen years around the selection and development of full-time teacher mentors, the tools and routines to support this specific work, and data systems to manage quality delivery. Mentoring new teachers is a complex professional practice, and Chicago needed to engage outside expertise in order to build its local capacity to carry this out well. In Era 4, new teacher mentoring became an explicit role responsibility for principals and network chiefs.

Trends in Consortium teacher surveys document the sustained gradual improvements in this domain beginning in Era 3 and into Era 4. Assignments of formal mentors had been routinized, and increasingly school staff were making conscious efforts to welcome new colleagues into their community. They invited them into their classrooms to observe and to get feedback and receive support through their early years of learning to teach. (See figure 3.4.) This was a far cry from Chicago of the 1980s, where new teachers were given their assignment and might be reminded to keep their lesson plans and attendance records up to date.

Through these efforts a larger improvement lesson again came into view: inventing a new program with strong design features was possible, but achieving quality outcomes reliably at scale remained the challenge. Strengthening new teacher induction was just the opening salvo in what would become a twenty-plus-year effort to raise standards for educators' practice and students' learning. Chicagoans were grappling with how complex, time-consuming, and challenging the journey ahead truly was.

Supporting an Expansive National Board Certification Initiative. The Office of Professional Development also joined with the CTU's Quest Center, the mayor's office, and the Fund to support CPS teachers applying for National Board Certification (NBC). The Quest Center had prioritized

Figure 3.4 Improved mentoring support for new teachers over time

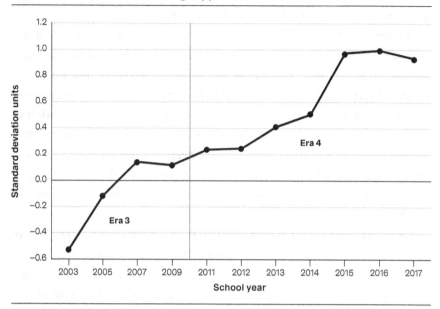

Source: UChicago Consortium on School Research, 2021.

Note: Trend is based on a Rasch measure for the socialization of new teachers constructed from three survey items collected by the Consortium in repeated 5E surveys. The measure tracks the extent to which new teachers are welcomed by their colleagues and provided feedback on their instructional practices.

this toward the end of Era 2. Early in Era 3, Duncan set a goal to certify 1,000 teachers by 2008, and this goal was reached.[54] Both the Quest Center and the district's Office of Professional Development operated programs to prepare teachers for National Board Certification. Participating teachers universally rated their professional preparation experiences for Board certification outstanding—often declaring it among the best professional development they had ever experienced.

The Quest Center's program demonstrated remarkable success, with four out of five teachers earning certification within two years. Their model, which included intense coaching, produced twenty to twenty-five certified teachers annually. The CPS program, which aimed to serve hundreds of candidates annually, was less successful: only one in three teachers earned a certificate.[55] This is another instance where the system's ambition outstripped its extant capacity to execute with quality at scale.

Judged against the Quest Center's priorities, the National Board initiative was highly successful. It demonstrated that the practice of many Chicago teachers met the profession's highest standards. These teachers deserved recognition and additional remuneration to remain in the classroom. National Board Certification, along with the teacher evaluation efforts described earlier, brought the professional standards movement to improve teacher quality into the city's conversation. Both initiatives demonstrated that teaching standards could be assessed. This was an important contribution that deepened civic conversations about how to improve teaching quality.

While individual teachers benefited, the National Board Certification program was never designed as a school improvement initiative. Some classrooms of students likely benefited from having a board certified teacher, but no evidence ever emerged, in Chicago or elsewhere, that schools improved as a result. Some them became teacher leaders in their buildings, and stronger professional communities operated in a small number of places where clusters of them worked together with a strong principal. A Consortium study concluded, however, that even here, it was the nature of principal leadership that largely determined whether these teacher groups actually coalesced and mounted productive collective action.[56] On balance, nothing in the National Board Certification process explicitly focused on teachers leading school improvement, and Board certified teachers struggled just as much as others to work productively with colleagues.[57] Basically, the certification process was able, on average, to identify better teachers and provide positive professional development experiences, but it was limited to that. From an improvement science perspective, there was no working theory about how 1,000 certified teachers in a system of more than 600 schools might result in improved system outcomes.[58]

Such is the nature of innovation: good ideas do not always take you where you want to go. Sometimes doing improvement means trying something, taking stock, and then taking a new direction. To its credit, the

Fund, which had invested in preparing teachers for National Board Certification, also commissioned a set of Consortium studies on its implementation and effects. Based in part on what was learned, the Fund subsequently shifted course and prioritized all its investments toward principal development instead.[59] CPS, as part of its collective bargaining agreement with the CTU, continued to support teachers' preparation for certification and offer a modest salary increment for those who succeeded.

To sum up, an ensemble of human resource initiatives emerged across Era 3—each designed to address an immediate need. The need to address chronic teacher shortages and improve the quality of teacher candidates led to an outreach beyond traditional sources. When large numbers of new teachers were hired during the 1990s, this raised concerns about their success and retention. In response, mentoring supports were invented. For existing teachers, as detailed in chapter 4, comprehensive teacher professional development was designed in literacy, math, and science, and advanced professional learning opportunities were created for those taking on new coaching roles to support teacher learning. Coming next into the mix, and now challenged by the new alternative certification entrepreneurs on the scene, was preservice preparation programs. As discussed below, colleges of education were pressed to move from a generic model to one that would develop teachers to succeed in some of Chicago's most challenging school communities.[60]

Moreover, a focus on continuous improvements characterized each effort. Initial designs often came up short in varied ways, but CPS leaders and their external collaborators were in constant conversation with one another: learning how to make all of this work better—by trial and error, by attending to Consortium research findings, and by lessons emerging more generally in the field. Whether the focus was on teacher preparation, recruitment, retention, professional development, or content-focused initiatives, broad-based organizational learning was occurring both inside CPS and in its exoskeleton. Summarized in figure 3.5, a coherent human resource development pipeline for strengthening the quality of teaching had emerged in Chicago by the end of Era 3.

Figure 3.5 Major initiatives in the evolution of a teacher development pipeline

Core pipeline elements	Era 1: 1988–1995	Era 2: 1995–2001	Era 3: 2001–2009	Era 4: 2009–2017
Initial professional preparation	Teachers for Chicago 1993 →	GEO & Golden Apple 1998 →	Teach For America 2003 → Academy for Urban School Leadership (AUSL) → UIC innovates on teacher prep 2003 → Council of Chicago Area Deans of Ed form around CPS teacher ed needs 2003 →	
Recruitment & hiring			CPS broadens outreach to IHEs 2002 → HR department initiates improvements 2003 →	
New teacher mentoring		MINT Program 1998 →	GOLDEN 2002 ↓ CPS contracts with New Teacher Center 2009 →	New teacher mentoring embedded in network chief and principal roles
Ongoing professional development		Chicago Annenberg Challenge 1996 →	New Office of Professional Development, CPS 2002 → PD programs, CTU 2002 → National Board Certification, CTU, CPS, & Fund → New CPS instructional coach roles and area instructional offices 2002 →	
Teacher evaluation & feedback system			Excellence in Teaching Project 2008 →	REACH CPS Teacher Evaluation system

Note: The → in this figure indicates the evolution of programmatic efforts across eras and in a few instances within eras. In cases where no text follows in the next era, the → means that the initiative continued forward in that era.

THE LAST MISSING PIECE IN THE PIPELINE: STRENGTHENING ENTRY INTO THE PROFESSIONS

Most system initiatives that began in Era 2 and moved into Era 3 focused on immediate needs associated with hiring new teachers and developing current staff. Noted earlier, there also was a local and national dialogue occurring about weaknesses in the initial preparation of teachers and school leaders. This issue became a focal point in Era 3, and headway was made when UIC stepped up to become a major institutional partner with CPS.[61]

Transforming Teacher Preparation: The UIC Case

Larry Braskamp, dean of UIC's College of Education, agreed to take responsibility for LSC training as part of the 1995 Amendatory Act. He quickly learned that his faculty, most of them recruited for their research and teaching abilities, had limited capacity to address this need. Moreover, few were experienced with the practical hands-on work of improving teaching and leading in urban schools that faced considerable challenges. When Vicki Chou was appointed dean in 1997, she recognized that operationalizing UIC's new urban mission entailed a broad-based transformation for the college. It required rethinking programs, recruiting new faculty, inventing new faculty lines, strengthening the clinical apprenticeships in its programs for both teachers and school leaders, and creating new policies around hiring, promotion, and faculty voting rights.

This was another instance where Martinez, then at the MacArthur Foundation, was an activating agent. Following Chou's appointment, Martinez offered her his own version of a challenge grant. If the school "stopped doing business as usual," he told Chou, funding would flow, with one additional condition: "whatever was proposed, both the faculty and chancellor had to be on board."[62]

Chou decided that "stop doing business as usual *meant* making good on the promise of public education" in Chicago. She led a collaborative process of reinventing the college's identity. In Chou's telling, it took extensive dialogue with her faculty, data, a continuous improvement orientation, and time to accomplish this.[63] Considerable political acumen was also needed since colleges and academic departments inside research universities are akin to a holding company organized largely around the research interests of individual faculty members. They are not easily led centrally. Orchestrating a transformation on this scale was truly countercultural.

At the start, Chou used regular faculty meetings to challenge her colleagues: Was the college meeting its potential as an institution of the city? What more could be done? She brought in speakers from other prominent urban public universities that were making progress recruiting students and faculty of color, strengthening supports for student teaching in high-need schools, and figuring out how to turn a social justice mission statement into constructive action.[64] Her efforts were resisted at first—by teacher education faculty who had long-standing working relationships with school educators that they were reluctant to give up, and from some research-oriented faculty who had different priorities. Shaping a new narrative about how these practice-based efforts might complement and support the institution's research mission was central to these conversations.

To create an analytic underpinning for this improvement effort, Chou hired staff to develop new data systems that merged information from the Illinois Teacher Data Warehouse with the college's in-house data. This provided faculty with formative and summative evidence about candidates' progress in their program and through their early years of teaching. The data helped faculty see their own leaky pipelines—places in the process where the college was not offering candidates needed support while in preservice preparation. Then, as candidates moved into teaching positions, the data also offered insight about factors that might be affecting their success and retention in schools. Once a specific problem was identified, the faculty could move to address it. And as new programmatic initiatives emerged, this data analytic capacity provided critical feedback on how these improvement efforts were working, and where or whether they were succeeding—all of which informed conversations about what the faculty might do next.

One of the hardest problems to tackle was field placements for student teachers. In the past, individual faculty had identified these and built relationships with individual schools, but many of the placements were in suburban schools or those serving affluent city neighborhoods. They were not in under-resourced schools in Chicago's most distressed neighborhoods. The programmatic contradiction was obvious: aspiring teachers were not learning how to succeed in the places that needed good teachers the most and where positions were most likely to open. Moreover, the program needed field supervision standards. Because past practices had been idiosyncratic to individual faculty, bringing faculty together to tackle this was a heavy lift. The college also introduced a summer institute for teacher mentors to improve the nature and quality of their supports to student teachers. It also sharply reduced the number of partner schools, to better focus and strengthen the school community experience for aspiring new teachers.

Both internal funding and new grants that Chou secured enabled this transformation. New tenure-line and clinical faculty were hired who demonstrated commitment to "making good on the promise of public education," and many were faculty of color. Chou also encouraged working relationships with colleagues in the arts and sciences and supported joint tenure-line and clinical hires with their academic departments. New job descriptions and norms for promotion for clinical faculty, analogous to those for the clinical teaching faculty in a medical school, were crafted. Admissions processes were changed to ensure that candidates themselves were committed to the program's goals. Courses were redesigned to prepare teachers to work in schools that faced many challenges. The net effect was a substantial increase in the numbers of new teachers prepared specifically for CPS.[65]

The college's new priority on strong clinical preparation diverged from its own past practice and that of many other research universities where tenure-line faculty considered field supervision secondary to their research commitments. A revolving door of graduate student assistants or adjunct personnel were typically assigned to supervise student teachers. These adjunct appointments, however, had no other connection to the college or its programs.[66] In contrast, the new UIC clinical faculty devoted themselves full-time to teaching professional preparation courses and supervising field experiences as their primary responsibilities. They also served as primary connectors with the college's academic faculty and mentors in partner schools.

Chou and her UIC colleagues also worked collaboratively with other local colleges of education as part of UIC's broader institutional commitment to strengthen teacher preparation.[67] Chou took a turn as chair and then cochair of the Council of Chicago Area Deans of Education (CCADE), and used this opportunity to energize connections between CCADE institutions and CPS. Eason-Watkins attended many of their meetings and frequently met individually with the deans in this group. She listened to what they were doing and candidly told them where she needed their help to advance her priorities. A productive give-and-take developed, and over time additional local colleges of education expanded their programming for CPS in varied ways. Duncan and Eason-Watkins had opened the system to new partnerships, and these institutions were coming through the door.

Transforming Principal Preparation

A basic framing for a CPS principal development pipeline had developed by the end of Era 2. The CPAA initiatives described earlier aimed to enhance the knowledge and skills of current principals, support those newly appointed, and offer additional preparation for those who already held administrative certification but did not meet the new Chicago-based standards. As these efforts continued into Era 3, attention moved toward the longer-term horizon: where would the next cohort of school-based leaders come from, and how could they be better prepared than their predecessors? Responding to this challenge would take a major investment of new resources and the better part of ten years to develop and mature.

The law allowing CPS to add eligibility requirements for principals, SB1019, had brought scrutiny to weaknesses in extant principal preparation programs and the need to raise certification requirements. But questions raised then were still percolating: What were the schools of education doing? Why were educators with type 75 certification and advanced degrees still so ill prepared to lead improvements in Chicago schools?

These questions contributed to a growing drumbeat nationally about the seeming irrelevance of schools of education to the needs of urban schools. This critique had surfaced relative to teacher preparation, and UIC transformed its efforts in response. The same critique applied to leadership preparation programs at UIC and necessitated a similar set of organizational changes. In the same way that TFA represented a challenge to traditional teacher preparation providers when it came into Chicago, New Leaders offered a comparable challenge to leadership preparation. An external questioning of the institutional legitimacy of professional preparation programs, coupled to a clearly recognized local need, fueled innovative developments. Two major contributors in this regard are described below.

New Leaders for New Schools.   New Leaders launched in New York City and Chicago in 2001 and added ten more cities over the next few years.[68] Its initial aspiration was to develop principals for the many charter and contract schools that were opening at that time. As part of its entry into Chicago, it was pressed by CPS to broaden its mission and serve all of Chicago schools. New Leaders accepted the challenge.[69] Like their TFA colleagues, New Leaders was critical of programming in colleges of education. Also, like TFA, they initially sought to bring new talent in by recruiting individuals who were skeptical of conventional certification programs.[70] In designing their Chicago program, New Leaders focused on the actual work of leading school improvement. An intensive yearlong clinical apprenticeship in a CPS school was a core component. (No state requirement existed then or even now for such an experience.) Like the LAUNCH initiative, New Leaders' curricular foci were anchored in the ISLLC standards as elaborated in Chicago and included the still-evolving CPS Principal Competencies.[71] Also, LAUNCH had already piloted a semester-long clinical apprenticeship and, most important, had convinced CPS to fund each candidate's work alongside a current Chicago principal. This CPS funding precedent carried over to New Leaders and into the UIC program that was soon to emerge as well.

In addition, New Leaders hired local practitioners as instructors and in coaching support roles. In essence, they too were operationalizing a role akin to the clinical professors described above. Bertani and Martinez, who both were now faculty at UIC, served as instructors. Since state law did not allow New Leaders to certify candidates or award advanced degrees, the group partnered with colleges of education who controlled this space.[72] While New Leaders had been reluctant to enter into this arrangement at first, with time they saw value in the theoretical foundations for school leadership that was the traditional emphasis in the colleges of education. And New Leaders' press on strengthening the clinical apprenticeship influenced university leadership departments in the other direction.[73] Cooperation between these programs, with CPS at the center, developed into a productive learning relationship.

Interestingly, like earlier CPAA initiatives, New Leaders was challenged early on by the limited base capacity among educators in Chicago. Leading the transformation of weak Chicago schools toward better student experiences and learning outcomes was new work. Principals who had the practical expertise to lead it remained in short supply in 2001. The design of this innovative program, and supportive policies to implement it, were just enabling first steps. Achieving quality reliably at scale was the ongoing challenge. New Leaders, like TFA, learned that simply recruiting new talent, from new sources, was insufficient.[74] A new learning system for both the candidates and those who sought to support them had to be invented.

Making all of this go depended on the active engagement of the CPS's Office of Principal Preparation and Development (OPPD), which had developed from the Human Capital Initiative discussed earlier. New Leaders collaborated with OPPD to identify qualified mentor principals, to work out the logistics necessary to place residents in their schools, to create a funding pool for the yearlong residency, and to ensure that the preparation mandates in Illinois School Code and SB1019 were being met. CPS and

New Leaders also jointly engaged in continuous program improvements as efforts got underway. Together they looked at data on placement rates for New Leaders' graduates, the subsequent performance of students in their schools, teacher and student reports on the 5Es, and data on teacher evaluations and retention rates.

In the past CPS had been a largely passive consumer of the candidates produced by colleges of education, and the colleges considered their graduate students their primary clients. In contrast, New Leaders regarded the school system as its client, and together they were learning how to improve school leaders—the system's most important human resource. Decentralization had placed its bets on them, Consortium research documented that what they did mattered, and the continued civic press to improve the city's schools sustained attention to them. These were enabling conditions for the truly innovative work to emerge.

The Urban Education Leadership Program at UIC.   The same year that New Leaders launched its first cohort, UIC approached CPS with a partnership proposal to develop its own principal preparation program.[75] In contrast to the more time-limited programs like LAUNCH and New Leaders, UIC envisioned a four-year program, culminating in a doctorate of education (EdD). Principal candidates would receive their state license to lead after the first year of full-time internship and coursework.[76] Then, over the next three years, coursework would continue, and they would be coached as they moved toward a data-based capstone project that demonstrated their ability to lead improvement in a CPS school. Woven through their entire professional preparation were the tools, methods, and mindsets of what came to be known as Improvement Science. This made sense since leading improvement was the core work of an effective principal.

The college's willingness to jettison a standard program in favor of this untested innovation was grounded in UIC's new urban mission, support from Chou, and strong advocacy by Tozer, a senior faculty member who chaired its Educational Policy Studies Department. Tozer was intrigued with the potential to redress persistent inequities in urban education at scale. At the time, Illinois was the nation's fifth-largest state, but it only needed 400 new principals annually, 20 percent of whom were Chicago principals. If higher education could embrace a new model for principal preparation, he believed that wide-scale impact was possible.

The existing school administration program at UIC was a master's program. It was nonselective and relatively inexpensive to operate, because it only required students to take nine courses. These courses were either already being taught by full-time faculty or could be covered by low-cost adjuncts. Course content and materials were determined by individual instructors and for the most part did not include field experience. Most students were part-time, and they took courses in any sequence that fit their work schedules. Because the college did not track its graduates, there was no data on whether the program was producing effective school leaders, or even if graduates were employed as school leaders. In short, the program operated as if it were a general liberal arts master's program rather than professional preparation.[77] UIC was not alone in these shortcomings: it looked like thirty other programs in the state, and hundreds in the nation, as highly publicized critiques would soon document.[78]

The proposed professional doctorate to be awarded by the new program stirred debate among UIC faculty, who were concerned that it would be a watered-down version of the PhD. Here again the local foundation community played a significant role by bringing substantial new dollars to the table. A MacArthur planning grant supported the program's initial design effort. Once the program was armed with that new design and once state approval was secured, more Chicago-area foundations offered support, including the Fund, Chicago Community Trust, Joyce, and the McDougal Family Foundation.[79] The Fund was a key early investor in both the UIC and New Leaders programs, and it now had considerable political cachet in the city. As part of its investment in leadership development, the Fund pressed both UIC and New Leaders to regularly collect data and conduct analyses on their programs and candidates. The Fund became an active learning partner in this domain and an influential political actor here as well.

UIC's program had a novel orientation: Like New Leaders, their primary clientele were no longer individual professionals seeking an administrative credential, but rather the school system and the youth it served, who deserved a good principal. Coupled with this was a big question: What would it take for a university to produce principals who significantly improved student outcomes in their schools, not as an exception, but as a rule? In short, the group at UIC knew what they wanted to accomplish but had to figure out how to get there.

Their initial logic model drew heavily on 5Es research, which showed that student learning outcomes were dependent on the organizational capacities of the school catalyzed by its school leaders. Turning this logic into an instructional design meant dropping some courses, inventing others, and modifying still more. Three major program strands that closely aligned with Consortium findings organized candidates' experiences across the four years. They included instructional leadership, organizational leadership, and practitioner-led improvement inquiry.

In a research-intensive university such as UIC, few faculty had been school principals earlier in their careers. Consequently, much as in the reform of its teacher preparation programs, UIC created new clinical faculty lines and began hiring colleagues who had improved schools, almost all in CPS. The university funded several of these positions, and foundation grants sustained others. Criteria for hiring new academic faculty now included research and practice-based experiences along with an expressed interest in building a more effective principal preparation program.

As this new effort gained momentum, academic and clinical faculty, as well as leadership coaches, met regularly. They formed a community of professional practice focused on supporting, challenging, and assessing individual candidates as each moved through professional preparation and took up new roles in CPS. These collaborative routines became part of how the program did business. With encouragement and financial support from external funders, UIC also was able to invest in the creation of a database that provided ongoing information about how their principals were performing relative to others districtwide. The data gathered focused on elementary school achievement gains, high school OnTrack data, dropout reduction, principal retention, the 5Es, and more. The learning from these data led to major program revisions in admissions processes and helped to further strengthen clinical preparation for leading in CPS's most underperforming schools. This evidence kept raising new challenges for program leaders, and each challenge fueled their next round of improvement efforts.[80] This commitment to evidence-based continuous improvement became a hallmark of the program and would subsequently earn it extensive state and national recognition.[81]

UIC's story offers a poignant example of the vitality of Chicago's exoskeleton—how still another key city organization stepped up in response to evolving needs identified in the long-term process of improving the city's public schools.

ERA 4
SUSTAINING PROGRESS THROUGH
CHURN AT THE TOP

Mayor Daley appointed another noneducator, Ron Huberman, CEO in 2009. Described in chapter 1, Huberman's aggressive performance management strategy contrasted sharply with Duncan and Eason-Watkins's professional capacity-building approach. When Eason-Watkins resigned early in 2010, the top of the system became a revolving door. As seen in figure 3.6, 11 different individuals filled the CEO and CEdO roles in CPS over the next eight-year period. This churn rippled through central office as new CEOs rearranged organizational responsibilities and several department leaders left. This instability, coupled with the aftermath of the severe economic recession of 2008 and then a subsequent financial impasse between the Illinois legislature and governor, resulted in an unprecedented two years without a state budget. Absent consistent sense of leadership direction and reduced and uncertain funding, it was a dispiriting time for those who remained in the district. For all practical purposes, it wasn't until Janice Jackson's appointment as CEdO in 2015 that any sense of stability and direction reappeared.

During this period of instability, operations in both the human resources and the professional development offices, which had been major priorities

Figure 3.6   CPS system-level leadership churn during Era 4

Year	CEO/CEdO
2009	Ron Huberman, CEO
	Barbara Eason-Watkins, CEdO (resigns 2010)
2010	Terry Mazany, interim CEO
	Charles Payne, interim CEdO
2011	Jean-Claude Brizard, CEO
	Noemi Donoso, CEdO (resigns 2012)
2012	Barbara Byrd-Bennett, CEO (resigns 2015)
	No CEdO
2015	Jesse Ruiz, interim CEO
	No CEdO
2015	Forest Claypool, CEO (resigns 2017)
	Janice Jackson, CEdO
2017	Janice Jackson, CEO
	LaTanya McDade, CEdO

for Duncan and Eason-Watkins, suffered. Matt Lyons, chief of human resources in Era 4, described the turmoil at the end of Byrd-Bennett's term:

> Essentially no work was happening with teacher recruitment or development—everything was outsourced to AUSL, Golden Apple, Teach For America. I am not even sure we had formal contracts [with those groups] at that point. . . . There was no concrete human capital plan or strategy as an organization. . . . If you have no centralized capacity to do recruitment [for example], every principal was [again] out there doing it on their own.[82]

During this time, the Office of Professional Development as a coordinating and coherence-oriented entity also disappeared, and its responsibilities were dispersed to other offices. Many of the network- and district-level positions focused on literacy, mathematics, and science professional development that had been built up in Era 3 were also cut back.

The Exoskeleton Operates as a Stabilizing Force

This constant turnover in senior system leadership during Era 4 could have precipitated a major setback in the improvements made in the CPS human capital infrastructure during Era 3, but it did not. A decade of investments had penetrated the system deeply enough to defend against its erosion. Mid-level staff in central office departments, and the large numbers of newly prepared principals and assistant principals in schools, had been influenced by the professional learning culture fostered by Duncan and Eason-Watkins. Their relationships with external partners carried the work forward despite senior leadership churn.

The school board's agenda during this period was dominated by navigating budget constraints and everything surrounding the massive school closings. While this slowed developments in some areas, it did not derail most of the work to improve teaching and learning that had been initiated in Era 3. The extensive relationships that key leaders in Chicago's exoskeleton had with individual board members helped to sustain these priorities. The Fund continued to play an important role promoting principal development efforts.[83] Further, when Illinois adopted Common Core in 2010, multiple foundations committed substantial resources to enable a good rollout by CPS. This work is considered in chapter 4.

Also significant were relationships between CPS department heads and network chiefs (formerly AIOs) with leaders in key external organizations, such as New Leaders, TFA, AUSL, and UIC. Much of this relational activity was out of the public eye, but it too helped CPS stay focused on the core work of improving teaching and learning. And the Consortium continued its studies around teacher evaluation and dug deeper into how principals led meaningful school improvement. This ongoing reporting helped sustain civic attention to the importance of continued human capital developments so that more progress could occur.

Leaders in civic institutions also rose to buffer out potentially derailing initiatives when these inevitably popped up. This was another way they acted to sustain the work. Emanuel referred to himself as an education mayor when he first ran for office in 2011. Apparently unaware of developments already in Chicago, one of his campaign promises was the creation of a new "principals academy," modeled after New York City's Leadership Academy. The Fund had already invested significantly in both New Leaders and the Urban Education Leadership Program at UIC and was an active learning partner with them. With support from well-positioned Fund board members, Tozer presented Emanuel's transition team with an alternative proposal to establish a Chicago Leadership Collaborative (CLC) among CPS, New Leaders, UIC, TFA, and Loyola University. Its formation in 2012 productively expanded and deepened efforts already underway in Chicago.

Over time, the Fund worked collaboratively with CLC leaders and continued to identify new problems and advocate for additional improvement initiatives. Beyond developing new principals, principal retention had become a recognized priority. Nationally nearly 25 percent of principals leave their schools each year.[84] Chicago, like all districts, had an interest in retaining its principals, and especially its strongest ones. In response, the Fund encouraged the creation of an Independent School Principals designation that would give successful principals more autonomy.[85] These principals were granted greater control over their school budgets and purchasing; they were not subject to network supervision, and they could choose their own arrangements for professional learning support outside the district's network structure. They were also afforded opportunities to engage directly with the CEO and CEdO and have a voice in shaping new system policies. In addition, the Fund, along with Crown Family Philanthropies, initiated a principal fellows program that offered advanced professional development opportunities for this group and engaged many of them in work groups to advise CPS on various problems. In a few short years, this created a well-prepared talent pool ready to move up into the most senior district-level roles. By so doing, it put in place one more piece

Figure 3.7 Trends in teacher reports about the quality of their school-based leadership

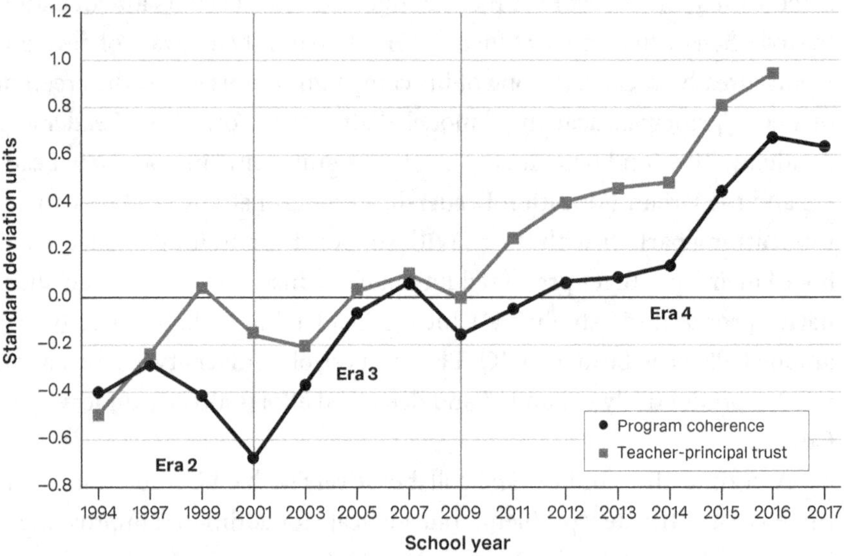

Source: UChicago Consortium on School Research, 2021.

Note: Trends are based on Rasch measures constructed from survey items collected by the Consortium in repeated 5E surveys. Program coherence measures teachers' views of whether school programs are consistent with and processes align with one another toward advancing goals for student learning. Teacher-principal trust captures the quality of the relationships that teachers perceive between themselves and their principal.

in a robust human capital pipeline. In total, over 400 new principals for CPS were prepared by the end of Era 4.

The transformation in how CPS principals carried out their work can be seen in Consortium survey data from teachers on the quality of their local school leadership. While the content of these surveys shifted some over time, two measures in this domain remained stable between 1994 and 2017. As seen in figure 3.7, elementary school teachers reported increasing coherence in the program improvement efforts at their school and greater trust with their principal. (Comparable survey results from high school teachers exist as well.) Beginning at a low base in Era 2, improvements began to appear in the second half of Era 3 (2005–2009) and grow steadily thereafter. As Era 4 progressed, a large and increasing number of principals had been trained in high-quality programs and were receiving sustained support from network offices and the Fund. The teacher survey reports affirm that these individuals were making a difference in their schools.

And one more good thing was happening. An increasing number of these principals had begun moving up into major leadership positions in the district. In Era 4 they took on roles as network chiefs and moved into senior positions in the central office, including the CEO and CEdO and as heads of the Department of Principal Quality, Office of Early Childhood Education, Office of Language and Culture, and Office of Network Support.[86]

Jackson's Promotion: Returning Attention to Strengthening the System's Capacity to Improve

It was an inauspicious time when Janice Jackson was appointed CEdO in 2015. Years of churn had taken its toll at central office. Jackson also faced conflicts still roiling from the massive school closings, a budget crisis that forced layoffs, the elimination of several important central office positions, and a culture of fear instilled by Huberman's performance management system.[87] This angst was further amplified by widespread teacher and principal bashing in the national press during those years. Michelle Rhee, chancellor of District of Columbia Public Schools, had literally fired a principal "live" on national television.[88]

Amid these tensions, Jackson brought a more human-centered approach as she returned attention to the district's capacity-building efforts. She repurposed elements of Huberman's performance management system toward continuous improvement instead of single-minded "accountability." Evidence about student, teacher, and school performance continued to matter, but now it was about informing improvements rather than what some privately described as "taking names and kicking ass." She continued district efforts to improve the quality of teachers and school leaders, and she also turned her attention to enhancing the work of network chiefs and central office heads.[89]

Much like Duncan's Era 3 strategy to focus on a small number of key initiatives, Jackson's priorities were evident in the three workgroups she established with support from the Fund. They were principal quality, district-level supports for schools, and improving high schools. Each workgroup included school leaders, members of the foundation and business communities, and local community stakeholders. Each was cochaired by a CPS district leader and someone external to CPS. Jackson personally cochaired the Principal Quality Workgroup with a board member from the Fund and a member of the Chicago Board of Education. As a former teacher, principal, and network chief, and an early leader in the movement that gave rise to the citywide Network for College Success, Jackson brought extensive firsthand improvement knowledge into these deliberations.[90]

Jackson engaged external partners to advance her agenda with the same openness that had characterized Eason-Watkins in Era 3. These relationships had been important to Jackson when she was principal at Al Raby and at Westinghouse high schools. She valued the capabilities resident in these organizations and recognized the important role that they continued to play in scaling district-wide improvements.[91] These partnerships were building blocks in how the system center in Chicago supported a decentralized system of schools. Jackson now sought to formalize these arrangements as a core mechanism for furthering systemwide change.

A new Chicago Principal Partnership, for example, emerged out of the Principal Quality Workgroup. It was a collaborative, led by the Fund and CPS, and it brought together nonprofit, university, and funding partners. It operated as a think tank for collecting and analyzing school leadership data as the basis for devising additional improvements efforts.[92] These included programs that support aspiring leaders, policy and program efforts designed to improve principal hiring in a decentralized context, and specialized surveys that informed the work of all partner organizations. Complementing this, a newly restructured Department of Principal Quality inside CPS regularly engaged with the Independent School Principals, mentioned earlier, to glean insights from their efforts. Taken together, an improvement learning system around the principalship had formed that combined systemwide data with in-depth insights from successful work on the job floor.

Network Leader Development

Simultaneous with the actions on principal quality, the workgroup on district-level supports for schools focused on strengthening the professional capabilities of network chiefs and core central office instructional leaders and on building a professional learning community among them.[93] The professional development line from teacher leaders and principals to network chiefs to senior district-level staff was targeted to drive toward a clearer and more consistent focus on instructional improvement. The human capital developments in schools and in the area offices that had emerged by the end of Era 3 created the base human resources necessary to make this reinvention of the line possible, and Jackson seized the opportunity.

All of this, however, was taking place as fiscal constraints worsened at CPS. When dollars are tight, it is commonplace for districts to attempt to preserve staffing allocations at schools and cut everywhere else. So, the infrastructure that had been building in Era 3 to support school improvement became a natural target for cutbacks during Era 4. Enter *Crain's Chicago Business*, which published a critique of the costs attached to the CPS network structure and called for eliminating network offices and network chiefs.[94] While reductions in force did occur at central office, the Board of Education did its best to protect core efforts aimed at improving teaching and learning. The network structure was sustained and continued to develop.

With regard to the network chiefs, Jackson returned to the professional work orientation that Eason-Watkins had established with the AIOs. She rebalanced their role responsibilities, away from punitive accountability as Huberman had been moving it, and back toward support for school improvement. Aligned with this, Jackson instituted further professional development for the chiefs and a new evaluation system that prioritized the professional learning of the educators in their networks and schools. It held chiefs accountable for supporting their principals as instructional leaders and for creating effective adult learning communities among them. Specifically, it signaled the importance of high-functioning instructional leadership teams in schools and emphasized that it was the chiefs' job to assure that their principals knew how to form and maintain the necessary team roles, routines, and relationships for this to happen.[95] Embedded here was an endorsement of the importance of school-based professional learning communities among school administrators, teacher leaders, and teachers. This long-standing element from the 5Es was finally formalized in an evaluation protocol.

The system's logic model in Era 4 envisioned teacher development as dependent on high-quality school leadership, which itself depended both on strong principal preparation partnerships and on network chiefs who could sustain principals' ongoing professional learning through individual coaching and networked activity.[96] The principal's priority in every school was improving teacher and student learning; network chiefs and central office focused there. This emphasis was consistent with a decentralized district organization. It also reflected one of the major findings of the last twenty years of research on principal effectiveness.[97]

Throughout this period, the Board of Education maintained its investments in principal quality as a key lever to improve student outcomes. This Board of Education conviction was strongly supported by leaders at the Fund and others in the exoskeleton. It was reinforced by Mayor Emanuel, who made a habit of visiting schools and meeting with their principals, and it was vitalized among board members when Emanuel appointed successful former principals, such as Mahalia Hines and Carlos Azcoitia, to the board itself.[98] Board members also held firm in contract negotiations with the CTU, which sought restrictions in principals' authority to act in their buildings. When money is tight, districts regularly give ground on issues like this, but that did not happen here. A dense relational network citywide sustained the system's focus on the principalship amid the turmoil of Era 4.

And through it all, the principalship, and the pipeline to it, stayed diverse. Among principals, the percent African American remained stable from 1990 forward, at about 45 percent, even as African American student enrollments reduced substantially. The percent of white principals declined, from 48 percent in 1990 to 35 percent by 2017, and Latino leadership increased during this same period, from 6 percent to 16 percent. In addition, the system's ongoing support for the recruitment and preparation of assistant principals aimed to assure a diverse cadre going forward. In 2017, the pool of assistant principals, who were primary candidates for promotion to principalships, was 36 percent Black, 33 percent white, and 23 percent Latino.[99] Maintaining a diverse leadership workforce is a challenge for urban districts, and Chicago's decade-plus efforts at developing its human capital pipeline left the district in good position as Era 4 closed.

New Teacher Development

Efforts from Era 3 to improve the basic academic preparation of new teachers persisted in Era 4. Contract organizations such as TFA, AUSL, and Golden Apple continued as part of a sustained effort to address chronic teacher shortages. They brought in 15 to 20 percent of Chicago's new teachers each year.[100] Selective enrollment universities, including DePaul, Loyola, National Louis University, and UIC, all contributed increasing numbers of new teachers. (Three of the four universities were part of an earlier federal grant, designed in collaboration with Eason-Watkins in Era 3, to transform their teacher education programs to be more responsive to the needs of Chicago's schools.) The percentage of teachers from the University of Illinois, Urbana-Champaign and from Illinois State University also increased during this time.

The workforce challenges of 1987—chronic shortages and lacking teacher qualifications—had become largely a thing of the past by the end of Era 4. The strategy of both expanding teacher recruitment from multiple higher education institutions and increasing placements from alternative providers had made a difference. The district went from one struggling with mass vacancies to one that had vacancies only in select positions that challenged urban school systems nationwide: hiring more teachers of color to better "match" student populations that were predominantly Latino and African American, and meeting specific shortages in STEM, special education, and bilingual and bilingual special education. Hiring teachers of color became even more challenging in Era 4 after the state cut budgets for students' college financial aid following the 2008 recession. These cuts depressed enrollments in the state institutions serving the largest numbers of students of color, and this, in turn, depressed the number of prospective teachers of color coming through. (Chicago State was threatened with closure due to state budget shortfalls.) In addition, in 2010 when the Illinois State Board of Education (ISBE) sharply raised the "cut score" on the basic skill test required of all teacher education candidates, the number of newly certified Black and Latino teachers declined further.[101]

Shaping State Mandates to Further Improvements

Although Chicago maintained considerable autonomy as a district across the thirty years of reform, state policy influenced it in multiple ways beyond the major legislation passed in 1988 and 1995. Importantly, as professional and civic capacity grew in the exoskeleton, its leaders began to influence subsequent statewide actions that further enabled efforts in Chicago. Advance Illinois formed as a statewide educational advocacy group in 2008. Its board membership included several civic and educational organizational leaders who had been active in Chicago school reform. The organization quickly became an important player that pressed for new teacher evaluation mandates, new principal certification requirements, and extending the use of the 5Es statewide.[102] Additionally, a state mandate that began taking shape in Era 3 required every principal preparation program in the state to close by 2012 and reapply for state approval under new rules. These new guidelines required partnerships with school districts, selective admissions, rich clinical experiences, better faculty-student ratios, and other program components. Tozer chaired the legislative task force that advanced these recommendations and involved leaders from other major principal preparation programs serving CPS, including LAUNCH and New Leaders. In these ways, Tozer's ambition to scale was being realized. The innovators who had been figuring out how to prepare better principals for CPS, and the organizations supporting them, were now shaping the regulatory process statewide toward stronger, more rigorous program requirements.

Era 4 also presented opportunities to advance the initiative on teacher evaluation begun in Era 3. The state now mandated that those conducting teacher evaluations, usually principals and assistant principals, be formally trained. They also specified that the intent of these evaluations was both formative and summative, which meant that evaluations needed to occur regularly throughout the school year and not just at the end. CPS worked with its partners to refine the observation protocols based on the Danielson Framework for Teaching, discussed in chapter 4, to assure that administrators could use them reliably. CPS's chief talent officer, Matt Lyons, reflected that these new processes motivated "tens of thousands of conversations about high quality teaching between administrators and teachers each school year."[103] In so doing, they advanced the development of both teachers and school leaders.

A New Problem Identified: High-Churn Schools

Regardless of the advances discussed above, analytic work at UIC revealed that a large number of neighborhood elementary schools still shared common challenges, including high rates of chronic absence, student mobility, and homelessness. The research team referred to these as "high churn" schools. Most were embedded in neighborhoods that overlapped substantially with what sociologist William Julius Wilson had called "truly disadvantaged communities"—a term that the authors of *Organizing Schools for Improvement* drew upon in 2010.[104] Though it was obscured in national reports about successes in some "90/90/90 schools"—90 percent student success rates in schools with 90 percent minority and 90 percent low-income enrollments—Consortium researchers had illuminated that school communities that shared the latter two ascriptive characteristics were not all the same. When analysts dug below simple gross comparisons, very different and much more problematic contextual conditions were discerned. There was a subset of schools in Chicago that had confronted extraordinary and stubborn challenges for decades, regardless of the interventions tried. These challenges seemed impossible to overcome.

Additionally, at a time when principal development efforts were showing success citywide, new principals still struggled to lead this group of schools. To address this, UIC partnered with CPS to create a professional learning community for the principals in high-churn schools. The district also supported efforts to figure out how to recruit to those schools teachers who showed clear interest in working in them, and central office leaders began trying to figure out how to strengthen system center supports for them. This was no longer the story of a power struggle between central office and local schools—as it had been during Era 2 of reform. That was a zero-sum game. In contrast, the more nuanced perspective that took root in Era 3, and continued to evolve in Era 4, guided central office initiatives entirely compatible with Chicago's decentralization. While preserving principals' decision-making authority to select their own staff, the district developed a specific program to recruit and support teachers in high-churn schools.[105] These efforts represented one more marker of the CPS functioning as a system of schools guided by a district-wide improvement orientation. Equally important, CPS now had capacity in central office to act on this orientation.[106]

In sum, progress continued during Era 4, despite churn among the system's senior leaders. Key in this regard were the resilience and continued commitments of diverse organizations in Chicago's exoskeleton. By staying the course and maintaining relationships with Board of Education members, district departments, network offices, and school-based leaders, they helped to sustain the developments that had blossomed in Era 3. Moreover, the professional and social capital that they nurtured became a resource for renewed growth in district-led actions once senior leadership stabilized.

By the end of Era 4, Chicago had strong systems in place for teacher recruitment and development, for teacher leader development, for initial principal preparation, and for their continued development through the Office of Network Support. Opportunities for teachers as mentors of aspiring and novice teachers; as instructional coaches and team and grade-level leaders; and as members of instructional leadership teams existed in virtually every district school. These experiences as school-based instructional leaders, in turn, enabled a deeper and better-prepared pool of candidates to compete for admission into new and more rigorous principal preparation programs, such as those at New Leaders and UIC. It had taken some twenty years of investments in human capital development among teachers and principals, but by the end of Era 4, returns on these investments were also being realized at the highest levels of the system itself. As mentioned earlier, the capabilities of individuals moving into senior leadership roles had grown enormously, and they were a powerful new resource for future efforts.

By the end of Era 4, an impressive human capital development pipeline had emerged. It was rooted in strengthening teachers' initial preparation, recruitment, and mentoring. Ample opportunities were created for these educators to grow further through new school-based leadership roles, and then deep investments were made in principals' preparation and support. As a result, a very different cadre of educators was leading CPS in 2017 compared to 1987. Figure 3.8 highlights how these elements now aligned: a revitalized and strengthened teacher pipeline fed into a transformed principal development pipeline and eventuated in transformed system-level leadership as well.

Figure 3.8 The architecture that emerged in Chicago for professional human capital development

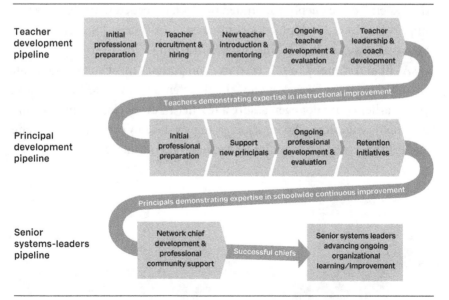

Ironically, no one set out to build these pipelines. Rather, at various points in time over this thirty-year period, immediate problems presented themselves and the district as well as its external partners responded. Interventions were introduced: Some laid a foundation for subsequent initiatives that replaced them, like GOLDEN for teachers and teacher leaders, LAUNCH for principals, and area instructional officers for principal support and development. Some endured but were less prominent drivers of change, such as National Board Certification and National Teachers Academy. And some continued to influence change at local and national levels, such as New Leaders and UIC's Urban Education Leadership Program. Even though early efforts appeared disconnected, the individuals involved—inside CPS and out, from higher education to foundations to community organizations and beyond—were learning about the depth of changes needed and developing expertise to lead such work. They were beginning to see potential connections for better aligning the system. Through the many individuals and organizations in the exoskeleton working to improve the system's human resources, coupled with reporting from both the Consortium and *Catalyst*, these learnings became more broadly shared. Diverse citizen actors were coming to "see the system" more deeply and understand what needed to be done next to improve it. The developments summarized in figure 3.8 represent the extraordinary product of this systems' learning.

As final testimony to this account, and perhaps most surprising of all, what had been the "worst public school system in America," which thirty years earlier could not even assure a teacher in every classroom, was now developing educators who were increasingly valued by other school systems and being recruited into senior leadership roles outside the city.[107]

4

Improving Teaching and Learning

When the US Secretary of Education called the CPS the "worst in the nation," Chicagoans were outraged, but few disagreed. A history of patronage appointments, a dysfunctional and largely interest-based school board, and state underfunding, all grounded in a century of institutional racism, were among the forces that made it so. Alongside this story, however, was another one that recalled a different past. Prior to the 1970s, there had been educational bright spots in Chicago's racially isolated African American neighborhoods. One of these was DuSable High School, which opened in 1935 in the Bronzeville community on Chicago's south side. Its "hall of fame" showcased dozens of alumni, including Harold Washington, Dinah Washington, Redd Foxx, John Johnson, and Nat King Cole, who went on to stellar careers in business, politics, law, medicine, the performing arts, and professional sports.[1] DuSable was exceptional but not unique. Most urban districts had a few DuSables back then. Drawing on the experiences of the segregated south, these schools excelled because their communities, faculties, staff, and principals were committed to educating and caring for their children when no one else would. By the 1980s economic and social forces had ravaged Bronzeville, and those assaults, coupled with failed school integration efforts, diminished DuSable too. But

219

hope came in the form of the School Reform Act, which reenvisioned schools as responsive community institutions led by educators who truly cared about the children.

We tell the story of CPS's instructional improvement through the lives of three African American educators—Sara Spurlark, Barbara Eason-Watkins, and Janice Jackson. Their careers spanned overlapping eras of reform. As principals early on, each worked with her faculty and the broader neighborhood and civic community to reinvent teaching and learning in her school. They then took what they learned into increasingly significant professional roles that eventually transformed the district. Their stories offer a window into organizational development and learning over time, describe how the tone and substance of leadership matters, and show how the strongest leaders never do this work alone. Their stories also illumine how each reform era built upon the last and how Chicago's exoskeleton kept learning, adapting, and deepening its capacity to contribute.

Yet, their stories are not the whole story. As noted in the introduction, African Americans had finally reached positions of power in CPS and the city at the start of reform. During Eras 1 and 2 when few Latinos were among district leaders, or even well represented among the staff, the educational needs of Latino students, and the English learners among them, received scant central office attention. Over the next twenty years Latinos became the district's largest student group, and their rising numbers signaled the next chapter in Chicago's ethnic succession. Early on, however, decentralization gave them influence in their local school communities. LSCs in Latino neighborhoods contracted with new principals who were younger and better "matched" to their communities and its needs, and the teachers these principals hired were different too. The stories of Jorge Sanchez and Carlos Azcoitia, along with pioneers like Adela Coronado-Greely and Janet Nolan, demonstrate how they used the authorities and resources of the 1988 legislation to reinvent their schools—just as their African American colleagues were doing. Learning how to effect local change and better serve Latino students and English learners were some of the things these principals carried when they too began to move into more senior district leadership positions toward the end of Era 3 and into Era 4. Here too, it took a city, with external allies and organizations playing critical roles.

SARA SPURLARK: SOUTHERN ROOTS, NORTHERN PROBLEM SOLVING

Sara Spurlark's grandparents were enslaved in South Carolina.[2] She grew up on the integrated campus of Johnson C. Smith University—an HBCU where her father was president. Marian Anderson, Paul Robeson, and Langston Hughes were among the family's houseguests whenever they toured the south, since hotels were closed to them. The family moved to Chicago in the 1940s when Spurlark's father was among the first Black students admitted to UChicago as a graduate student. Twenty years later Spurlark started a PhD program in biochemistry there, but family obligations rerouted her to the CPS. Her first assignment was to teach AP chemistry at Kelly High, which served a white, working-class neighborhood on the southwest side. She was one of the first to integrate its faculty, and she faced a hostile school community when she did. She also was the first African American in CPS to teach an AP chemistry class, and during her years at Kelly she mentored dozens of students on to college and careers. In the late 1960s Spurlark became the assistant principal of Kenwood Academy, a new high school, and in the 1970s she headed Ray Elementary School. Both served Hyde Park, the integrated southside community that is home to UChicago. Over the years Spurlark was a member of the district team that negotiated contracts with CTU president Jackie Vaughn, and she was a mayoral appointment to the School Finance Authority and School Reform Nominating Commission. When she retired from CPS in 1989 to be a cofounder of the Center for School Improvement, it was her approach to teaching and learning and her understanding of school community development that made her essential to the path the Center sought to forge. Her experience and reputation in the larger civic context were assets too.

Spurlark had attended southern Black schools. She and her siblings knew that they had to be twice as good to get half as far. Her teachers knew that too. Her parents told her that the only real failure was a failure to try, and that those who have more must give more. As an educator Spurlark made it her life's work to motivate her students, teachers, and families. She then figured out the supports they needed to succeed. Spurlark's CPS career preceded the push toward ambitious instruction by several decades, but it was not a new approach—just one typically reserved for privileged others. Spurlark felt that the root of many of the discipline and behavioral problems that she saw in CPS was students' boredom with the work they were asked to do and the adult belief that it was all they could do. In Spurlark's view, the cure was to give students more engaging, meaningful work, instill in them the belief that they could be successful if they persisted, and then, most crucially, ensure that they were. She understood the power of a "growth mindset" long before it had an academic name. Similarly, for students who fell behind, it was common practice to relegate them to remedial classes where they were exposed to less content, and where teaching proceeded at a snail's pace and was repetitive in ways that had failed them before. Going slow does not help students catch up or build self-esteem, but it was swimming upstream to say otherwise. Spurlark did not blame students or try to fix them. Instead, she looked for ways to motivate adults to change their ways and then taught them how. Much of what would emerge as Chicago's instructional improvement agenda is rooted right here.

Spurlark embodied the role of instructional leader before it too had a name. She encouraged her teachers to work together: to take joint responsibility for students' success and well-being, to be humane and consistent regarding discipline, and to use a common pedagogy so that students' experience from course to course and grade to grade did not feel like whiplash and so their skills and knowledge built over time. Trained as a scientist herself, she wanted her students (and their teachers) to feel the excitement that comes from being steeped in a discipline—a stance that put her at odds with "back to basics" adherents in CPS and nationally. She was a master at "counseling out" teachers who did not want to come along or work hard. Her teachers rarely filed grievances. On the rare occasions when they did, she never lost, because her documentation was meticulous and, as a negotiator with CTU, she knew the rules better than they did.

Spurlark mastered the mechanics of school leadership too. As assistant principal she did her best to align the school's budget and schedule to instructional priorities, although these were mostly immovable objects pre-reform. Spurlark also made sure that her high school students were programmed into the right classes in the right sequence to keep them on track to graduate, and she constantly checked their progress. She predated Freshman OnTrack by more than a decade.

Spurlark was also an early and vocal advocate for increasing instructional time. CPS had instituted a "closed campus" policy in the 1960s. It was intended to keep students indoors during the school day and safe from gang activity, and a 2:30 dismissal meant they could be home before street violence escalated in the late afternoon. But closed campus had insidious consequences. Relative to other urban districts, CPS students were shorted three years of instructional time across their K–12 years.[3] Moreover, a shortened day meant that young children had no recess, and teachers rarely got more than a few-minute break themselves. Regardless, the CTU had defended closed campus ferociously since its inception, largely because early dismissal put teachers on the road home ahead of rush hour. Closed campus required a 60 percent vote of a school's faculty to overturn. Few reached that threshold.

Finally, an ethos of Spurlark's southern upbringing was that "it takes a village." This was manifest when her parents fostered children, in the hospitality they extended to travelers (luminaries and those who just needed a bed), and from all of the adults who took it upon themselves to quash any child's questionable behavior and then tell the child's parents. Spurlark brought this sensibility to her schools. She knew the parents, grandparents, or guardians of every student and, somehow, could recall their names and stories during chance encounters at a grocery store or restaurant decades later. Parents felt "known," and part of knowing was figuring out the supports and resources that would help them be the kind of parents they wanted to be. The drive for community schools that began in the 1990s developed from cultures where community was the norm.

Forming the Center for School Improvement

Spurlark turned down many other offers when she decided to join Bryk and Greenberg in founding the Center in 1989, and her decision was noticed by funders, community, civic, and district leaders. She chose the Center because its proposed work resonated with her earlier efforts, and reform created new potential for their realization. Moreover, the Center's vision of working with a network of schools was a new way for her to reach even more educators and families. Spurlark brought her reputation, experience, and energy to this new reform organization. It might not have launched without her.

The Center was among the groups that offered training to new LSCs. In addition, LSC members were asked if their school community wanted to partner with the Center and an "affinity" network of like-minded schools, to help them build the schools they truly wanted for their children. The Center's first network comprised three southside elementary schools that each anchored a low-income, African American neighborhood.[4] In those schools, and those that joined the network subsequently, Center staff worked alongside the principal, faculty, and staff to develop a comprehensive school development initiative. Its design built eclectically from current research, professional practice, and school community input. Drawing from the Comer Project, for example, the Center created a social service coordinator role and supported someone from the faculty who might assure attention to "the whole child" and strengthen parent and community engagement. It borrowed organizational insights from Success for All, including the use of interim assessments to chart progress and the grouping of students to accelerate their learning through push-in resources and supplemental tutoring. To advance more ambitious teaching and learning overall, the Center drew on emerging work in New York City's district 2 and the Early Language and Literacy Center at The Ohio State, both of which had roots in Marie Clay's literacy work in New Zealand. The Center also created a literacy coordinator role, which was an analogue to the social service position. The coordinator provided school-based teacher professional development and classroom-embedded coaching. Through this work, Center staff brought new ideas and practices into the daily work of school communities that had been neglected for decades, and Center staff learned about the real opportunities and challenges of neighborhood schools.

To inform the implementation of its initiatives, the Center cocreated several tools with network colleagues. The STEP primary grade reading assessment system was a formative tool that built from Clay's observation survey.[5] Across twelve steps it identified the progression of knowledge and skills that started with the conventions of print and led to proficient reading and writing by the end of third grade. This enabled teachers to track each student's progress frequently. The tool also offered teachers guidance about how to advance students at each step. From an improvement perspective, STEP stood in stark contrast to norm-referenced tests, which were in wide use then and by design necessitated that half or more of students be "below norm." One tool provided a pathway toward a desired aim; the other reinforced deficit thinking.

STEP's developmental orientation, coupled with routine progress monitoring, revealed a leaky pipeline problem. Auxiliary services existed in these schools for struggling students, but as a system the services were failing. A student in need might not be referred by her teacher; she might be referred for extra support, but the designated staff might not get to her; a service might not be regularly provided, or it might be the wrong service or an ineffective one. For too many students the process was a dead end. In response, the Center developed an academic and social service support system (AS3). Conceptually akin to STEP, it tracked students' flows through the school's supplemental support system and pinpointed leaks. Once identified, they could be fixed.

Finally, the Center's "grand rounds" were a half-day event that generally took place in the spring—and only after educators were brave enough to open classroom doors. Preparation included observations, self-evaluation, and analysis of student work and student and school data. These self-studies and the conversations organized around them aimed to help the school's leadership team see how their system actually worked—the progress made, the problems visible, and the necessary steps ahead.

The Center was an anomaly in Chicago. It was not a service provider offering a menu of options, it was not a research group looking for an urban context to study, it had none of the authorities of a central office, and it had no ambition to take on large numbers of schools. Instead, by working small and being embedded in school communities, and by advancing comprehensive school development, Center staff were trying to understand

how to facilitate improvement and figure out the intermediate space between the system center, schools, and academia. The Center was deliberately straddling the research-practice divide and sharing responsibility with
schools for results. At a time when Chicago was preoccupied with governance reform, the Center was focused on the next horizon: instructional
improvement and all that had to happen for it to occur.

BARBARA EASON-WATKINS: LEARNING SMALL TO GO BIG

A few miles from the Center, another school development initiative was
taking best advantage of reform. This one was spearheaded by the school's
principal. Barbara Eason-Watkins was one generation removed from the
south. Like Spurlark, she had grown up knowing that she needed to be twice
as good to get half as far. Her mother had been educated at an HBCU in
Alabama and then moved to Detroit where she taught first grade. When
her daughter followed in her footsteps and was a new first-grade teacher
still living at home, her mother never asked "How was your day?" when
she came home but went directly to "Let's look at your students' work."
Prior to reform, Eason-Watkins moved to Chicago and became principal
of two southside elementary schools—Mollison and then McCosh.[6]

Eason-Watkins described base conditions at McCosh as dire in 1988,
when she was appointed principal, and also emblematic of the system as a
whole at the start of Era 1.[7] Reflecting back, she said:

> McCosh back then was one of the 100 lowest performing schools. . . . It had
> lots of traditions and competitions but teaching and learning was so weak.
> Teachers yelled at kids from the front of the class. Students did worksheets,
> at best. There was no critical thinking, no academic challenge. Kids were
> bored. They stayed out of class, ran the halls, got into fights. It was CPS at
> the time.
>
> My teachers? Everyone did their own thing. McCosh was two
> buildings—K to 3 and 4 to 8. Teachers didn't talk to each other in either
> building and there was no communication across the two. So, there was a

real lack of coherence and just so little knowledge—about reading and math, and also about middle school and the early adolescent child. That lack of knowledge wasn't their fault. They hadn't had opportunities to learn.

Ten years later McCosh was recognized as one of the district's most improved schools in reading and math. There was more to do, but the progress had been considerable.

Eason-Watkins described her method as "figuring it out as I went along and pulling in a lot of smart people to think with me, bring resources, and help." One of the things she "figured out" was how to start building professional community in her faculty:

> How did I get started? . . . I had to come up with ways for the teachers to get to know me—and each other. I started a monthly breakfast club and cooked breakfast for the teachers. It was voluntary; just a time to eat and talk.

Eason-Watkins found her teachers' professional knowledge inadequate, but she never blamed them. "Black teachers back then were limited in terms of the preparation programs they could go to," she said, "and CPS professional development—well, what can I say?" Her efforts to build their knowledge of content and pedagogy entailed collaborative work, coaching from her, and coursework. Like Spurlark, she held the door open for teachers who did not want to work hard and work together. She nudged several toward it, and about half the faculty "vamoosed" during her first few years.[8] These were teachers who did not believe that their students could learn, and so felt little pressure to teach. Their departure was celebrated quietly by others because their negativity had depressed and curtailed the rest.

Eason-Watkins navigated a delicate transition with her teachers toward public practice and away from their closed-door norm. This included opening their classrooms to each other, to the teacher leaders that she was developing in-house, and to external partners that she was bringing in. This was a monumental shift, and by easing their way, Eason-Watkins gained her teachers' trust and respect. She also started with her lower grades—the level where she was most knowledgeable as a former first-grade teacher, and where teachers were most open to trying something new. She reasoned that a good start there also might be noticed by the rest of the faculty and soften their resistance. And much like the conversations she had with her mother, she created a safe context for looking at student work and data that helped her faculty see bright spots in their instructional practice and pinpoint weaknesses to work on:

> I started with a focus on primary literacy. I helped teachers look at student writing together, share articles and talk about how to apply the ideas we read about to their practice. We started grade level meetings and 5 week reading assessments. That kind of work started to change the culture of the faculty and the building. Teachers asked if they could get into each other's classes.

> Phase one was primary literacy. Phase two was primary math. Phase three was my middle school.

> I arranged for lane or course credits for my [middle school] teachers—so they could learn about the "adolescent child." I also got a grant for teachers to take classes in reading, math, and science to deepen their content knowledge. . . . . . . I taught one of the classes. . . . [But] deepen is the wrong word because some of them didn't have any content knowledge. Most of my teachers had only had one class in reading for their certification and it was totally irrelevant.

> It was a culture of trust that was building at McCosh that enabled my teachers to do these things together. I wasn't paying them extra. [After a while] they just wanted to learn and get better together.

Eason-Watkins focused first on her youngest students. She reasoned that a good start and support to stay on track would spare them the trauma of failure followed by remedial and retention programs down the road—interventions that are costly, rarely successful academically, and erode students' confidence and self-esteem.[9] This explains her starting points in primary literacy and math (grades K–3), followed by upper elementary and middle school initiatives (grades 4–8).

She also believed that teachers needed opportunities to learn to teach in new ways. Locally, the Consortium and *Catalyst* were teaching the city about "ambitious intellectual work," and the Center was introducing this pedagogy to its network. Nationally, educators like Anthony Alvarado and Elaine Fink and Irene Fountas and Gay Su Pinnell were learning how to create capacity for ambitious instruction in the primary grades. The transition was a heavy lift in CPS because it was so contrary to earlier district efforts.[10] It also was anathema to the scripted lessons and teaching to the test that Vallas was mandating at the same time for probation schools.[11] In contrast, ambitious instruction in the 1990s was the same concept that Spurlark had espoused a decade earlier. It depends on teachers helping students master the fundamentals, for example, phonics in early literacy and multiplication tables in math. But developing basic skill was coupled with opportunity for students at every grade to work with complex texts, tackle interesting problems in academic disciplines, engage in higher-order thinking and elaborated written and oral communication in that discipline, and make meaningful connections to life beyond the classroom.[12] When Eason-Watkins taught a demonstration class for her middle school teachers, analyzed children's writing with her primary faculty, or reconfigured the schedule to assure dedicated time for teachers to collaborate, she was helping her teachers learn new ways to teach and learn.[13] As one of her teachers said, "She really does lead. . . . You feel like someone is always behind you."[14]

Eason-Watkins's cultural competence also gave her insight into what needed to be done to support a "fragile" school community like McCosh.[15] Like Spurlark, she knew all the students' names, their stories, and their families. She started a partnership with Even Start for her primary grade parents.[16] She also organized a grandparents' club, because she "had more grandparents raising students than parents." Eason-Watkins coordinated activities and resources with her community's five churches, started a partnership with the city's Metropolitan Family Services, and convinced some of the social service agencies that had left the neighborhood to return. A playwright from the theater group ETA Creative Arts Foundation helped her sixth graders rewrite *The Watsons Go to Birmingham*, to make it more relevant to them. When the playwright directed the students' performance, their script reading progressed from halting to fluent. These are some of the ways that the arts and student and family services, which had been cut by successive fiscal crises, were reinstated and reconceived to meet the moment.[17] In retrospect, Eason-Watkins, and other principals like her, had freedom under reform to figure out the essential supports specific to advancing each of their school communities—work that the Consortium would later frame as part of the 5Es.

Eason-Watkins did not rebuild McCosh alone. Rather, she distributed leadership among her team and enlisted members of her academic network and funders to help.[18] In the early years, she recalled, she brought in George Olson (Roosevelt), Gloria Pleasant (Chicago State), Carol Lee (UChicago, then Northwestern), Louis Gomez and James Spillane (Northwestern), and Marty Gartzman (University of Illinois, Chicago) to be her thought partners and work directly with her teachers. Grants from Chapman at Joyce "kept making it possible for me to get people into my building," she said. She also used grants "to get [all of her] teachers out into the world", where they could be exposed to more new people and ideas.[19] "Don't forget the invitation to my faculty to a retreat and speakers' series the Center did. And the dinner with Gay [Pinnell]."

Then there were the people who sought her out:

> Tony [Bryk], Melissa [Roderick] and John [Easton] came a-calling one day. They were doing some ITBS score analysis and comparing scores between McCosh and [a school nearby].[20] We had similar students, families, teachers. We were in the same community and their question was, What was I doing that my kids' achievement was so much better? That started my conversation with Tony—which has never ended. . . . Louis [Gomez] introduced me to Jim [Spillane]. Jim came and he watched me work with people and even put a name on it—"distributed leadership." Who knew it had a name? It just made sense.

This list of people and institutions grew over Eason-Watkins's years at McCosh.[21] A common bond was their recognition that building the capabilities of fragile schools required melding diverse bodies of research knowledge with practical expertise. Eason-Watkins was drawing that research knowledge from the outside into her school. Less than a mile away, the Center staff was addressing this same problem, but from the other side.

About ten years into her stint at McCosh, Eason-Watkins, and the school itself, were ready for something new. A natural next step was collaborating with the Center. After extensive negotiations with the Board of Education, Eason-Watkins joined the Center's leadership team half-time as associate director for professional school development, and McCosh was poised to become the Center's second professional development school. As such it would complement a new school that the Center had designed and opened two years before and extend and deepen the Center's reach.[22] That plan derailed, however, when Duncan was appointed CEO a few months later and he asked Eason-Watkins to become the district's chief education officer.

From One School to 600+

Eason-Watkins had achieved a measure of success and celebrity at McCosh, and what she learned there informed what she did downtown. How to improve teaching and learning from a still dysfunctional central office and in a decentralized district where many schools continued to struggle, was, however, another ballgame entirely. At the start of Era 3, central office had minimal capacity, and the need was tremendous.

Nevertheless, there was some good news. A growing number of schools (like McCosh and others featured below) were progressing under reform, and this set of schools, and the educators in them, were resources for the system.[23] The Consortium, *Catalyst*, and Annenberg had brought attention to the importance of professional learning and school-based professional community. This helped pave the way for new, more-open ways for adults to learn from each other. Groups additional to the Center also had launched since Era 1 to partner with schools around instructional improvement, as discussed below. These were new, organically grown fruits of reform, even if none was fully embedded in the system.

Eason-Watkins knew that building central office's capacity to help schools improve instruction was her biggest challenge. She also knew it was an effort that would extend far beyond her term—regardless of how long she lasted. To recall Chapman's language again, her job was to "step up and choose the right path," hew to it, call on the "collective us" to help, and try to seed new norms and capacities strong enough that they might persist and keep growing when she left. She focused intensely on two of the 5Es—building a professional learning community, and capacity for more ambitious instruction.

The Chicago Reading Initiative.   Eason-Watkins started the Chicago Reading Initiative (CRI) in her first weeks as CEdO. It focused initially on the primary grades. In 2001, 114 elementary schools were on probation. Eason-Watkins had authority to mandate their curriculum, materials, and pedagogy, as Vallas had done. But many had resented his mandates even if fiats from above seemed an efficient way to deal with low performers. In contrast, Eason-Watkins thought that "constrained choice" would be more palatable to a decentralized system. She and her team vetted materials and offered probation schools their pick among three reading series. This was the most she felt central office could possibly support.

Eason-Watkins did not shy away from directive steps toward probation schools, but these were broached as support to get better, not command from above. Her team created a new role for area reading coaches (ARCs) and recruited, hired, and assigned them to work directly with the school-based reading specialists in their "area's" schools. (The new "area" structure is described in chapter 3.) Many of the ARCs had been reading specialists in the past; in that capacity most had only worked with students.[24] Now they were introduced to a new adult educator role, and a literacy framework, with the expectation that they would help teachers learn how to devote at least two hours of instruction each day to the "four blocks" of word knowledge (which includes phonics), fluency, comprehension, and writing. This framework was the choice of Tim Shanahan, a UIC literacy professor who had been tapped to direct CRI. The Four Blocks program was a relatively simple starting place, which seemed appropriate given capacity issues at that time. It also was compatible with the Bush administration's Reading First program and the federal funding that supported its implementation in districts. Otherwise, the Four Blocks did not take sides in the nation's "reading wars" that pitted back-to-basics against more-holistic approaches. It was an anodyne framing that could deepen and complexify as teachers, their coaches, and the system being built to support them learned more about ambitious instruction.

Initial support to help the ARCs teach the Four Blocks to the reading specialists in their buildings included content workshops and instructional rounds (discussed below). DIBELS, a commercial tool designed to assess students' reading development in grades K–3, was introduced, as were progress monitoring tools akin to the five-week assessments that Eason-Watkins had developed at McCosh.[25] ARCs would help school-based reading specialists learn to administer these data check-ins quickly and frequently so that students' learning glitches might be caught early. When paired with guidance about what to try when a problem was identified, these tools could help educators learn how to intervene, rather than letting difficulties fester.

Area instructional officers (AIOs) also were recruited to mentor principals and facilitate the instructional improvement work in their buildings. Theirs was another new instructional leadership role in CPS. Virtually all of the new AIOs had been principals and among the system's best, having led some of the "actively restructuring schools" identified by the Consortium. Others came from Annenberg network sites or had been involved with two other initiatives discussed below—the Teaching Academy for Math and Science, and a curriculum initiative of the National Science Foundation. The AIOs' role focused on developing principals as instructional leaders who would work with their faculties to improve teaching and learning and orient school operations around that goal. Unsurprisingly, the AOIs, like the ARCs, needed support to execute their new roles.

The ARCs and AIOs participated in the same literacy professional development so that they would have a common knowledge base, their methods and messaging would cohere, and they could reinforce each other's work. Each group also received role-specific training. Both drew from ongoing learnings at the Center and from how Eason-Watkins had conceived her own role, at McCosh, and from that of Geralynn Wilson, her homegrown literacy leader. It was an effort at scaling up, but one that recognized the enormous challenges involved in building the norms and capabilities necessary to enact it well at scale. The AIOs and ARCs were trained in year one of CRI. They engaged their new roles, with continuing central office support, beginning in year two.[26]

Eason-Watkins also extended CRI beyond probation sites. Schools that were "stuck" just above probation were invited to join the new Advanced Reading Development Demonstration Project and partner with an area university to build literacy capacity.[27] The rest of the elementary schools were offered a full-time literacy leader if they joined CRI.[28] Eason-Watkins hoped that most schools would come into the new work through one of these avenues, but those that chose to fly solo, could. Options like these made system alignment harder to achieve, but they also functioned as a release valve. And whatever was achieved was also likely to be more authentic and better embraced because it had been chosen.

Absent capacity at central office to mentor the AIOs and ARCs, Eason-Watkins enlisted her network of external colleagues to help. They now signed on as thought partners, designers, developers, coaches, and trainers. They populated her "kitchen cabinet" too. Some took leaves, others accepted CPS leadership positions, and still others consulted or had their time bought out. To name a few, Shanahan, from UIC, directed CRI its first year; Greenberg, from the Center, took responsibility for a monthly workshop for AIOs and ARCs (discussed below); and Bertani offered role-specific AIO training through the district's new Office of Professional Development.

Eason-Watkins also drew on processes that had been incubated externally, including instructional rounds. Greenberg had learned this process from proteges of Alvarado and Fink and developed her own practice of it in the Center's network. Now, Eason-Watkins asked her to tailor it to CRI's new instructional leadership group. So, Greenberg and her Center colleagues led a monthly two-day workshop for AIOs and ARCs during the reading initiative's first year.[29] Eason-Watkins participated in many of the sessions, and her team participated in all of them so that there could be an eventual hand-off. Each workshop included instructional rounds in two elementary schools.

Introducing the process had its challenges. The first was convincing principals and teachers that they were not being judged if a few dozen CPS educators descended on their building and took turns observing classrooms in small groups. Another hurdle was convincing the AIOs and ARCs that they could and should go into classrooms and then talk about what they saw. They resisted: "What can you see in five minutes?" "It's so disruptive!" "It's like a judgment drive-by!" Unnerved about the "opening up" aspect of the rounds, someone compared it to the police screaming "Open up" and then kicking in the door. An extreme metaphor, but heads nodded when they heard it.

Eason-Watkins asked the group to "give it a try," and Greenberg met them at a school. She put them in groups of five or six and sent each group into a first-grade classroom to "look for" specific instructional or management practices they might otherwise miss. In the early rounds these were straightforward questions like, Who is sitting at the back of the room? Does the teacher ever ask students to "say more"? Can *you* understand her directions? Is the lesson review or new material? What can you learn about writing instruction from scanning the room? How many students are paying attention?[30]

At the five-minute mark the AIOs and ARCs met briefly in the hallway with Greenberg to share both what they saw and questions that were raised for them. Then they would rotate among the rooms, or go into more first grades, or another grade, with the same questions, or perhaps new questions that the first round surfaced. At day's end they would debrief as a whole group about the professional development implications of their visits. Greenberg might prompt: "Across first-grade classrooms, what commonalities did you see? What about differences from grade to grade? If this were your faculty, and given these observations, where would you focus professional development?" Resistance to the process wilted in the face of learning. Socialized as compliance managers, some had never really looked at classroom teaching before. These were smart, committed people and among the system's best, but few had ever been asked to look closely at instruction.

The rounds also were a window into culture—in a classroom, a school, or between them. Based on earlier experiences at the Center, Greenberg deliberately rotated visits between buildings serving African American and

Latino students. She paired places where the achievement levels were similar but the school cultures different. The AIOs and ARCs often described the Latino buildings, and especially those serving second-generation children, as a "more relaxed . . . positive . . . gentler" climate for student learning. Because most of the group had spent their careers in racially segregated CPS schools, the contrast surprised and unsettled some of them, but no one brought it up in the debriefs. Privately Eason-Watkins encouraged a couple of the AIOs she knew well to speak up, and tentative remarks became a conversation. It modeled a practice about facilitating difficult conversations that the AIOs and ARCs might bring into their own schools.

The Chicago Math and Science Initiative.   Eason-Watkins started planning a Chicago Math and Science Initiative (CMSI) as soon as the literacy work launched. The challenges were similar and similarly overwhelming: How should they address a profound content and pedagogical knowledge deficit among educators about both disciplines? How should they navigate the move from private to public practice, and from didactic pedagogies to more ambitious instruction? How should they address the incoherence and lack of alignment that had always plagued the district but now was stoked by decentralization and by vendors selling textbooks and other instructional materials directly to individual schools? And, as discussed in chapter 3, how should they scale in a system where new adult educator roles needed to be designed, new people needed to be hired and assigned, but virtually everyone would need extensive professional preparation and support to fill those roles, yet central office had no capacity to provide it?[31]

To start CMSI, Eason-Watkins again asked for "a little help from her friends."[32] Marty Gartzman had begun his career as a science teacher and bilingual coordinator at Juarez High School, and then he had joined UIC's Institute for Mathematics and Science Education as a program and curriculum developer. He was among a group of university-based educators in Chicago that had NSF funding to codevelop with CPS teachers a new math and science curriculum and professional learning supports for its use. He met Eason-Watkins when she volunteered McCosh as a codevelopment site during Era 2. The NSF-funded efforts sought to enliven the NCTM standards that had debuted in 1989, which were themselves another push toward ambitious instruction. At every grade they called on students to learn basic skills in the context of investigating real-world problems that must be solved through using disciplinary reasoning, methods of inquiry, and procedural knowledge. Guidance embedded in the science curricula, for example, encouraged teachers to organize students in small groups to conduct experiments. This introduced students (and their teachers) to collaborative work, the scientific method, and a sampling of each discipline's tools.

Eason-Watkins asked Gartzman to design and lead CMSI and join her cabinet as a "direct report."[33] This was the same arrangement she had with Shanahan, the CRI director. The direct reporting tied Eason-Watkins into both initiatives and signaled that improving instruction was the CEdO's priority. Notably, this organizational arrangement differed from typical practice in large urban districts, then and now, where similar roles are buried in the bowels of a central bureaucracy, and where they typically create separate, uncoordinated silos of guidance to schools that compete for control of central-level resources. Eviscerated by Chicago's decentralization reform, central office had little ability to resist Eason-Watkins's reinvention of this problematic organizational design.

When Gartzman came on board in 2001, he said most CPS faculties were "entrenched" in old ways of thinking about instruction that still called for students to memorize facts, formulas, and algorithms; solve rows of problems on work sheets; and take meaningless chapter tests. In Era 2 Vallas had used an NSF grant to offer individual schools small incentive grants, and he had directed math and science staff in central office to offer citywide teacher professional development workshops focused on the new math and science standards. Once reform cracked open the door, colleagues of Gartzman in university-based math and science centers had started offering teacher workshops that introduced the NSF materials.[34] Gartzman described all of this earlier work as "lots of activity. A lot was good but without an over-arching vision there was no coherence and no systemic improvement."[35]

An exception was the Teachers Academy for Math and Science (TAMS). Launched in Era 1 by Nobel laureate Leon Lederman at the Illinois Institute of Technology, TAMS offered a comprehensive approach, more akin to that of the Center for School Improvement than the efforts described above. It implemented:

> a rigorous program of classroom-based . . . modeling and support [for teachers] provided by TAMS trainers . . . that focused on [math and science] content and concrete teaching strategies. . . . Trainers worked side by side with teachers . . . including seasoned veterans . . . [who were] eager to learn . . . and evaluations showed that they successfully changed their instructional practices.[36]

When TAMS's funding wound down at the start of Era 3, the program did too, but an important deposit had been laid down. Some TAMS principals became AIOs, and some of the teacher leaders TAMS developed would later move on to leadership roles in CMSI and central office. They became a resource to the system.

Within CMSI Gartzman built a leadership team drawing from a network of CPS colleagues he had known for years.[37] Many had spent time away from the district in Eras 1 or 2 as "teachers on leave," working in one of the externally funded, university-based projects mentioned above. Gartzman reflected that their time "outside" helped them deepen and broaden their understanding of their fields and strengthened their pedagogy in ways that would have eluded them had they never stepped away. At the same time, they also brought a much-needed practitioner lens to the university-based activities. As a story of permeable boundaries, this is another demonstration of how the system and its exoskeleton supported each other and grew together. It also illustrates how the external projects of Eras 1 and 2 developed people who crossed boundaries and became integral to the district's work in Era 3.

Gartzman also invited central office science and math staff into the fold. Most had been successful classroom teachers prior to working downtown. But they lacked experience as instructional coaches, similar in role to the area reading coaches being developed in CRI, and one of their responsibilities would be to coach school-based math and science specialists.[38] They too needed support for their new role. The NSF instructional materials that would become CMSI's organizing framework, much as Four Blocks grounded CRI, were also unfamiliar to most of them. These curricula were much more elaborated and specified than the Four Blocks, but they too functioned as boundary objects that brought people together around a common conceptualization of instruction, a common disciplinary content, a common language, and common goals for teacher and student learning. Additionally, teachers deepened their own understanding of the content by using the curricula. This was especially important for CPS elementary teachers, since most held generalist credentials and typically had limited preparation in math and science through their college coursework and certification programs.

Attacking a High-Leverage Instructional Problem.   Algebra 1 is a notorious gatekeeper course for low performing students. CMSI's internal data and OnTrack analyses showed that failing it in ninth grade was highly predictive of dropping out of high school, and 40 percent of CPS ninth graders were failing the class at that time.[39] For high performing students, in contrast, *when* the course was offered was key. If students took it in middle school, then they had room in their high school schedules for more-advanced coursework, and this made them more college competitive. Because only a handful of CPS selective enrollment middle schools offered the course, however, many qualified eighth graders had no opportunity to take it. Additionally, few middle school teachers were qualified to teach it, and most of them were not in neighborhood schools. The algebra problem had many ramifications, raising a complex set of issues to solve. Over several years Gartzman organized what was eventually called the CPS Algebra Initiative. It aimed to address these problems, one by one.

One reason freshmen failed algebra 1 was weak instruction in their eighth-grade pre-algebra classes. Few CPS teachers were prepared to teach that course well either. A change strategy was for more middle school teachers to become endorsed in math. But the endorsement courses were expensive. To reduce that barrier, CMSI offered area universities a subsidy to bring down costs. Several accepted, and then competition among some of them dropped rates even further. Over several years this change enabled hundreds of CPS teachers to be endorsed, and CPS came close to realizing the goal of a qualified math teacher in every middle school. It also more tightly connected institutions in the exoskeleton to each other and to CPS.

Another target was making it possible for top students to pass algebra in eighth grade. In 2002, 35 percent of students nationally were entering high school with algebra behind them, while only 4 percent of CPS students were doing so, and most of those students attended selective schools. Gartzman aimed for every "well-prepared" eighth grader to have access to a rigorous algebra course in his or her neighborhood elementary school.[40] But again, this depended on a qualified teacher in every middle school to teach it. Here CMSI encouraged UChicago, UIC, and DePaul to offer a comparable one-year preparation program specific to a new CPS elementary specialist credential. In response, these universities created a common end-of-program exam and agreed to schedule the course at times that accommodated working teachers. This program became the heart of the CPS Algebra Initiative, which is ongoing. Well over 500 teachers have been credentialed, and the eighth-grade pass rate climbed to about 20 percent after several years. This was still below the national average, and it left room for further improvement, but it was a huge increase over 4 percent.

CMSI also focused on supporting students directly. Efforts included a summer transition program for at-risk eighth graders. Students who opted in were offered counseling, literacy, and math support. In CPS this program broke new ground because it was invitational rather than mandated, supportive rather than punitive, and it offered a range of services and an approach that was not remedial. Students signed on, and it was embraced by CPS.

Yet another effort was a "double dose" of algebra for freshman students whose academic background placed them at risk for failing algebra 1. This group was offered one period of general math support, intended to address their knowledge and skill gaps so that their progress might accelerate, and one period of algebra that aimed to help them understand new material. The double dose was jettisoned after a few years, however, as administrators complained that it complicated students' course scheduling; some faculty argued that it minimized students' time for other subjects, including more-engaging electives; and improved academic outcomes were not immediately apparent. This rush to judgment was unfortunate, since a follow-up study evidenced long-term benefits including improved algebra test scores and pass rates, high school graduation rates, and college enrollment and completion rates for some double dose students.[41]

Taken as a set of reforms, the specific Algebra Initiative plus CMSI's more general efforts to strengthen teacher professional learning and the system's human capital all pointed toward one goal: creating academic opportunity and support for students who had never had it before. In the context of doing this work, what had been centrifugal forces in university math and science centers (where everyone acted on their own) became centripetal and pulled in several colleges of education. These developments strengthened CPS and, much like the stories told in chapter 3, encouraged this sector to respond to specific district needs. This was the "collective us" in action again. It was also an extraordinary result in the higher education sector that had been only minimally invested in the reform of teaching and learning in CPS prior to the Annenberg Challenge.

The initiative took a hit when Huberman came along with his performance management systems, which alienated many educators, including those who had been sustaining CMSI. Some CMSI staff left central office to become school principals. Others moved to positions in the university centers that partnered with CMSI.[42] Budget cuts in 2010 further depleted the central office math and science staff.[43] Regardless, the work persisted as the Chicago Community Trust stayed engaged in both CMSI and CRI and adapted to regime change by shifting its working relationship from direct engagement with system leaders to engagement with those mid-level directors who had stayed in place.[44] The Trust also continued funding CMSI's higher education partners so that the Algebra Initiative could continue to evolve.[45]

Consequently, much of the Era 3 work and the people who fueled it persisted, even if its coherence, for a time, was undermined. When Jackson became CEdO a few years later, one of her challenges was similar to that of all the king's horses and all the king's men when they had to put Humpty Dumpty back together again.

Summing Up CRI and CMSI.   Eason-Watkins's messaging was clear as soon as she walked into central office. She emphasized teachers' professional learning, a transition to public practice, and the formation of school-based professional learning communities. She embraced select frameworks that centered and aligned efforts among educators within schools with those in area and central offices and were integral to the human capital development initiatives discussed in chapter 3. Her efforts directly addressed in an integrated fashion three of the 5Es—instructional guidance, professional capabilities, and principal leadership. Each of these in turn had also been designed to engender conversations pressing toward a more student-centered learning climate (the fourth of the 5Es.). Although the 5Es framework was originally designed to inform improvement in individual school communities, it also increasingly shaped and transformed how the areas and central office built infrastructure to support local schools.

Early in Era 3, when central office capacity was limited, CRI and CMSI both relied on individuals and institutions in the exoskeleton to catalyze change. Over time, the efforts of individual university-based faculty gave way to institutional partnerships—much the same as described in chapter 3 relative to principal and new teacher preparation and support. Also similar to that story, funding (and in-kind support) for these innovations came from local foundations, higher education, the CPS, and for CMSI, a second NSF grant.

All of this required that a critical mass remain committed to the improvement of this work as it evolved, regardless of transitions in the C suite. The payoff is evidenced by improved teacher reports over time in select Consortium measures about the "quality of professional development" experiences (see figure 4.1); the character of school-based professional communities, including educators' capacity to work together ("collective responsibility"); and their trust in faculty colleagues as they opened their classroom doors ("teacher-teacher trust"). CPS had stagnated on all three measures in Era 2, but major improvements that began in Era 3 continued to develop in Era 4.

Figure 4.1   Improving trends in elementary teachers' reports on professional development and community

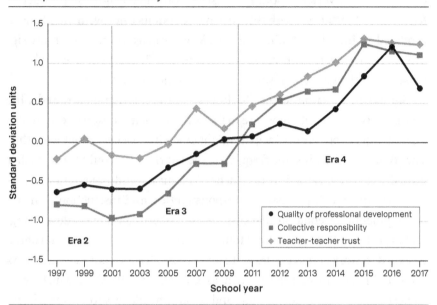

Source: UChicago Consortium on School Research, 2021.

Note: Trends consist of Rasch measures over time created from 5E survey items. Quality of professional development measures teachers' reports of whether professional development is rigorous and focused on student learning. Collective responsibility indicates teacher perceptions of their shared responsibility for student development, school improvement, and professional growth. Teacher-teacher trust represents teacher perceptions that their peers are supportive and respectful of one another. High school teacher survey reports show similar trends over time.

Improving Teaching Quality and Supporting Principals as Instructional Leaders

In 2005 Eason-Watkins set her sights on another chronic and controversial problem—a dysfunctional teacher evaluation system. She aimed to curb principals' penchant for giving virtually every teacher a high rating irrespective of the actual quality of classroom instruction.[46] Central to addressing this problem was the introduction of the Danielson Framework for Teaching (FFT).

The FFT was first introduced to CPS in 1998 as part of LAUNCH, the new principal development initiative. Back then the principal's role was just beginning to shift nationally from compliance manager to instructional leader. Earlier work at the Center made clear that CPS principals lacked a common framework for looking at instruction and engaging in productive feedback conversations with their teachers about its improvement. The FFT provided an initial scaffolding for this. Moreover, as the press for more rigorous teacher evaluation came forward in Era 3, the FFT already had a presence in the CPS as a resource for instructional improvement.

Similar in function to the "look fors" in the instructional rounds, the FFT cued principals about where to focus their teacher observations. It also offered hints about how principals might talk with teachers about what they saw. When used with some frequency, the rubrics also could track teacher growth. The FFT zeroed in on teachers' planning and preparation, classroom environment, professional responsibilities, and instruction. It had a developmental orientation that distinguished between novice, developing, and expert practice across these four domains. It also was a general rubric, designed to work across grades K–12 and across all subjects and teachers. As such it differed from rubrics such as CLASS and PLATO, which were subject-matter- and grade-specific and became available several years later.

Eason-Watkins encouraged broader uptake of FFT in CPS several years before it took its place of prominence in Race to the Top and the Gates-funded Measures of Effective Teaching study.[47] She saw its potential to build some coherence around how principals and teachers observed instruction across grade levels and subjects. The design of the FFT was valuable for this purpose precisely because it was a general tool. As discussed in chapter 3, her move put the CTU on alert, however, and especially when its use began to shift from professional development to teacher accountability.

Even so, the FFT contributed to educator learning. Like the NSF texts described earlier, it helped educators develop a common language to think and talk about teaching and learning. Next, and consonant with this, it enabled some shared understanding about what "good" is, at least insofar as good related to the generic categories of the tool—planning and preparation, classroom environment, professional responsibility, and instruction.[48] It also generated evidence, and encouraged the regular reporting of evidence, about teacher growth. In so doing, the FFT was functioning as another core boundary object. It offered a common language for training teachers and principals, central office and CTU actively supported it, it aligned work at different levels of the system and across different roles and institutions, and it generated evidence about educators' progress that prompted further reflection and action on how to improve. A few years down the road, the FFT was brought into university preparation programs in the Chicago area, and its use was formally sanctioned by the state in 2010 under the Illinois Performance Evaluation Reform Act. In 2012 the state legislature made it a required component in teacher tenure decisions. Needless to say, these developments had certainly caught the CTU's attention: changes in teacher evaluation became a major point of contention in the 2012 contract negotiations.

From the Outside In: Chicago Philanthropy and Its Arts Community Fill a Gap

The CPS suffered many fiscal crises beginning in the 1970s, and in each, arts education was among the first programs to go. Both before and after decentralization, affluent parents often found ways to compensate in their children's schools—which meant that the gap between the haves and the have-nots was stark and growing. The Chicago Community Trust initiated a study to understand the contours of that inequity just as Duncan and Eason-Watkins were taking office. Among the findings was that "on average elementary school children were getting 45 minutes of art a week, [but] in some schools, children had as many as four different weekly arts engagements, and in other schools they had none." The study identified two hundred active external providers, but there was no coordination among them, and few knew which schools were saturated, nor was there awareness of all the providers that might be in the same building, or what they were providing.[49]

The Trust study gave rise to the Chicago Arts Education Collaborative—an ongoing and largely outside-in effort to support equitable, high-quality arts education in CPS. The Collaborative began with several aims: build a citywide infrastructure to ensure quality and equity in programming across schools, focus on student learning over time (and not just performance and engagement), align efforts with district goals, and engage the city's best resources in the visual and performing arts. It also identified three obstacles: CPS leadership transitions and leaders' differing commitment to arts education; the absence of stable funding to withstand fiscal crises; and a lack of coordination that made programming, and its quality, uneven and inequitable.

Duncan and Eason-Watkins welcomed the Collaborative. They valued arts education but were leading a system that had neither funding nor expertise to take this on. Eason-Watkins met regularly with Collaborative leaders to jointly plan and coordinate efforts, and she opened a Department of Arts Education in 2006 to signal her commitment and create a foothold for the future. Regarding funding, the Collaborative's membership included more than twenty funders between 2001 and 2011, and the Collaborative helped support the new department.[50] In 2011 the Collaborative transitioned to Ingenuity—another new organization emerging in Chicago's exoskeleton—to continue to drive the partnership. Over the next decade, and guided by Ingenuity, art was added to student report cards as a core subject, and Illinois was the first state to include art as an indicator of K–12 success. Ingenuity raised millions in grants for CPS schools, offered them technical support for art programming, and developed standards of practice for its arts partners.[51] Importantly, Ingenuity developed an equity-focused data-mapping platform that is used in Chicago and beyond. The information it generates is used to continuously improve on the initiating problem: how to ensure that every student has a quality arts education?[52]

Improving Ties Between Families and Schools: Chicago's Community Schools Movement

When Spurlark was growing up in South Carolina, community schools were all she knew. Families and educators shared responsibility for children's well-being, and in the best of those places, students excelled. Eason-Watkins grew up a generation later in Detroit in better circumstances. But strong relational ties and an integration of school and neighborhood were still needed to withstand pervasive discrimination. As principals, both Spurlark and Eason-Watkins did their best to build up their students, families, schools, and communities. Their inclination was to go back to their roots.

The genesis for community schools in CPS dates to 1996 when the Polk Bros. Foundation launched a "full-service initiative" in three schools. A positive evaluation three years later led to six more sites. In 2002, a group of funders met with Duncan and Eason-Watkins and proposed opening one hundred more sites within five years. CPS footed half the bill, with the rest raised through a campaign cochaired by Polk and the CPS. Some twenty-three private, corporate, and family foundations joined in. In 2002 CPS won a federal 21st Century Community Learning grant to partially support this as well. In 2004, JPMorgan Chase gave $1 million to the UChicago School of Social Work to start a graduate program that would prepare community social workers. This was an example of CPS innovating still another new role, of school-community social workers, much as it had pioneered the AIO role and put its own stamp on instructional coaching. Much like the leadership program at UIC, the UChicago program was another instance of the city's educational institutions leading the way to develop human capital specific to CPS needs. By 2010 CPS was operating 154 community schools.

What are community schools, and what explains their embrace? Suzanne Doornbos Kerbow was director of education programs at Polk and an early champion. She described them as a way to "reduce barriers to learning for students and improve parent engagement in the school and in their child's education."[53] The national Coalition for Community Schools later defined a community school as "a place and a set of partners" that develop wraparound services addressing children's academic, health, recreational, and social service needs.[54] Chicago community schools resonated with tenets of southern Black culture and, as discussed below, those of many Latino communities as well. They linked historically to Chicago's settlement houses as a defense against the poverty, discrimination, and lack of resources that challenged many immigrant neighborhoods.[55] Their extended day, summer, and weekend programming promised an engaging, safe harbor for children, and the programs became a lifeline for the local organizations contracted to run them. Many of Chicago's community schools fell victim to school closings and weakened system support in Era 4, and there has been little local impact analysis.[56] But the urgent needs they aimed to fill did not dissipate. They were the systems-level response to support the fifth of the 5Es—strengthening school, family, and community ties. Indeed, the need to strengthen this social fabric surrounding schools heightened when the CPS started closing buildings and large numbers of students traveled to schools outside their neighborhoods.

Taking Stock of a Decade's Work

When the system first began to open up in 1988, Eason-Watkins and principals like her had newfound authority to chip away at local concerns. Each problem solved tended to reveal another, and through this process an integrated framework for school development, captured in the 5Es, came into view. Eason-Watkins lived the framework at McCosh. Once in central office, it helped her "see the system" that she was now responsible for. What she saw was a profound need to build the knowledge and skills of school-based educators and central office staff. Principals needed support to take on their new instructional leadership role. Other new roles, for instructional coaches and community social workers, needed to be developed, and the people moving into those roles needed to learn how to support more collaborative ways of working—building relational trust and operating as professional learning communities—so that more ambitious teaching and learning might take hold. New forms of partnership with individuals and institutions in the exoskeleton needed room to be invented and flourish too. All of this capacity building would take time, and especially in a system where there were so few people at the start who knew this work and could guide others. In Chicago's decentralized context, leaders also needed to learn how to thread the needle between top-down and bottom-up efforts to move ahead. Such was the work of Era 3.

By Era 3's end, and contrasted with its start, central office was a different place. Moreover, the exoskeleton that supported CPS was different: The civic architecture had expanded, and the organizations in it were more expert, more aligned around instruction; more collaborative within and across sectors; and in service to both central office and local schools. Central office itself had been reconceptualized and new norms were forming. In Era 2, Vallas had aspired for central office to transition from a failed state to a functional central bureaucracy that told school people what to do and aimed toward higher test scores. In Era 3 and under Duncan and Eason-Watkins, central office was recast in service to a system of schools that sought to expand teachers' capacities for ambitious instruction, and students' opportunities to learn. Incredibly, in the CEO churn that followed Era 3, core instructional and human capital development efforts persisted. Board members did their best to keep the internal work intact, and exoskeleton leaders looked to middle management to sustain it. Gartzman expressed the views of many when he said that "a critical mass in central office worked incredibly hard under difficult and changing circumstances" to carry the work forward.[57] And the system continued to develop and create opportunities for educators like Janice Jackson.

JANICE K. JACKSON: FROM KINDERGARTENER TO CEO

Janice Jackson grew up in a southside two-bedroom apartment. Her father drove a cab. Her mother was a dispatcher. Jackson and her four siblings attended their neighborhood elementary school, as well as selective-enrollment programs and high schools. Jackson went to college at Chicago State and then returned to CPS as a history teacher at South Shore High School. That is where, as a novice teacher, she first realized that absent a common and ambitious pedagogy across teachers, grades, and courses, students were being shortchanged:

> I learned that even with my best efforts and the efforts of some of my colleagues, if you don't have coherence, you're not going to see much progress. So, I noticed that my students didn't write much. I went through this whole process about everybody has to do a research paper before they pass my class to graduate. It was a big deal. And I felt very proud of myself, but it was still this isolated activity that kids only did in my class.[58]

Spurlark had flagged this same problem thirty years before.

In 2004 Jackson wrote a proposal to the Gates-funded small-school initiative to open a new westside high school. When Al Raby opened, Duncan asked her to be its first principal. At age 27, she was possibly the youngest CPS principal ever appointed. The small-school push later was abandoned because measurable benefits failed to materialize quickly.[59] Nevertheless, it created a path for Jackson's rise. Jackson next led Westinghouse High School, which had just reopened with a STEM focus and in a state-of-the-art, new facility. At a time when the city was roiling over the first round of school closings and student displacements, she maintained Westinghouse as a destination for neighborhood students that also welcomed more-affluent ones. Westinghouse, like Raby, thrived under her leadership.

In 2014 Jackson was appointed as a network chief. To this new role she brought her experiences as a CPS student, high school teacher and principal, and charter member in the Network for College Success. Along the way she had acquired her EdD through UIC's program on urban education leadership. As network chief she oversaw twenty-six schools—a network that included elementary and high schools and was diverse in terms of principal and faculty capabilities, student demographics and achievement, and most everything else. From this perch the system's "variability problem" came into focus and became an enduring concern for her. A year later Jackson was tapped to be CEdO. Like Eason-Watkins, she supported the CEO's and the mayor's agendas and in turn had latitude to focus on instruction. Our story ends in 2017 when Mayor Emanuel appointed her CEO. She was thirty-nine years old and the seventh appointment in nine years.

As CEdO in 2015, Jackson walked into difficult circumstances: a fiscal crisis; a strengthened, adversarial CTU; the aftermath of successive rounds of school closings; and redrawn and unstable alliances within the reform coalition. And nationally, Common Core, Race to the Top, and bilingual education had all become partisan battlegrounds. Jackson also had social media and a 24-7 news cycle to contend with—making leadership far more taxing than in the days when Vallas controlled the message and Duncan and Eason-Watkins exerted considerable influence.

Central office had a split personality as well. There was a culture of suspicion and fear left over from Huberman's brief tenure, uncertainty brought on by leadership churn and episodes of corruption, and a return to teachers' strikes after a long hiatus. Balancing this, and offering new affordances, was a staff that had grown into new roles in Era 3 and had managed to keep the district focused on improving teaching and learning through the first years of Era 4. Huberman's performance management system was ill-conceived, but its attention to data was a strength Jackson wanted to build on, and the exoskeleton that enveloped reform had continued to grow more vibrant, sophisticated, targeted, and impactful. Central office needed healing *and* it was a dynamic place to lead.

Shifting the Culture Toward Continuous Improvement

Key to Jackson's central office recovery plan was recasting Huberman's performance management reviews as support for continuous improvement. UIC's graduate program had formalized her intuitive grasp of this methodology, and she reflected that it was the most important thing she learned:

> I didn't know the language [of improvement science] until I got into the UIC program, and I didn't learn how to operationalize it and make it a part of my ways of thinking and doing every single day [until then]. That took time and it evolved over time.[60]

As CEdO, Jackson did her best to make continuous improvement the district's way of "thinking and doing" as well. This orientation continued the transition Eason-Watkins had begun: toward collaborative problem solving and away from compliance management.

One of Jackson's first steps was eliminating Huberman's dashboard of "really narrow, easily quantifiable measures" that had at best a tangential relationship to ambitious teaching and learning.[61] She replaced it with indicators focused on leaders' developing ability to mentor, coach, and teach other adults and support school-based improvement efforts that would expand students' opportunities to learn. Data on these new metrics then informed evaluations at every level of the system. Importantly, her team took a "teaching and learning" approach to accountability. It supported adults' growth as improvement leaders.

Jackson's efforts to transform the culture permeated all that she did. She commented that her challenge as CEdO was less to innovate, as Eason-Watkins and her team and partners had needed to do, and more to sustain, enrich, deepen, adapt, and extend the most impactful district initiatives and partnerships from earlier years, especially those focused on instruction, and keep going from there.[62]

Freshman OnTrack

As a former first-grade teacher, Eason-Watkins had been especially concerned with elementary schools. Jackson had been a high school teacher; high schools had shown the least progress under reform; she was committed to their improvement, and they progressed under her watch. Reflecting back, she said that OnTrack, discussed in chapter 2, was key to the gains students made. When Jackson was still at Raby, Roderick had invited her to join the principal group that was workshopping the process. Jackson called OnTrack "empowering" because it brought educators together around seemingly baked-in problems and then offered practical, data-guided pathways to solve them:

> As a principal, I felt empowered. I felt like I could do something. I remember going to those briefings with NCS (Network for College Success) even before NCS was NCS and learning about OnTrack. We were early adopters and implementers—using it to identify where students were and provide support. We really bought into what we saw in the data, which was if we could keep students on track, they would increase their graduation rate so much. So that at Al Raby, where I was principal first, our graduation rate was well over 90 percent when the rate for [the rest of] the west side was below 50 percent. . . . I saw other schools doing that [too]. I honestly think teachers, principals, and counselors just felt more empowered: We had a roadmap to do this work.

Jackson thought that frameworks like OnTrack needed to be fully integrated into districts' processes, much as the Danielson Framework for

Teaching had been: "First OnTrack was voluntary. . . . [Later], it became something we had to do but not much happened until there was support for it. Then it just took off. It played a huge role and changed the trajectory."[63]

Jackson remarked that OnTrack also emboldened her team to strengthen high school graduation requirements beyond where Vallas had set them twenty years before:

> When people hear that our [graduation] rates went up, they think, "Oh, they made it easier to graduate." But the opposite is true. We strengthened the requirements to graduate and it's because of the OnTrack data: The tools and protocols that were built around that showed us that students could do more if we expected more and put in the guardrails.

OnTrack fostered a student-centered learning climate in high schools by attending to key drivers that keep students progressing, such as getting them to attend class, helping teachers realize that personal connections still mattered to older students, and emboldening leaders to raise requirements in ways that respected students' potential. Jackson's embrace of it was also an example of her penchant for putting into place frameworks that pulled people into a common discourse, guided what previously had been disparate efforts, and focused on what was valued:

> I always try to put a framework around things. So, we're not talking about equity or customer service or continuous improvement without a framework.[64] With a framework, even if [a group of educators doesn't] immediately fix the problem, [they] are set on a path to improve.[65]

Common Core

When Jackson was principal at Westinghouse, CPS began its implementation of Common Core State Standards, a national push toward more ambitious teaching and learning. The standards articulated the content knowledge that students should learn from kindergarten through high school in math and English language arts, complemented with attention to the "soft" skills that were needed for work in a twenty-first-century world. Importantly,

Common Core was consistent with the instructional improvement work begun in CRI and CMSI—another step on the path to more ambitious instruction.

By most accounts, Chicago's embrace of the Common Core, its preparation, early rollout, and then persistent effort over the next decade were well executed and consistent. Formally, this took place under CEOs Brizard and Byrd-Bennett, but it was another instance where sustained and targeted foundation support, much of it from the Chicago Community Trust, was key. The Trust brought both money and people who staffed the initiative and pushed it forward.[66] Main strategies included professional development for teachers to help them understand the standards, and a collaboration between central office departments and early adopter schools to develop and test instructional materials and the assessments aligned to them. Teacher leaders also received training so that they could introduce the standards to their faculty colleagues in each school and guide their uptake. Erikson Institute and DePaul University agreed to support educators in several networks. The Trust also brought in Aida Walqui, a bilingual expert, to embed second-language and academic language acquisition strategies in teachers' professional development about the standards.[67] The Quality Teaching for English Learners framework that she introduced to CPS provided an instructional framework that supported English learners (ELs)—and really, all learners and their teachers. The Trust's support for EL instruction, and its integration into all of their instructional improvement grants, would deepen through Common Core and other initiatives in the years ahead.[68]

Jackson said that Common Core, and the system's support for implementation, gave educators direction and more insight into their system:

> I know the national debate went in all different directions, but I was educated and taught in CPS. We never had a lot of direction on what we should be teaching and doing at each [grade] level. There were attempts. But Common Core was the first time most people agreed that it was the right approach. And when we started to really understand the standards better, we understood how far behind our students were.

There was considerable variation in uptake of Common Core by CPS schools over the next several years, as might be expected in any system and certainly a decentralized one. There also was positive impact. A Consortium analysis of the Common Core math effort concluded that mathematics achievement improved districtwide during this period (2012 through 2018) for students at all achievement levels. Echoing an earlier Annenberg finding, the Consortium reported that improvements were greater in schools with extensive faculty participation in professional learning focused on Common Core, and this was especially the case among students with low, prior-year achievement.[69] Once again, the schools that invested most heavily in professional development had the strongest improvement trajectories.[70]

A Press Toward a More Coherent Learning System

Jackson was positive about what had been accomplished relative to Common Core, but she also felt that its full potential had not been tapped yet. Professional development had been offered, some new instructional materials and assessments had been developed, and some schools and networks were focusing on instructional practice. But these discrete efforts had not "created [in every school] a strong instructional core and foundation that has instruction, PD, and assessment all tied together as opposed to loosely coupled." As a former principal and network chief mentoring twenty-six principals, Jackson understood their central role in leading school improvement. She also had seen "wide variation in [their] capacity to think strategically, engage colleagues, collaborate, and organize for instructional improvement."[71] She reasoned that yoking the principal evaluation process to Common Core was essential to achieving an integrated effort:

> So, I created this instructional core rubric [tied to Common Core]. I trained the principals on it and said, "We're going to come into your school and look at curriculum, instruction and assessment and see how those things are linked. Then [we'll ask] 'What systems and structures do you have in place to support this coherence?'" Only one of my 26 schools got a

distinguishing score. . . . Most got a basic score, which annoyed all the principals. They were like, "This is not how everybody else is rated."

Jackson also aligned Common Core with the instructional rounds process that Eason-Watkins and Greenberg had initiated in 2001. In its first iteration Greenberg had prompted simple "look fors" like, How many students are paying attention? In 2015, Jackson and her team guided educators toward a more complex vision of "what they *should* be noticing" about curricular rigor, instructional approaches, and assessment strategies.[72] She made the process a part of each high school's audit of their continuous improvement plans and by doing so replaced and oriented toward new norms the documentation Huberman had required for performance reviews.[73] Two years into these changes, Jackson said, "I feel like the quality of the conversation has improved . . . elevated. . . . So, I'm always pushing them, always reflecting, [What] did people learn from this?"[74] As a vignette about adult teaching and learning, the tone and substance of these activities indicated both the distance traveled and the journey ahead.

Jackson and her team also focused on curricular alignment so that a student's academic experience at any particular grade was neither remedial nor repetitive. She remembered that when she was teaching high school, her attention to students' writing fell short because there was no systematic build from grade to grade, teacher to teacher.

> Schools like to talk about instruction . . . target an instructional area . . . and instructional strategies. [But] people do not have a documented curriculum that is fully aligned both horizontally and vertically. . . . If you laid everything out from the beginning to the end of the year, from grade to grade, you'd see overlap in the progression and you'd see that rigor over time is not happening.[75]

The "fully aligned . . . documented curriculum" Jackson described echoes back to the NSF curricula that anchored CMSI more than a decade before.

The cumulative effects of the instructional improvement work, begun in Era 3 and then deepened and intensified in Era 4, are reflected in changing student reports about the nature of instruction in core subject areas,

Figure 4.2 High school students reporting more ambitious instruction in core academic classes

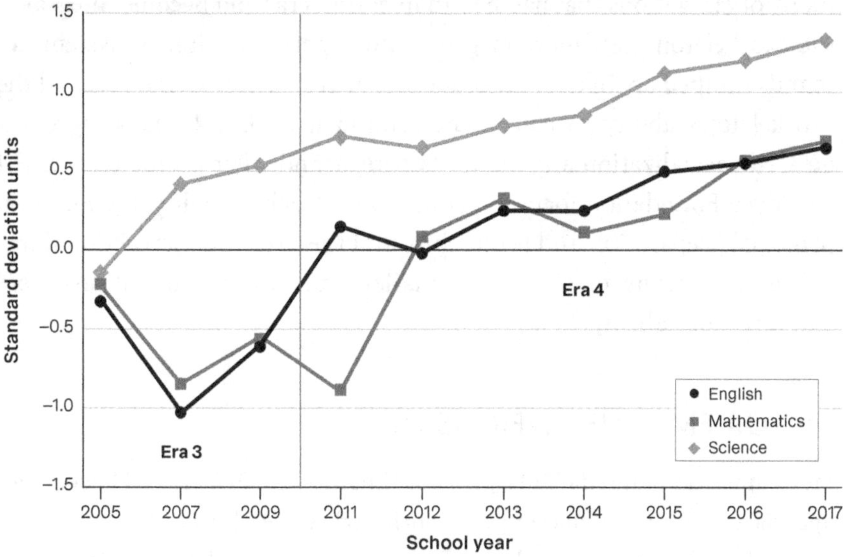

Source: UChicago Consortium on School Research, 2021.

Note: Trends are based on Rasch measures constructed by the Consortium from repeated 5E survey items. English instruction measures whether students perceive that they interact with course material and one another to build and apply critical reading and writing skills. Math instruction concerns whether students perceive that they interact with course material and one another to build and apply knowledge in their math classes. Science items ask students whether they conduct scientific investigations, test hypotheses, write lab reports, and use lab equipment.

including English language arts, science, and mathematics. Figure 4.2 display trends in Consortium surveys from high school students on a set of measures added to the survey system in 2005. (Data from elementary school students shows a similar trend.) Reports about science instruction show steady improvement from 2005 that tracks back to CMSI's start. Initial reports in English and mathematics remained mixed through the end of Era 3, then began to rise steadily through Era 4—contemporaneous with the introduction of Common Core professional development in Era 4 and increased central office attention to English learners (discussed subsequently).

Throughout this period, the exoskeleton was also evolving in line with the larger political environment and Jackson's press toward coherent instruction. Each organization confronted its own challenges as priorities and funding changed and as local and national policies shifted. Even so, many organizations that had begun in earlier eras and become integral to the exoskeleton grew more targeted and expert over time as system demands ramped up. In fact, the organizational structure of the 5Es, and the exoskeleton's ability to coordinate around it by Era 4, encouraged increased specialization aligned to its core strands. For example, by Era 4 the Joyce Foundation focused primarily on teacher quality, the Fund on principal preparation and leadership, and the Trust on instructional improvement. Many of Chicago's smaller and family foundations were similarly specializing.[76]

MAYOR EMANUEL WEIGHS IN

Jackson was appointed CEO by Mayor Emanuel in 2017. He had backed her agenda as CEdO, and his support continued. Since his first election he had focused on doing whatever he could to strengthen public education in the city. While multiple controversies complicate his legacy, including school closings and the problems brought on by his revolving door of CEOs, he did advance initiatives that expanded the city's resources for improving student outcomes.

A legislative fight around fair funding for the CPS had been ongoing for fifty years. Emanuel brought it closer to the finish line when he maneuvered a change to the state's funding formula. Fair funding had been a main goal of the 1988 reform, and the battle to achieve it had been raging all along.[77]

Emanuel also goaded the governor into releasing funding for full-day kindergarten. He then threw his weight behind universal preK and emphasized the need for high-quality seats where high quality meant, among other things, an instructional focus appropriate to young children. (Eason-Watkins, working with Barbara Bowman from the Erikson Institute, had begun efforts to strengthen early childhood education fifteen years earlier.)[78] By the time Emanuel beat this drum, universal preK was trending nationally—a factor that helped tip the scales. In addition to strengthening early childhood, Emanuel supported partnerships with city and community colleges, which then expanded to include private universities, to increase the college-going options for Chicago's youth. Crucially, none of these were one-and-done efforts. Rather they focused on system change—building an infrastructure that would support Chicago's children, from early childhood through college at no cost to their families.

Emanuel also championed specific reforms internal to CPS. Following the publication of a Consortium report, he called for expanding Advanced Placement classes and the number of schools offering the International Baccalaureate program.[79] Noted in chapter 1, he also negotiated a longer school day, even if the price was a CTU strike in 2012 and a settlement that compensated teachers for the additional time.[80] This was a victory long in the making. Spurlark had tried to increase instructional time when she was on the CPS negotiating team in the 1980s; the problem had been a focus of a 1998 Consortium report, *It's About Time*, and Duncan brought it into each of his contract negotiations with CTU.[81] A parent survey conducted in Era 4 indicated overwhelming support for increasing instructional time, and CTU could no longer say no.[82] Even so, getting this over the finish line was an enormous accomplishment. While these changes and Emanuel's other reforms arrived too late to explain the academic gains documented in the introduction, Emanuel felled some big, old dragons and by doing so, he put the CPS, and its exoskeleton, in good position to sustain its ongoing improvement journey.

CPS'S LATINO STUDENTS AND ENGLISH LEARNERS: LESS INVISIBLE THAN BEFORE

Chicago's Media Shines Another Light

The *Tribune* had captured the city's attention when it published the Worst in America series in 1987. The *Chicago Reporter* aimed to do the same in 2017. "English Learners Often Go Without Required Help at Chicago

Schools" accused CPS of chronically neglecting its Latino population, and its English learners in particular.[83] While admonishing the state for persistent underfunding, the report took primary aim at a slew of problems that CPS had allowed to fester over the entire sweep of reform. The list of concerns was familiar to Chicagoans because it echoed the findings of two earlier studies—one published in 2010 by the Bilingual Education and World Language Commission, and another by the Council of Great City Schools in 2013. The system failed to provide oversight to schools that were out of compliance with the 1980 desegregation consent decree; bilingual services and programs were insufficient; and there was a chronic and severe shortage of Spanish-speaking teachers and teachers endorsed to teach in dual-language, bilingual, or English as a second language programs. Of most concern was the average achievement for EL students; it was weak year after year. This group always lagged behind that of white students and weighed down the system's overall performance. These average annual test scores were cited as a key indicator in each of these reports.[84]

A remarkable Consortium study published in 2019 offered a very different perspective and "busted the myth" about the poor learning of ELs in CPS. It revealed that 76 percent of EL students who began their education in the CPS achieved English proficiency by the end of fifth grade. By the end of eighth grade, that group had caught up to their peers on standardized tests administered in English, and they were on track for high school success at rates equivalent to the rest of the CPS.[85] In fact, ELs' rapid learning gains were actually pulling up student achievement trends for the district and the state overall.

To reach these conclusions, Consortium analysts problematized the traditional accountability-based statistics that had been used in reports cited above. Such analyses examine only the students currently receiving services, and that group is always changing as some students graduate out of services and new students come in. By definition, then, the current population of EL students is always "behind." There simply was no way to know how well the district was educating these students from this kind of analysis.

In contrast, Consortium researchers analyzed students' development over time: how students were doing as they moved through EL services *and* after they transitioned out. Three cohorts of kindergarteners who entered CPS in 2008, 2009, and 2010 were followed. By examining their flows through the grades and into general education, Consortium researchers changed the angle of view and reached conclusions that were brighter and more accurate. At base here is an important analytic feature of improvement research. To deeply understand a problem and develop reliable evidence of student progress toward solving it, the flows of students through educational systems over time must be examined. Analyses of fixed points in time like annual test score reports, and grade-level studies, often obscure the actual dynamics at work.

The Consortium report was well received, but it posed a puzzle: How did these students in fact do so well during the many decades when they and their schools received so little notice or district support and so many were out of formal compliance with the consent decree? On balance, the consent decree relied on indicators that are easy to measure, like the annual test scores and teacher certification data, but not always the most meaningful evidence of what is actually happening on the ground. Even so, this still left unanswered a big question: how did this improved learning among EL students actually accrue in Chicago?

The Consortium's state of reform analysis in 1993 documented that strong democratic practice had emerged in many elementary schools serving predominantly Latino students, and many of these schools were actively restructuring.[86] Subsequent research also reported relatively high levels of relational trust in these school communities, and collective efficacy in their neighborhoods; both are core enabling social resources for school improvement.[87] Reaching back even earlier into the 1970s, two parents working inside their local neighborhood had managed to start Inter-American—an innovative dual-language elementary school. Fifteen years later, when Eason-Watkins used reform's affordances to reinvent McCosh, principals in some Latino schools, like Jorge Sanchez and Carlos Azcoitia, were working with their communities to do the same. Improvement was developing from the bottom up, and in this case often enabled by progressive state policy and external resources. To the broader public, however, this good news was either not noticed or invisible.

The District's First Dual-Language School

As legend has it, "two moms (who were also CPS teachers) dreamed of a multi-lingual, multi-cultural school that would bring English- and Spanish speaking children together to learn one another's languages, traditions and histories."[88] Adela Coronado-Greeley and Janet Nolan lived in what was then a diverse northside neighborhood near Wrigley Field, home of the Chicago Cubs. They shared their dream with neighbors. Seeing organized community interest and apparently little risk, the Board of Education approved in 1975 a preschool that would prepare Spanish-speaking children for kindergarten.[89] Coronado-Greeley and Nolan were its first teacher leaders. At the end of the school year the Board moved to close the preschool, but parents resisted, and a kindergarten was added instead. Over the years, Inter-American cultivated an engaged, protective parent group, and because the school was small and operating outside CPS strictures, Coronado-Greeley and Nolan were able to recruit teachers who had bilingual expertise and believed in the mission. That, combined with its students' academic success, made the school too strong to close.[90] Inter-American grew to be a prekindergarten through eighth grade elementary school, received magnet designation, and finally moved into its own building in 2006 as Inter-American Elementary Magnet School.

Inter-American aimed for students to become bilingual, biliterate, and multicultural. In contrast to English as a second language and some other transitional bilingual approaches, its dual-language program extended across the curriculum and built up children's Spanish and English. Today it continues to hold pride of place as one of the district's strongest dual-language schools: applications currently outnumber seats by about one hundred to one.[91] Additionally, it has long been a training ground for teachers who have gone on to open similar schools, become principals, and moved into central office. Inter-American was a dream that became an early engine of innovation and specialization, and an educator pipeline for the district.

Jorge Sanchez: A Dual-Language School for His Community

Coronado-Greeley and Nolan were not the only dreamers. Jorge Sanchez was new to the principalship when he was appointed to Thomas School a year before reform.[92] He took over from a white principal who did not speak Spanish and whom parents had accused of diverting resources earmarked for the bilingual program to the "general," English-only one. Thomas's 900 preK–6 students filled an ancient main building, a leased branch located blocks away, and "temporary" decrepit mobile units that had been there for years. Moms who had started volunteering when their oldest children were in Head Start had won most of the seats on the first LSC. They knew each other and the school; they did not yet know Sanchez.

Sanchez's dream, which he announced at his first faculty meeting, was for Thomas to become:

> a really bilingual school, where all of you are bilingual and can talk with all of the students . . . where there's no split between the instructional programs and teachers and students don't look down on each other. . . . A school for this community.[93]

Many teachers were taken aback. Those in the general program who did not speak Spanish felt threatened, and the bilingual faculty was shocked that Sanchez would openly address these cleavages at a first convening. Similarly, a year later when the LSC was first seated, Sanchez extolled members to break the bonds of colonialism: "Schooling is a very domesticating experience," he said. "[Educators are] trying to colonize the students, to make them think like we do." Some on his council were so unsettled by these remarks, they were unable to hear the role he hoped parents would play if Thomas became a "school for this community":

> In the past, parents were only asked to bring coffee and cake. . . . In terms of restructuring, rethinking, reforming schools—it's time to establish a real

partnership. . . . The school provides the tools, and the home contributes the values. So, the values of the home become the values of the school.

Sanchez later marveled at his own naivete. It would be four more years, and working through two LSC elections, annual budgets, and school improvement plans, before the faculty and parents had developed sufficient knowledge and trust in each other and him to actually entertain what it might mean to pursue this vision. A fight between two groups of fifth-grade girls—one group still in the bilingual program and another that had already transitioned out—set the ball in motion when it spilled into a hallway and required teachers from both programs to settle it and summon parents to the school.

The fight gave voice to all that had been silenced before: the split between the two programs that cleaved the faculty into interest groups that vied for enrollments—and the funding, resources, and teaching positions tied to them. The silence also kept the faculty from ever discussing what their academic and language goals for the children were, when best to transition them from bilingual to the general English-only program, and what constituted an "equal" education. Additionally, the silence made it impossible to address the rifts among children. Students who had already transitioned to English assumed an air of superiority for being more "cool" than the rest. "Cool" amounted to worse behaved and less respectful of adults. They deemed themselves smarter too because they had already exited the bilingual program. The silence also exacerbated the dilemma of parents who wanted their children to learn English but also saw their language, values, culture, and behavioral expectations drain away as their children acquired it. Silence also kept parents and faculty from ever addressing their frustrations with Sanchez for being too lenient about discipline. Ironically, the fight opened the Pandora's box that had been slammed shut when Sanchez first told teachers he wanted to create a "truly bilingual school" and had urged parents to break free from their "colonialist mentality." Four years of collaboration around the responsibilities of reform prepared them to tackle all that was in that box.

Reflecting back, a teacher in the general program, named Marie, said the fight had been a "blessing." Years before, when she had transferred to Thomas, its "gentle" tone had surprised her. She was not in the bilingual program but said it was the "demeanor of the bilingual kids and their families . . . the way they respected teachers" that made Thomas such a "special place to teach." (Some area instructional officers similarly were surprised when they visited Latino schools for instructional rounds.) Marie said Thomas was a place where she had "learned a lot too." Early on, she thought the "cure [for Spanish speakers] was just teach them English." In time she "realize[d] there's value in knowing two languages." The fight and its aftermath emboldened her to ask her colleagues questions that had never felt "politically correct" for a general teacher to raise before: When was the right time to transition children? Is the goal to replace Spanish with English or add to it? Questions like these from Marie and others went to one of the school's planning teams. It deliberated and made its recommendation to the LSC:

> The research shows that children do better if they stay in bilingual longer, stay in their own language past third grade. So, a maintenance program with dual language is what we recommend. Children taught together with Spanish dominant teachers instructing in Spanish, and English dominant in English. . . . Research shows long lasting academic benefits from that approach. So, we want one program that equates the value of English and Spanish so kids will respect each other and behave the same.

The LSC approved the reorganization, and teachers and parents from both sides of the aisle assumed planning responsibilities. The initiative became the focus of the Thomas School's improvement plan, and professional support for the faculty was prioritized in the budget.

Thomas's decision to become a dual-language school surfaced a central policy concern regarding the education of ELs in the CPS and elsewhere: What is the best approach? When a district or state tries to answer the question and then impose its choice, it inevitably creates winners and losers. Even if the research lines up mostly on one side, as it did here regarding dual language, other views persist. In contrast, Chicago's decentralization pushed this question down to local school communities to determine their own way. Thomas chose dual language as its central focus, other schools made different decisions, but having chosen, these school communities were invested in making their choices work.

Carlos Azcoitia: Community Schools Responsive to a Mexican Immigrant Community

Prior to reform, Spry Elementary School was "among the most troubled schools in the system." In 1988, 100 percent of Spry's 1,357 kindergarten through eighth grade students were from low-income families, 96 percent were Latino, 51 percent were ELs, and the composite IGAP score was 174 (when the state average was 250).[94] Spry was one of many schools in Chicago's Little Village community that had exploding enrollments and little capacity to address student and family needs. A few years later, in 1993, Spry was profiled in the Consortium's *State of Reform* report as an "actively restructuring school." How so?

The answer at Spry was similar to that at other actively restructuring schools. A new principal, Carlos Azcoitia, was a good "match." He was bilingual, open toward everyone, and had been a middle school teacher at another overcrowded Latino school. He also was able to look past the present to envision Spry as "a safe haven . . . a central institution of a strengthened community life that expands civic participation and reclaims the public spaces of the neighborhood from drugs, gangs and violence."[95]

Azcoitia was an early champion of community schools—years before they had a clear nomenclature or Congressional funding, before the Polk Bros. Foundation got interested, and before central office mounted its press. Over the next thirty years, Azcoitia would move into central office as deputy chief of education (Eras 2 and 3), back to Spry as the founding principal of the John Spry Community School (Era 3), and into the role of network chief (Era 4). After retiring, he was appointed to the Board of Education (Era 4) and took on a post with National Louis University. He was another Chicago boundary spanner, bringing to others what he had learned through each of these roles and expanding social connections across the "collective us." In his writings and speeches, Azcoitia expressed deep commitment to community schools and advocacy for them, while tailoring the concept to a Latino community seeking to overcome hardships and achieve agency and voice. "Rather than lament the prevalence of outside negative factors . . . poverty, gang violence, undocumented status, language barriers and more," Azcoitia said, "schools must seize opportunities to connect families and students to resources and support. They must become a way of thinking, acting, and working together [that is about] inclusion, self-determination, localization, agency, and an integration of services. . . . By expanding the boundaries . . . [community schools] represent the core values of democracy." His rich definition posited civic participation as the path to school renewal—exactly what the activists who wrote the School Reform Act had dreamed of.[96]

Inter-American was an early innovator. Its story started more than a decade before reform. In contrast, the 1988 legislation kickstarted changes at Spry and Thomas. Absent support from central office, Sanchez and Azcoitia paved their own way, as did a number of other principals and schools in Latino neighborhoods. Some developed as community schools, like Spry, or dual-language schools, like Inter-American. Still others, like Thomas, evolved as a mix of the two. While the central office did not begin to show interest until late in Era 3, these principals were not entirely on their own. Beginning in the 1970s, key enablers were active in state legislative bodies and professional groups. A developmental English language proficiency assessment proved helpful too.

Early Enablers

The State Senate's Education Champion.   Miguel del Valle's parents came to Chicago from Puerto Rico. He attended four CPS schools and never crossed paths with an educator who "looked like me," much less spoke his family's language.[97] Del Valle's first job was as a youth community organizer in West Town. It was the 1970s and the neighborhood's dropout rate was around 70 percent. About 1,000 Black and brown youth were murdered in the streets each year. Del Valle helped organize a funeral procession that carried a coffin down Division Street to a rally on the steps of Clemente

High to drive home the connection. He once took a youth group to observe a senate session in Springfield. It was his first time in chambers.[98] "While sitting in the gallery with the kids I thought about how they deserved better schools," he said. "That afternoon I told my brother I was going to run for senate to get kids those better schools."[99] Del Valle was elected the Illinois Senate's first Latino member in 1987, and he was seated just in time to ensure that the School Reform Act passed and that provisions important to his community remained intact: that LSCs have authority over principal hiring, budget, and the school improvement plan; and that undocumented parents and community members have the right to vote and be elected to LSCs. Like others mobilizing for reform, del Valle thought that local control was the only viable option in a district that had turned a blind eye to his community.[100]

Del Valle opened the door for other Latino candidates to run for office. Over the next twenty years, he led the Latino caucus and organized and chaired the senate's education committee and every other committee and task force concerned with education. He also sponsored or signed onto numerous bills aimed at protecting and advancing the rights of marginalized students.[101] The fight for fair funding for CPS overall, and for bilingual programming specifically, was never-ending, and his faction lost most battles (until recently). Importantly, however, they prevailed on many other substantive issues that impacted ELs and Latino students in the CPS and statewide. In the 1970s and 1980s, the education of Latino students was not a "wedge issue," just one that was largely ignored. In states like Illinois, where there were advocates and allies, enabling legislation often passed with bipartisan support even as full funding was regularly voted down.

State Law and the Illinois Resource Center.   In the early 1970s a small group of CPS and Chicago-based bilingual education advocates approached legislators in Springfield. They had drafted a bill intended to secure students' right to high-quality transitional bilingual education services statewide and needed a sponsor. This was years before del Valle reached the senate, but a Republican legislator volunteered, and the bill passed in 1974 on a bipartisan vote.[102] In addition to spelling out entitlements, the new law required that Illinois adopt professional standards for bilingual teachers, and it identified specific course requirements for their preparation and continuing education. (The coursework provision eventually led to a state bilingual endorsement, and a State Seal of Biliteracy followed that.) Over the years the legislature expanded protections for Latino students and ELs.

The 1974 bill also set aside funds for a new organization, the Illinois Resource Center (IRC), to provide the prescribed coursework for teachers statewide and meet their ongoing needs for professional learning. Headed by Josie Yanguas since 2006, IRC's courses and coaching guided teachers toward research-based instructional practices that support ELs.[103]

The state directly picked up the tab for IRC services in every Illinois district except Chicago. Instead, and prior to the 1988 reform, CPS received an annual funding appropriation. The reports and articles mentioned earlier all criticized central office for misusing these and other categorical funds designated for bilingual services. However, when the 1988 reform pushed control of these discretionary resources into schools, those that wanted support, like Thomas, were able to contract with IRC (or another provider) directly. So even though central office paid little attention to the education of Latino students and the professional needs of their teachers before Era 3, IRC developed externally to fulfill this critical function. In this domain, it was often state actors and institutions, rather than civic ones, that formed the exoskeleton.

The ACCESS English Proficiency Assessments.   No Child Left Behind had drawn attention to the nation's ELs. Passed in 2001, the act required English language proficiency instructional standards and required that districts assess and report student performance. Shortly thereafter a multistate collaborative, WIDA, formed and developed an English language acquisition assessment.[104] Conceptually similar to the STEP and DIBELS developmental assessments discussed earlier, ACCESS measures students' growth in English proficiency in listening, speaking, reading, and writing. These are the foundational elements of language learning. (Importantly, these same elements also are foundational to young children's literacy development, and attention here supported ELs' literacy learning.) Academic language, defined as students' developing capability in the discourse of each academic discipline, also was assessed by the tool. Noted earlier, academic language is an aim of ambitious instruction.

ACCESS was designed as a formative assessment tool, and initially it was low stakes—intended to help teachers understand and track students' progress in their ability to listen, speak, read, and write in English and to indicate when and where interventions might be needed.[105] Over time, however, as the accountability press grew in public education, WIDA member states, including Illinois, began using it as a gatekeeper test to determine whether a student stayed in a bilingual program or transitioned out. Much like the Danielson Framework for Teaching (FFT) discussed earlier, this transition from formative to summative assessment made it high stakes for students, teachers, and schools who all now were judged by the information it provided.[106] Even so, and similar to FFT, it functioned as a boundary object that brought teachers together, focused attention to things that mattered (which in this case were the specific elements that supported language *and* literacy learning), and created a data feedback loop that guided reflections toward continuous improvement. Combining that with mentoring by a professional group like IRC, was a one-two punch—in a good way.

As the national landscape politicized around the education of Latino and EL students across the years of reform, Illinois largely sidestepped these partisan battles, probably for a few reasons. One was the strength of the Latino caucus that del Valle had nurtured in the Senate and its commitment to working collaboratively with other lawmakers. Continued activism by allies and advocates led to the appointment of supportive members to the Illinois State Board of Education too. Chicago's decentralization also made it possible for individual school communities to set their own paths, rather than fight the district about whatever paths it chose for them. In essence, Illinois created enabling resources for improvement rather than entering this contested political space or commanding "one best way." Moreover, these resources supported both the local school efforts described above, and district capacity building once central office got involved, discussed below. The absence of voter-initiated propositions in Illinois also offered some protection against narrow interest groups, and increasingly privately financed ones, hijacking state policy to their own ends, such as the propositions in California that banned bilingual education in 1998 and its reinstatement in 2016. This boomerang suggests how narrow interest group politics are often ill-equipped to resolve complex issues that depend on expertise, sustained effort, and empathy tailored to local context.[107]

A History of District Neglect Begins to Give Way

Prior to Era 3, and with only a handful of Latinos on staff or at mid- or senior-level positions in central office (or city government), CPS leaders seemed to suffer a "continuing amnesia" about Latino students.[108] Duncan had fast-tracked a new high school for Little Village in his first months as CEO, and a small number of charters opened in Latino neighborhoods too. These relieved overcrowding somewhat, but most charters were going into African American communities where schools had been underenrolled and closed, and vacant facilities could house them.

In her bid to change that narrative, Eason-Watkins appointed Diane Zendejas chief of the Office of Language and Cultural Education (OLCE) in 2007. Zendejas was one of the first Latinas in central office with sufficient rank to raise awareness of this population's strengths and needs. Over the next three years she aimed to improve program consistency across schools and bring more schools into compliance with the federal desegregation consent decree. With support from the Trust, her office also developed a guidebook for starting and developing dual-language programs. All of these initiatives started small; there was little capacity to do otherwise. These efforts chugged along and also stayed under the radar for the most part, because most of central office was not paying attention.

Eason-Watkin also convened a Bilingual Education and World Language (BEWL) Commission in 2007 and asked Zendejas to lead it. The commission's charge was to "better understand bilingual education and to close the gap between English Learners (ELs) and other students."[109]

Overall, the commission's report was hopeful and future oriented, even as it identified significant challenges to raising the achievement of Latino students. These included a lack of standards across programs and approaches; limited knowledge in central office and among school-based educators about this group and how best to teach them; limited data about program enrollment, implementation, or effectiveness; a shortage of certified bilingual and special education bilingual teachers; and woefully insufficient funding. The report described several approaches to bilingual education and the evidence base behind each. It made recommendations about best practices, specifically citing dual-language programs that nurtured children's native language while helping them acquire a second one.[110] Such programs, when effectively implemented, kept children connected to their families, communities, and culture; built self-esteem; and had strong academic outcomes long-term. Inter-American and Thomas Schools, profiled earlier, implemented dual language for many of these reasons.

Additional to addressing ELs' needs, the BEWL report argued for *all* students to develop proficiency in a second language, noting that dual language would raise academic achievement for all and make CPS students more competitive with their counterparts worldwide who routinely learn a second language. Similarly, the authors claimed that there were "practical and personal, social and cognitive, emotional and economic" benefits to *all* students becoming bilingual and biliterate.[111] Mayor Daley's ambition for Chicago to become a "global city" depended on such a citizenry. The authors also asserted that the lack of attention to academic language across the curriculum was depressing the achievement of all students, not just ELs.[112] Its explicit teaching was described as critical to success in a knowledge economy.

By the time the BEWL report was published in 2010, 15 percent of the district—some 48,000 students—were ELs. Over one hundred languages were spoken among them, but 86 percent were second-generation Spanish speakers in the elementary grades. Both Zendejas and Eason-Watkins had left their positions by then. The interim leadership team of Mazany and Payne referenced BEWL in the report they prepared for the next CEO. But

Evaluating Our Vision for Learning was sidelined in the immediate leadership churn.[113] During his short stint as CEO, Brizard downgraded the OLCE to a department. This was a setback, but program staff continued most of their capacity-building efforts nonetheless.[114]

When Barbara Byrd-Bennett became CEdO and then CEO later in Era 4, she was the next senior district leader after Eason-Watkins to recognize the district's responsibility to educate this marginalized group, and the growing political imperative to do so. Byrd-Bennett convened a citywide Latino advisory committee. She also commissioned a study, this one by the Council of Great City Schools, in 2013 to determine "why [Latino and EL students] were achieving at the [low] levels they were, and to make recommendations and proposals for improving [their] academic performance."[115] Among its findings was variability among predominantly Latino schools in the city: CPS had some of the best schools with regard to education for ELs—consistent with the school-level efforts described earlier—while others remained problematic. Again, concerns were raised about compliance with multiple federal, state, and court-ordered mandates. A program audit that same year—the first of its kind initiated by Jesse Ruiz when he became interim CEO—found 71 percent of the sampled schools failed to comply with one or more provisions of state code. Charters were the worst offenders.[116]

Byrd-Bennett also restored the OLCE and appointed Karen Garibay-Mulatierri its chief in 2014. Because Byrd-Bennett was amenable and the district now had more Latino students than any other group, Garibay-Mulatierri could build on Zendeja's earlier efforts and also be more aggressive. Similar in strategy to the efforts in CRI and CMSI when these launched several years before, much of OLCE's work focused on professional development for central office staff and school-based educators: What did each group need to know and be able to do so that Latino students and ELs might be better served? The OLCE also developed a plan for building educators' understanding of the interconnections between literacy and language development.[117] Enabled by funds from the Trust, language development subsequently became integral to CPS instruction in all the core content areas, and as noted earlier, it became a mainstay of all the instructional improvement work that the Trust supported, including Common Core.

The Great Schools report was published in 2015. By then Byrd-Bennett was under indictment, and Ruiz, who was an interim appointment, had been replaced by Claypool. Following their departures, and similar to what was going on more generally in central office regarding instructional improvement, continuing efforts to better serve Latino students and their teachers remained the purview of mid-level leaders and staff. They sustained this work amid more leadership churn, and with support from the Board of Education, which by then had several Latino members and allies. When Jackson became CEdO in 2015, and then CEO in 2017, she held the megaphone to champion this work and committed resources to advance it further, including more staff and senior-level leaders with relevant expertise. Her team's efforts were substantive and aggressive and bode well for continued improvement beyond what was documented in the Consortium study that analyzed the progress of earlier cohorts of EL students.[118] By the end of Era 4, the district was finally shining more than a flashlight on its Latino students.

As noted earlier, the good news about English learners was celebrated when the Consortium published its report in 2019. But how did a success story fly under the radar for so long, and what propelled Latino students' progress when much of the district seemed disengaged much of the time?

As it turns out, this is another story rooted in the DNA of Chicago's decentralization reform. While many of the educational, linguistic, and cultural needs of Latino students were distinct, the mechanisms by which problems were solved early on are familiar: from new principals and their school communities up, and with support from the outside in—although in this case it was state actors, and state policy, that formed much of the protective exoskeleton. Internal to central office, it was not until late in her tenure that Eason-Watkins was able to turn her attention here and make some first, capacity-building moves. Unlike the big initiatives launched at the start of Era 3 including CRI and CMSI, efforts in this domain started small and stayed small for the next several years—mostly in one office and with a few commissions, advisory councils, and reports. They remained small because the broader political will to do more was not yet there, and fiscal constraints following the 2008 recession were operant too. The work also took time to grow because, as with CRI and CMSI, the expertise and capacity had to be built, but the base capacity in the district and its exoskeleton was not as extensive. Leadership churn tested the resilience of this work, but it did persist, and over time central office developed capacity to better serve Latino students and the educators who worked with them.

5

Learnings and Reflections

Chicago's school reform story began in 1987. By almost any indicator of student outcomes—test scores, student attendance, graduation rates, and college success—Chicago's was a very troubled school system. Although the data on the quality of its educator workforce was more limited, it spoke to similar concerns. Many in the city had concluded that this system could not be reformed from within. In response, an unusual alliance formed among business leaders and neighborhood-based organizers to change the governance of the system.

Back then, little in Chicago seemed primed for the transformation that unfolded. And it happened under circumstances that were far from ideal: fourteen different superintendents/CEOs over the next thirty years; recurring fiscal crises; and a highly segregated city where many neighborhoods were devastated by deindustrialization, deinstitutionalization, and a long history of racial disparities in healthcare, housing, employment, and education. From this angle of view, Chicago was an unlikely context for broadscale improvement efforts to be sustained over time and consolidate into a coherent corpus of action. Yet that is what occurred, and in the preceding pages we have tried to share what unfolded and how it happened. While it is a distinctly Chicago story, important improvement lessons can be drawn from it.

WHAT HAPPENED AND HOW

We have described how an extraordinary community of individuals and organizations made it happen. Participants came from advocacy groups, the business and philanthropic communities and the media, citywide educational organizations and higher education, local and national foundations, as well as parents, community members, and local school educators. Many schools improved, a hundred new schools opened, and a considerable number of neighborhood schools closed. Interwoven through the story of *How a City Learned to Improve Its Schools* is an account of two dominant and interrelated dynamics orchestrating these improvements: an institutional-political reframing and a social learning one.

An Institutional-Political Reframe

Figure 5.1 affords an overview of the institutional-political dynamics that shaped these efforts. As discussed in chapter 1, Chicago's journey grew out of an unusual alliance that joined neighborhood and community-based groups with business leaders. This was democracy at work—challenging and ultimately upsetting what had calcified as a dysfunctional power structure. A hopelessness about the status quo forced a moral reckoning that the normal politics governing the city's schools was entirely insufficient to address the disgrace that was then the CPS. It was civic outrage and civic organizing that initiated reform and continued to advance it in response to changing circumstances across a thirty-year period. On the political front, it helped to sustain reform through leadership churn in Era 1 and again in Era 4; and it functioned as a buffering resource during the early stages of mayoral control in Era 2, when decentralization—reform's original organizing idea—was challenged. Institutionally, it catalyzed and supported the emergence of new organizations and a renewal of existing ones that would play major roles in revitalizing the overall school system.

A distinctive set of intellectual roots, alive in the late 1980s, set Chicago's path. It was a time of perestroika and glasnost on the international

Figure 5.1   CPS systems development levers for change

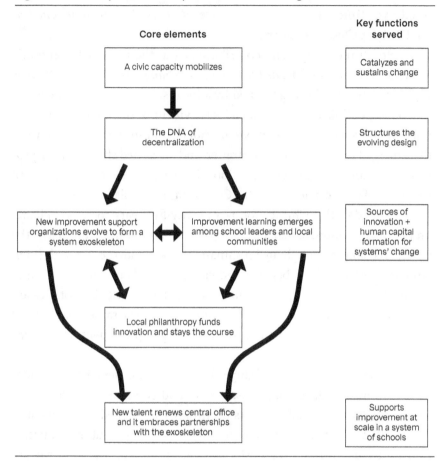

scene, a corporate environment focused on downsizing in response to stagnation in American industry, and educators advancing ideas about school-site management and decision-making. School system decentralization, in the form of local community control of neighborhood schools, became Chicago's initial lever for reform, but this proved to be much more than a starting point. Decentralization shaped much of what followed over the next thirty years, even as the salience of the term itself diminished over time. From our perspective, *decentralization functioned as the DNA for Chicago's reform.*

One of its most important contributions was the sustained attention it brought to the *local school as the key unit of change.* This was equally true whether that school was governed by a local school council or a charter school board. This distinctive focus was evident in the ways Chicago developed and supported school-based leaders, and in the innovative work that emerged regarding their preparation and associated efforts to raise professional standards. Decentralization also shaped the most significant programs of work carried out by the Consortium. The 5Es framework, which has remained vital in Chicago for over twenty-five years, focuses explicitly on organizing improvements in local school communities. Similarly, the powerful changes wrought by Freshman OnTrack and To&Through (high school to postsecondary) began in individual high school communities and in their self-organizing as an improvement network. In both cases, school-based educators and school-community leaders, rather than central office actors, were the key figures for advancing improvements in their local settings.

To accomplish productive change, decentralization demanded a fundamental mindset shift among these school and community leaders. Historically, they were implementors of initiatives designed by others, and those initiatives often were not especially well thought out or resourced. In contrast, decentralization positioned local leaders as lead improvers in their own communities. While the take-up of this new local agency varied among them, the best in this group, in both neighborhood schools and charters, proved transformative for their schools. Subsequently, many of these educators moved into network and central office roles in CPS and into leadership positions in other educational organizations around the city. And because they were grounded in the everyday work of improving their schools, they brought a very different set of experiences, know-how, and mindsets to their new positions.

And so, a previously closed system opened to new ideas, new people, new centers of power, and new energy. New leaders emerged from diverse walks of life and were committed to making a difference. They stayed engaged and gradually, bit by bit, helped to make CPS better. Some moved up into senior positions with formal school system authority. Others took on important middle-level administrative roles inside CPS. Still others became leaders in various organizations across the city. Together they substantially shaped the course of reform. Our story gives voice to many of these individuals. Had a longer account been possible, many more voices could have been added.

Accompanying this burst of human capital development was the emergence of a distinctive civic architecture—an *exoskeleton* supporting school system reform. Beginning in Era 1 and growing from there, entities within the exoskeleton increasingly took on the direct work of improving the city's schools. Brand-new organizations emerged in Chicago, and new centers of work developed within existing organizations, including several of the city's colleges of education, the Chicago Principals Association, and the Chicago Teachers Union. National groups, including Teach For America and New Leaders for New Schools, brought new talent streams into the system as well. Derivative reform organizations, with specific responsibilities and interests, were launched and supported by Chicago's business community, including LQE and the Renaissance School Fund. Organizations in the exoskeleton directly advanced a revitalization of arts education in Chicago schools and an expansive community schools effort. A significant transformation in the internal operations of local colleges of education also occurred. We have highlighted efforts at UIC, the city's major public research university. Complementary changes happened in many other colleges in metropolitan Chicago as well.

Each of these organizations specialized around distinct professional capacities needed by the city's schools. These included developing, recruiting, and mentoring new teachers; preparing principals to lead change in some of Chicago's most challenged school communities; supporting the large-scale professional learning needs of educators as more ambitious academic goals emerged; and sustaining ongoing analysis and reporting to continue to inform the city about the conditions of its schools, the progress of its reform efforts, and the work still ahead.

Fueling much of the development of this new improvement infrastructure was primary work for Chicago's local philanthropic community. They stayed in for the long course of district transformation, learning as they went, and supported a cooperative space for schools and organizations in the exoskeleton to innovate and develop over time. Local foundations worked collaboratively, rather than competing with each other. They jointly invested in good people and good ideas and combined this with a social-venture capital orientation. Like venture investing generally, many initially supported projects failed to achieve at a breakthrough level, but several of their bets did become significant contributors to reform.

Last, and equally key, was a shift made by district leaders, beginning in Era 3, as they sought to resource directly the CPS's new mission of supporting a system of schools. Although the exoskeleton emerged organically, supported by the local foundation community, it was *district leaders' innovative embrace of partnerships* with these external organizations and their leaders that moved these developments from the periphery to the center of district transformation. Partnerships became a central part of the CPS strategy for building an improvement infrastructure for the entire system. The professional resources needed for this purpose had been growing in the exoskeleton in Eras 1 and 2, but beginning in Era 3, many of these organizations began working directly with the district. They aimed to be responsive to district needs, but were not controlled by the district. This came about in large part because significant funding for the initiatives came as "public-private ventures," with the local foundations contributing resources and expertise to these partnerships. Especially noteworthy in this regard were two developments: the CPS collaborating with the Chicago Public Education Fund, New Leaders, and UIC on new principal preparation; and the Network for College Success (NCS), supported by multiple local foundations, partnering with CPS to enable high school success for many more students. Strong professional norms directed these partnerships, and collectively they exercised a kind of gyroscopic effect on evolving district actions. They functioned as a sustaining force that kept core initiatives moving forward during critical periods of leadership instability, budget cutbacks, labor-management conflicts, and the aftermath of contro-versial school closings in Era 4. This was especially the case with regard to human capital and instructional improvement initiatives.

The ability of these external organizations to stay the course is especially important because institutional capacity building, which generates practi-cal problem-solving knowledge and expands the base of people who know how to use it, takes longer to develop than the typical terms of a CEO or board member. In addition, whatever capacity is built can be quickly evis-cerated if new district leaders suddenly press in a different direction. The importance of staying the course was especially evident in Era 4, where de-spite CEO churn, the district's core improvement initiatives around teach-ing and learning and enhancing the quality of its human resources largely endured.

In broad strokes then, Chicago's account mirrors academic writings about civic capacity as a mobilizing force for public problem solving.[1] A base civic capacity challenged a dysfunctional status quo and set Chicago on a path toward school system transformation. As this civic capacity be-came more expansive and expert over time, it evolved into a kind of com-munity synergy that sustained reform in the face of slow progress while maintaining focal attention on core infrastructure building. The organ-izations making up this enterprise came to touch virtually every aspect of the school system, and the capabilities within these organizations contin-ued to develop through this activity. In a complementary fashion, system leaders increasingly worked collaboratively with them. Together, the city learned how to get better at advancing targeted aims.

So this is what Chicago's reform history looks like when viewed through an institutional-political lens. But this is only part of our story—an account of a stunning array of new people, new energy, and new activity vitalized in schools, in the exoskeleton, and eventually inside the central office it-self. Still left unanswered is one big question raised at the beginning of this book: How did coherent changes emerge out of this stew of activity absent strong, central control directing it? Many individuals and organizations were doing and learning different things; a competition for attention could easily have emerged and pulled the system apart, but this did not happen. How then did the many different change initiatives that evolved from the DNA of decentralization come to work productively together?

A Social Learning Frame

As noted above, much improvement learning occurred among school-based educators: individuals who typically were young and relatively new to school-leadership roles. They had been activated as agents for local school improvement by the decentralization reform of 1988 and following that were largely buffered from competing demands from the central office because of the limits that reform had placed on its authority. Barbara Eason-Watkins, Carlos Azcoitia, and Jorge Sanchez were a few such leaders called out in our story. Others too were moving along similar paths. Because the central office was too incapacitated to send directives their way, these educators could sustain their focus instead on learning how to improve their particular schools. This first round of school-leader improvers in turn were followed by a second generation whose early socialization into the profession was shaped in the new school-community improvement spaces that had opened up. Janice Jackson's early career opportunities to lead two high schools and become a charter member of the NCS exemplifies this. Many, like Jackson, were also being trained in new professional education programs specifically designed to support them as school improvement leaders. The best of this talent eventually moved up into larger leadership roles in the system and brought these learnings with them.

Complementing this learning-by-doing among CPS educators were similar efforts occurring in the exoskeleton. This too was catalyzed by the 1988 reform. The Center for School Improvement (the Center) was an early leader focusing on elementary schools; the NCS, which emerges a bit later in this history, focused on high school improvements. The Annenberg initiative in Era 2 challenged individual faculty in colleges of education to move beyond their particular research specialties into how this knowledge could productively be used to improve schools. Beginning in Era 3, professional education programs were being reinvented that focused explicitly on developing educators to succeed in Chicago schools. These programs garnered regular feedback regarding the success and failures of their graduates, and this data continued to press them: "How do we get still better?" Typically, these initiatives struggled early on, as judged against the expansive needs in Chicago. This was especially true for those programs that attempted to work quickly at large scale. Regardless, all over the city individuals were learning, and what they learned, and how they learned in colleagueship with others, fueled subsequent gains.

Improvement Learning Becomes Broadly Shared. Chicago's civic architecture did not have a formally designated citywide coordinating body guiding its efforts. Rather, it operated more along the lines of a dynamic social network. A variety of mechanisms enabled individual learning to become widely held and transformed into broadly usable knowledge for improvement. Taken together, these mechanisms functioned as the invisible hand bringing coordination and coherence to reform efforts citywide.

Conversation spaces for social learning Numerous contexts operated in Chicago, where individual learnings were shared, tested through dialogue, and further refined. Several of these were deliberately organized "rooms where it happened" that brought people into sustained conversation around improving Chicago's schools. At the school community level, and by far the "rooms" that engaged the largest number of people, were local school councils (LSCs). An innovation of Chicago's reform, an LSC brought together the principal and two teachers, chosen by their faculty colleagues, with elected parents and community leaders to chart a course for improving their school.

Simultaneously, this social learning was occurring in numerous other institutional settings across the city. The Civic Committee of the Commercial Club (composed of Chicago's business leaders) set up specific suborganizations where these conversations were ongoing. A revitalized Council of Chicago Area Deans of Education brought leaders from the area's colleges and universities into this discourse. The active funding of school reform by the city's various foundations regularly ensured that their staff and board members were part of this as well. When charter schools began to open, each with its own board of directors, these became still another context for school improvement learning. Many charter board members came from the elite sectors of the city where thin air conversations about the intellectual merits of competition and choice abounded. Now they confronted concrete concerns about how one really makes a school work, regardless of how the larger system may be governed. In addition, some new contexts emerged in Chicago that were deliberately designed to bring different interests and perspectives into conversations with one another. Two especially significant in this regard were the Consortium's steering committee and *Catalyst*'s editorial board.

The boundary spanners and linkers   The individual learning of early leaders in schools and in the exoskeleton, and the new relationships forming among them, became "the things they carried" with them as they moved over time into other professional roles. School-based leaders took on influential district roles beyond their schools. Others brought their learnings into the exoskeleton. Some, whose professional work located them external to the district initially, eventually went to work inside the district for periods of time. Many crossed back and forth. Introduced in our text are some fifty-two individuals whose work histories crossed over two or more of the institutional domains identified in the introduction. Figure 5.2 documents their career paths and the dense institutional connections they created.

In addition, other individuals introduced in our account were active reformers who linked with others through their membership on various local and state boards focused on school reform. The overall density of educational leaders in Chicago interacting with one another across this institutional space, as illustrated in figure 5.3, is compelling. Especially noteworthy are the numerous connections created through the Consortium steering committee and *Catalyst*'s editorial board, and also the broad-based engagement of faculty and staff from university improvement centers and schools of education. This is how both local and national

Figure 5.2   Chicago reform boundary spanners

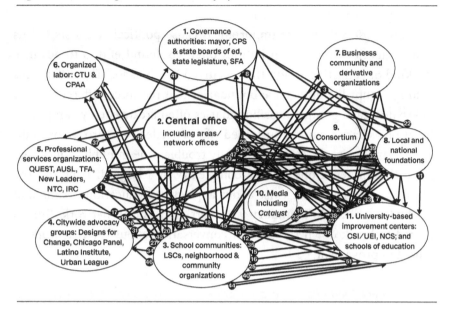

Figure 5.3   Reform conversation spaces: interconnected board memberships

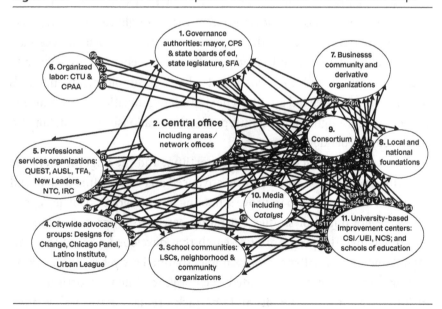

research-based knowledge continued to pulse through Chicago's social learning environment.

These observations are important because political scientists tell us that contentious intergroup politics often confound efforts to advance the kind of collective action that occurred in Chicago.[2] The differences among groups literally create boundaries that reinforce different beliefs internal to each group. These boundaries often create enemy camps and function as barriers to the sustained efforts needed to improve how public institutions work. This is especially troublesome in public education, given the immense operational complexity of a large district and the pluralism of views that exist about appropriate educational aims and methods. Chicago's boundary spanners and social network linkers helped to break down the silos of conversation about the real work of school improvement.

Civic knowledge-building organizations[3]   At the center of this social learning enterprise were two new institutions that launched soon after Chicago's decentralization law was passed. Both *Catalyst* and the Consortium vitalized the notion that an informed, activated, and educated citizenry was reform's most critical resource. They brought research evidence, rigorous analysis, and in-depth descriptive reporting to the table. Their accounts deliberately sought to engage a diverse audience and give voice to their experiences and concerns about what was unfolding in the city's schools and what needed attention next. Both organizations were external to the district, sought to maintain a productive relationship with it, but also remained independent throughout.

The studies conducted by the Consortium, and the ongoing citywide convenings organized around them, advanced an evolving line of data and argument about efforts to improve schooling in Chicago. Consortium projects were not one-shot studies but rather extended programs of inquiry and reporting. The program of research that developed around the Chicago Annenberg Challenge, for example, spanned six years. The work on ending social promotion extended to eight years. The Consortium's two major contributions—the 5Es and OnTrack—remain active today, more than twenty years after their start. Topics central to improving the technical core of schooling—principal leadership, teacher quality, a student-centered learning climate, and the character of instruction itself—were identified as priorities early on and returned to on multiple occasions. Likewise, over its twenty-five years of operation, *Catalyst* sustained attention to this same set of issues and connected them to local efforts to strengthen school communities citywide. *Catalyst* told the stories of parents, students, and school educators experiencing reform and simultaneously brought to these same audiences the best of external ideas and emerging research and analysis.

A compelling set of boundary objects   All of this takes us to the last key ingredient: the development of skillfully crafted improvement frameworks that created the potential for shared learning to emerge across the city. Social learning theorists refer to these as *boundary objects*. They are anchored in a conceptual framework, require regular data feedback systems tied to the framework, and involve social processes for engaging participants around the evidence produced.[4] They can be manifested in a host of different tools, such as protocols for instructional rounds, personnel evaluation rubrics, and school surveys. The key test is not just whether such tools exist, but rather their capacity to focus, sustain, and inform conversations about the core improvement challenges that need to be addressed. Interestingly, when such conversations are broadly occurring within different organizations, and across different roles and levels within organizations, they foster the development of the shared understandings necessary to coordinate action and promote coherence even among individuals and groups who may never have been in the same "room" together.

The two major boundary objects discussed in chapter 2—the five essential supports for school improvement (5Es) and the concept of Freshman OnTrack—played this role. Both frameworks were rooted in the structures, routines, and norms that ground day-to-day work of schools and are instrumental to the outcomes achieved. Both articulated an explicit set of causal mechanisms that produced the unsatisfactory results of the past and helped to identify targets for ongoing improvement. Continuous data about these mechanisms, and how they in turn connected to the student outcomes observed, was central to the Consortium's analytic work and became a regular part of the reporting back to schools, to system leaders, and into the city. Consortium reports attended to conventional school quality indicators, such as standardized test scores, student attendance, graduation rates, and grade point averages, but were not fixated on the small jiggles in these indicators occurring from one year to the next. Instead, studies focused on the progress being made in improving *the major work processes and systems* controlling teaching and learning and the evidence that linked changes in these processes and systems to *discernable trends* in student outcomes over time.

We also saw in chapter 3 how an evolving set of professional standards for preparing school-based leaders and assessing their competencies played a similar role organizing what previously had been a weak and incoherent professional education space. Likewise, as detailed in chapter 4, the introduction of a framework for improving teaching, and efforts to generate reliable evidence about the quality of teaching, created a wedge to move what previously had been a domain of highly variable autonomous practice toward a more coherent one. Although less well documented, the ACCESS assessment system played a similar formative role focusing improvement efforts for English learners. The embrace of Common Core showed promise for accomplishing similar goals going forward.

Interestingly, much of this standards raising was catalyzed nationally. On their own, however, standards are inert resources; they educate no one. Turning inert standards into productive local actions was the actual work of Chicago educators, enabled by a social learning system, anchored in district partnerships with organizations in the exoskeleton, and resourced and guided by strategic investments made by local foundations. This is how, despite a cacophony of activity unleashed by the DNA of decentralization, it was possible for shared understandings to develop and for coherent system actions to emerge that broadly transformed practice in schools.

To sum up then, a core set of moves supported systems transformation in Chicago. First, district leaders acted as collaborators with other organizations facilitating this system renewal, rather than seeing themselves as the sole authoritative actor. Formal power remained with them, and civic actors engaged with this. They supported its use on some occasions, and they pushed back at other times. As Chicagoans learned from the leadership team of Duncan and Eason-Watkins, sometimes the most effective action by system leaders was the reflective choice not to exercise power in traditional ways.

Second, the Chicago story highlighted the extraordinary array of organizations and individual actors attempting to improve specific aspects of public schooling and the learnings they acquired through such activity. This was not a district's five-year strategic plan or a foundation's six-year program of work. It was a generation's effort. The public-private partnerships in Chicago that supported and sustained an innovation and improvement learning space was a core driver in the system's transformation.

Third, the chief actors in Chicago's exoskeleton were not just involved in passive debates about what other people should do. Rather, they were attempting to actually make their ideas work. They were citizen activists, proximate to the real work of improving schools, and learning by doing. Chicago's decentralization made possible this reorientation of civic attention.

Fourth was the centrality of well-crafted working theories of action. These frameworks explicated the causal mechanisms (often tacitly) assumed by reformers in their advocacy for some change, and then repeatedly tested those assumed linkages against evidence. This applied research aimed to both inform the efforts of people on the ground trying to make these changes work, and guide subsequent system policies and practices so that better outcomes might be more broadly achieved. Multiple spaces were created for these conversations to occur, and in their creation, opportunities for deeper and more broadly shared understandings emerged. In this regard, Chicago's transformation involved a long-term commitment to community education about the improvement of public education. This is how Chicago learned to improve its schools.

IMPROVEMENT LESSONS FROM CHICAGO FOR OTHERS

We have had a unique opportunity to bring a contemporary historical perspective to bear on the transformation of a major public urban education system. Chicago's efforts entailed the invention of a host of new organizations that formed an improvement infrastructure for the city's schools. This infrastructure enhanced the capabilities of educators to work in new ways and extended and deepened relationships among school communities and the larger civic context. This institutional renewal occurred within a postmodern democratic polity that bears little resemblance to the social context of De Tocqueville's *Democracy in America* and efforts to build common schools in support of that social and political world. Chicago's reform directly challenged the dominant paradigm that took root in the twentieth century of a public bureaucracy administered by educational professionals who managed a "one best school system."[5] We draw out below a few larger lessons from Chicago for improving public education systems more broadly.

Governance Reform as a Transformative Lever

Over this thirty-year period, debates raged in the city about reforming the governance of its schools, and these continue. As noted in the introduction, four big ideas—community control, mayoral takeover of the public bureaucracy, charters and choice, and professionalism—developed local advocates who competed with each other. Each group saw its answer as *the* answer to improving public education. Each had periods of ascendancy, all contributed in different ways, but each also manifested distinctive weaknesses internal to its design.

Chicago's reform began with community control of schools, which brought parents and community organizations to the forefront, renewed agency among school-based educators, and redirected them to strengthen their ties to students, parents, and their local community. This feature taps into a core improvement science principle that those engaged in the work are central to its improvement. Rather than exclusively looking up into the system for direction on the next new program to implement, school-based leaders were empowered to identify local problems and go to work at solving them. Decentralization created space for different improvement ideas to be tried out in different places. As a result, it redirected much of the interest-group-based organizing, typically pressing to advance their favored solutions over the entirety of the school system, into attempting to make their specific ideas actually work in some schools. Thus, decentralization functioned as a powerful initiating lever for system transformation. But Chicago's record is also clear that when school communities were left largely on their own to improve, some succeeded and others were left behind. And the latter result was especially true in the most challenging neighborhoods in the city. See more on this below.

Next came direct mayoral control over the district bureaucracy. It accomplished some good things as well—expanding the fiscal resources for the system, achieving an extended stretch of labor-management peace, and advancing some operational improvements, including renovating buildings and opening some new ones. And without question, direct mayoral control over the school board further tempered the contentious interest-group-based politics that plagues public education systems. But strong centrally directed action can also result in missteps; we have documented multiple instances of these too.

Choice and charters, in their turn, brought new schools into existence. Like community control, this effort activated agency and ownership for improvement at the school site and allowed for varied solutions to emerge. Charters expanded the number of educators leading change in local schools and engaged civic actors as board members in the actual tasks of learning how to get a good school to work. Charters expanded the choice possibilities for parents; some new "good seats" became available, and some not great ones too. So just shifting to having markets as the control mechanism did not assure success either. Moreover, Chicago's experiences made visible a value previously ignored in these conversations. By replacing neighborhood schools with a marketplace of charter schools, many communities lost a core neighborhood institution—their school—and that change destroyed relationships that residents cared deeply about. Indeed, this sense of loss around the closing of neighborhood schools proved so profound that it propelled a political backlash in Chicago that stopped charter expansion in its tracks.

Latest to the scene was the rise of professional normative control. As our story closes, it is still too early to write its full case. Its strength is in its laser-like attention to bringing the best research-based practices in teaching and learning to bear as organizers for an improvement support system. It played a key role in Eras 3 and 4 as CPS aimed to move classroom practice toward more ambitious standards. These aspirations posed enormous challenges for individual schools to resolve on their own; they clearly needed a support system to accomplish this. But one cannot be fully sanguine about professional normative control as the sole "answer" either. Competition about the "right ideas and practices," and the warrant for many so-called research-based practices remains suspect. Like mayoral control, there is an ever-present possibility of ideological dogmatism outrunning its evidence base. Also unanswered are questions about how parents and local communities achieve voice about what they want. Control exercised by professional elites, like mayoral control, needs to be disciplined by an ecumenical spirit in response to this civic pluralism, but professional control has no track record showing how it might actually go about doing so.

In sum, one lesson from Chicago is that reframing school system governance—who gets to exercise what power—was central to its transformation. But there is also a corollary: no simple answer emerged for how best to accomplish this. A hybrid system evolved in Chicago that extracted some of the promise offered by each of the four competing governance ideas—decentralization, mayoral control, choice and charters, and standards/professional norms—while also addressing their silences. Such a hybrid arrangement may well be the most productive template for other districts going forward.

Whatever the path chosen by others, effective governance reform must confront simultaneously (1) the complex and time-consuming character of transforming a public school system and (2) the pluralist views its citizens hold regarding the proper aims and methods for schooling. (Research can certainly inform the latter, but neither technical elites nor a mayor can dictate this.) Given the institutional location of public schools—partway between the wishes and values of families and local communities, and the public needs for a civil and economically viable society—schools operate in an intrinsically contested political space. Recognizing this grounds the challenge for governance reform in support of district transformation. The only thing that is clear is that doing nothing is not the answer. Here too, another improvement science mantra speaks: if we continue to do what we have always done, we will continue to get what we have always gotten. The public's disdain for what we have always gotten is the political problem to solve. It was Chicago's problem in 1987 and remains education's problem to solve today.

Achieving Reforms at Scale

There is no shortage of good ideas about reforming schools, but the technical know-how and expertise necessary to execute on them is woefully underdeveloped. And so, districts often fall victim to an organizational problem common across institutions and sectors. In *Scaling Up Excellence*, Sutton and Rao call this the clusterfug.[6] (The term originated with the military, but Sutton and Rao sanitized the spelling.) Three phenomena join here. The first is illusion—a belief that what is being scaled is so powerful that it will overwhelm any pedestrian logistical constraints. Second is incompetence—a failure to recognize and appreciate the expansive knowledge and skill needed when trying to spread some change at scale. And third is impatience—a belief that events can be achieved faster than the facts warrant. In contrast, scaling well requires building the necessary know-how to execute effectively on a new idea, developing early cohorts who succeed in advancing these changes and who can in turn teach others, and nurturing on-the-ground evangelizing leaders whose enthusiasm helps to spread the work.

The limits imposed here arose on multiple occasions in the Chicago story. The expansive initial ambitions of the Chicago Annenberg Challenge, described in chapter 1, ran headlong into them. The first efforts at high school reform through small schools, and the end-of-social-promotion initiative in Era 2, did so as well. As described in chapter 3, while small and intensive efforts to mentor new teachers and prepare National Board certified teachers showed considerable success, efforts attempting to achieve the same objectives faster and larger struggled.

In this regard, Chicago does offer examples of getting scaling right. One of the most successful large-scale improvements in public education anywhere—the OnTrack to high school success initiative—started in a very small network of principals organized by Melissa Roderick. Operating within the improvement learning space afforded by the DNA of decentralization, this group took on the hard work of turning a promising idea into tools, routines, and new ways of working together. Out of these successful early efforts grew the Network for College Success and a district partnership to spread this work. Based on what was learned by collaborating in those early efforts, the district then designed supporting data systems, professional development offerings, and new specialized roles. Subsequently, it revised the feedback and evaluation processes for principals and network leaders to align with this. The sequence that these changes followed was literally constrained; one cannot jump to the end without going through the "learning how-to" beginning and middle.

The OnTrack account is one of several in this book that illumine a hard reality about limits on the reach of a district's improvement efforts. A district can allocate funds to create new roles such as instructional coaches, new principal mentors, and network chiefs. A district can roll out entirely new initiatives such as a new curriculum or a tutoring program, but vitalizing these developments to achieve quality outcomes reliably at scale is an entirely different matter. These are typically developmental learning challenges, places where professional expertise must grow. They are not simple training and straightforward implementation problems. Consequently, they share a character analogous to organic growth.

As is true of all organic growth, the rate of change at any given point in time is constrained by the phenomenon's current state. When the base capacity is limited, growth will be slow; but if supportive environmental conditions are established, the rate of growth will accelerate as the base capacity expands. By analogy, the process is akin to planting a seedling in a garden. Initially it doesn't look like much. Even with appropriate attention, for a long while it seems like little is happening. While only a few small new leaves may appear aboveground, beneath the ground a vibrant root system is growing and taking hold. And then the plant begins to "come alive." New and larger leaves emerge, and rapid growth now occurs. But none of this is possible without the development of that strong root system.

This points to a very different way of thinking about advancing reform at scale. It means moderating the traditional premium placed on rapid broad-based implementation of new programs and policies. Such actions do respond to a felt public need to act big and fast, but they also lead to promising more than is realistically possible. Some successes can emerge here and there from quick-fix programs and policies, but overall improvements remain limited, and those school communities most in need often are the least likely to benefit. This was true in Chicago in the period prior to reform, and it continued episodically over the next three decades. Mediocrity just repeated from flawed attempts to scale too quickly. In contrast, the big effects documented in the Chicago story were anchored in sustained commitments to build an improvement infrastructure in the city's exoskeleton, in the district's central office, and in the partnerships between them. Continuous attention was paid to developing the capabilities needed to design, refine, and enact coherent, aligned, instructional systems while the actors continued to learn how to get better at what they sought to achieve.

At work, then, in the conventional practices of educational reform are versions of the clusterfug anchored in misguided beliefs that with the right new leadership, all will be well because these leaders are smart, committed, and caring. All of these leadership characteristics are essential, but they must be coupled with hard-nosed thinking about what it will actually take to reach the changes aspired to. These leaders must also be truthful with the public in these regards. Absent this, they effectively undermine the legitimacy of their host institutions and breed deep public pessimism about whether better is actually possible.

This lesson is especially salient today in the context of increasing calls to reimagine schooling in America. This movement has been afoot for some time, for example, in calls for schools to focus more attention on developing "21st century skills." This press has grown stronger of late in revisiting our nation's failures with regard to its indigenous people and those enslaved. The narrow focus of accountability systems on academic skills in literacy and math has caused schools to underattend to the education of students as whole persons, and this need has become even more visible in the post-pandemic period. In his essay "Possible Futures: Toward a New Grammar of Schooling," Jal Mehta brings voice to these new aspirations.[7] He calls for schooling that creates agency and purpose for students who become users and creators of knowledge— where they learn through apprenticeships and are judged by the products they create and through their own accounts of learning, rather than solely by standardized tests. Schools should become places where leadership is distributed broadly rather than top down; where the boundaries of conventional subject matter and disciplines are crossed; where the conventional eggcrate structure of classrooms and uses of time are opened up; and where education occurs not only in schools, but also in communities and workplace settings. As soon as one shifts from such envisioning, however, to contemplating the actual work of systems transformation, the scope and daunting character of the tasks become immediately manifest. This is not a call for marginal change, but fundamental systems transformation. It would demand an innovation space on a vast scale to learn how to execute on each of these aspirations, and it would surely challenge current governance structures, as they are not designed to support such innovation and improvement learning. This would require expansive actions even more complex than the ones recounted in this book. All of the lessons learned in Chicago's transformation apply here big time.

Massive Returns from Investing in an Improvement Infrastructure

Regularly accompanying calls for reform are calls for more public funding for schools. This was and continues to be an essential need in Chicago. Such funding is best understood as a facilitating resource—it makes things possible that otherwise would be impossible. But, alone funding does not assure success. Achieving more effective outcomes, a more efficient use of resources, and a more person-centered environment for the work of both students and educators is a systems design and improvement problem. Chicago made substantial headway this past thirty years through critical investments in building and by sustaining an improvement infrastructure. Several key elements stand out.

First was the focus on strengthening human capital pipelines and especially the development of principals, given their key role as change leaders in their local school communities. The CPS Department of Principal Quality estimates spending about $10 million annually on its principal development efforts. Extensive research has documented that such investments are remarkably cost-effective.[8]

Second, much the same can be said about the extended investments made in the Consortium's informing of improvement efforts citywide. Their annual budget amounts to about $5 million a year. Third was the support provided for public media, like the role that *Catalyst* played. And then fourth was the need for a generous pool of resources to support innovation efforts, akin to the roles played by the Center, NCS, and UIC. These last two concerns—public media support and an innovation fund—add roughly another $20 million a year.

Taken together, this amounts to an investment of about $35–40 million annually on Chicago's improvement infrastructure. To put this in perspective, this total set of commitments amounts to about half of 1 percent of the school system's annual budget. In dollar terms this is equivalent to spending about $100 per student per year to better leverage how the remaining $17,700 per year are spent.[9] The results from Chicago speak powerfully to why such a commitment matters and how it can create enormous momentum for positive change. Sustained infrastructure building needs to be funded as such. System improvement is not free.

Appreciating the Time Demanded for Systems Change

Yet another key lesson from Chicago is that systems transformation is a long-term undertaking. To place this in perspective, we turn to a different large-scale Chicago initiative that occurred during this same time period.

In 2001, Mayor Daley announced a major project for another of Chicago's public service systems—the addition of a new runway, a new highway access, and a new terminal at O'Hare Airport. Chicagoans were told it would take twelve years to accomplish this, and nobody blinked an eye. Think about this in comparison to the ways that large-scale improvement efforts in public education are scrutinized. If that same logic were applied to the O'Hare project, three or four years out, people would be clamoring to know "Is this working? I don't see the new runway, and where is that terminal you promised?" Clearly, this would be a silly way to judge the progress of a project of such scope and complexity.

To the point, like the O'Hare expansion, school system transformation is also a big infrastructure development project. So similarly, we need to appreciate and set realistic expectations about what advancing progress on an effort of this scope actually entails. Yet many public figures don't think about district improvement in this same way. Take for example efforts that have been underway for some time to introduce the Common Core standards. What does the Chicago story teach us here?

The standards call for a major transformation in what educators teach and how they teach it. To jump-start this change in Chicago, extensive professional development was needed for its current teachers, and system educators more generally, to just learn what the standards were about and why they were needed. This was a very basic first step before any serious classroom use and this took a couple of years. Preservice preparation programs also needed to be overhauled to prepare the next generation of teachers to teach in these new ways, as many new teachers continued to come into these schools. This wasn't directly under CPS control and required considerable conversations with local professional preparation providers. These colleges of education, of course, work at their own pace. Then to move beyond the early stages of novice implementation of the Common Core, the development of an instructional coaching capability for each role—teachers, principals, instructional leadership teams, and network and district staff—was needed. But here Chicago, like other districts, confronted a start-up problem. Few educators had ever taught in these ways before, and consequently coaching expertise simply didn't exist. With a commitment of resources, it could be built, but this too took time as a critical sequencing constraint was structured into the process. The coaches have to have done this work themselves as teachers of the Common Core before they can support others. So the coaching role can be created immediately, but expert execution is several years out. In addition, an immense set of new instructional artifacts had to be designed, tested, and refined. Entirely new curricula and instructional resources needed to be developed that align with these standards. New sources of evidence, such as exemplary student work products, standardized assessments, and classroom observational protocols, needed to be created to inform continuous improvement. While everyone might start to work with these new resources, ultimately the biggest improvements would be expected to flow from the base up: first strengthening preprimary and primary education, then building on this stronger base to deepen students' middle school experiences, which in turn sets the stage for students engaging in much richer intellectual work in high schools. Clearly, a very long time lag exists before the full consequences of such a district transformation can be seen.

Realistically, pulling all of this together is more than a decade's work. Many separate programmatic pieces have to be developed, tried out, and refined. All of these separate pieces have to be integrated together and must join well with other, extant school district processes. Surely some of the latter would likely be redundant or, worse yet, send conflicting signals about what is valued. But then, identifying and removing them from a school system is typically not straightforward either. And all along the way, these efforts remain subject in one form or another to democratic political control, which can slow the process and possibly derail it.

In sum, an extensive improvement infrastructure needs to be built, and building it just takes time. This observation is equally true about redeveloping an airport or transforming our nation's public schools. And just like the O'Hare project, one has to keep the existing system running while its workings are being fundamentally transformed. By the way, that O'Hare Airport renovation that was supposed to take twelve years actually took closer to twenty and included huge cost overruns, and then, the city announced the airport's next major improvement project.

So why have we come to think that districts could accomplish major changes in their core work in just a fraction of the time needed to add another runway and terminal at Chicago's airport? Why are we so patient about one and so frustrated by the other? To the point, more forthright discussions are needed about the temporal dynamics of school district change efforts and how one might more appropriately evaluate their unfolding. Systems transformation cannot be captured fully ahead of time in a strategic plan; rather, it has a substantial evolutionary character to it. Issues arise in the course of doing the work: setbacks occur, and new problems become visible that simply weren't seen at the outset. All of these are common in complex construction efforts like the O'Hare project. Not surprisingly, they are part of the life of district transformation too.

Key Roles Played by Core Civic Institutions

Throughout this volume we have focused on the key roles played by select civic institutions in the reform of Chicago's schools. Several of these institutions took innovative turns that proved central to how reform played out. Embedded here too are important lessons for others.

Private Philanthropy.   Foundations investments played a major role in catalyzing and sustaining school reform in Chicago. While different organizations and individuals in this sector established different particular priorities, they also operated as a community investing together in developing and sustaining a broad base of external organizations focused on school improvement. As conditions afforded it, they advanced partnerships between the system, various external organizations, and their own staff. They stayed focused on core systems improvement issues and did not pivot wildly every three to six years, as many foundations are accustomed to doing. Nor for the most part did they use their resources to press controversial and untested initiatives. By funding broadly, and not creating just a few winners and many losers, they afforded reasons for all involved to stay at the table. Consequently, the foundation community was able to function as a lubricant for organizations in the exoskeleton to work cooperatively with each other and with the central office. In these ways, they were able to hold and maintain a broadly respected civic position. Given current criticism about possible undue influence surrounding the uses of private monies in the public sphere, Chicago offers a strong example of the productive role that private philanthropy can play in advancing the public good.

Universities and the Public Schools.   The relationship between public schools and universities has been a problematic space since schools of education opened.[10] Beginning in the 1980s, John Goodlad and colleagues advanced the idea of school-university partnerships to improve the preparation of new teachers. This effort gave rise to a movement to create professional development schools.[11] While the analogy to medical teaching hospitals was frequently used in these conversations, the depth of institutional transformation that this concept would have required, had it been taken seriously, did not occur. Most partnerships were narrowly conceived, did not deeply engage the core problems of school reform, nor struggled to reframe the boundaries between public schools and universities.[12] Nevertheless, they did contribute a compelling idea: the potential for revitalizing schools through collaborative problem-solving efforts between academics and practitioners.

This is another instance where two decades later Chicago offers a proof point. Our account has highlighted the extensive contributions that developed from the involvements by faculty and staff at both the University of Chicago and University of Illinois at Chicago with CPS practitioners. On the professional education side, the reforms at UIC engaged Goodlad's original aspiration to strengthen teacher preparation so that new teachers were more likely to succeed in challenging urban schools. This work eventually expanded to include the preparation of school-based leaders. The sustained partnership and direct funding for new principal preparation, from both the CPS and the Fund, also concretize the depth of the interinstitutional support commitments that Goodlad sought. On the applied research side, we have highlighted the distinctive contributions made by the Center, the Consortium, and the Network for College Success at UChicago. NCS and the Center offer rich examples of codesign efforts involving researchers and school-based educators attacking important school-based problems along the lines of what is now called design-based implementation research.[13] The activities carried out in partnership between the Consortium and CPS informed subsequent district actions while also advancing a new model for how applied research engages the public and, in so doing, reconceives its relationship to civic life.

The combination of these varied domains of work—of stimulating innovation, improving professional preparation and development, and research informing reform—depicts what a school of education committed to the improvement of public education should look like in its teaching, research, and community engagement.

Central to each of these efforts was the concept of partnership. This term has been picked up rapidly in education, but like many new ideas in this field, it can have the character of putting new labels on old bottles of wine. For this reason, the extensive descriptions included in this book bring specificity and detail into how this concept was vitalized in Chicago. At the center of each partnership was one or more specific problems of practice and a shared aim to actually getting better at solving them. A partnership, with this as its primary purpose, grounds a different kind of collective thinking and action. It is the difference, for example, in the professional development space, between a university-based professional education program that aligns its course of study with the highest standards of the field, and one that also embraces ownership for the success of its candidates in its partnering district(s). We saw in the UIC story how it, the Fund, and the district jointly owned the success of the principals prepared to lead CPS schools and engaged in continuous improvement toward this end. Likewise, in the preparation of teachers, UIC and CPS jointly owned the classroom success of novice teachers and their continuing careers in some of the district's most challenging schools.

Similar features were manifest in the vignettes about the Center and NCS. These applied research initiatives weren't primarily about testing or deploying some favored theory, applying some new research methods, or gaining an opportunity to access administrative data stores, although all of that and more did happen. These partnerships evolved a new way of being in action together. University partners did not judge themselves primarily by the academic papers published, and the district didn't see the primary value of these activities as the next new initiative to tout. Instead, working together, they focused on the ultimate concern—improving the lives and learning of their students and the public school educators who work with them. This shared sense of value is what moved their work beyond the particulars that may initially have brought participants together, and into the collective action needed to actually solve a problem. In short, these partnerships were about *problem solving*; participants lived a belief that if they actually stayed the course long enough, they would accomplish something of value together. Absent this centering, productive work can occur at the partnership boundary between universities and the schools, but the traditional distinct and separate identities of the participants remain unchallenged.

Correspondingly, different relational understandings anchor partnership of this sort. Again, as noted in the UIC story, the university came to see the district, rather than the tuition-paying students, as its client. In a reciprocal fashion, the district encouraged candidates for such advanced training and sustained financial support for these arrangements so that a strong program remained viable despite the ebbs and flows in budgets year to year. Taking on these new responsibilities and the corresponding relational reframing is central to a genuine partnership and distinguishes it from a more conventional contract for services. In Chicago each party had a vested interest in the long-term well-being of the other.

When leaders stepped up in these different organizations, a new form of social contract, akin to a trust agreement, emerged among them. Each needed and respected what the other brought to the table and learned about the constraints under which the other worked. Broadly speaking, each was vulnerable in different ways to the other. For CPS leaders, there was the worry that they might be blindsided and constantly called out for failures. On the university side, researchers were anxious: Would their access to data and schools be blocked; could they count on supportive administrative action and in some cases direct operational support? While much can be detailed in a contract, these very basic human and relational concerns demand consistent integrity in action—the heart of a trust agreement between parties. It is this attention to first principles—why we are here, why we work together—that maintains efforts through the inevitable challenges that arise given the contested political space that is public education.

Media: A Challenge of Informing Reform

Media played a complicated role in engaging the public around efforts to improve Chicago's schools.[14] Acting as a watchdog over societal institutions, Chicago's media frequently brought troublesome issues to public attention. This was true of the *Tribune* series that galvanized reform in the 1980s and in their reporting on the weak college success of CPS students in the early 2000s. Likewise in 2001, a *Sun-Times* exposé on the prevalence of teachers failing basic skill tests highlighted serious weaknesses in the academic preparation of faculty in some Chicago schools. Such efforts are highly consistent with the basic training for journalists and journalistic reward systems. Their social role is to hold institutions accountable, and naturally they focus their attention on instances of failure, corruption, and malfeasance. Correspondingly, they hold a well-honed sense of distrust for accounts offered by institutional leaders, recognizing that they are self-protective regarding the organizations they lead. This is true regardless of who the leaders happen to be; it is simply about the social role these leaders hold and the expectancies that their attendant role power creates in others.

But when this is all that people read and hear about, it fuels a pessimism about our actual ability to improve our public institutions. Chicago's reform was a complex and difficult story to capture. There was not a "silver bullet" solution, nor was there a charismatic superintendent who just fixed things. These are the easy stories that media tends to gravitate toward in terms of the success accounts that they do report. Legacy media, and this is equally true for much of its modern social media counterpart, is just not well designed institutionally to engage the complexity of systems transformation, given its evolutionary character and long timeframe.

In her monograph *Districts That Succeed*, Karin Chenoweth recounted what happened when Sean Reardon presented the findings discussed in the introduction at a conference of education writers. One Chicago reporter listened and then simply said, "We don't believe it."[15] Given all the many stresses that the school system had been under by 2015 when the conference took place—a major teacher strike, multiple episodes of CEO churn and malfeasance, school closings, and fights with the state over continued underfunding—Reardon's results made no sense to the reporter. This exchange visibly illustrates the public's difficulty comprehending the developmental character of systems change and the difficulty it poses for the media that seeks to inform it. Discrete initiatives that have temporally immediate and direct effects—we introduced "x" this year and "y" improvements occurred by the end of the year—are relatively easy to digest and report. But again, district improvement efforts are not like this; typically they are a complex and very long game. We saw, for example, in chapter 4 how the Consortium's longitudinal analyses of the progress of English learners in Chicago, tracking them from 2008 forward for some ten years, challenged a long-standing and inaccurate account about the system's success educating them. As for the Reardon findings, this research documented large learning gains for students educated in CPS between 2009 and 2014. The Reardon team, however, made no causal claim as to *how* or, equally important, *when* these improvements actually occurred. These interpretations were left to others, and this is where the challenge of informing the public arises. The genesis of the strong elementary school learning gains reported by Reardon likely developed out of the vast array of efforts, documented in this book, that occurred in Era 3 to improve the system's human capital and the quality of teaching and learning in its classrooms. A key fact supporting this explanation is that the enlarged learning gains reported by Reardon were present as early as 2010 and remained stable over the next five years.[16] Recall from the introduction that in 2001, average learning rates in Chicago were approximately one year of learning for a year of instruction. By 2010 these numbers had risen to 1.2 years of learning per year. This means that the enhanced learning gains had emerged over the course of Era 3 but were not added to during Era 4. And actually, maintaining stability, rather than decline, amid all of the upset in CPS from 2010 through 2015 might well be seen as an accomplishment unto itself. So, the reporter had good reasons to doubt, but her analysis was flawed. The results were real, and the reporter's assumptions about causal mechanisms and timing were misspecified.

In short, skillfully crafted, descriptively rich and balanced accounts of progress are not media's strong point. This work requires an institution specifically designed, organized, and supported to carry out such studies and to engage the community around understanding both the findings and their implications for continuing efforts to improve. This is where the combination of the Consortium and *Catalyst* added great value to the public problem-solving space in Chicago.

An unresolved challenge for Chicago is how it sustains this important public function going forward. Local philanthropy supported the development of both organizations for extended periods of time. Then, when core support atrophied, *Catalyst* left the scene. Fortunately, individual civic actors recognized the public value served by the Consortium, and a new enterprise emerged to provide some continued core support. Keeping this function vital, however, remains an ongoing concern. Given its distinctive public role, the Consortium cannot be primarily supported and governed by the same institution that it studies—the Chicago Public Schools. It also needs assurance of free and unencumbered access to student-level and system data and permission to engage field studies. Counterbalancing this, this activity cannot be the sole purview of academic researchers who live in the world of technical analysis and critique, but who may have little or no connection to the actual work of doing improvement. Its investigators must remain proximate to school communities and the concerns arising within them. They must remain open to the questions others want explored, concerns about how these questions will be explored, and possible alternative explanations of findings that merit consideration. To accomplish this, the enterprise needs a public engagement and accountability mechanism along the lines deployed by the Consortium throughout most of its history.

Absent an institution enlivening this distinctive mission, efforts would devolve into something more conventional: a congeries of separate projects each separately funded and dependent on district approval. Good work initiated by different individual researchers could still happen on discrete aspects of reform, but the public-informing role would inevitably atrophy, and the researchers' relationship to the district would likely return to a more conventional "advisor to the prince" role. In addition, no one would hold responsibility for trying to make sense of the complex "whole" of district transformation, make its core elements visible, and articulate the interconnections among them. This would be a great loss.

CHICAGO'S WORK IS NOT DONE: THE SCHOOL COMMUNITIES LEFT BEHIND BY REFORM

We began this book with a quick introduction to a vast body of evidence that major improvements in student outcomes occurred in the Chicago Public Schools over the last thirty years. Our account aimed to explain how this district went from "worst in America" to one of the best at getting better. Moreover, these improved outcomes accrued in a district that continues to serve students primarily from low-income families of color. Much has been accomplished, but as is also generally true of improvement efforts, success also helps to illumine the next challenge.

As early as 1997, Consortium data identified a subset of communities on the south and west sides of the city where no improvement in student learning rates had been seen. (See figure 5.4.) These elementary school communities were described as stagnating; they did not improve in Era 1 as Chicago embraced local community control, nor did they get better under centrally directed interventions in Era 2. Twenty years later, schools in many of these same communities continue to struggle. (See figure 5.5.)

Figure 5.4   Location of stagnating elementary schools: what it looked like in 1997

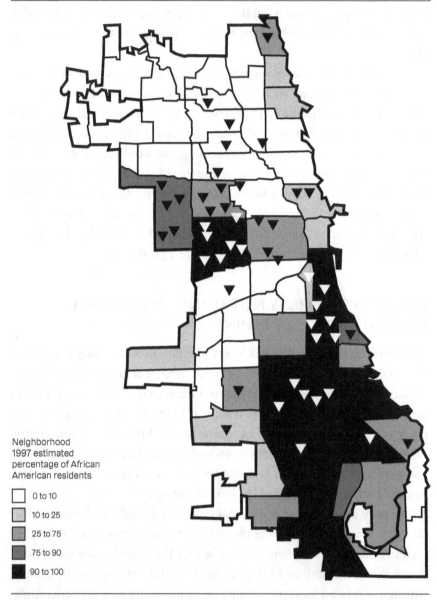

Neighborhood
1997 estimated
percentage of African
American residents

☐ 0 to 10
◻ 10 to 25
▨ 25 to 75
▩ 75 to 90
■ 90 to 100

Source: Bryk et al., *Organizing Schools for Improvement,* 161.

Note: Stagnating schools had flat or declining trends in their learning rates.

Figure 5.5 Location of elementary schools that received long-term intensive district support: what it looked like in 2017

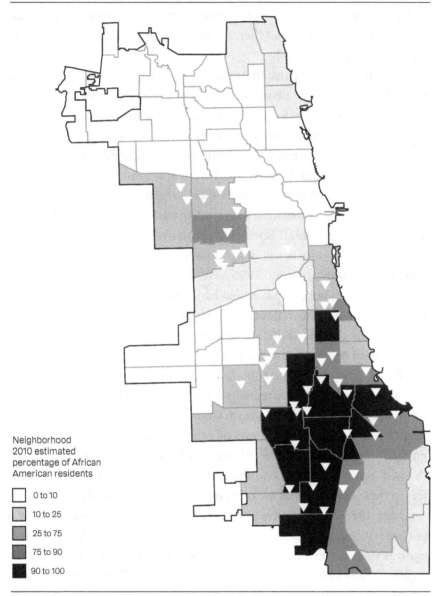

Neighborhood
2010 estimated
percentage of African
American residents

- 0 to 10
- 10 to 25
- 25 to 75
- 75 to 90
- 90 to 100

Source: New Schools Chicago, *Who Is Sitting in Those Seats?* (Chicago: New Schools Chicago 2017), 40–42.

Note: These schools were classified as on probation and receiving intense support for ten or more years.

These schools have been on "intensive district support" for ten or more years, and have been targeted for every conceivable intervention—restructuring, reconstitution, restaffing, closure, and reopening. Nevertheless, they continue to fail their communities. Clearly, this is a problem that Chicago has yet to solve.

On balance, the expansion of choice initiatives during Era 3 allowed many families in these neighborhoods to choose other schools, and this improved opportunities for some, especially at the high school level.[17] Even so, relying primarily on choice initiatives also bankrupted these neighborhoods of a critical community institution—their local elementary schools. To be clear, the schools that closed were academically very weak and chronically so. Even in the worst of these schools, however, some educators maintained relationships with students and their families that were highly meaningful to all involved.[18] Moreover, there were histories to these relationships—older siblings had attended the school and often parents had too. In these most basic ways, the schools were valued in their respective communities—places that had been ravaged over the decades by disinvestment, deindustrialization, and neglect. Not surprisingly, their residents saw the closings of their schools, and the breaking of these relational bonds, as just one more instance in a long history of systemic racism.[19]

How to create strong neighborhood schools, as anchors in the rebuilding of these communities, remains a major civic problem for Chicago to solve. In truth, the problem is much larger than just schools, as it interconnects with dysfunction in a web of other public institutions, including public safety, community health, and social services. All of these affect the well-being of families and their efforts to raise their children. Educators in these communities are often overwhelmed by how this larger environment affects all who live and work there.[20] Taken together this is a public service system that reproduces failure over and over. When one recognizes this, as was the case in the mobilizing for school reform in Chicago in the late 1980s, the answer is not just adding still more new programs into this dysfunctional system. The larger system itself must become the target for change.

To truly take this on, a city needs to take a step back to engage students, parents, and leaders in these communities about the challenges affecting them and their children. Beginning these conversations, and hearing these voices, is the root action for genuine improvement efforts. In addition, these efforts also demand a critical perspective as to how long-standing and complex these problems truly are. In such circumstances, improvement science cautions humility. This is a learning-to-improve challenge on a vast scale, arguably even larger than the scale of the problem that Chicago took on when it passed reform legislation thirty years ago. Given the scope of the problem, and its resistance to change, it pushes back toward the most basic improvement stance: can it actually be solved somewhere, in just one school community; then can it be solved in a handful of places; and then, based on what has been learned, it might be possible to solve in many more places. As noted earlier, there is a developmental arc to improvement, and it is generally impossible to get to the end except through enduring the improvement journey.

This challenge is by no means peculiar to Chicago. Neighborhoods like these are common across other major urban centers, and a vast array of initiatives have been directed nationally to similar schools with similar non-results. To Chicago's credit, the city and its school leaders see the problem. The city has good analytic capacity that could help everyone involved to better understand it and inform future efforts to improve. Chicago has also built a strong civic architecture to both continue the press for such change and grow the capabilities needed to make it happen. Thirty years ago Chicagoans joined together, did the work, and got something done. That process needs to capture the city's will and skill again.

CLOSING

Over the course of thirty years, a reimagined central office and Board of Education emerged in Chicago and transformed how teachers teach and how students learn. As Era 4 closed, the district was poised to push further still. The leadership learning that Janice Jackson brought into the district, when she was appointed CEO in 2017, positioned it to work at a new level. She also confronted extraordinary challenges, however: some lingering from the school closings, and some that had been festering for decades. And then there were the sudden and unprecedented demands of navigating a school system through a pandemic, and a renewed attention to the institutional racism that gripped Chicago and the nation. By the time we finished this book, Jackson and her team had stepped down, the Illinois legislature had changed CPS governance again, labor-management conflicts were bitter and pervasive, and renewed financial concerns were on the horizon.

Like districts across the country, Chicago now confronts still more extraordinary challenges: addressing the pandemic-induced trauma and learning loss among tens of thousands of students; and simultaneously, responding to a growing press to seize this moment as an opportunity to upend traditional notions of schooling and reinvent it entirely. And do all this, while not losing sight of the need to dramatically improve the school communities that still remain left behind. The city has proven resilient in the past; it is being tested again. The broad-based civic engagement, coupled with a shared orientation toward improvement learning, that mobilized, supported, and sustained the long work of reform in Chicago in the recent past is needed now—perhaps more than ever.

In closing, we return to a comment offered by Warren Chapman in chapter 1. He reflected that Chicago "chose a good path [when its] collective us stepped up for its poor, Black and brown children." At almost every juncture, Chicago's collective us sustained its commitment to keep learning how to get better. The road has zigged, zagged, detoured, taken some terrible turns, but it continues. By 2017, the CPS was a system of schools rather than a failed bureaucracy. This was unprecedented progress, and light-years from where it was thirty years before. Chicago should be proud of what has been done even as it recognizes that the CPS continues to fail some of the children and neighborhoods most dependent on it. This too is the character of genuine improvement: initial successes shed light on what is next, and the challenge to do better renews.

Appendix A

Study Contributors

The work of over ninety individuals is told through the pages of this book. Many gave generously of their time as participants in one or more of the multiple convenings that we organized to launch this project, informed its efforts along the way, and read and critiqued an early draft of the manuscript. A substantial number also sat for interviews typically lasting from sixty to ninety minutes. We aimed as authors to bring their diverse voices to bear in the crafting of this account, although we alone are responsible for the interpretations offered here. The individuals enumerated in chapter 5 as boundary spanners and board linkers are also listed below.

	Interviewee	Convening participant	Boundary spanner	Board linker
Elaine Allensworth	x	x		
Heather Anichini	x	x	x	x
John Ayers	x	x	x	
Carlos Azcoitia		x	x	x
Stephanie Banchero		x	x	
Cynthia Barron		x		
Albert Bennett			x	x
Al Bertani		x	x	x

	Interviewee	Convening participant	Boundary spanner	Board linker
Larry Braskamp			x	
Anthony Bryk		x	x	x
Warren Chapman	x	x	x	x
Sherly Chavarria		x		
Lynn Cherkafsky-Davis		x		
Vicki Chou	x	x		x
Greg Darneider	x	x		
Marisa de la Torre	x			
Miguel del Valle	x		x	x
Tracy Dell'Angela		x	x	x
Suzanne Doornbos Kerbow	x	x		
Arne Duncan	x			
Sarah Duncan		x	x	x
Barbara Eason-Watkins	x	x	x	x
John Easton	x	x	x	x
Shayne Evans		x		
Camille Farrington			x	
Don Feinstein		x		
Lorraine Forte	x			
Marty Gartzman	x	x	x	
Pat Graham	x	x		
Sharon Greenberg		x	x	
Anne Hallett		x	x	x
Martha Hebert		x		
Fred Hess			x	
Zipporah Hightower		x		
Mahalia Hines			x	
Janice Jackson	x	x	x	
Ascensión Juarez	x	x	x	
Kylie Klein	x			
Yolanda Knight	x			
Tim Knowles		x	x	x
Janet Knupp				x
Martin "Mike" Koldyke	x		x	x

	Interviewee	Convening participant	Boundary spanner	Board linker
John Kotsakis				x
Emily Krone Phillips		x	x	x
Michael Lach			x	x
Carol Lee			x	x
Charles "Chuck" Lewis				x
Jim Lewis			x	x
Karen Lewis			x	x
Rachel Lindsay	x			x
Phyllis Lockett	x	x		x
Gudelia Lopez	x	x	x	
George Lowery			x	
Debbie Lynch	x		x	x
Matt Lyons			x	
Peter Martinez	x	x	x	x
Terry Mazany		x	x	
Dea Meyer				x
Shazia Miller			x	x
Don Moore			x	x
Peggy Mueller	x		x	
Jenny Nagaoka	x	x		
Matt Niksch	x			
Charles Payne	x	x	x	x
Paige Ponder	x		x	x
Sylvia Puente		x	x	x
Barbara Radner		x	x	
Greg Richmond		x		
Melissa Roderick	x	x	x	x
Ken Rolling			x	x
Amy Rome	x	x	x	x
Jesse Ruiz		x	x	
Albert Sanchez	x			
Lauren Sartain	x			
Penny Sebring		x	x	x
Tim Shanahan			x	x

	Interviewee	Convening participant	Boundary spanner	Board linker
Jesse Sharkey	x		x	x
Barbara Sizemore			x	x
Nancy Slavin	x			
Aneesh Sohoni		x		
Sara Spurlark			x	x
Robin Steans		x	x	x
Elizabeth "Beth" Swanson	x		x	x
Steven E. Tozer		x	x	x
James Troupis		x		
Beverly Tunney			x	x
Arie van der Ploeg		x	x	x
Andy Wade		x		
Alicia Winkler	x		x	
Josie Yanguas	x	x	x	x
Paul Zavitkovsky	x	x	x	x

Appendix B

Data on Boundary Spanner and Board Service

The individuals numbered 1 through 52 are the boundary spanners included in figure 5.2. Individuals 53–66 are linkers who are included along with the boundary spanners in figure 5.3.

Out of this group of sixty-six, no relevant board service information was reported or could be found for fourteen individuals; therefore, they are not included in figure 5.3. We have limited our enumeration of board connections to those organizations directly influencing school reform in Chicago. Many of the listed individuals were active in other organizations as well. Service on the Consortium steering committee and the *Catalyst* editorial board is included in these data.

The **Boundary Spanner data** for figure 5.2 is organized as a historical flow for each individual as that person moved across institutional domains over time. An institutional domain may appear more than once in an individual's work history, as numerous individuals moved back and forth.

The *Board service data* for figure 5.3 is presented as ego-centric for each actor. The first number is the individual's principal institutional affiliation during Chicago reform. Subsequent numbers are the other institutions that they connected into. Since many of these individuals occupied multiple roles in different organizations, their principal affiliation is designated by their longest work tenure.

The data streams highlighted below in bold are for the **Boundary Spanners** included in figure 5.2. The data streams highlighted in italics are for *Board Service* displayed in figure 5.3.

Name Data streams	Organizations
1. Heather Anichini **5,3,2,5,8**	2001–2007 Consultant for Umoja Student Development Corporation 2002–2006 Chicago Public Schools (teacher and central office) 2006–2012 Teach For America (national team) 2012– The Chicago Public Education Fund
8,3,5,7	*Board Service* *Lighthouse Academies Charter School Board; Umoja Board of Directors; Teach For America Chicago/Northwest Indiana Advisory Board; Commercial Club, Economic Club; The Chicago Network*

2. Carlos Azcoitia
 	
3,2,3,11,2,1
	1989–1995 Chicago Public Schools (principal K–8)
	1995–1996 Chicago Public Schools (assistant superintendent)
	1996–1997 Chicago Public Schools (director of community
	            relations)
	1997–2003 Chicago Public Schools (deputy chief of education)
	2003–2007 Chicago Public Schools (principal preK–12)
	2007–2017 National Louis University (distinguished professor of
	            practice)
	2012–2013 Chicago Public Schools (network chief)
	2013–2016 Chicago Public Schools (school board member)
	2017– Mentor GEM (Great Expectations Mentoring)

2,10,11,3,5,1	*Editorial board, Catalyst Chicago* *Board Service* *Coalition of Community Schools, Steering Committee member; trustee, Northeastern Illinois University; Chicago HS for the Arts (ChiArts); Governor's Task Force on Educational Accountability; Teach For America, Steering Committee member; Illinois State Board of Education, Bias Review Committee; Challenge; Advisory Board, Collaborative for Academic, Social and Emotional Learning; Advisory Board, City Year Chicago; founding member, Latinos United for Priorities in Education (LUPE) Support Undocumented Students; member, Chicago Public Schools Budget Equity Task Force; School and Community Initiatives, Evaluation Committee*

Name Data streams	Organizations
3. John Ayers **7,3,7** *7,9,10*	1987–2005 Leadership for Quality Education 1990–1992 Chicago Public Schools (local school council, 　　　　　　community member) *Steering committee, UChicago Consortium on School Research* *Editorial board, Catalyst Chicago*
4. Stephanie Banchero **10,8**	1997–2010 *Chicago Tribune* (education reporter) 2010–2014 *Wall Street Journal* (national education reporter) 2014–　　　Joyce Foundation (Education and Economic Mobility 　　　　　　Program director)
5. Albert Bennett **2,8,11** *11,9,10*	1985–1988 Chicago Public Schools (central office) 1988–1991 Chicago Community Trust 1991–　　　Roosevelt University *Director, UChicago Consortium on School Researchh* *Editorial board, Catalyst Chicago*
6. Al Bertani **11,6,2,11,7** *11,9,7,2*	1990–1998 Center for School Improvement, UChicago 1998–2001 Chicago Principals and Administrators 　　　　　　Association 2001–2005 Visiting Faculty, New Leaders for New Schools 2002–2005 Chicago Public Schools (central office) 2005–2009 University of Illinois Chicago 2005–2017 Urban Education Institute, UChicago 　　　　　　(senior advisor) 2015–2017 LEAP Innovations *Board Service* *Advisor, UChicago Consortium on School Research; Principal* *Assessment Center Advisory Committee, Civic Committee; Advisory* *Group, Re-Engineering Project, Chicago Public Schools; Human* *Resources Advisory Committee, Chicago Public Schools; UChicago* *Impact*
53. Larry Braskamp *11,9*	1989–1995 University of Illinois Chicago (dean) *Steering committee, UChicago Consortium on School Research*
7. Anthony Bryk **11,9,2,11** *11,8*	1989–2004 University of Chicago (cofounder, Center for School 　　　　　　Improvement) 1991–2004 University of Chicago (cofounder, Consortium on 　　　　　　Chicago School Research) 1993–1994 Chicago Public Schools (on loan to central office) *Board Service* *The Chicago Public Education Fund Advisory Board*

Name Data streams	Organizations

8. Warren Chapman
 	
1,11,8,7,11,5
	1986–1992 Illinois State Board of Education
	1986–2002 University of Illinois at Urbana/Champaign
	1992–2002 Joyce Foundation (Lead Education Program
	  officer)
	2002–2004 BankOne Foundation (BankOne vice president)
	2004–2006 JP Morgan Chase (vice president of corporate
	  philanthropy)
	2006–2012 University of Illinois at Chicago (vice chancellor,
	  external affairs)
	2012–2014 Columbia College Chicago (senior vice president)
	2014–2016 Chicago Lighthouse (vice president of advancement)

8,7,10,9,4,11,3	*UChicago Consortium steering committee* *Editorial board, Catalyst Chicago* *Board Service* *Chicago Donors Forum; Funders Committee; Chicago Annenberg* *Challenge; Executive Committee, Grant Makers for Education;* *member, Business Roundtable; Board of Directors, Community* *Renewal Society; Advisory Board, Herr Research Center for Children* *and Social Policy, Erickson Institute; Board of Directors,* *Noble Street Charter Schools; Board of Directors, ChiArts* *High School*
54. Vicki Chou *11,9,2,8,7,1,3*	1996–2013 University of Illinois Chicago (dean, College of Education) *Steering committee, UChicago Consortium on School Research* *Board Service* *Advance Illinois, NCTQ Teacher Preparation Program Evaluation* *Advisory Council; Chicago Annenberg Challenge; Chicago School* *Leadership Cooperative; Chicago Metropolis 2020, Chicago Public* *Education Fund, Leadership Council* **Chicago Public Schools** *(multiple CPS advisory groups)* *City Colleges of Chicago, Academic Advisory Council; Civic Commit-* *tee of the Commercial Club of Chicago, Teacher Task Force;* *Committee on Inter-institutional Cooperation (CIC); Council of* *Chicago Area Deans of Education (CCADE), member, chair, and* *cochair; Illinois Association of Deans of Public Colleges of Education;* *Illinois Mathematics and Science Academy, Board of Trustees; Illinois* *P-20 Council, Subcommittee on Teacher Effectiveness; Museum of* *Science and Industry, President's Council Education Committee;* *North Lawndale College Preparatory High School; University of* *Illinois P-16 Task Force Initiative*

Name Data streams	Organizations
9. Miguel del Valle **3,1**	1980–1986 Association House (executive director) 1987–2006 Member of the Illinois Senate 2006–2011 City Clerk of Chicago 2019– Chicago Public Schools (president, Board of Education)
1,4,3	*Board Service* *Advance Illinois; chairman, ISBE PreK-20 Council; Josephinium High Schools; Latino Institute; Spanish Coalition for Housing; Federation for Community Schools; Illinois Students Assistance Commission; Advisory Council on Latino Affairs*
10. Tracy Dell'Angela **10,11,8,5**	1995–2007 *Chicago Tribune* 2007–2009 UChicago Consortium on School Research 2011–2013 The Chicago Public Education Fund 2013–2014 100Kin10 Urban Education Institute—UChicago 2014–2016 Education Post 2017–2021 LEAP Innovations
10,3	*Board Service* *2011–2013 Board Member, Garfield Park Preparatory Academy*
11. Sarah Duncan **8,11**	1991–2004 Ariel Education Initiative 2004–2006 UChicago Crown Family School of Social Work, Policy, and Practice 2006– UChicago Crown Family School of Social Work, Policy, and Practice Community Schools and Network for College Success
11,3,8	*Board Service* *Ariel Education Initiative, local school council member; McDougal Family Foundation; Young Women's Leadership Charter School*
12. Barbara Eason-Watkins **3,11,2**	1985–2001 Chicago Public Schools (principal) 2000–2001 Center for School Improvement, University of Chicago (partner school) 2001–2010 Chicago Public Schools (chief education officer) *Steering committee, UChicago Consortium on School Research* *Editorial board, Catalyst Chicago*
2,9,10,8	*Board Service* *The Chicago Public Education Fund; Principal Advisory Board, UChicago Consortium on School Research*

Name Data streams	Organizations
13. John Easton **2,4,2,9,2,9,8**	1984–1989 Chicago Public Schools (central office) 1989–1994 Chicago Panel on Public Policy (director of research) 1994–1997 Chicago Public Schools (central office) 1997–2002 UChicago Consortium on School Research (deputy director) 2001–2002 Chicago Public Schools (on loan to central office) 2002–2009 UChicago Consortium on School Research (executive director) 2009–2014 Institute of Education Sciences—USDOE (director) 2014–2018 The Spencer Foundation (distinguished senior fellow)
9,10,2,1	*Director, UChicago Consortium on School Research* *Steering committee, UChicago Consortium on School Research* *Editorial board, Catalyst Chicago* *Board Service* *SQRP Advisory Board, Chicago Public Schools; Illinois Economic Security Advisory Board; Illinois Workforce and Education Research Collaborative*
14. Camille Farrington **3,11,9**	2000–2006 Young Women's Leadership Charter School, Chicago Public Schools 2010–2015 University of Chicago School of Social Service Administration 2015–2017 UChicago Consortium on School Research
15. Marty Gartzman **3,11,3,2,11**	1977–1986 Chicago Public Schools (teacher) 1986–2002 University of Illinois Chicago 1990–1992 Local School Council Member (community) 2002–2006 Chicago Public Schools (central office) 2006–2010 University of Illinois Chicago 2011–2016 UChicago STEM Education
16. Sharon Greenberg **3,11**	1977–1984 Chicago Public Schools (teacher) 1988–2004 University of Chicago, Center for School Improvement (cofounder)

Name Data streams	Organizations

17. Anne Hallett
 	
4,8,5
	1982–1983 Chicago Panel on School Policy
	1986–1995 Wieboldt Foundation
	1993–2003 Cross City Campaign for Urban School
	         Reform
	1995–2000 Chicago Annenberg Challenge, Chicago School
	         Reform Collaborative
	2004–2005 Consultant: Education, Community,
	         Philanthropy
	2005–2014 Grow Your Own Illinois
	
	Steering committee, UChicago Consortium on School Research
	Editorial board, Catalyst Chicago

8,9,10,4	*Board Service* *Citywide Coalition for School Reform; Algebra Project; Community Organizing and Family Issues; Chicago Public Education Fund Leadership Council*
18. Mahalia Hines **3,2,1**	1969–1983 Chicago Public Schools (teacher) 1983–2000 Chicago Public Schools (principal) 2001–2009 Chicago Public Schools (central office) 2011–2017 Chicago Public Schools (school board member)
19. Fred Hess **4,11** *4,9,11*	1983–1996 Chicago Panel on School Policy 1996–2006 Northwestern University *Steering committee, UChicago Consortium on School Research*

20. Janice Jackson
 	
3,2
	1982–1995 Chicago Public Schools (student)
	1995–1999 Chicago State University (student)
	1999–2004 Chicago Public Schools (teacher)
	2004–2014 Chicago Public Schools (principal)
	2014–2015 Chicago Public Schools (central office network
	         chief)
	2015–2017 Chicago Public Schools (chief education
	         officer)
	2017–2021 Chicago Public Schools (chief executive
	         officer)

Name Data streams	Organizations
21. Ascención Juarez **2,3,2**	1985–1987 Chicago Public Schools (central office) 1988–1991 Chicago Public Schools (principal) 1992–1994 Chicago Public Schools (central office) 1994–2010 Chicago Public Schools (central office, chief of human resources)
55. Tim Knowles *11,7,1,9*	2003–2008 University of Chicago (director, Center for Urban School Improvement) 2008–2015 University of Chicago (director, Urban Education Institute) 2015–2017 University of Chicago (director, Pritzker Urban Labs) *Steering committee, UChicago Consortium on School Research* *Board Service* *New Schools for Chicago; Illinois Education Policy Steering Commit-* *tee; The Renaissance Fund; Urban Teacher Residencies United;* *Advance Illinois; UChicago Impact; Chicago Beyond; Chicago Public* *Education Fund; After School Matters; A Better Chicago; Chicago* *Science Works*
22. Martin "Mike" Koldyke **8,1,5** *7,1,8,11,5*	1985– Golden Apple Foundation for Excellence in Teaching (founder) 1992–2010 School Finance Authority, Chicago Public Schools (chairperson) 2001– Academy for Urban School Leadership (founder) *Board Service* *Golden Apple Foundation Board; Academy for Urban School* *Leadership Board; Commercial Club of Chicago; Civic Committee;* *The Economic Club of Chicago; After School Matters Board; The* *Chicago Public Education Fund; Chicago Community Trust; Big* *Shoulders Fund; lifetime trustee, Northwestern University*
56. John Kotsakis *6,9*	1988–2000 Chicago Teachers Union (cofounder of the QUEST Center) *Steering committee, UChicago Consortium on School Research*
57. Janet Knupp *8,9,10,5*	1994–1999 Communities in Schools (executive director) 1999–2011 The Chicago Public Education Fund (founding president and CEO) *UChicago Consortium steering committee* *Editorial board, Catalyst Chicago* *Board Service* *Golden Apple Foundation; Teach For America*

Name Data streams	Organizations
23. Emily Krone Phillips **10,11,8**	2005–2009 *Daily Herald* (education reporter) 2009–2015 UChicago Consortium on School Research 2016–2018 Spencer Foundation grantee (authored *Make or Break Year*) 2018–2019 The Spencer Foundation (communications director)
9,10	*Director, UChicago Consortium on School Research* *Editorial board, Catalyst Chicago*
24. Michael Lach **11,2,11**	2000–2001 Northwestern University (lead curriculum developer) 2006–2010 Chicago Public Schools (director of Math & Science and officer of High School Teaching & Learning) 2011–2019 University of Chicago (director of STEM and Strategic Initiatives)
11,10	*Editorial board, Catalyst Chicago*
25. Carol Lee **3,11,3,11**	1969– New Concept School, Institute of Positive Education 1989–1991 Center for School Improvement, UChicago 1991–2017 Northwestern University 1998– Betty Shabbazz Charter School (founder) 2005– Barbara A. Sizemore Academy (founder)
11,9,10	*Steering committee, UChicago Consortium on School Research* *Editorial board, Catalyst Chicago*
58. Charles "Chuck" Lewis 7,11,3,10,9	1997– Lewis-Sebring Family Foundation (chairman) *Board Service* *Commercial Club of Chicago; University of Chicago, trustee; UChicago Impact; UChicago Charter School; Museum of Science and Industry; Chicago Public Media*
26. Jim Lewis **4,11,8**	1990–1999 Chicago Urban League (vice president) 1999–2007 Roosevelt University (director, Institute for Metropolitan Affairs) 2002–2015 Chicago Community Trust (senior program officer and director of evaluation) 2016– University of Illinois Chicago (senior researcher)
4,9	*UChicago Consortium steering committee*
27. Karen Lewis **3,6**	1988–2010 Chicago Public Schools (substitute teacher and teacher) 2010–2014 Chicago Teachers Union (president)
6,9	*UChicago Consortium steering committee*

Name Data streams	Organizations
59. Rachel Lindsay *11,9,3*	1976–2006 Chicago State University (professor and dean) 2017– Chicago State University (interim president) *Steering committee, UChicago Consortium on School Research* <u>Board Service</u> Morgan Park Academy
60. Phyllis Lockett *7,8,5*	1998–2004 Civic Consulting Alliance (executive director) 2004–2014 New Schools for Chicago (president and chief executive officer) 2014– LEAP Innovations (chief executive officer) <u>Board Service</u> *The Chicago Network; The Economic Club of Chicago; Chicago Scholars Foundation; Future Founders; Civic Consulting Alliance*
28. Gudelia Lopez **2,11,2,8,11**	1976–1989 Chicago Public Schools (student) Summer 1994 Chicago Public Schools (central office) 1995–1998 UChicago Consortium on School Research 1998–2007 Chicago Public Schools (central office) 2007–2015 The Chicago Community Trust 2015–2016 UChicago Center for Elem. Mathematics and Science Education 2016–2017 Independent consultant
61. George Lowery *11,9*	1997–2006 Roosevelt University (dean of the College of Education) 2006–2016 Roosevelt University (faculty member) 2016–2022 Roosevelt University (professor emeritus) *UChicago Consortium steering committee*
29. Deborah Lynch **6,3,6,3,11** *6,9,1*	1992–1995 QUEST Center, Chicago Teachers Union (director) 1995–2001 Chicago Public Schools (teacher) 2001–2004 Chicago Teachers Union (president) 2004–2011 Chicago Public Schools (teacher) 2011–2017 Chicago State University (professor) *Steering committee, UChicago Consortium on School Research* <u>Board Service</u> *Executive Board Illinois Federation of Teachers and Chicago Federation of Labor; University Professionals of Illinois, CSU Chapter Executive Board*
30. Matt Lyons **2,8,2**	2009–2013 Chicago Public Schools (central office) 2014–2015 The Chicago Public Education Fund 2015–2021 Chicago Public Schools (central office)

Name Data streams	Organizations

31. Peter Martinez
 	
4,7,8,11
	1984–1991 Latino Institute
	1985–1991 Chicago United Civic Committee (cochair and
	                Latino Institute deacon)
	1991–2001 MacArthur Foundation
	2001–2002 Visiting Faculty, New Leaders for New
	                Schools
	2001–2015 University of Illinois Chicago

8,9,10,4,2,7,1	*Steering committee, UChicago Consortium on School Research* *Editorial board, Catalyst Chicago* *Board Service* *Multiple CPS advisory committees; Chicago United Civic* *Committee; Chicago Academy for School Leadership (CASL)* *Advisory Board; Chicago Principal Assessment Center; Illinois* *Consortium for Education Leadership; Governor's Commission* *for Teaching and America's Future; Donors Forum Grant Makers* *in Education*

32. Terry Mazany
 	
8,2
	2001–2011 Chicago Community Trust
	                (president)
	2010–2011 Chicago Public Schools (interim chief executive
	                officer)

62. Dea Meyer *7,10*	1994–2022 Civic Committee of the Commercial Club (executive vice president) *Editorial board, Catalyst Chicago*

33. Shazia Miller
 	
11,2,5,11
	1998–2003 UChicago Consortium on School Research (associate
	                director)
	2003–2005 Chicago Public Schools (central office)
	2005–2011 Learning Point Associates (director of
	                evaluation)
	2011–2017 American Institutes for Research (director of
	                evaluation and managing director)

5,9,10	*UChicago Consortium steering committee* *Editorial board, Catalyst Chicago*
34. Don Moore **3,4**	1970–1977 Chicago Public Schools, Metro High School (teacher) 1977–2012 Designs for Change (executive director)
4,10	*Steering committee, UChicago Consortium on School Research*
35. Peggy Mueller **3,8**	1990–1992 Chicago Public Schools (local school council member) 1994–1999 The Spencer Foundation 1999–2009 The Chicago Community Trust 2009– Independent consultant

Name Data streams	Organizations

36. Charles Payne
 	
11,3,2,11
	1985–1998 Northwestern University
	1990–1997 Institute for Policy Research (faculty affiliate)
	1998–2007 Duke University
	2007–2017 UChicago School of Social Service
	            Administration
	2007–2017 UChicago Consortium on School Research
	            (faculty affiliate)
	2007–2009 Carter G. Woodson Institute, Center for Urban
	            School Improvement
	2008–2009 Educational Research for Community Leaders
	            (lecture series)
	2009–2011 Woodlawn Children's Promise Community
	Feb.–May 2011 Chicago Public Schools (interim chief education
	                     officer)

11,9,10,4,8,3,7	*Steering committee, UChicago Consortium on School Research* *Editorial board, Catalyst Chicago* *Board Service* *Chicago United to Reform Education (CURE); Chicago Corporate* *Community School Planning Group; Chicago Algebra Project;* *MacArthur Foundation, Chicago Education Funding Review* *Committee; Chicago Annenberg Challenge, Research Advisory* *Committee; Wendell Phillips High School, Community Advisory* *Board; Chicago Metropolitan Agency for Regional Planning, K–12* *Advisory Committee; Chicago Public Education Fund, Research* *Advisory Committee; Woodlawn Children's Promise Community,* *Board of Directors*
37. Paige Ponder **5,2,5**	2002–2007 The Grow Network/McGraw-Hill 2007–2011 Chicago Public Schools 2011–2012 Project Exploration 2012–2017 One Million Degrees
5,9,11	*Steering committee, UChicago Consortium on School Research* *Board Service* *Advisory Council, To&Through UChicago Consortium on School* *Research; Advisory Council for Harrison Pathways, National Louis* *University*

Name Data streams	Organizations
63. Sylvia Puente 4,9,2,1	1990–1998 Latino Institute 2001–2009 Center for Metropolitan Chicago Initiatives, Institute for Latino Studies 2009– Latino Policy Forum *Steering committee, UChicago Consortium on School Research* *Board Service* *Chicago Panel on School Policy; Chicago Public Schools Blue Ribbon Advisory Committee on Capital Improvements; Advance Illinois; Education Funding Advisory Board; Education Transition Team for Governor Pritzker; Education Transition Team for Mayor Lightfoot, City of Chicago*
64. Barbara Radner 11,9	1990–2017 DePaul University (faculty and center director) *Editorial board, Catalyst Chicago*
38. Melissa Roderick **11,2,11** 11,9,3	1991–2001 UChicago, School of Social Service Administration 2001–2003 Chicago Public Schools (central office) 2003–2017 UChicago, Network for College Success 2003– UChicago, Crown Family School of Social Work, Policy, and Practice *UChicago Consortium on School Research, Board member North Lawndale Charter H.S. (director)*
39. Ken Rolling **8,4,5**	1990–1995 Woods Charitable Trust 1995–2001 Chicago Annenberg Challenge (executive director) 2002–2008 Parents for Public Schools 2009– Community Learning Partnership
40. Amy Rome **3,11,3,5,1** 5,3	1994–2000 Chicago Public Schools (teacher and curriculum coordinator) 2001–2004 University of Illinois Chicago (codirector, GATE Program) 2005–2012 Chicago Public Schools (assistant principal and principal) 2012–2015 Academy for Urban School Leadership (director) 2015–2021 Leading Educators (vice president, chief program officer, president) 2019–2021 Chicago Public Schools (school board member) *Board Service* *Chicago Tech High School*

Name Data streams	Organizations
41. Jesse Ruiz **1,2**	2004–2011 Illinois State Board of Education (chairman) 2011–2013 U.S. Department of Education 2013–2014 Leadership Greater Chicago (fellow) 2011–2015 Chicago Public Schools (board member) 2015–2016 Chicago Public Schools (interim CEO) 2016–2017 Chicago Park District
65. Penny Sebring *9,10,8,1,7*	1990– UChicago Consortium on School Research *Director/Cofounder, UChicago Consortium on School Research* *Editorial board, Catalyst Chicago* *Board Service* *Chicago Public Education Fund; Northwestern University School of* *Education and Social Policy; cofounder of the Investors Council,* *UChicago Consortium on School Research; Lewis-Sebring Family* *Foundation; Kids First Chicago*
42. Tim Shanahan **11,2,11** *11,5,1*	1980–2013 University of Illinois Chicago 2001–2002 Chicago Public Schools (central office) *Board Service* *Illinois Reading Council; Illinois Right to Read*
43. Jesse Sharkey **3,6** *6,9*	1998–2010 Chicago Public Schools (teacher) 2010–2018 Chicago Teachers Union (vice president) 2018–2022 Chicago Teachers Union (president) *UChicago Consortium steering committee*
44. Barbara Sizemore **3,11** *11,9*	1950–1967 Chicago Public Schools (teacher and administrator) 1992–2004 DePaul University (dean) *Steering committee, UChicago Consortium on School Research*

45. Sara Spurlark
 	
3,1,11
 	
11,10,9
	1955–1990 Chicago Public Schools (teacher, assistant principal,
	          and principal)
	1987–1991 School Finance Authority
	1988–1995 School Board Nominating Commission
	1990–2005 Center for School Improvement, University of
	          Chicago
	
	Editorial board, Catalyst Chicago
	Advisor to UChicago Consortium on School Research

Name Data streams	Organizations
46. Robin Steans **3,4,7,3,4**	1988–1990 Chicago Public Schools (teacher) 1992–1994 Chicago Public Schools (local school council, 　　　　　　　community member) 1994–1997 Small Schools Coalition 1997–1999 Leadership for Quality Education 2005–2009 Local School Council (parent member) 2008–2017 Advance Illinois
7,10,3,5,8	*Editorial board, Catalyst Chicago* *Board Service* *North Lawndale College Prep Charter High School; Legacy Charter School; Chicago Communities in Schools; National Louis University; Ingenuity; Illinois Network of Charter Schools; Steans Family Foundation*
47. Elizabeth "Beth" Swanson **2,8,1,8**	2002–2009 Chicago Public Schools (central office) 2009–2011 The Pritzker Traubert Family Foundation 2011–2014 City of Chicago (deputy mayor for education) 2014–2019 Joyce Foundation 2019–　　　A Better Chicago
2,9,4,8	*Board Service* *Federation for Community Schools; City Year Chicago; Chicago Arts Partnerships in Education (CAPE); Next Generation Leadership Advisory Council; Illinois Network of Charter Schools (INCS); Chicago Public Education Fund; One Million Degrees; founder and board chair, Thrive Chicago; Illinois P-20 Council, College and Career Readiness Committee chair; The Partnership for College Completion, board chair*
66. Steven E. Tozer	1978–1994 University of Illinois Urbana Champaign (professor 　　　　　　　and department chair) 1995–2018 University of Illinois Chicago (professor, department 　　　　　　　chair and cofounder of EdD Program and Center for 　　　　　　　Urban School Leadership)
11,2,1	*Board Service* *Human Resources Advisory Committee, Chicago Public Schools; Governor's Council on Educator Quality; Joint ISBE and IHE Illinois School Leader Legislative Task Force; Illinois School Leader Advisory Council; Illinois Education Research Council; ISBE/UIC Task Force on Teacher Licensure in Illinois*

Name Data streams	Organizations
48. Beverly Tunney **3,6** *6,9*	1956–1981 Chicago Public Schools (teacher) 1981–1993 Chicago Public Schools (principal) 1993–2003 Chicago Principals and Administrators Association 　　　　　　(president) *Steering committee, UChicago Consortium on School Research*
49. Arie van der Ploeg **2,5** *5,9*	1976–1992 Chicago Public Schools (central office consultant) 1992–2004 North Central Regional Educational Laboratory 　　　　　　(senior program associate) 2004–2010 Learning Point Associates (senior program associate) 2010–2013 American Institutes for Research (principal 　　　　　　researcher) *Steering committee, UChicago Consortium on School Research*
50. Alicia Winkler **2,8**	2009–2014 Chicago Public Schools (central office) 2017–　　　 Golden Apple Foundation (president and chief 　　　　　　executive officer)
51. Josie Yanguas **11,5** *5,9,3,2,1*	1988–1993 Center for School Improvement, UChicago 1989–2006 Illinois Resource Center 2006–2017 Illinois Resource Center (director) *Steering committee, UChicago Consortium on School Research* *Board Service* *Little Village High School (CPS) Transition Advisory Council (TAC);* *Illinois Advisory Council for Bilingual Education; Illinois Early* *Learning Council; Latino Advisory Committee for the Chicago Public* *Schools*
52. Paul Zavitkovsky **3,7,11** *11,10,2,1*	1991–2001 Chicago Public Schools (principal) 2001–2004 Civic Committee of the Commercial Club of Chicago 2004–2017 University of Illinois at Chicago *Editorial board, Catalyst Chicago* *Board Service* *Teachers Supporting Teachers Board; Illinois Education Research* *Council Advisory Board; Statewide Assessment Review Committee,* *Illinois State Board of Education; Data, Assessment and Accountabil-* *ity Committee, Illinois P-20 Council*

ENUMERATION OF THE 11 INSTITUTIONAL DOMAINS USED IN THE CODING ABOVE

1. Governance authorities: mayor, CPS and state boards of education, state legislature, SFA
2. Central office including area and network offices
3. School communities including LSCs, neighborhood and community organizations
4. Citywide advocacy groups: Designs for Change, Chicago Panel, Latino Institute, Urban League
5. Professional services organizations: QUEST, AUSL, TFA, New Leaders, NTC, IRC
6. Organized labor: CTU and CPAA
7. Business community and derivative organizations
8. Local and national foundations
9. Consortium
10. Media including *Catalyst*
11. University-based improvement centers: CSI/UEI, NCS, and schools of education

Notes

Introduction

1. This text is adapted from the prologue of Bryk et al., *Charting Chicago School Reform*.
2. For early results see Allensworth, *Graduation and Dropout Trends in Chicago*. For more recent data see Malone et al., *Educational Attainment*.
3. This is for the total graduation rate by 2017, including students in options schools. Without the options school graduates, the rate was 75% as reported in chapter 2. For more details see Malone et al., *Educational Attainment*.
4. Considerable debate now exists as to the most appropriate language convention for describing students and families of Hispanic origins. In an early draft of our text, we introduced the gender-neutral term *Latinx*. However, the overwhelming feedback we received on that draft text from Chicago participants was that the term was inconsistent with their native language. It was neither used by the school system nor embraced by the school and community leaders we interviewed and who participated in different convenings that we organized as part of the development of this book. In an effort to remain sensitive to their feedback, we returned to the term *Latino* as the general descriptor used in this book.
5. Beginning in 2016, the SAT replaced the ACT as the required high school assessment.
6. "Appendix A: Background on the Degree Attainment Indices," in *The Educational Attainment of Chicago Public Schools Students: 2018* (Chicago: University of Chicago Consortium on School Research, 2019), https://consortium.uchicago.edu/sites/default /files/2019-11/DAI%202018%20Technical%20Appendix-Nov2019-Consortium.pdf.
7. See Bryk, "No Child Left Behind."
8. The 2016 results come directly from the Educational Opportunities Project report from Stanford. The earlier results are based on analyses conducted by the Consortium on Chicago School Research and can be found in Bryk, "No Child Left Behind."
9. Joyce Foundation, *Progress and Promise*.
10. Zavitkovsky and Tozer, *Upstate/Downstate*.
11. The 1989 data come from the *Public Schools DataBook* published by the Chicago Panel on School Finance. The data from 1991 and thereafter come from tabulations compiled by the UChicago Consortium on School Research.

12. Tabulations compiled by the UChicago Consortium on School Research.
13. Reardon and Hinze-Pifer, *Test Score Growth*.
14. Data compiled by Paul Zavitkovsky, Center for Urban Education Leadership, University of Illinois at Chicago.
15. Allensworth et al., *High School Graduation Rates*.
16. Barrow and Sartain, "Expansion of High School Choice."
17. On this characterization of Chicago's schools, see publications from the Illinois Network of Charter Schools; for example, Kalata and McEwen, *Chicago: A Choice District*.
18. Gwynne and Moore, *Chicago's Charter High Schools*.
19. Allensworth et al., *High School Graduation Rates*.
20. Gwynne and Moore, *Chicago's Charter High Schools*. Computations provided by Elaine Allensworth.
21. For a case of an individual charter school success in Chicago, see Hassrick, Raudenbush, and Rosen, *Ambitious Elementary School*. For more general evaluation findings see Center for Research on Educational Outcomes, *Urban Charter School Study Report on 41 Regions*. See also Sampson, *Chicago Charter Schools*.
22. As is customary with each school system leadership transition, a "plan" was developed in 2002 entitled "Every Child, Every School." Much of its rationale was anchored in research published by the Consortium in the late 1990s, and it was developed through a broad citywide consultation process. It involved a long list of priority initiatives, many of which emerged in some form over time. The plan itself, however, achieved little public recognition, and few saw it as a driving force for change.
23. This quote acknowledges and draws from Lisa Delpit's essay on this topic: Delpit, *Other People's Children*.
24. For a further discussion on this topic, see Katz, "Chicago School Reform as History." He describes how community control's earliest roots were in the rural schools of the American frontier and how the development of urban, immigrant neighborhoods also gave rise to an alternative system of schools organized by local churches and, in some cities, synagogues. The purpose was to protect their children from what were deemed hostile outside influences determining who would teach them and the content and values their children were to be exposed to. The policy contest about the content and values that children are exposed to in schools remains highly salient today.
25. Chicago's efforts to transform its school system around the principle of community control was not unique in modern times. New York City's installation of community boards in the late 1960s drew on this same ideology. Don Moore, a key architect of the 1988 reform, had carefully studied the NYC experience, including the controversies that sprang up in Ocean Hill-Brownsville. He was troubled by how interest group politics still could overwhelm doing right by the children. He believed in democratic control of public schools exercised at the school-site level where the decision-makers' only concern was their children's well-being.
26. In 1981, Chicago United, a derivative of the Civic Committee of the Commercial Club, undertook a massive review of the managerial processes of the Chicago Public Schools. It resulted in 253 recommendations as to how the management of the district should improve. In 1987, Chicago United undertook a reexamination of the progress of the

district on this set of recommendations. They concluded that the most important recommendations from 1981 had simply not been implemented. So, within the business community, improving the management of the system remained a major challenge as the mobilization for reform began.

27. Shipps, *School Reform, Corporate Style.*
28. The literature here is voluminous and anchored in Dan Lortie's seminal work on sociology of teaching. Numerous major contributions on this topic include writings from Susan Moore Johnson and Linda Darling Hammond. The American Federation of Teachers and the National Educational Association have been major advocates on the national scene. The invention of the National Board for Professional Teaching Standards was a major innovation in this area. While often this has translated into efforts to improve salaries, career ladders, and working conditions for teachers, at its heart is the central question, "Who should control public education?"
29. The argument that the designed fragmentation in the governance of US public education created incoherence in schools has been articulated by Cohen and Spillane in "Chapter 1: Policy and Practice." It can also be found in O'Day and Smith, "Systemic Reform and Educational Opportunity."
30. Stone, "Civic Capacity and Urban Education."
31. We are indebted to Charles Ashby Lewis, who articulated this analogy in "A Memorandum on Chicago's 'Education Exoskeleton,'" revised January 4, 2022.
32. We are indebted to Clarence Stone for his account of the important functional roles played by applied research and media in nurturing capacity for productive civic actions. Stone, "Rhetoric, Reality and Politics."
33. For an account on San Diego, see Hubbard, Mehan, and Stein, *Reform as Learning.* On New York City see O'Day, Bitter, and Gomez, *Education Reform in New York City.* On New Orleans see Harris, *Charter School City.*
34. Bryk et al., *Learning to Improve.*

Chapter 1

1. Greenberg served as a note-taker for the mayor's office at all of the PCC forums. In that capacity she noted the location of each forum and the name, race, gender, and approximate age of each speaker (and title if it was shared), took verbatim notes, and developed an analytic summary that captured the testimony, tone, and prevalent themes. The discussion presented above and the quoted remarks are based on that earlier analysis.
2. The CPS central office was housed in three abandoned buildings near the Chicago stockyards on Pershing Road at that time. Built in 1905, the three originally were part of the Chicago Manufacturing District and repurposed as an armory and then a morgue in World Wars I and II.
3. Housing covenants were later deemed illegal, a result of a case brought by the father of Chicago poet Lorraine Hansberry when he was unable to purchase a home. Villarosa, "Black Lives Are Shorter in Chicago."
4. Todd-Breland, *Political Education.*
5. John Ayers, personal communication, January 2022.
6. Baron, *Chicago Public High School for Metropolitan Studies.*
7. Shipps, *School Reform, Corporate Style*, 103.

8. *The Bottom Line: Chicago's Failing Schools; Dropouts for the CPS: An Analysis; Caught in the Web.*
9. We use "Latino" rather than "Latinx" throughout, as it was the term in use during this time period.
10. O'Connell, *School Reform Chicago Style.*
11. Stone, "Rhetoric, Reality and Politics"; Stone et al., *Building Civic Capacity.*
12. National Commission on Excellence in Education, *Nation at Risk.*
13. Todd-Breland, *Political Education,* 165.
14. Among their earlier projects was the underwriting of Daniel Burnham's *Plan for Chicago.* See Civic Consulting Alliance, "Our History."
15. Civic Consulting Alliance, "Our History."
16. John Ayers, memo, January 2022.
17. In 1989 the Civic Committee also launched Leadership for Quality Education to support the implementation of school reform.
18. The Designs and Panel studies cited earlier concluded that a majority of CPS graduates were functionally illiterate.
19. Lenz, "Missing in Action."
20. Leon Jackson, quoted in Shipps, *School Reform, Corporate Style,* 93.
21. Shipps, *School Reform, Corporate Style,* 94–95.
22. Superintendent Hannon left town as soon as the reforms were announced and ahead of getting fired. Byrne appointed Angelina Caruso (a CPS insider) as interim superintendent.
23. Todd-Breland, *Political Education,* 150.
24. *Report of the 1981 Special Task Force on Education.* Chicago United had offered to conduct audits for previous superintendents, and their advice was usually heeded. Shipps, *School Reform, Corporate Style,* 100.
25. Love was replaced after two years by Manford Byrd. Byrd was an African American CPS "lifer" who continued to ignore Chicago United's recommendations. Shipps, *School Reform, Corporate Style,* 107.
26. Recounted by John Ayers, who is one of the sons of the late Thomas Ayers, CEO of Commonwealth Edison. He was an observer at many of these conversations with his father and his corporate colleagues. John Ayers, interview, April 7, 2021.
27. Washington appointed an African American CPS educator, Frank Gardner, to the BOE in 1984. Gardner became BOE president in 1987, shortly after Washington's death.
28. For evidence on dismal high school student test scores as reform began, see Allensworth, Kochanek, and Miller, *Student Performance.*
29. John Ayers, interview, April 7, 2021. Ayers attributes this comment to state senate leader Pate Philip.
30. Hal Baron, Mayor Washington's chief of staff, shared these views with Greenberg in a 1988 interview.
31. Learn Earn was appealing for several reasons: as an economic incentive program that would increase the number of job-ready CPS graduates, it responded to business concerns. Economic development also was an area where Washington had expertise and leverage, especially because he planned to run the new program out of the Mayor's Office of Employment and Training, which he controlled, rather than the CPS, which he

did not. He also conceived it as a partnership with City Colleges, which were a key institutional resource.

32. Byrd had come up through the system. He had been passed over when both Caruso and Love were appointed, then appointed superintendent in 1982 when Love left.
33. Hal Baron and John Kotsakis both said this when interviewed by Greenberg in 1988.
34. "History of Chicago Public Schools."
35. Wilson, *Truly Disadvantaged*.
36. O'Connell, *School Reform Chicago Style*, 1991.
37. "Stranglehold" was a term that parents used at the PCC forums.
38. Hal Baron, interview, 1988.
39. Baron, interview, 1988.
40. See O'Connell, *School Reform Chicago Style*, 40, for a list of PCC members.
41. Baron, interview, 1988.
42. Washington deliberately chose a West Coast lab, hoping that its counsel would be objective and free from conflicts of interest. Baron, interview, 1988.
43. Shipps, *School Reform, Corporate Style*, 114, discusses the "elevation" of parents and community in the PCC. She also discusses middle-class African Americans employed by CPS, as well as established African American community groups including Operation Push, KOCO, and TWO, being opposed to reform. Shipps, *School Reform, Corporate Style*, 107. Relatedly, Todd-Breland discusses the changing nature of class coalitions across time in the African American community and refers to middle-class Blacks, and the groups that represented them, as having "something to lose" by the late 1980s. Todd-Breland, *Political Education*, 186.
44. O'Connell, *School Reform Chicago Style*; Katz, "Teachers College Record."
45. John Kotsakis complained that advocacy groups like Designs for Change and the Chicago Panel on Public School Finance had no constituents, but each had a vote. He had one vote too, but was representing 38,000 teachers. Kotsakis, interview, 1988.
46. PCC organizers accused NWREL of disrespecting parents in its early analysis of forum testimony and asked the lab to leave. Baron, interview, 1988.
47. O'Connell, *School Reform Chicago Style*, 40, lists thirteen written proposals that were presented to the PCC.
48. In the mid-1980s, Project CANAL established local school improvement councils in CPS. A precursor to LSCs, they were advisory only.
49. John Ayers, interview, April 7, 2021. This group included his father, Thomas Ayers, Perkins, Koldyke, Weber, and Bacon.
50. Todd-Breland, *Political Education*, 168.
51. Shipps, *School Reform, Corporate Style*, 107, 114, 119; O'Connell, *School Reform Chicago Style*, 22; Peter Martinez, interviews, February 19, 2021, and March 5, 2021.
52. Martinez, interviews, February 19, 2021, and March 5, 2021.
53. The Speaker of the House informed CTU leadership that reform was going to happen with or without labor at the table, and it was their choice to determine which optics their membership would prefer. Martinez, interviews, February 19, 2021, and March 5, 2021.
54. State Chapter 1 was designed to bring additional funds into schools that served a high-poverty population. Funding was based on the number of students in a specific school who qualified for free or reduced lunch.

55. While Martinez was bringing the factions together around points of agreement, Moore secured funding to hire a legal consultant to help him draft the new law, he hired a public relations firm and a lobbyist, and he (and others) had buses ready to take parents to Springfield to demonstrate outside legislative chambers. Martinez, interviews, February 19, 2021, and March 5, 2021.

56. Wilkerson, "New School Term." In Wilkerson's article, Michael Kirst is quoted calling Chicago's reform the "biggest change in American school control since the 1900s . . . the most drastic . . . absolutely precedent breaking . . . a bold experiment." Chester Finn called it "unique." Johnson in "Illinois Legislature Moves to Give Parents Control of the Chicago Schools," 7. quotes Moore saying "This is the most far-reaching reform of any big city school system in the last 20 years. It basically brings accountability and decision-making down to the local level."

57. As quoted in Wilkerson, "New School Term," Danny Solis, director of UNO, called the legislation the "largest experiment in grass-roots democracy the country has ever seen. We have a community with people who are not citizens. We are now suddenly able to leapfrog into . . . positions of real power."

58. This was an instance where Chicago's segregation, which created racially and economically homogeneous communities, may have facilitated decision-making in positive ways.

59. Those potential consequences might include, for example, interest group meddling, a disregard for professional expertise, and racialized personnel decisions that could be perceived as beneficial or problematic, depending on perspective.

60. Efforts to achieve community control of schools had been tried in the past, most notably New York City's installation of a community board in Ocean Hill-Brownsville, which was the size of many midsize city districts. In Chicago, the first of a handful of independent, community-controlled Afrocentric schools opened in the 1960s. Todd-Breland, *Political Education*, 81–87.

61. Groups including UNO, which was active in Latino communities, organized slates of their members to run for LSC seats in specific schools.

62. Gorov, "Hispanic Radio." Similarly, WVON, which was founded as the "Voice of the Negro" in 1963, kept reform on the airwaves.

63. O'Connell, *School Reform Chicago Style*, 28.

64. LSC members' calls for help are well documented. For a sampling see list of "councils' needs." Menacker et al., "Most Principals, Councils Get Thumbs Up," 2. Reporting on Chicago school reform for the *NYT*, Wilkerson also mentions reticence on the part of some LSC members. Wilkerson, "New School Term." See also case studies of the early implementation of reform by Rollow and Bennett, "Participation and Chicago School Reform"; and Rollow and Yanguas, *Road to Emergent Restructuring*.

65. Joravsky, "Money Made the Difference," 12.

66. McKersie, "Strategic Philanthropy and Local Public Policy."

67. McKersie, "Strategic Philanthropy and Local Public Policy."

68. McKersie, "Strategic Philanthropy and Local Public Policy."

69. Warren Chapman, interview, January 8, 2020.

70. The spending was more like the venture capital we would now associate with Silicon Valley—although it predated Silicon Valley's social investing efforts by a decade.

71. Chapman, interview, January 8, 2020.

72. Noted earlier, the Community Renewal Society was Chicago's first settlement house. It also published the *Chicago Reporter*, which continues to be a newsletter focused on issues of race and class.

73. Linda Lenz, "To Our Readers."

74. "Diaries."

75. Martinez, interviews, February 19, 2021, and March 5, 2021.

76. Lorraine Forte, interview, November 25, 2020.

77. The Center was the focus of a case study developed by Chicago Community Trust staff for their January 9, 1990, Executive Committee Meeting Book. In addition to the Center's focus on instructional improvement, program officers stated that the Center was "building the institutional capacity of schools by working with professional staff, parents and community residents" to achieve it. Additionally, through its principal network and summer institute it "created a network of adult leaders across the school system . . . and [sought to] link the insights and experiences of teachers, parents and principals with policy makers." McKersie, "Strategic Philanthropy and Local Public Policy."

78. Deborah Lynch, interview, October 1, 2020.

79. Quest's first initiative was to invite proposals from teacher teams to support innovation in their schools. Conferences and "hands-on" courses tailored to the expressed needs of CPS teachers followed.

80. Albert Shanker, conversation with Anthony Bryk, 1990.

81. Warren Chapman, interview, January 8, 2020.

82. Michael Koldyke, interview, November 30, 2020.

83. Michael Koldyke's work developed in stages: starting in the 1980s a Golden Apple Awards program that honored individual teachers and a Golden Apple Scholars program that supported and prepared college students aspiring to become exemplary teachers. In Era 2 Koldyke started LAUNCH, which aimed to bring new talent into school leadership roles, and then developed the Academy for Urban School Leaders (AUSL). AUSL "turned around" a group of Chicago's chronically lowest-performing schools in Eras 3 and 4.

84. Michael Koldyke, interview, November 30, 2020; and John Ayers, interview, April 7, 2021. An article in the *New Yorker* also describes this generational shift among civic leaders: Enos, "How Greenwich Republicans Learned to Love Trump."

85. John Ayers, interview, April 21, 2021. See also Bernstein, "Daley v Daley," for a discussion of the second Mayor Daley's break with the Chicago machine—an action that made him more palatable with this faction of the business community.

86. Philip is the state senator who had referred to CPS as "a Black hole." John Ayers, memo, January 2022.

87. Andy Wade, interview, April 8, 2022; and Ayers, "Picking Principals," 133–140.

88. The moratorium on negotiations would not be overturned until 2020. "After Decades-Long Struggle."

89. This change was phased in such that the fifteen-member reform board was disbanded in 1995. A "superboard," with five members appointed by the mayor, replaced it until 1999. In 1999 a new board replaced that one, again with the mayor appointing all members.

90. CPS contracted with the College of Education at UIC to provide this training.

91. Lenz, "What's in the New Law?"
92. The standoff recalled the activism three decades earlier when a group of Pilsen moms also used hunger strikes to call attention to their demand for a new high school in their Latino community. When they finally prevailed in 1977, the bilingual banner announcing their new school's opening read "Benito Juarez High School Was Won by Community Struggle, Not by Politicians." The Little Village debacle also portended a future struggle, when Dyett parents in Bronzeville resisted their school's closing. Ewing, *Ghosts in the Schoolyard.*
93. Principals and faculty in impacted schools complained about their new status, and when interviewed by *Catalyst,* Bryk said that "crude measures" had been used to determine which schools were put on probation. Williams, "Probation Stuns Schools."
94. At that time not many external partners were experienced supporting this cohort of schools—the Center and TAMS, discussed subsequently, being exceptions. Finnigan and O'Day, *External Support to Schools on Probation.*
95. Finnigan and O'Day, *External Support to Schools on Probation.*
96. Chapman previously had directed the Illinois Coalition of Essential Schools, which was a national Annenberg Challenge affiliate.
97. McDonald et al., *American School Reform,* 94.
98. This anecdote was shared with Bryk in a conversation with Vartan Gregorian, then president of the Carnegie Corporation. Gregorian was working directly with Walter Annenberg at that time to launch the challenge.
99. Patricia Graham, interview, October 7, 2020.
100. Andy Wade, interview, April 8, 2022. Vallas's continuing effort to control principal appointments prompted the CAC to team with LQE to launch the Chicago Schools Leadership Collaborative. It lobbied downstate for LSCs to retain control over principal appointments. That struggle eventuated in passage of SB 652, another compromise bill. For further discussion see Ayers, "Picking Principals," 133–140.
101. See discussion in chapter 4 about the participation of staff and faculty from university math and science departments.
102. McDonald et al., *American School Reform,* 99; Chapman, interview, January 8, 2020.
103. Fendt et al., *Successes, Failures, and Lessons for the Future.* See appendix A for a list of CAC grantees.
104. McDonald and colleagues distinguish between the civic and professional expertise that different CAC partners brought to the table, arguing that education improvement expertise was in short supply at that time. McDonald et al., *American School Reform,* 101.
105. McDonald et al., *American School Reform,* 103.
106. Ayers, "Picking Principals," 141–150.
107. Warren Chapman, interview, January 8, 2020.
108. Albert Sanchez, executive director of the Children First Fund, as quoted in Lopez, memo, May 3, 2021.
109. It is likely that Duncan came to the mayor's attention by virtue of working with After School Matters. Duncan, *How Schools Work,* 31–33.
110. Weissmann, "What's Next? Who's Next?," 13.
111. Arne Duncan, interviews, February 18, 2021, and February 28, 2021.
112. Warren Chapman, interview, January 8, 2020.

113. "Every Child, Every School."
114. Duncan, *How Schools Work*, 49.
115. Rossi, Beaupre, and Grossman, "Failing Teachers." This is discussed in chapter 3. The college success rate exposé is taken up in chapter 2.
116. Newmann, Lopez, and Bryk, *Quality of Intellectual Work in Chicago Schools*; and Newmann, Bryk, and Nagaoka, *Authentic Intellectual Work and Standardized Tests*.
117. "Children First Fund."
118. This group, discussed in chapter 3, included National Board Certification, the New Teacher Project, and Teach Plus.
119. Barbara Eason-Watkins, interviews, June 24, 2020, August 28, 2020, October 20, 2020, and November 17, 2020.
120. Lopez, memo, May 3, 2021.
121. Simmons, *School Reform in Chicago*.
122. Lopez's colleagues at the Office of Post Secondary included John Q. Easton and Greg Darneider, both introduced in subsequent chapters.
123. Philanthropy-district partnerships, like the research-practice partnerships described subsequently, were another product of Chicago's reform that developed in Era 3 when Duncan and Eason-Watkins were leading.
124. The exception to this labor–management harmony was the school closings discussed below.
125. Eason-Watkins, interviews, June 24, 2020, August 28, 2020, October 20, 2020, and November 17, 2020.
126. Lenz, "Missing in Action," 129.
127. Deborah Lynch, interview, October 1, 2020.
128. Jesse Sharkey, interview, April 9, 2021.
129. For another discussion of Daley's "lock" on the city, see Bernstein, "Daley v Daley."
130. Arne Duncan interviews, February 18, 2021, and February 28, 2021. Eason-Watkins agreed, saying that the challenge was to "draw from the strengths of the district *and* charter schools that were succeeding, so that we could have a more effective district." Eason-Watkins, interviews, June 24, 2020, August 28, 2020, October 20, 2020, and November 17, 2020.
131. Thomas Ayers is deceased; however, one of his sons, John Ayers, spoke with us about his father's views. Our discussion of Thomas Ayers, and his quotes, draws from our interview with John Ayers.
132. John Ayers told us that at home his father said Martin was "rabidly, pathologically, vehemently opposed to organized labor and the CTU." Others we interviewed, including Arne Duncan, Peter Martinez, and Jesse Sharkey, described him as "anti-CPS," "rabidly anti-union," "just rabid," "ideologically driven," "ruthless," and "impervious to facts he doesn't like—I mean just apoplectic." In sum, there was a convergence of unsolicited opinion—all of it extreme.
133. The same phenomenon, but in a different context, is described in Enos, "How Greenwich Republicans Learned to Love Trump."
134. In 1995 Chicago had so poorly managed its public housing that HUD took it over. The first demolitions took place under HUD's watch in 1996 and 1997. In 1999 Mayor Daley won back control on the strength of his *Plan for Transformation*. It promised that 18,000 units would be razed and 25,000 new units developed within five to seven years.

Moreover, it promised that all who lived in Chicago's public housing would have access to these new, mixed-income communities and the new schools that would anchor them. Bittle, Kapir, and Mathani, "Redeveloping the State Street Corridor"; *Plan for Transformation*.

135. Prevalent at that time was the notion that mixed-income schools would advantage lower-income students. Bittle et al., "Redeveloping the State Street Corridor"; *Plan for Transformation*.

136. Williams, "Mid South: Linking Schools and Communities."

137. Ewing, *Ghosts in the Schoolyard*.

138. Civic Committee of the Commercial Club of Chicago, *Left Behind*. In addition to Martin, the committee's twelve members included Andrew McKenna (chair of the Illinois Republican Party and the McDonald's Corporation), John Rowe (chairman and CEO of Exelon), John Rogers (chairman and CEO of Ariel Capital), Tim Schwertfeger (chairman and CEO of Nuveen), and Harrison Steans (financier and philanthropist).

139. Civic Committee of the Commercial Club of Chicago, *Left Behind*, 3.

140. Paul Zavitkovsky, interview, December 8, 2020.

141. Civic Committee of the Commercial Club of Chicago, *Left Behind*, 3.

142. The original FRAC group, which came together following a request for assistance by Mayor Washington, consisted of seventy civic leaders. Subsequently, FRAC's scope of work expanded to broader challenges of governmental and municipal management, and in 2005 it was rebranded the Civic Consulting Alliance. Ayers, memo, January 2022. See also Shipps, *School Reform, Corporate Style*, 110; and Civic Consulting Alliance, "Our History."

143. Lipman, "Making Sense of Renaissance 10 School Policy in Chicago," 9.

144. LQE, a committee of the Civic Club, did its best to fend off Vallas's and Daley's attempts to take principal appointments away from LSCs. Ayers, memo, January 2022; Wade, interview, April 8, 2022. For further discussion see Ayers, "Picking Principals," 133–140.

145. The argument was somewhat disingenuous since thousands of African American families had been opting out of their neighborhood schools since choice programs were first offered the 1960s. An advantage of Ren10 neighborhood charters, at least in theory, was that they would alleviate the travel burden. In a city racked by gang violence, keeping students close to home was a priority for many families.

146. Lipman, "Landscape of Education 'Reform' in Chicago,"

147. Payne, *Still Crazy After All These Years*, 5.

148. The federally funded Project CANAL in the 1980s was an effort that predated reform.

149. By 2006, and using this 50 percent criterion, 147 schools were underutilized. Later, CPS changed the policy, and less than 65 percent of capacity in use was defined as under-enrollment and underutilized. Gwynne and de la Torre, *When Schools Close*, 11.

150. See, for example, Bittle, Kapir, and Mathani, "Redeveloping the State Street Corridor."

151. Gwynne and de la Torre, *When Schools Close*.

152. Sharkey, interview, April 9, 2021.

153. Sharkey told us that CORE teachers attended and often led protest meetings focused on their own schools, and soon were attending the meetings of other targeted schools to show solidarity. Some parents and community members were doing the same. Sharkey, interview, April 9, 2021.

154. Eason-Watkins interviews, June 24, 2020, August 28, 2020, October 20, 2020, and November 17, 2020; Ewing, *Ghosts in the Schoolyard*.

155. When AUSL worked with a school, the student group stayed intact, the adults were replaced, and AUSL then managed the school. Koldyke, interview, November 30, 2020.

156. Underutilized was defined as below 65 percent of capacity. Low performing schools were those that had been on probation at least one year but their students had not improved academically. Gwynne and de la Torre, *When Schools Close*.

157. We draw these numbers from the 2009 Consortium report and an internal Consortium list that enumerates school closings and openings and identifies the management group between the years 1994 and 2020. We also note that the exact numbers are difficult to pin down, because they vary across reports and articles, depending on the time frame analyzed, the many different types of schools that came into being, and the evolving terminology that was used to describe them.

158. This report analyzes the closings that had transpired through 2006. Gwynne and de la Torre, *When Schools Close*.

159. We borrow the phrase from an article by Sarah Karp, "Grading Mayor Rahm Emanuel's Educational Legacy." She writes that "improvement in a time of turmoil and scandal will forever be the contradiction that is Emanuel's educational legacy."

160. Whalen, *Transforming Central Office Practices for Equity*, 40; Payne, interview, February 18, 2021.

161. Payne, interview, February 18, 2021.

162. Sharkey, interview, April 9, 2021.

163. Whalen, *Transforming Central Office Practices for Equity*, 7–8.

164. The CTU's willingness to collaborate was contingent on the Consortium being selected to conduct the research that would accompany a pilot of this project. When CPS agreed, a collaborative effort ensued. John Q. Easton, interview, May 17, 2021, and May 21, 2021.

165. Beth Swanson, interview, April 19, 2022.

166. In 1998, for example, the Consortium had published Smith, *It's About Time*.

167. Emanuel, *The Nation City*, 22.

168. This was a big-ticket item for a district that was cash strapped. That CPS put its money here speaks to the importance it attached to the issue.

169. Civic Committee of the Commercial Club of Chicago, *Still Left Behind*, 18.

170. Ewing discusses this drop in Bronzeville and the city more generally. See Ewing, *Ghosts in the Schoolyard*. There is other reporting that documents that families had limited options to find new housing in the city when the projects came down, owing to segregation and low incomes. This forced many to move to segregated collar suburbs or leave the area altogether. See, for example, Villarosa, "Black Lives Are Shorter in Chicago."

171. Beth Swanson, memo, January 2022.

172. As quoted in Ewing, *Ghosts in the Schoolyard*, 2.

173. As quoted in Ewing, *Ghosts in the Schoolyard*, 100.

174. Beth Swanson, interview, April 19, 2022. Ewing's critique of the board's "deep analysis" is withering. See Ewing, *Ghosts in the Schoolyard*.

175. Swanson, interview, April 19, 2022; Jesse Ruiz, interview, March 2, 2022.

176. Swanson, memo, January 2022; Ruiz, interview, March 2, 2022.

177. Swanson, memo, January 2022; Ruiz, interview, March 2, 2022.

178. Karp, "50 School Closings Approved at Raucous Board Meeting." See also Ewing, *Ghosts in the Schoolyard*, 2, 4.
179. Ewing, *Ghosts in the Schoolyard*, 2; Karp, "Minimal Cost Savings for Closing Schools."
180. Bryk et al., *Charting Chicago School Reform*.
181. See Ewing, "Mourning," in *Ghosts in the Schoolyard*, 125–156.
182. The "murder mayor" nickname was also a reference to the city's murder rate during Emanuel's tenure.
183. Lewis, "On Baseballs and Budgets."

Chapter 2

1. Most steering committee members either held grants from one or more of these foundations or aspired to receive one in the future. These meetings created a regular place where informal sidebar conversations could occur with foundation staff. This offered a bit of incentive for steering committee members to attend regularly. On the flip side, when conversations within these meetings became contentious, as they sometimes did, the foundation's presence helped to sustain the modicum of civility necessary for collective action to persist.
2. This view was espoused on the national scene by Albert Shanker, who had been president of the United Federation of Teachers in New York City in the late 1960s and was president of the national American Federation of Teachers, as Chicago's version of community control was emerging. Understood as a proposal for community control of schools, Shanker's experiences from the highly controversial Ocean Hill-Brownsville community district initiative in New York City in the late 1960s quickly entered into the conversation.
3. Some of Bryk's previous research had focused on how diverse stakeholders might be better engaged in the process of evaluating public programs. See Bryk, *New Directions for Program Evaluation*.
4. *Catalyst*, for example, reported on the *State of School Reform* as part of its September 1993 issue. Interestingly, the role of research in informing local improvement efforts in Chicago was still unsettled at this point. This was the first time that *Catalyst* directly reported on Consortium work in a section toward the end of the issue titled "Updates." In subsequent years, findings from Consortium studies would move to the front, often becoming a lead story in a given issue.
5. Unfortunately, many failed to comprehend the mediating role that small size plays and viewed it instead as the next "silver bullet" reform. Taken alone, small size is not a direct instrument of school improvement. At best, a smaller organization affords possibilities for more intimate connections that act as a facilitating factor for productive change. Ironically, policy interest in small high schools subsequently waned before longer-term studies, both in Chicago and in New York, began to document that significant improvements did occur.
6. This topic is taken up both in Elizabeth Todd-Breland's account of Black politics and education reform in Chicago and in John Boyer's history of the University. Todd-Breland, *Political Education*; Boyer, *University of Chicago*.
7. A small additional grant of $15,000 followed from the Illinois State Board of Education. This was facilitated by another early steering committee member, Al Ramirez, at the Illinois State Board of Education.

8. This sequencing of events was another key element of stakeholder engagement. Bryk worried that if they had started with the researchers, their interests would have dominated the process. Engaging their expertise was critical, but the agenda setting process needed to focus them on the specific problems and concerns being brought forward by the reform community in Chicago.

9. Bryk and Sebring, *Achieving School Reform in Chicago*.

10. Peter Martinez, interview, March 12, 2021.

11. Patricia Graham, interview, October 25, 2020. At that time, Spencer had a rule that a principal investigator could hold only one grant at time from the Foundation, and Bryk already had a grant for a set of coordinated case studies on Chicago's school reform. Graham felt that that rule could be finessed as this would be formalized as a grant for the Consortium, with UChicago as the fiscal agent, rather than a grant to Bryk as principal investigator.

12. Interestingly, only years later would Bryk discern a connection to a core idea from Improvement Science called the Pareto Principle. As an empirical generalization, the Pareto Principle guides that 80% of the variation in outcomes is often tied to just 20% of the causes. Large-scale progress is possible if you can identify these drivers and sustain attention to their improvement. In essence the Consortium was building frameworks organized around a small set of key drivers and related measures and would continue to report back on them. Bryk et al. were following this principle even though its roots were unknown to them at that point in time. For a general discussion of the Pareto Principle, see Langley et al., *Improvement Guide*, 436. For a discussion of this in an education context, see Bryk et al., *Learning to Improve*, 176.

13. All of the ideas presented in this section were first articulated in the 1991 *Research Agenda*. For a further explication of this public philosophy and supporting academic citations, see Bryk et al., *Organizing Schools for Improvement*, appendix H, 252–255.

14. See Lewin, "Action Research and Minority Problems"; Lewin, *Resolving Social Conflict*. Also see Schein, "Kurt Lewin's Change Theory."

15. Bryk was influenced in this regard by his mentor David Cohen and early colleagueship with Carol Weiss and Bob Stake. See, for example, Lindblom and Cohen, *Usable Knowledge*. Earlier related arguments can be found in Dewey, *Public and Its Problems*. See also Weiss and Bucuvalas, *Social Science Research and Decision Making*; Stake, "Program Evaluation, Particularly Responsive Evaluation"; Warnick, "Rethinking Educational Research"; Dockrell and Hamilton, *Rethinking Educational Research*, 72–87.

16. This conclusion was anchored in the early work on research utilization by Carol Weiss and Bob Stake and subsequent developments by Michael Patton on Utilization Focused Evaluation. These arguments shifted attention away from the "go/no go" decisions embedded in simplistic forms of summative evaluation toward a more developmental evaluation focus.

17. This concept, rooted in social organizing, brings moral arguments to bear on institutionalized inequities. See Wildavsky, *Speaking Truth to Power*. He brought this framing to the work of policy analysis and program evaluation in its first big wave of this activity in the 1970s.

18. Schneider, like Sebring, was also at NORC at the time working on the High School and Beyond Survey system. Bryk had consulted with them on the survey's design, which

opened up the connections that brought both of them into research on Chicago school reform.

19. Following completion of this study, the executive director of the Principals and Administrators Association became an institutional member of the steering committee.

20. The report's prologue specifically stated that judged against this standpoint virtually any plan proposed for reforming a major urban school system would surely be viewed a failure (3).

21. Bryk et al., *View for the Elementary Schools.* The report can be found at https://consortium.uchicago.edu/publications/view-elementary-schools-state-reform -chicago. A fuller explication of theorizing undergirding this research can be found in Bryk et al., *Charting Chicago School Reform.*

22. This framing was anchored in insights from Benjamin Barber on participatory politics that was explicated by Sharon Greenberg. She subsequently developed this further in her dissertation. Greenberg, "Grounding a Theory of School Community Politics."

23. For a summary of the work on effective school restructuring available at that point in time, see Newmann et al., *Authentic Achievement.*

24. The field staff in each of the two separate case study projects were asked to classify their schools based on the typologies that had been created for local school politics and improvement efforts. (At this point, they had no knowledge of the survey-based results for their schools.) Their classifications were then compared to the survey data. The field reports and survey data agreed over 90% of the time on both frameworks. This bolstered confidence in the report's claims about the prevalence of each phenomenon and how they were distributed among different school communities around the city.

25. Interestingly, this term was never used in the report itself, and the description was only an approximation of the actual accounting presented in the report.

26. The 1988 reform delegated this responsibility to another new governance structure: area-wide school councils made up of representatives from local school councils. Little in the line of resources and training was offered to these councils. In addition, the basic design was flawed in that it called on council members to police other council members.

27. Another important finding in this regard was that the early implementation of reform was more problematic in schools with high levels of student mobility. Relationships between parents and professionals were more transient in schools where the student body was not stable, and subsequent Consortium studies documented that the relational trust necessary to advance local improvement was harder to initiate and sustain in these places. So, a critical aspect about schools as organizations—the mobility in their student populations—had come into focus. Previously, student mobility was just accepted as a fact of life in poor urban neighborhoods. It remained a Consortium topic for research, and reducing it became a target for improvement efforts that continue to this day in many Chicago schools and surely many other urban districts as well.

28. The report discussed the kinds of indicators central to such an accountability system. It argued that they should clearly signal the full range of knowledge, skills, competencies, and basic dispositions that were valued for all of Chicago's children. The then current state or local testing programs did not come anywhere close to this, nor for that matter do current assessment programs.

29. John Ayers, interview, April 7, 2021.

30. At that time Bryk held a major leadership role in both the Center for School Improvement and the Consortium. Both were still very early in their organizational development, and separating completely from both seemed unfeasible.

31. For a further discussion of the rationale and implementation plan for an accountability council, see Bryk et al., *Charting Chicago School Reform*, 289–304.

32. As noted in chapter 1, the Amendatory Act of 1995 split the traditional superintendent's role into two new roles: a chief executive officer (CEO) and a chief education officer who reported to the CEO. The title "superintendent" disappeared.

33. Payne, *So Much Reform, So Little Change*, 13. This is also the source for the quote from the *Catalyst* editors.

34. With the exception of CPS senior leaders, the sending of delegates to the steering committee meetings was frowned upon as a practice. If an individual member did not maintain regular attendance, one of the committee cochairs would reach out to explore why and discern whether that individual should continue as a member. This issue rarely arose for individual members of the committee. It was sometimes problematic for the institutional members from CPS, CTU, and the Principals Association, and simply maintaining connections here was always the primary consideration.

35. School Reform Achievement Award to the Consortium on Chicago School Research presented by the Chicago Association of Local School Councils, June 6, 1998.

36. On a humorous note, it was only well after Paul Vallas departed from Chicago that Bryk learned from him during a public event at the University of Pennsylvania that his staff were actually reading Consortium reports, talking about them, and often finding them helpful. When Bryk expressed some surprise, Vallas responded, "Oh that other stuff, that was just politics."

37. For a more in-depth description of the theory of action undergirding Chicago's promotional gate grades, see Roderick, Jacob, and Bryk, "Impact of High-Stakes Testing."

38. The results summarized in the next two paragraphs draw from seven reports over a five-year period, from 1999 through 2004, in the Consortium's series on *Ending Social Promotion*. See the following: Roderick et al., *Results from the First Two Years*; Roderick, Nagaoka, and Easton, *Update: Ending Social Promotion*; Roderick et al., *Results from Summer Bridge*; Tepper Jacob, Stone, and Roderick, *Responses of Teachers and Students*; Nagaoka and Roderick, *Effects of Retention*; Allensworth, *Dropout Rates in Chicago*.

39. A core proposition in Improvement Science is that to improve outcomes, you have to see how the system operates to produce its current results and likewise be especially alert to possible unintended consequences emerging as one intervenes in a complex system. This orientation too was central to Consortium research programs.

40. *Catalyst* (Spring 2011). This was also subsequently reported in *Education Week*: Karp and Catalyst Chicago, "Chicago's Social Promotion Ban Quietly Fades."

41. In a final report on this research program, Nagaoka and Roderick concluded that neither social promotion nor retention helped to close the achievement gap for low-performing students. They recommended early identification of students experiencing difficulties in the primary grades, long before the first promotional gate at third grade. Waiting until third or sixth grade to intervene was not a judicious use of resources. See Nagaoka and Roderick, *Ending Social Promotion*.

42. Meeting Notes for Steering Committee of the Consortium on Chicago School Research, late 2003.

43. See *Catalyst Chicago*, May 2004.

44. The DNA of decentralization pulsed through the CAC proposal. For a detailed description of this influence, see Shipps, Sconzert, and Swyers, *Chicago Annenberg Challenge*.

45. Martinez, "City Teachers Rate Training as Ineffective."

46. For a summary of the evidence on changes affecting the annual test score reports during the Vallas years, see Bryk, "No Child Left Behind." A 1999 Test Trend report, authored by John Q. Easton et al., brought attention to the use of annual student learning gains as a better measure of the changing productivity of the Chicago Public Schools. Easton et al., *Annual CPS Test Trend Review, 1999*. Improvements in student annual learning gains had begun to emerge toward the end of Era 1 in 1994 and continued through the first year under the high-stakes accountability of the Vallas era. They then flattened out and subsequently showed some signs of decline. Another report by Elaine M. Allensworth and John Q. Easton, *Calculating a Cohort Dropout Rate*, challenged district claims regarding improving high school dropout rates.

47. On the immediate evaluation results, see Smylie et al., *Chicago Annenberg Challenge*.

48. This was reflected in a shift late in CAC funding to direct priority to a smaller number of networks, and "breakthrough schools" within these networks, that were specifically focused on teacher development and professional community and school leadership, including relational trust building out to parents and community, to directly enhance teaching and learning. See Smylie et al., *Chicago Annenberg Challenge*.

49. Weissman, "What's Next, Who's Next?"

50. Bryk, Camburn, and Louis, "Professional Community in Chicago Elementary Schools."

51. Newmann et al., "Instructional Program Coherence."

52. The very first work on this measure was advanced by David Kerbow at the Center for School Improvement. The labels for the 5Es have evolved some over the years. In this book we draw on the terminology set out in Bryk et al., *Organizing Schools for Improvement*.

53. The framing for the Consortium's measures here benefited from early work on measuring curricular demand initiated by another Restructuring Center Principal investigator, Andy Porter.

54. In *Organizing Schools for Improvement*, the term *instructional guidance system* was used for this essential support. In other publications it has been called *quality instruction* and/or *ambitious instruction*.

55. Foundational work that informed these developments included Bryk's earlier collaboration with Valerie Lee and Peter Holland on the academic and communal organization of effective urban Catholic high schools, and also Shouse, "Academic Press and Sense of Community."

56. The first public report on this is a working paper by Bryk and Schneider, *Social Trust*. It was subsequently published in book form in Bryk and Schneider, *Trust in Schools*. The evolution of the relational trust in school improvement was informed by discipline-based scholarship in social psychology and especially the theorizing by James Coleman on the notion of social capital. (See, for example, Coleman, *Foundations of Social Theory*.) It was also influenced more generally by new developments in urban

community sociology, much of it anchored in Chicago, by numerous scholars, including William Julius Wilson, Mary Patillo, Tony Earls, and Rob Sampson.

57. Payne's work also helped to identify a weakness in the survey system in the school leadership domain. While the emphasis on a strategic orientation and inclusive leadership seemed well placed, the measures underattended to a more basic managerial dimension. This was manifest in the most problematic schools where basic aspects of school life—a poorly run principal's office, supply shortages, nothing starting and ending on time, poor communications to parents and staff—characterized some places. Payne also directed attention to how the productive use of a principal's role of authority was a key lever to advancing meaningful change.

58. For a further elaboration of the five essential supports for school improvement, see Bryk et al., *Organizing Schools for Improvement.*

59. Sebastian and Allensworth, "Student Learning."

60. See Hart et al., *Supporting School Improvement*; and Hart et al., *5Essentials Survey in CPS.*

61. As discussed in chapter 3, in response to the changes wrought by the decentralization reform and challenges to the relevance of the organization, the Principals Association changed its mission and broadened its membership late in Era 1. It expanded out to include both principals and administrators and changed its name correspondingly.

62. Chicago Principals and Administrators Association, *Chicago Standards for Developing School Leaders.* This work was led by Al Bertani, formerly at CSI and then at the Chicago Principals and Administrators Association, who was in charge of developing the first system-wide efforts for principal professional development.

63. For a review of this work, see Akkerman and Bakker, "Boundary Crossing and Boundary Objects."

64. Put somewhat differently, the presence of such boundary objects resolves the "Tower of Babel Problem," where many people may be working hard to address a complex problem but, absent a common language to organize their efforts, simply cannot succeed.

65. This began as a separate project between CSI (Bryk) and the Chicago Panel (Easton) and then was absorbed under the Consortium umbrella as it took several years to solve.

66. Formally, the research on academic productivity developed a value-added measure for a school's contribution to student learning each year, and the indicator of improvement was the trend in these value-added estimates over time. The key evidence in generating these value-added estimates is the observed annual learning gains. (The correlation between the observed gain and the value-added estimate typically exceeded 0.9.) To simplify the presentation here, we refer to the evidence as learning gains. For details on this work see Bryk et al., *Academic Productivity of Chicago Public Elementary Schools.*

67. Bryk and Raudenbush, "Toward a More Appropriate Conceptualization of Research on School Effects."

68. Hart et al., *Supporting School Improvement.*

69. Smylie et al., *Chicago Annenberg Challenge,* 29.

70. It would take several more years of analytic efforts, probing the details in these rich data, including connecting evidence backward to 1990 and then forward through 2005, to fully validate this evidentiary system. The first full report was shared with the city in 2006 and then published in Bryk et al., *Organizing Schools for Improvement,* in 2010.

71. Koeneman, *First Son.*

72. Duncan and Easton had met by chance while Duncan was starting Ariel Community Academy in the North Kenwood neighborhood of Chicago. Unable to obtain reliable information from the CPS about the students and schools in the community that the Academy aimed to serve, he realized that he could obtain this information from the Consortium. After Duncan went to work for Vallas in 1997, he continued to reach out to the Consortium for data as accessing information, even internal to CPS, remained hard. Easton, interview, November 8, 2020. See also Duncan, "The Consortium."

73. While Roderick was new to working in the CPS, Easton had considerable previous experience, first as a data analyst in the Department of Research and Evaluation in the late 1970s, then as a research specialist in the Office of Equal Educational Opportunity in the mid-1980s, and finally as the director of research and evaluation at the launch of the Vallas Era.

74. For further details see Sebring, *Research Agenda 2004–2008*.

75. This work was led within CPS by Larry Stanton, previously on the staff of Chapin Hall at the University of Chicago, who recruited Heather Anichini, who subsequently developed a strong working relationship with the Consortium, to join him on this project. Anichini had previously worked for several years in the National TFA organization and eventually became president of the Chicago Public Education Fund, where she worked closely with the central office around principal leadership development. She is another exemplary boundary spanner—directly working inside the CPS, engaged in the social entrepreneurial space, a leader in the foundation community, and with strong connections to the applied research occurring at the Consortium around principal leadership development discussed in chapter 3. By infusing core frameworks from Consortium research into the CPS and the Public Education Fund, she advanced shared learnings about the improvement of the city's schools.

76. Earlier in the 1980s, results had emerged on public versus Catholic school sector effects on high school achievement and dropping out. Informed by this ongoing line of research, there was now good reason to believe that differences in how high schools were organized contributed to the observed inequities in student outcomes. This led to the study by Anthony S. Bryk and Yeow Meng Thum, "The Effects of High School Organization on Dropping Out: An Exploratory Investigation." The paper subsequently received the Palmer Johnson Award in 1991 from the American Educational Research Association for its distinguished contribution to the field.

77. Bryk was also affiliated at that time with the Center for Students' Placed at Risk at Johns Hopkins, another federally funded research center. He was able to access a subaward from them to support this study.

78. First shared with the city in the Consortium's report *Charting Reform in Chicago: The Students Speak* (1996).

79. For the 2002 report see Allensworth, Reed Kochanek, and Rafiullah Miller, *Student Performance*. Shazia Miller, a coauthor of this report, undertook the analysis work, with guidance from Roderick, Bryk, and Camburn, that resulted in the first "on track" indicator. For the 2005 report see Allensworth and Easton, *The On-Track Indicator as a Predictor of High School Graduation*.

80. See Krone Phillips, *Make or Break Year*, 98.

81. Melissa Roderick, interview, March 30, 2021. Corroborating evidence can also be found in Krone Phillips, *Make or Break Year*.

82. Mindsets/dispositions is one of the core domains for improvement leadership. See the discussion of this topic in Biag and Sherer, "Getting Better at Getting Better."

83. For a further discussion of the organizing principles and strategies deployed by NCS, see Pitcher et al., *Capacity Building Model for School Improvement*.

84. These CPS individual school reports expanded on an idea for individual reports to high schools first piloted by the Consortium in 1999. See both Easton, *How Do Kenwood Graduates Perform*; and Easton, *How Do Barton Graduates Perform in CPS High Schools*.

85. Paige Ponder, interview, February 23, 2022.

86. For a further discussion of the OnTrack initiative in Chicago as a task of "going upstream," see Heath, *Upstream*.

87. Allensworth and Easton, *What Matters for Staying On-Track*.

88. Ponder, interview, February 23, 2022.

89. For a further discussion of all this, see Krone Phillips, *Make or Break Year*, 100–107.

90. Krone Phillips, *Make or Break Year*, 104.

91. Krone Phillips, *Make or Break Year*, 171.

92. Leaky pipeline problems are common in education. For a further discussion of this idea, see chapter 1 of Bryk, *Improvement in Action*, where this frame is applied to efforts in the Fresno Public Schools to improve students' college going and address an under-matching issue.

93. Heath, *Upstream*, identifies this as a common class of problems found in many organizations.

94. Lopez's senior undergraduate thesis focused on issues affecting college attainment for Latino students; the work with CPS would anchor her PhD thesis at UChicago. She developed a senior exit survey about CPS students' graduation plans and the myriad factors that might interfere between postsecondary aspirations and actual attainment.

95. Greg Darnieder, interview, February 24, 2022.

96. Greg Darnieder also ramped up the program, Advancement in Individual Determination (AVID), so that it eventually reached 50,000 students. But in his view, it was the investment in counselors and the data infrastructure that principally drove the improvements that emerged.

97. John Easton, interview, June 15, 2021. This was also recounted by former Consortium director of communications Emily Krone Phillips in a memo of September 2, 2021, on the role of the media.

98. Easton, interview, June 15, 2021.

99. Roderick, Nagaoka, and Allensworth, *From High School to the Future*.

100. Roderick, Coca, and Nagaoka, "Potholes on the Road to College."

101. It wasn't until 2013 that the Consortium began formally documenting its efforts in this domain. According to the Consortium's own records, they made over one hundred presentations annually to diverse audiences, ranging from CPS leaders and school groups to national conferences. The Consortium also contributed to over one hundred media stories, evenly divided between local and national sources, including the *Chicago Tribune, Chicago Sun-Times*, local radio/TV, *Washington Post, New York Times,* and *Wall Street Journal*. By 2016 they had close to 100,000 website visitors each year.

102. Elaine Allensworth, communication with authors, 2020.

103. The collaboration with Ounce of Prevention also resulted in the formation and testing of the 5Es framework and measurement system for preschools. See Stein, Pacchiano, and Luppescu, *Essential Organizational Supports for Early Education*.

104. A significant number of new positions were created at the central office to support the work in schools on graduation pathways described in this chapter and instructional improvement efforts described in chapter 4. Some of this was disbanded by Huberman as he shifted attention to his performance management priorities coupled with budget crises derivative first of the Great Recession in 2009–2010 and then again as a result of a state budget crisis in 2013–2014.

105. Personal confirmation, Penny Sebring, 2021.

106. Follow-up responses from Darneider post interview, March 10, 2022.

107. Gwynne and De la Torre, *When Schools Close*.

108. Superintendent Byrd Bennett created the Commission on School Utilization to advise on how to consolidate schools in the district. The commission did its work in a four-month period of time and reported out in early March 2013. Consortium researchers had shared these findings with the Commission, but the wheels had already been set in motion to undertake the largest single-year closure of public schools ever in a US district.

109. Jesse Ruiz, interview, March 3, 2022.

110. Personal confirmation by author with Penny Sebring, 2021.

111. See de la Torre et al., *School Closings in Chicago*; and also Gordon et al., *School Closings in Chicago*.

112. The public release occurred at the Logan Center on the UChicago campus, and many parents, community organizers, and protesters came to the event. Laura Washington, a veteran *Chicago Sun-Times* reporter and editor, had been invited to facilitate a panel discussion following the presentation of findings. The event was often interrupted by angry audience reactions.

113. This included spending time with the CPS Office of External Research and Accountability, so that staff could further explain the results to others. Marisa de la Torre, interview, June 15, 2021.

114. Kalata and McEwen, *Chicago: A Choice District*; Barrow and Sartain, "Expansion of High School Choice."

115. This had been documented in independent qualitative studies, in school system report cards, and in Consortium findings. For one account along these lines see Payne, *So Much Reform, So Little Change*.

116. For a powerful account of the impact of the closures in the Bronzeville community, the home of the former State Street CHA public housing corridor, see Ewing, *Ghosts in the Schoolyard*.

117. Sampson, *Chicago Charter Schools*.

118. The University of Chicago established UChicago Impact, a not-for-profit organization wholly owned by the university that is dedicated to advancing evidence-based practices in K–12 schools and providing tools for teaching, learning, and leadership. Organizationally located, along with the UChicago Consortium, under the UChicago Urban Education Institute, its first order of business was to transform survey administration and reporting from a paper system to online.

119. On the emergence of the logic of performance management in Chicago, see the case study *Performance Management in the Chicago Public Schools*.

120. For a first report on this initiative, see Klugman, Gordon, and Sebring, *First Look at the 5Essentials in Illinois Schools*.
121. This move was also consistent with a growing call at that time for the use of multiple measures in these processes beyond test scores.
122. See Davis et al., *5Essentials Survey in CPS*.
123. See Hart et al., *Supporting School Improvement*.
124. In 2014, the Consortium and Urban Education Institute (its university home) established an operation derivative of the Consortium called To&Through, which provides educators, policy makers, and families with research, data, and training on the milestones that matter most for college success.
125. The Consortium continued its research programs in this area, building on Allensworth and Easton, *What Matters for Staying On-track*. Subsequent reports focused on students with disabilities and English learners and documented longer term outcomes.
126. One of the most significant in this regard, City Year, decided to deploy its mentors to work primarily with ninth-graders to make sure they understood the importance of attendance and commitment to their classes.
127. The department's name was eventually changed to the Office of College and Career Success.
128. Topics ranged from the limited academic challenge in students' (high school) senior year to the positive effects of International Baccalaureate on the paths to and through high school and college.
129. Farrington et al., *Teaching Adolescents to Become Learners*.
130. Farrington had helped launch the Young Women's Leadership Charter School in Chicago and began working at the Consortium while pursuing a doctorate in social psychology at UIC.
131. The initial review was supported by two national, non-Chicago foundations, Lumina and Raikes. Subsequent work was supported by the Wallace Foundation, which also aimed for a national audience.
132. See Allensworth et al., *Supporting Social, Emotional and Academic Development*.
133. See note 55.
134. It is well known that all organizations, including public bureaucracies, engage in self-protective defensive actions. Such actions can undermine internal organizational learning and, in the case of improving public schooling, also the broader-based social learning necessary to advance improvements citywide. For a further discussion on this account, see Argyris, *Overcoming Organizational Defenses*.

Chapter 3

1. Warren Chapman, interview, January 12, 2021. Also see McKersie's discussion of CCT history and especially their role moving beyond the confines of the 1988 reform law in McKersie, "Strategic Philanthropy and Local Public Policy."
2. Davidson and Kurtz, "Monitoring Project CANAL." Second quarter, year 2 progress report submitted to US Department of Education, April 1991 (Chicago Public Schools, Monitoring Commission for Desegregation Implementation, 1992) ED 359 298. Additional data on state and federal funding from Dr. Martha Hebert, director of funded programs for CPS 1985–1995; personal correspondence with Steven E. Tozer, July 7, 2020.
3. Bennett et al., *Charting Reform*.

4. McKersie, "Strategic Philanthropy and Local Public Policy."

5. A small grant for work with principals was also made to Roosevelt University during this same period. McKersie documents only minimal foundation dollars flowed in this direction during Era 1. McKersie, "Strategic Philanthropy and Local Public Policy."

6. The Leading Change Summer Institute was further supplemented by monthly follow-up sessions throughout the year. Al Bertani, personal correspondence with Anthony Bryk, January 20, 2021.

7. McKersie, "Strategic Philanthropy and Local Public Policy."

8. "Carving Out Time for Teacher Renewal"; Shore, "Teachers Academy to Resume Training."

9. Bryk et al., *Organizing Schools for Improvement*.

10. The Golden Apple Teacher Foundation was sponsored by Golden Apple, a local foundation launched by Mike and Pat Koldyke. Mike was among the "old guard" of senior business leaders discussed in chapter 1.

11. In 1992 CPS approached UIC to develop a program to help them expand the number of CPS teachers with a Type 29 ESL/bilingual education endorsement. See Sakash and Chou, "Increasing the Supply of Latino Bilingual Teachers."

12. *Tomorrow's Teachers; Tomorrow's Schools of Education*.

13. Phyllis Lockett, interview, March 9, 2022.

14. Payne, *So Much Reform, So Little Change*.

15. "History of Chicago Public Schools."

16. For a strong critique of the scripted, direct instruction curriculum under CEO Vallas, see Duffrin, "Direct Instruction Making Waves." Shortly thereafter, in an editorial, *Catalyst* editor Linda Lenz noted the Vallas decision to make the scripted curriculum nonmandatory. Lenz, "So What's a School to Do?" By the time that Duncan and Eason-Watkins took control, the scripted curriculum had faded from public reporting and increasingly from school implementation, soon to be replaced entirely by new curriculum initiatives as described in chapter 4.

17. Smylie et al., *Chicago Annenberg Challenge*.

18. Bryk et al., *Charting Chicago School Reform*.

19. Al Bertani, personal planning notes for discussion with Beverly Tunney, president of Chicago Principals and Administrations Association, October 1994.

20. Chicago Leadership Academies for Supporting Success (CLASS) Program Brochure (1998). LIFT (Leadership Initiative for Transformation), established in 1995, was a partnership between CPAA, CSI, and the Chicago Public Schools. It was designed to serve as a new principal induction program. Activities included monthly daylong learning sessions and regular coaching from retired and practicing principals. Program partners included Al Bertani, Center for School Improvement; Karen Carlson, Leadership for Quality Education; Arthur Fumarolo, Chicago Public Schools; Marcella Gillie, Kellogg Graduate School of Management; Dolores Gonzalez and Sallie Penman, Illinois Administrators Academy; and Beverly Tunney, Chicago Principals and Administrators Association.

21. Chicago Leadership Academies for Supporting Success Program Brochure (1998). CASL (Chicago Academy for School Leadership) was modeled after the California School Leadership Academy and, over several years, adapted its curriculum modules for Chicago (1996). CASL was led by Executive Director Karen Dyer and supported by

several former CPS principals including Don Anderson, Pat Anderson, Jackie Carruthers, and Cynthia Felton.

22. Chicago Leadership Academies for Supporting Success Program Brochure (1998). LAUNCH (Leadership Academy and Urban Network for Chicago) was conceived by Al Bertani, senior designer, and Beverly Tunney, president of the Chicago Principals and Administrators Association. It was led by Executive Director Ingrid Carney (former CPS principal and assistant superintendent for human resources in Anderson, Indiana). Carney and Frederick Brown led initial program efforts from 1998 to 2002, followed by Joan Crisler and Faye Terrell-Perkins between 2003 and 2008.

23. Social network data is not available for this period. Had it been, Tunney would have demonstrated "high betweenness centrality."

24. The 1995 Amendatory Act authorized the CEO to appoint interim principals in probation schools. For the majority of the system, however, this authority remained with LSCs. See Wade, "Site-Based Management During a Time of Centralization"; Wong, "The Big Stick."

25. Ayers, "Picking Principals," 133–139.

26. Lenz, "Principal Selection Process Needs Fine-Tuning."

27. Murphy and Shipman, "Interstate School Leaders and Licensure Consortium."

28. For a detailed history of the evolution of SB1019 and its implementation in determining requirements for Chicago principal eligibility, see Cafferty, "Historical Analysis of the Chicago Public Schools Policy."

29. Pick, "Business Group Launches Principal Assessment Center." Peter Martinez, program officer at the MacArthur Foundation, and Warren Chapman, program officer at the Joyce Foundation, helped fund the efforts to create it. Also noted by Cafferty, "Historical Analysis of the Chicago Public Schools Policy."

30. Sebring et al., *Essential Supports for School Improvement*; Bryk et al., *Organizing Schools for Improvement*.

31. Ascensión Juarez, interview, October 26, 2020.

32. Elmore, *Building a New Structure for School Leadership*.

33. See, for example, the web page "History: More Than a Century of Discovery and Service," University of Illinois Chicago, https://www.uic.edu/about/history/, which states: "In 1993, then UIC Chancellor (and later UI President) James Stukel launched the Great Cities Initiative to join UIC teaching and research community, corporate and government partners in tackling urban challenges. Renamed the Great Cities Community at its ten-year mark, the signature program integrates research with genuine community engagement."

34. Arne Duncan, interview, February 18, 2021, and February 26, 2021.

35. Juarez, interview, October 26, 2020.

36. Juarez, interview, October 26, 2020.

37. Nancy Slavin, interview, October 22, 2020.

38. Juarez, interview, October 26, 2020; Slavin, interview, October 22, 2020.

39. Orfield, Woolbright, and Kim, *Neighborhood Change and Integration in Metropolitan Chicago*.

40. Rossi, Beaupre, and Grossman, "Failing Teachers," 6.

41. According to statistics provided by the Consortium, CPS teaching staff trained at Chicago State and Northeastern declined from 25.3% in 2003–2004 to 18.6% by

2017–2018. Meanwhile, the total share of teachers graduating from Chicago-area institutions, including UIUC, UIC, DePaul, National-Louis University, and downstate ISU, increased in both degree categories. And Chicago was also now drawing substantial numbers of teachers from outside Illinois as well. Also significant, by 2017–2018 some 50% of new teachers held master's degrees, up from 42% in 2003–2004.

42. Koldyke, introduced in chapter 1, supported the development of both programs.

43. For a critical analysis of the low percentage of teachers of color in TFA in this era, and the displacement of teachers of color that resulted, see White, "Teach For America's Paradoxical Diversity Initiative."

44. Shohoni, "Teach for America Growth and Impact Snapshot"; Aneesh Shohoni (executive director, Teach For America), correspondence with the author, August 27, 2021.

45. Slavin, interview, October 22, 2020.

46. Data provided by Steven E. Tozer at UIC based on tabulations from ISBE Teacher Service Records. In 2001, 48% of teachers with less than 5 years' experience were white. By 2010 this number had jumped to 62%.

47. Jiang and Sporte, *Teacher Evaluation in Chicago.*

48. The "checklist" evaluation process in which virtually all teachers received high ratings was widely disparaged. More generally, attention to teacher evaluation received a boost in Era 2 when a joint task force led by UIC and the Illinois State Board of Education successfully recommended a two-stage state teaching license. Illinois School Code subsequently required that teachers perform satisfactorily during a three-year "initial license" period before they could be granted a standard Illinois teaching license, during which time these teachers would be formally evaluated annually and could be terminated. Article 21 "Certification of Teachers."

49. This widely cited quote is attributed to Linda Darling Hammond. For an account of Finland's education system, see Morgan, "Review of Research."

50. Jiang and Sporte, *Teacher Evaluation in Chicago.* Also see Sartain et. al., *Teacher Evaluation in CPS.*

51. Data reported as part of the Slavin interview, October 22, 2020.

52. Stoelinga and Mangin, *Examining Effective Teacher Leadership.*

53. Easton, Kapdia Matsko, and Coca, *Keeping New Teachers.*

54. *Profiles in Excellence.*

55. Kelleher, "CPS Gets Boost."

56. Hart et al., *Teacher and Principal Leadership in Chicago.*

57. Al Bertani, personal notes, 1995–2001. Witness the difficulties encountered when the CTU attempted to support turnaround efforts early in Era 2 and the sustained struggles experienced by the National Teachers Academy, a joint venture of CPS, CTU, and UIC.

58. The National Board for Professional Teaching Standards eventually recognized this weakness and approached the Carnegie Foundation for the Advancement of Teaching in 2014 to assist them in the formation of a Networked Improvement Community to develop such a working theory. Even so, the press to simply expand the numbers of certified teachers, which was core to NBCT's ongoing funding, often distracted from this organization building goal. By Era 4, Catalyst headlined that "City, District Leaders Pivot from National Board Certification." Kelleher, "City, District Leaders Pivot."

59. The last of these was Hart et al., *Teacher and Principal Leadership.*

60. This development as well was influenced by scholarship emerging in Chicago. See Kapadia Matsko and Hammerness, "Unpacking the 'Urban' in Urban Teacher Education."

61. We have highlighted the work of UIC in our account because it became a nationally recognized leader in transforming professional preparation and influenced both local and state policies in lasting ways. The *Chicago Sun-Times* attested to UIC's distinctive contributions in 2004 when its list of the ten most influential women in Chicago education included UIC Chancellor Sylvia Manning and College of Ed Dean Vicki Chou. Although it was Chicago's largest university and its most visible in CPS teacher and leader workforce development, UIC was not alone among education schools in rethinking how its programs could better respond to the needs of CPS. Several other colleges of education around the city, including DePaul, Northwestern, National Louis, and Northeastern Illinois University, also found new ways to respond to CPS personnel needs in teacher and principal preparation.

62. Peter Martinez, interview, February 19, 2022, and March 5, 2022.

63. Victoria Chou, interview, September 11, 2020.

64. City Universities of New York Graduate Center and UCLA's Center X were and are prominent examples of urban institutions that prepare educators for urban districts. See City Universities of New York Graduate Center, "A Public Graduate School in the Center of NYC" and UCLA Center X, "UCLA Prepares and Supports Educators."

65. At the beginning of Era 3, and dating back many years, Chicago State and Northeastern were preparing the most teachers for CPS. By the end of Era 3 and throughout Era 4, UIC, National Louis, DePaul, and Loyola were.

66. The College of Education at UIC eventually received national attention. It received three American Association of Colleges for Teacher Education Best Practice Awards. At the same time, it broke into the top fifty of *U.S. News & World Report*'s best education schools—what had long been the domain of more prestigious research-intensive institutions. Specific professional education programs were ranked even higher, such as the EdD program in urban education leadership, which peaked at #14 nationally for three consecutive years in Era 4.

67. Among its other activities under Chou's leadership, UIC joined with Loyola University, Northeastern Illinois University, and National Louis University to redesign their elementary teacher preparation programs in partnership with CPS as a result of a $16 million USDOE Teacher Quality Partnership grant. UIC, Loyola University, and National Louis University would become three of the top four university suppliers of new teachers to Chicago in Era 4. DePaul was the fourth, as noted above.

68. The program was conceived by three graduate students—Jon Schnur, Ben Fenton, and Monique Burns—at Harvard University.

69. Personal communication between Al Bertani, then head of the Office of Professional Development, and the then school board chair, Gerry Chico.

70. Over time, however, this changed to resemble more conventional recruitment and selection processes.

71. Murphy and Shipman, "Interstate School Leaders and Licensure Consortium." The CPS principal competencies were introduced above in the discussion of SB1019. Under the direction of Nancy Laho, the first chief of the Office of Principal Preparation and

Development, and in collaboration with leadership from LAUNCH, New Leaders, and UIC, the competencies were revised and then later revised again. Today's version of these competencies represents that evolution over time. "Competency A: Champions Teacher and Staff Excellence Through Continuous Improvement."

72. In 2008, an Illinois Legislative Task Force that included Launch, New Leaders, and UIC recommended that New Leaders could prepare candidates for the state endorsement on its own, a measure signed into law in 2010. For a detailed account of this history, see Hunt et al., *Reforming Principal Preparation at the State Level.*

73. Selected faculty from National Louis University offered the academic curriculum and provided the course credits required for administrative certification.

74. The struggles that TFA teachers faced, despite their selective-college preparation, are well documented in Crawford-Garrett, *Teach for America and the Struggle for Urban School Reform.*

75. From 1999 to 2000, a university bi-campus P-20 task force, co-led by a UIUC professor of educational psychology and Tozer as the chair of UIC's Education Policy Studies Department, called for all three campuses to take a greater role in improving student learning outcomes in the state's public schools. This helped catalyze the UIC redesign of principal preparation, and together the past and then current UI presidents, Ikenberry and Stukel, met with McArthur's president to discuss how the foundation might be supportive. Northwestern University had assisted CPAA's initiative in principal development, and in 2001 National Louis University started hosting the New Leaders program. It would be three years before a highly selective, residency-based model designed to meet the needs of urban schools replaced the traditional master's degree program at UIC.

76. This was subsequently revised to be one and a half years.

77. For a classic treatment of how professional preparation differs from traditional liberal arts education, see Flexner, *Medical Education in the United States and Canada.* See also Borrowman, *Teacher Education in America.*

78. See, for example, widely circulated critiques published in the early 2000s, such as Finn and Broad, *Better Leaders for America's Schools*; Levine, *Educating School Leaders.*

79. Subsequently, the department was able to leverage national sources as well, such as the Broad Foundation, Stone Family Foundation, and the US Department of Education.

80. By the end of Era 4 the commitment to use data to improve the program would result in a Spotlight Award for Continuous Improvement from the Carnegie Foundation for the Advancement of Teaching.

81. They would go on to receive national awards from the University Council on Education Administration, the Council on Great Cities Schools, and others. See Davis and Darling-Hammond, "Innovative Principal Preparation Programs." See also Walker and Tozer, "Towards the Continuous Improvement."

82. Matt Lyons, interview, March 15, 2021.

83. By 2012, the Fund had concentrated its initiatives on principal leadership development, offering design and scheduling workshops, peer-driven professional learning communities, succession planning, and even a Chicago Principals Fellowship at Northwestern University. Assistant principals who wanted to lead schools also received special opportunities. Eventually, almost half of the 650 principals and dozens of assistant principals took part.

84. *Keeping Chicago's Top Principals.*
85. *Chicago's School Leaders.*
86. CEdO and then CEO Janice Jackson was a UIC program graduate, as were the chief of the Office of Language and Culture, Ernesto Matias, and the chief of early childhood education, Michael Abello. New Leaders alumnae Elizabeth Kirby and Zipporah Hightower became the heads of the Office of Network Supports and the Department of Principal Quality, respectively. LAUNCH also produced several central office leaders, including Karen Saffold, deputy chief for the Office of School Networks; Antonio Acevedo, chief of the Office of Language and Culture; and Bogdana Chkoumbova, current CEdO. In addition, several graduates of LAUNCH, UIC, and New Leaders became network chiefs.
87. This was a theme of the video *Waiting for Superman.*
88. This originally appeared as part of a PBS special. See "Rhee Fires Principal."
89. Whalen, *Transforming Central Office Practices for Equity.*
90. Jackson, like many other high school principals, was assisted in her work at Westinghouse by the Network for College Success, founded at the University of Chicago in 2006. Among other programs of support for high school principals as leaders of learning communities, NCS partners with a cohort of fifteen to twenty high schools every year throughout Chicago in its Partner School Network, providing cross-school professional learning and job-embedded coaching. "Network For College Success."
91. Whalen, *Transforming Central Office Practices for Equity,* 79.
92. See the Partnership website: https://www.chicagoprincipals.org/. See also Fitzpatrick, "CPS Trying to Stanch Rapid Turnover of Principals."
93. Whalen, *Transforming Central Office Practices for Equity,* 31.
94. Knight, "Five Big Ideas for Chicago's Troubled Schools."
95. Whalen, *Transforming Central Office Practices for Equity,* 37–40.
96. Lyons, interview, March 18, 2022.
97. Darling-Hammond et al., *Developing Effective Principals.* This decentralized approach to supporting principals and teachers through network chief development was limited by the number of schools actually participating in networks. After the Independent School Principal program was instituted, about sixty of those schools were exempt from network participation, and that number would later grow. Also exempt were over one hundred charter schools and some fifty contract, performance, and specialty schools. Consequently, network chiefs had responsibilities over about two-thirds of the district's 650 schools.
98. Jess Ruiz, interview, March 2, 2022.
99. Source data from *Progress Report* and *Chicago's School Leaders.* As Grissom et al. point out, evidence demonstrates that students of color tend to be more successful in schools led by principals of color. Grissom, Egalite, and Lindsay, *How Principals Affect Students and Schools.*
100. Lyons, interview, March 18, 2022.
101. Koetting, "For the Record."
102. Manna and Moffitt, *New Education Advocacy Organizations in the U.S.*
103. Sartain et al., *Teacher Evaluation in Chicago Public Schools;* Lyons, interview, March 1, 2021.
104. Bryk et al., *Organizing Schools for Improvement;* Wilson, *Truly Disadvantaged.*

105. The Opportunity Schools program was designed during the Jackson administration to recruit and support teachers in what the district otherwise referred to as hard-to-staff schools. Lyons, interview, March 18, 2022.
106. Whalen, *Transforming Central Office Practices for Equity*. CEO Jackson would later elevate the continuous improvement focus further by hiring a director of strategic planning who had continuous improvement expertise.
107. For example, during Jackson's tenure as CEdO and CEO, CPS leaders have become superintendents of Chicago-area districts including DeKalb, Elmwood Park, Forest Park, Skokie, Westchester, and Kalamazoo, MI. Others during this period have become the chief academic officer of Indianapolis Public Schools, the superintendent of Prince William County, Virginia, the chief academic officer of the Illinois State Board of Education, and the director of school and district leadership for the Illinois State Board of Education.

Chapter 4

1. Briscoe, "Historian Timuel Black Celebrates DuSable High School at Black History Event."
2. Source material for the Spurlark discussion includes a series of audio recorded interviews conducted by Greenberg in 2000. Topics included Spurlark's family background, her childhood and schooling, and her professional career.
3. In his memoir, Emanuel compares the Houston public school system to CPS in terms of instructional time and states that the difference is 2.5 years. Emanuel, *Nation City*, 22.
4. Through Eras 1 and 2 the number of schools in CSI's network was typically five but some years as many as eight.
5. STEP was subsequently expanded to be a K–5 tool. For more information see Urban Education Institute, UChicago, https://uchicagoimpact.org/our-offerings/step.
6. Barbara Eason-Watkins, interviews, June 24, 2020, August 28, 2020, October 20, 2020, and November 17, 2020.
7. Eason-Watkins was one of the last principals appointed by the central office prior to the start of reform.
8. Pick, "Tour of Duties."
9. Children who are not proficient readers by third grade have less chance of graduating from high school on time or at all, less chance of college completion, and less chance of full employment as adults. See *Early Warning! Why Reading by the End of Third Grade Matters*. See also Moffitt, Arseneault, and Belsky, "Gradient of Childhood Self-Control Predicts Health, Wealth, and Public Safety"; Hernandez, *Double Jeopardy*; Lesnick et al., *Reading on Grade Level in Third Grade*. We also can put a price tag on the problem. The cost for retaining a student for a year is estimated at $10,700 (Weyer, "Third-Grade Reading Legislation"), and the cost of placement in special education is roughly double that (Harr, Parrish, and Chambers, "Special Education"; Verstegen, "Public Education Finance Systems"). Additionally, the lifetime earnings of a struggling reader who doesn't finish high school are estimated to be $260,000 less than the individual's peers with a bachelor's degree. Planty et al., *Condition of Education*.
10. One notable example was Chicago's failed effort implementing mastery learning districtwide. Banas, "Byrd Is Already Talking Reform."

11. By 1995 when Vallas took over, McCosh had progressed enough to be above probation and so not subject to the system's scripted curriculum.

12. Newmann et al., *Authentic Instruction and Standardized Tests.*

13. For further discussion see Duffrin, "Woodlawn School Shows What Can Be Done."

14. As quoted in Pick, "Tour of Duties."

15. "Fragile" is a term Eason-Watkins used to describe the McCosh school community and others like it. Eason-Watkins, interviews, June 24, 2020, August 28, 2020, October 20, 2020, and November 17, 2020.

16. Herrick, "Parents Learn to Read from Their Kids."

17. For further discussion see Fargo, "It Takes a Village to Raise a School."

18. Prior to her appointment at McCosh, Eason-Watkins had started a doctoral program at UChicago. This was her entree to the academic network that she would cultivate over her years at McCosh and when she became CEdO.

19. Chicago philanthropy made the McCosh story possible. Chapman, at the Joyce Foundation, was a sustained funder. The Chicago Community Trust underwrote much of the initial middle school work, and McCosh had been part of an Annenberg network that focused on the transition to high school.

20. We have omitted the school's name since this was a negative comparison.

21. The individuals mentioned reflect the range of expertise that Eason-Watkins was bringing into her building, including literacy, mathematics and science teaching and learning, project-based learning, leadership development, child and adolescent development, school administration, sociology, organizational development, applied statistics, social services, learning sciences, and school finance. In addition to the institutions mentioned above, colleagues from institutions including Loyola, the Chicago Panel on Public School Policy and Finance, the Center, and the Consortium also contributed.

22. McCosh had served as a professional development site in an Annenberg network and was the only CPS school to do so. Aspects of the Center's comprehensive restructuring had taken hold in individual schools, but none had achieved it fully. This led the Center to design, open, and operate the North Kenwood Oakland Charter Elementary School. See Hassrick, Raudenbush, and Rosen, *Ambitious Elementary School.*

23. A report by the Consortium in 2006 (with a follow-up study in 2010) documented that over one hundred elementary schools had achieved significant student learning gains prior to Eason-Watkins becoming CEdO in Era 3. Sebring et al., *Essential Supports for School Improvement.*

24. A few of the ARCs had previously participated in the Chicago Area Writing Project and the Illinois Writing Project, where they might have had some experience as adult educators.

25. For information about DIBELS, see "Dibels: Dynamic Indicators of Basic Early Literacy Skills."

26. Noted in chapter 3, to offer this level of support to schools, Eason-Watkins transitioned the district from six regions of one hundred schools to twenty-four areas of twenty-five schools. In Era 4, the areas transitioned to networks.

27. The Advanced Reading Development Demonstration Program (AARDP) was supported by Searle funds at the Chicago Community Trust. Initiated in 2002 as a partnership among the CPS, area universities, and schools, it engaged Northeastern, Roosevelt, Chicago State, University of Illinois, Chicago, National Louis, and the Center to each

work with a network of up to ten schools. Consistent with the CRI, AARDP did not offer one-shot professional development. Rather, it sought to build faculty and school capacity. Universities did not have to use a common approach; however, they did agree to spend time in their schools each week, meet monthly with CPS, school, and foundation leaders, and cooperate with an external evaluator. "Urban Literacy: Partnerships for Improving Literacy in Urban Schools"; and Russo, "Branches of the Reading Initiative."

28. Depending on funding at any given time, Eason-Watkins's office paid for one or two coordinator positions, and at other times the position was a cost share with the school.

29. Jennifer McDermott, Tom Nardone, MaryBeth Crowder-Meier, and Sharon Greenberg made up the Center's team. Both McDermott and Nardone had worked in New York City's District 2. At that time McDermott was also consulting in San Diego, where Alvarado was chancellor of instruction.

30. Quotes and information about the instructional rounds derive from Greenberg's personal memos and notes about the work as it was ongoing. Interviews with Eason-Watkins add corroboration. Eason-Watkins, interviews, June 24, 2020, August 28, 2020, October 20, 2020, and November 17, 2020.

31. An audit done early in Era 3 identified eighty-six elementary math textbook series, over two dozen algebra I textbooks, and several dozen science texts. For more information see Center for Science and Math Education, Scale UP: Systemic Reform of Math and Science Education in Chicago, Loyola University, http://scaleup.luc.edu/index.php.

32. Borrowing from a Beatles' song, Eason-Watkins used this as the title of a presentation at Rutgers University in 2021. Eason-Watkins, interview, June 24, 2020, August 28, 2020, October 20, 2020, and November 17, 2020.

33. Gartzman's quotes, and much of the description of the CMSI initiative, derive from interviews with Gartzman and several memos that he wrote for us. Marty Gartzman, interviews, July 7, 2021, and February 16, 2022.

34. These included the Institute for Math and Science Education at UIC, the University of Chicago Science and Math Project, the Department of Mathematics at DePaul, and the Illinois Math and Science Academy at the Illinois Institute of Technology. Their number was testament to both the wealth of such resources in the city and the excitement that seized the city when the reform legislation first passed and the "collective us" was motivated to pitch in. It is also notable that these were disciplinary departments and centers that were jumping in at this point, and not the city's colleges of education.

35. Marty Gartzman, interviews, July 7, 2021, and February 16, 2022.

36. *Never Too Late to Learn*, 1–2.

37. Quotes and source material for the CMSI discussion are from a series of interviews with Gartzman on July 7, 2021, and February 16, 2022, and memos he developed for Greenberg, with corroboration from Eason-Watkins, interviews, June 24, 2020, August 28, 2020, October 20, 2020, and November 17, 2020.

38. While both CRI and CMSI were developing instructional coaches in their respective disciplines, CRI was drawing mainly from reading coaches who had been working directly with students in schools. CRI was preparing them to coach the reading specialists in their area's schools. CMSI, in contrast, was developing central office staff to coach school-based math and scientist specialists. While many of those staff had

organized and delivered "sit and git" professional development in the past, most had been in central office and distant from schools for years.

39. Gartzman, interviews, July 7, 2021, and February 16, 2022.
40. CMSI also defined what was meant by "well-prepared." Gartzman, interviews, July 7, 2021, and February 16, 2022.
41. Nomi, Raudenbush, and Smith, "Effects of Double-Dose Algebra."
42. Gartzman, interviews, July 7, 2021, and February 16, 2022.
43. Jessie Ruiz, interview, March 2, 2022.
44. Piling onto the funding problem, the MacArthur Foundation had spent down its education money and did not refresh the pot, and by then the Joyce Foundation had specialized around teacher quality, not instructional improvement.
45. Gudelia Lopez, memo, February 8, 2021; and follow-up conversations with Sharon Greenberg.
46. CPS principals rated almost all of their teachers positively, regardless of student achievement, and they had little incentive to do otherwise. Low ratings had the potential to anger teachers or make them fearful. Prior to the 1988 reform, the hurdles to remove a problematic CTU member were close to insurmountable, and most principals were not the instructional leaders who could help that group improve. The 1988 and 1995 legislation weakened union protections, but the changes were insufficient. There was no upside to low ratings, while the downside was considerable.
47. It is notable that FFT was introduced in CPS prior to the federal Race to the Top education initiative that was announced in 2009, and prior to the Gates-funded Measures of Effective Teaching Project that studied the use and efficacy of Danielson and several other teacher observation and evaluation tools. "PLATO Protocol for Classroom Observations."
48. In an *Education Week* conversation with Rick Hess, Danielson makes this same point—that when used well, the tool functions as a powerful form of professional development because it focuses principals and teachers on instruction and gets them "on the same page" about what "good" is. Danielson, "Straight Up Conversation."
49. This information and quote are from the Lopez memo, May 3, 2021.
50. "Our Story: 10 Years of Art Education Progress."
51. Toward the end of Era 3, CPS and numerous art and community partners also collaborated to open in the Humboldt Park neighborhood a Chicago High School for the Arts. It opened in the fall of 2009.
52. "Our Story: 10 Years of Art Education Progress."
53. Suzanne Doornbos-Kerbow, interview, April 16, 2021; Lopez memo, May 3, 2021.
54. Coalition for Community Schools, "About."
55. Chicago still had several active settlement houses, including the Community Renewal Society, which housed *Catalyst*, and Association House. Miguel del Valle, whose story follows, was executive director of Association House early in his career.
56. National studies include https://www.americanprogress.org/article/building -community-schools-systems/, https://www.nea.org/student-success/great-public -schools/community-schools, https://learningpolicyinstitute.org/product/community -schools-effective-school-improvement-brief, https://www.rand.org/pubs/research _reports/RR3245.html.

57. This sentiment was shared with us in a number of interviews, including Beth Swanson, April 19, 2022; Jessie Ruiz, March 2, 2022; and Gudelia Lopez, personal communication, February 14, 2022.

58. Janice Jackson, interviews, June 14, 2021, and February 3, 2022.

59. See discussion, chapter 2.

60. Janice Jackson, interviews, June 14, 2021, and February 3, 2022. See also CPS Chief Janice Jackson comments on her experience at UIC. UIC Today, "I Made the Right Choice."

61. Charles Payne, interview, February 18, 2021.

62. Most of these efforts had been initiated in Era 3, while a few, like raising graduation requirements and expanding International Baccalaureate and Advanced Placement, started under Vallas in Era 2.

63. See chapter 2 for further discussion of these developments. See also discussion in Krone Phillips, *Make or Break Year.*

64. Whalen, *Transforming Central Office Practices for Equity*, 49; Gartzman, interviews, July 7, 2021, and February 16, 2022.

65. Whalen, *Transforming Central Office Practices for Equity*, 43.

66. That Common Core was implemented contemporaneously with the district's leadership churn makes its success even more remarkable. Lopez, a program officer at the Chicago Community Trust for much of this time, believes that foundation support, and the lack of interest, oversight, or interference from the system's top, enabled district department heads to prioritize and sustain its implementation. Gudelia Lopez, memo, February 8, 2021.

67. With support from the Trust, Walqui had already been consulting with the system's handful of dual-language elementary schools when she was asked to take on this broader role. Gudelia Lopez, personal communication, January 2022.

68. Lopez memo, July 2022.

69. Allensworth, Cashdollar, and Gwynne, "Improvements in Math Instruction."

70. Common Core's implementation also demonstrated a causal cascade: better teacher guidance (in the form of articulated standards) leads to better teaching, which leads to better learning, which leads to improved student achievement.

71. Whalen, *Transforming Central Office Practices for Equity*, 24.

72. Janice Jackson, interviews, June 14, 2021, and February 3, 2022.

73. As quoted in Whalen, *Transforming Central Office Practices for Equity*, 6.

74. As quoted in Whalen, *Transforming Central Office Practices for Equity*, 40.

75. As quoted in Whalen, *Transforming Central Office Practices for Equity*, 39.

76. Gudelia Lopez, memo, May 3, 2021.

77. The 1988 reform gave LSCs control of discretionary money, in part because early reformers like Moore and Hess did not believe they could achieve fair funding in Springfield. In their interviews, Miguel del Valle (June 8, 2021), Beth Swanson (April 19, 2022), Jessie Ruiz, (March 2, 2022), Josie Yanguas (February 25, 2021, July 1, 2021, and February 11, 2022) and Arne Duncan (February 18, 2021, and February 26, 2021) all talked with us about the ongoing fight for fair funding.

78. Eason-Watkins, interviews, June 24, 2020, August 28, 2020, October 20, 2020, and November 17, 2020; Yanguas, interviews, February 25, 2021, July 1, 2021, and February 11, 2022. In this fight Eason-Watkins and Bowman had support from Chicago's

academic and early childhood communities, from African American and Latino professional and community-based organizations, and even from former governor Blagojevich.

79. This was the first expansion of the AP and IB programs since Era 2 under Vallas.
80. Brizard was CEO when the 2012 contract was negotiated, but Emanuel takes credit for this reform in his memoir.
81. The 2001 Consortium report brought attention to this problem; time was also identified as a problem in a *Catalyst* article entitled "It's About Instruction, Stupid" and in Gordon, "Moving Instruction to Center Stage." The Annenberg Challenge identified time as one of the three biggest impediments to improving schooling. Fendt, *Chicago Annenberg Challenge.*
82. Swanson, interview, April 19, 2022.
83. Belsha, "English Learners Often Go Without Required Help in Chicago Schools."
84. While using test scores as its benchmark, the *Chicago Reporter* also acknowledged the need for a Consortium study that might analyze student progress over time.
85. De la Torre et al., *English Learners in Chicago Public Schools.*
86. Bryk et al., *View from the Elementary Schools*, 11, 19. For further discussion, see Bryk et al., *Organizing Schools for Improvement.*
87. Bryk et al., *Organizing Schools for Improvement.* Also, Bryk and Schneider, *Trust in Schools.*
88. Roberts, "Pride, Not Prejudice."
89. Inter-American Magnet School, "History."
90. Roberts, "Pride, Not Prejudice." Inter-American serves a student population that is half Spanish speaking and half English speaking. About 60% of the students are from low income families. Since the school's inception students routinely score above state average on standardized tests, and 60% have been college bound.
91. Roberts, "Pride, Not Prejudice."
92. "Thomas School" was the subject of a 1993 case study written by Greenberg (formerly Rollow) and Yanguas. Consistent with prior confidentiality agreements, we use pseudonyms for the school and all of the people mentioned. Rollow and Yanguas, *Road to Emergent Restructuring.*
93. As quoted in Rollow and Yanguas, *Road to Emergent Restructuring*, 10. This quote, and others relating to Thomas School, is drawn from this case study.
94. State of Reform report, 1993, 24.
95. State of Reform report, 1993, 36.
96. Quotes in this paragraph are from Azcoitia, "Community Schools Like Spry"; and a discussion of Azcoitia's work on the Community Organization and Family Issues (COFI) website, https://cofionline.org/COFI/. Azcoitia is a founding member of COFI. See Azcoitia, "Community Schools Like Spry"; and Lewis and Azcoitia, "For Equity in Alternative High Schools."
97. Quotes herein, and del Valle's story overall, are based on a June 8, 2021, interview.
98. He was then executive director of Association House, one of Chicago's first settlement houses. By the 1980s it had become a community-based social service agency.
99. Miguel del Valle, interview, June 8, 2021.
100. In addition to the dropout problem, as executive director of Association House, del Valle worked with families who complained that CPS was not providing services to

Spanish-speaking special education students, nor was it giving Latino neighborhoods a fair share of Head Start seats even as other communities were getting them. Del Valle, interview, June 8, 2021.

101. Absent oversight from central office, many schools remained out of compliance with these state laws, but for those schools that wished to comply, the bills offered guidance about how to do so. Yanguas, interviews, February 25, 2021, July 1, 2021, and February 11, 2022.

102. The bill was essentially copied from a new Massachusetts law, and it traveled to several more states after that. Yanguas interviews, February 25, 2021, July 1, 2021, and February 11, 2022.

103. Yanguas was another boundary spanner. Prior to her full-time appointment at IRC, Yanguas had been staff at the Center for School Improvement. She also cochaired or was a member of the Consortium Steering Committee for twelve years.

104. WIDA was initially a consortium of three member states: Wisconsin, Delaware, and Arkansas (from which it derived its name). It now has forty-one member states and territories. "Mission and History."

105. ACCESS was designed to help educators get a nuanced picture for how ELs were developing English-language proficiency and use of disciplinary academic language. When NCLB required an assessment, it was a state-level decision to use ACCESS to fulfill that part of the federal mandate, or another test. Then and now, WIDA cautions states to use ACCESS as a formative instrument only, but it cannot control that decision. Yanguas, interviews, February 25, 2021, July 1, 2021, and February 11, 2022.

106. Student performance on the assessment is high stakes for schools and teachers as well because it determines whether they stay in services or transfer out. The number of students enrolled in bilingual programs determines teaching positions and categorical funding.

107. Sanchez, "Bilingual Education Returns to California."

108. This invisibility was not an anomaly but endemic to American society. Recently, Joaquin Castro, a member of the US House of Representatives, wrote that even though the Latino population has climbed to 40% nationally, Latino stories remain "a missing narrative . . . written out of textbooks, film, TV, print and minimized in the halls of power." Taladrif, "Exclusion of Latinos."

109. *Language Education: Preparing Chicago Public School Students*, 1.

110. Additive approaches were also contrasted with "subtractive ones" like transitional bilingual that aimed to replace a child's native language with English.

111. *Language Education: Preparing Chicago Public School Students*, 1.

112. Research on academic language in bilingual education, and best practices to teach it, initiated in the 1960s and well ahead of it becoming a focus of literacy research. James Cummins, at the University of Toronto, OISE, was an early pioneer. Yanguas, interviews, February 25, 2021, July 1, 2021, and February 11, 2022.

113. Chicago Public Schools, *Elevating Our Vision for Learning*, 11.

114. Lopez, memo, July 2022.

115. *Raising the Achievement of Latino Students and English Language Learners.*

116. Charters run by the citywide Latino advocacy organization UNO were found to be the worst offenders. Belsha, "English Learners Often Go Without Required Help at Chicago Schools."

117. Garibay-Mulaterri offered Saturday workshops for teachers focused on the needs of ELs. She also convened a Principals Consortium on Dual Programs. OLCE created a new position for EL specialists, trained a cadre of specialists, and assigned one to each school network. In addition, OLCE trained and placed an EL program leader in most of the schools that had a significant EL population. OLCE deployed its budget toward these efforts, and supplemental support came from the Trust. Lopez, memo, July 2022.
118. As CEO, Jackson ordered a complete compliance audit and sent each school its results with the mandate that progress toward compliance become part of its continuous improvement plan. She also supported the start of more dual-language schools: she told us there were about five in 2017 when she became CEO and more than forty in 2021 when she left CPS. She brought expertise into central office from professional and academic groups and made internal promotions that positioned Latino leaders across central office rather than siloed in those departments focused solely on cultural and language concerns. Most importantly, she continued efforts begun by Eason-Watkins to recast the role of central office in service to the specific needs of individual schools. Jackson, interviews, June 14, 2021, and February 3, 2022.

Chapter 5

1. We are indebted on this account to the scholarship articulated by Clarence Stone. See Stone et al., *Building Civic Capacity*. Stone et al. focus on the conditions that enable a community to advance efforts that result in social betterment. They argue that successful change requires a sustained community synergy in the face of slow progress and to moderate competing demands as new "silver bullet" ideas arise and new individuals take up the reins of system leadership. Stone defines the existence of such productive institutional arrangements across a city as civic capacity.
2. This is a well-recognized and long-standing theme in the politics of education, and responding to it is a core concern in the writings on building civic capacity. See Stone et al., *Building Civic Capacity*.
3. See Stone, "Rhetoric, Reality and Politics," for his account of the important functional roles played by applied research and media in nurturing capacity for productive civic actions.
4. For a review of this research, see Akkerman and Bakker, "Boundary Crossing and Boundary Objects."
5. For the classic treatment on this topic, see Tyack, *One Best System*.
6. Sutton and Rao, *Scaling Up Excellence*, 25.
7. Mehta, "Possible Futures."
8. The extensive research on this topic can be found through links on the Wallace Foundation website: https://www.wallacefoundation.org/knowledge-center/school-leadership/pages/principal-pipeline-implementation.aspx.
9. According to statistics compiled by the Illinois State Board of Education, in 2020 the operating expenses in the Chicago Public Schools were $17,799. Illinois State Board of Education, https://www.illinoisreportcard.com/district.aspx?source=environment&source2=perstudentspending&Districtid=15016299025.
10. Powell, *Uncertain Profession*.
11. See Sirotnik and Goodlad, *School-University Partnerships in Action*.

12. These critiques are succinctly summarized in Puckett, Review of *School-University Partnerships in Action*.
13. For an introduction see Penuel et al., "Organizing Research and Development."
14. Karin Chenoweth raises a similar point in her *Washington Post* op-ed, "In Chicago, Public Schools Are Often Called a Mess. Truth Is, They've Improved—a Lot," August 26, 2021, https://www.washingtonpost.com/opinions/2021/08/26/chicago-public-schools -dysfunction-success-data-media/.
15. Chenoweth, *Districts That Succeed*, 151.
16. This appears in basic CPS descriptive tabulations provided by Paul Zavitkovsky from UIC.
17. A recent Consortium report documents that the rates at which students graduated from high school and went on to college were relatively similar regardless of what community area they lived in. This, however, is not true for college completion. See McKoy et al., *Approaching Chicago Student Attainment*
18. See, for example, the case study report on Thomas School in Bryk and Schneider, *Trust in Schools*. See also the account on Alexander School in Bryk et al., *Charting Chicago School Reform*. Similar reports on educator and family relations appear in the *Tribune* series on the Goudy school.
19. See Ewing, *Ghosts in the Schoolyard*.
20. For an account of the dysfunction in public social services affecting such neighborhoods, see Elliot, *Invisible Child*.

Bibliography

"After Decades-Long Struggle, Pritzker Signs Bill Restoring CTU Bargaining Rights."
April 2, 2021. https://www.ctulocal1.org/posts/after-decades-long-struggle-pritzker-signs
-bill-restoring-ctu-bargaining-rights/.

Akkerman, Sanne F., and Arthur Bakker. "Boundary Crossing and Boundary Objects."
Review of Educational Research 81, no. 2 (2011): 132–169. https://doi.org/10.3102
/0034654311404435.

Allensworth, Elaine. *Ending Social Promotion: Dropout Rates in Chicago After Implementation of the Eighth-Grade Promotion Gate.* Chicago: University of Chicago Consortium on
School Research, 2004. https://consortium.uchicago.edu/publications/ending-social
-promotion-dropout-rates-chicago-after-implementation-eighth-grade.

Allensworth, Elaine. *Graduation and Dropout Trends in Chicago.* Chicago: University of
Chicago Consortium on School Research, 2005. https://consortium.uchicago.edu
/publications/graduation-and-dropout-trends-chicago-look-cohorts-students-1991-2004.

Allensworth, Elaine, Sarah Cashdollar, and Julia Gwynne. "Improvements in Math Instruction and Student Achievement Through Professional Learning Around the Common
Core State Standards in Chicago." *AERA Open,* 7 (2021). https://doi.org/10.1177
/2332858420986872.

Allensworth, Elaine, and John Q. Easton. *Calculating a Cohort Dropout Rate for the Chicago
Public Schools.* Chicago: University of Chicago Consortium on School Research, 2001.

Allensworth, Elaine, and John Q. Easton. *The On-Track Indicator as a Predictor of High
School Graduation.* Chicago: University of Chicago Consortium on School Research, 2005.
https://consortium.uchicago.edu/publications/track-indicator-predictor-high-school
-graduation.

Allensworth, Elaine M., and John Q. Easton. *What Matters for Staying On-Track and
Graduating from the Chicago Public Schools: A Focus on Students with Disabilities.*
Chicago: University of Chicago Consortium on School Research, 2012.

Allensworth, Elaine, and John Q. Easton. *What Matters for Staying On-Track and Graduating
in Chicago Public Schools.* Chicago: University of Chicago Consortium on School
Research, 2007. https://consortium.uchicago.edu/publications/what-matters-staying
-track-and-graduating-chicago-public-schools.

Allensworth, Elaine M., Camille A. Farrington, Molly F. Gordon, David W. Johnson, Kylie Klein, Bronwyn McDaniel, and Jenny Nagaoka. *Supporting Social, Emotional and Academic Development.* Chicago: University of Chicago Consortium on School Research, 2018. https://consortium.uchicago.edu/publications/supporting-social-emotional -academic-development-research-implications-educators.

Allensworth, Elaine M., Julia A. Gwynne, Kaleen Healey, and Rene Crespin. *High School Graduation Rates Through Two Decades of District Change.* Chicago: University of Chicago Consortium on School Research, 2016.

Allensworth, Elaine, Julie Reed Kochanek, and Shazia Rafiullah Miller. *Student Performance: Course Taking, Test Scores, and Outcomes.* Chicago: University of Chicago Consortium on School Research, 2002. https://consortium.uchicago.edu/publications/student -performance-course-taking-test-scores-and-outcomes.

Allensworth, Elaine, and Shazia Rafiullah Miller. *Declining High School Enrollment.* Chicago: University of Chicago Consortium on School Research, 2002. https://consortium .uchicago.edu/publications/declining-high-school-enrollment-exploration-causes.

Argyris, Chris. *Overcoming Organizational Defenses: Facilitating Organizational Learning.* Needham, MA: Allyn and Bacon, 1990.

Article 21, "Certification of Teachers," Chapter 105 Schools, 105 ILCS 5/ School Code, in *Illinois Code.* Springfield: Illinois State Board of Education, 2010. https://law.justia.com /codes/illinois/2021/chapter-105/act-105-ilcs-5/article-21/.

Ayers, John. "Picking Principals: Vallas Goes Too Far." In *School Reform in Chicago: Lessons in Policy and Practice,* edited by Alexander Russo, 133–141. Cambridge, MA: Harvard Education Press, 2004.

Azcoitia, Carlos. "Community Schools Like Spry Could Expand Nationally After This Election." *Chicago Unheard* (blog), September 24, 2020. https://chicagounheard.org/blog /community-schools-like-spry-could-expand-nationally-after-this-election/.

Banas, Casey. "Byrd Is Already Talking Reform." *Chicago Tribune,* May 26, 1985.

Baron, Paula, ed. *The Chicago Public High School for Metropolitan Studies,* October 2021. http://www.metrohschicago.com/book.pdf.

Barrow, Lisa, and Lauren Sartain. "The Expansion of High School Choice in Chicago Public Schools." *Economic Perspectives* 41, no. 5 (2017).

Belsha, Kalyn. "English Learners Often Go Without Required Help at Chicago Schools." *Chicago Reporter,* June 28, 2017. https://www.chicagoreporter.com/english-learners-often -go-without-required-help-at-chicago-schools/.

Bennett, Albert L., Anthony S. Bryk, John Q. Easton, David Kerbow, Stuart Luppescu, and Penny Bender Sebring. *Charting Reform: The Principals' Perspective.* Chicago: Consortium on Chicago School Research, 1992.

Bernstein, David. "Daley v Daley." *Chicago Magazine,* September 10, 2008.

Biag, Manuelito, and David Sherer. "Getting Better at Getting Better: Improvement Dispositions in Education." *Teachers College Record* 123, no. 4 (2001): 1–42. https://doi .org/10.1177/01614681211230.

Bittle, Jake, Srishti Kapir, and Jasmine Mathani. "Redeveloping the State Street Corridor." *South Side Weekly,* January 31, 2017. https://southsideweekly.com/chicago-unfulfilled -promise-rebuild-public-housing/.

Borrowman, Merle L. *Teacher Education in America: A Documentary History.* New York: Teachers College Press, 1965.

The Bottom Line: Chicago's Failing Schools and How to Strengthen Them. Chicago: Designs for Change, 1985.

Boyer, John W. *The University of Chicago: A History*. Chicago: University of Chicago Press, 2018.

Briscoe, Tony. "Historian Timuel Black Celebrates DuSable High School at Black History Event." *Chicago Tribune*, February 25, 2018. https://www.chicagotribune.com/news/ct -met-timuel-black-dusable-high-school-20180225-story.html.

Bryk, Anthony S. *Improvement in Action: Advancing Quality in America's Schools*. Cambridge, MA: Harvard Education Press, 2020.

Bryk, Anthony S., ed. *New Directions for Program Evaluation: Stakeholder-Based Evaluations*. San Francisco: Jossey Bass, 1983.

Bryk, Anthony S. "No Child Left Behind, Chicago Style." In *No Child Left Behind? The Politics and Practice of School Accountability*, edited by Paul E. Peterson and Martin R. West, 242–268. Washington, DC: Brookings Institution, 2003.

Bryk, Anthony S., Elaine Allensworth, John Q. Easton, Penny Bender Sebring, and Stuart Luppescu. *Organizing Schools for Improvement: Lessons from Chicago*. Chicago: University of Chicago Press, 2010.

Bryk, Anthony S., Eric Camburn, and Karen S. Louis. "Professional Community in Chicago Elementary Schools: Facilitating Factors and Organizational Consequences." *Educational Administration Quarterly* 35, no. 5 (1999): 751–781. https://doi.org/10.1177 /0013161X99355004.

Bryk, Anthony S., John Q. Easton, David Kerbow, Sharon G. Rollow, and Penny Bender Sebring. *A View from the Elementary Schools: The State of Reform in Chicago*. Chicago: University of Chicago Consortium on School Research, 1993.

Bryk, Anthony S., Louis M. Gomez, Alicia Grunow, and Paul G. LeMahicu. *Learning to Improve: How America's Schools Can Get Better at Getting Better*. Cambridge, MA: Harvard Education Press, 2015.

Bryk, Anthony S., and Stephan W. Raudenbush. "Toward a More Appropriate Conceptualization of Research on School Effects: A Three-Level Hierarchical Linear Model." *American Journal of Education* 97, no. 1 (November 1998): 65–108.

Bryk, Anthony S., and Barbara Schneider. *Social Trust: A Moral Resource for School Improvement*. Chicago: University of Chicago Consortium on School Research, 2018. https://consortium.uchicago.edu/sites/default/files/2018-10/socialtrust_amoralresource forschoolimprovement.pdf.

Bryk, Anthony S., and Barbara Schneider. *Trust in Schools: A Core Resource for improvement*. New York: Russell Sage Foundation, 2002.

Bryk, Anthony S., and Penny Bender Sebring. *Achieving School Reform in Chicago: What We Need to Know*. Chicago: University of Chicago Consortium on School Research, 1991. https://consortium.uchicago.edu/publications/achieving-school-reform-chicago-what-we -need-know.

Bryk, Anthony S., Penny Bender Sebring, David Kerbow, Sharon Rollow, and John Q. Easton. *Charting Chicago School Reform: Democratic Localism as a Lever for Change*. Boulder, CO: Westview Press, 1998.

Bryk, Anthony S., and Yeow Meng Thum. "The Effects of High School Organization on Dropping Out: An Exploratory Investigation." *American Educational Research Journal* 26, no. 3 (1989): 353–383.

Bryk, Anthony S., Yeow M. Thum, John Q. Easton, and Stuart Luppescu. *Academic Productivity of Chicago Public Elementary Schools*. Chicago: University of Chicago Consortium on School Research, 1998. https://consortium.uchicago.edu/publications/academic-productivity-chicago-public-elementary-schools.

Cafferty, Siobhan M. "An Historical Analysis of the Chicago Public Schools Policy on the Requirements for the Selection of Principals, 1983–2008." EdD diss., Loyola University, 2010. http://ecommons.luc.edu/luc_diss/60.

"Carving Out Time for Teacher Renewal." *Catalyst* 2, no. 5 (February 1991).

Caught in the Web. Chicago: Designs for Change, 1982.

Center for Research on Educational Outcomes. *Urban Charter School Study Report on 41 Regions*. Stanford, CA: CREDO, 2015.

Charting Reform: The Teachers' Turn. Report no. 1. Chicago: Consortium on Chicago School Research, 1991. https://consortium.uchicago.edu/sites/default/files/2018-10/Charting%20Reform_The%20Teachers%20Turn.pdf.

Chenoweth, Karin. *Districts That Succeed: Breaking the Correlation Between Race, Poverty, and Achievement*. Cambridge, MA: Harvard Education Press, 2021.

Chicago Principals and Administrators Association. *Chicago Standards for Developing School Leaders*. 1998.

Chicago Public Schools. *Elevating Our Vision for Learning: Improving Schools for All*. Chicago: Chicago Public Schools, 2011.

Chicago's School Leaders: 2020–2021. Chicago: Chicago Public Education Fund, 2021. https://thefundchicago.org/wp-content/uploads/2021/03/2020-21-Chicago-Principals-Overview-1.pdf.

"Children First Fund." Chicago Public Schools, 2022. https://www.cps.edu/about/departments/children-first-fund-cff/.

City Universities of New York Graduate Center. "A Public Graduate School in the Center of NYC." https://www.gc.cuny.edu/.

Civic Committee of the Commercial Club of Chicago. *Left Behind: Student Achievement in Chicago's Public Schools; A Report of the Education Committee*. Chicago: Civic Committee of the Commercial Club of Chicago, 2003.

Civic Committee of the Commercial Club of Chicago. *Still Left Behind: Student Learning in Chicago's Public Schools*. Chicago: Commercial Club of Chicago, 2009.

Civic Consulting Alliance. "Our History." https://www.ccachicago.org/about/history/.

Clifford, Geraldine, and James Guthrie. *Ed School: A Brief for Professional Education*. Chicago: University of Chicago Press, 1988.

Coalition for Community Schools. "About." Institute for Educational Leadership. https://www.communityschools.org/about/.

Cohen, David K., and James P. Spillane. "Chapter 1: Policy and Practice: The Relations Between Governance and Instruction." *Review of Research in Education* 18, no. 1 (1992): 3–49. https://doi.org/10.3102/0091732X018001003.

Coleman, John S. *Foundations of Social Theory*. Cambridge, MA: Belknap Press of Harvard University Press, 1990.

Community Organization and Family Issues (COFI). https://cofionline.org/COFI/.

"Competency A: Champions Teacher and Staff Excellence Through Continuous Improvement to Develop and Achieve the Vision of High Expectations for All Students." Office of Accountability—Educator Effectiveness, September 2015. https://www.cps.edu

/globalassets/cps-pages/careers/school-leadership/principal-quality/principal-eligibility
/principalevaluationrubric.pdf.

Crawford-Garrett, Katy. *Teach For America and the Struggle for Urban School Reform:
Searching for Agency in an Era of Standardization.* New York: Peter Lang, 2014.

Danielson, Charlotte. "Straight Up Conversation; Teacher Eval Guru Charlotte Danielson."
Education Week, June 23, 2011.

Darling-Hammond, Linda, Marjorie Wechsler, Stephanie Levin, Melanie Leung-Gagne, and
Steve Tozer. *Developing Effective Principals: What Kind of Learning Matters?* Palo Alto,
CA: Learning Policy Institute, 2022.

Davis, Laura, Andria Shyjka, Holly Hart, Vanessa Gutierrez, Naureen Kheraj, Christopher
Young, Alicia Chen, and Elaine Allensworth. *5Essentials Survey in CPS.* Chicago:
University of Chicago Consortium on School Research, 2021. https://consortium
.uchicago.edu/publications/5Essentials-survey-in-CPS-2021.

Davis, Stephen H., and Linda Darling-Hammond. "Innovative Principal Preparation
Programs: What Works and How We Know." *Planning and Changing* 43, no. 1/2
(Summer 2012): 25–45.

de la Torre, Marisa, Alyssa Blanchard, Elaine Allensworth, and Silvana Freire. *English
Learners in Chicago Public Schools: A New Perspective.* Chicago: University of Chicago
Consortium on School Research, 2019.

de la Torre, Marisa, Jennifer R. Cowhy, Paul T. Moore, Lauren Sartain, and David Knight.
School Closings in Chicago. Chicago: University of Chicago Consortium on School
Research, 2015. https://consortium.uchicago.edu/publications/school-closings-chicago
-understanding-families-choices-and-constraints-new-school.

Delpit, Lisa. *Other People's Children: Cultural Conflict in the Classroom.* New York: New
Press, 2006.

Dewey, John. *The Public and Its Problems.* New York: Holt Publishers, 1927.

"Diaries." *Catalyst* 1, no. 1 (1990): 26–36.

"DIBELS: Dynamic Indicators of Basic Early Literacy Skills." University of Oregon. https://
dibels.uoregon.edu/about-dibels.

Dockrell, W. Bryan, and David Hamilton. *Rethinking Educational Research.* London: Hodder
and Stoughton, 1980.

Dropouts for the CPS: An Analysis of the Classes of 1982, 1983, 1985. Chicago Panel on Public
School Finance, 1985.

Duffrin, Elizabeth. "Direct Instruction Making Waves." *Chicago Reporter,* July 25, 2005.
https://www.chicagoreporter.com/direct-instruction-making-waves/.

Duffrin, Elizabeth. "Woodlawn School Shows What Can Be Done." *Catalyst,* September
1998.

Duncan, Arne. "The Consortium." In *How Schools Work,* 67–84. New York: Simon and
Schuster, 2018.

Duncan, Arne. *How Schools Work.* New York: Simon and Schuster, 2018.

Early Warning! Why Reading by the End of Third Grade Matters. Baltimore: Annie E. Casey
Foundation, 2010. ED509795.

Easton, John Q., Robert M. Gladden, Shazia Rafiullah Miller, and Stuart Luppescu. *How Do
Barton Graduates Perform in CPS High Schools?* Chicago: University of Chicago
Consortium on School Research, 1999. https://consortium.uchicago.edu/publications
/how-do-barton-graduates-perform-cps-high-schools.

Easton, John Q., Robert M. Gladden, Shazia Rafiullah Miller, and Stuart Luppescu. *How Do Kenwood Graduates Perform?* Chicago: University of Chicago Consortium on School Research, 1999. https://consortium.uchicago.edu/publications/how-do-kenwood-graduates-perform.

Easton, John Q., Kavita Kapdia Matsko, and Vanessa M. Coca. *Keeping New Teachers.* Chicago: University of Chicago Consortium on School Research, 2007. https://consortium.uchicago.edu/sites/default/files/2018-10/keeping_new_teachers012407.pdf.

Easton, John Q., Todd Rosenkranz, Anthony S. Bryk, Brian A. Jacob, Stuart Luppescu, and Melissa Roderick. *Annual CPS Test Trend Review, 1999.* Research Data Brief. May 2000. https://consortium.uchicago.edu/sites/default/files/2018-10/p0a05.pdf.

Elliot, Andrea. *Invisible Child: Poverty, Survival and Hope in an American City.* New York: Random House, 2021.

Elmore, Richard F. *Building a New Structure for School Leadership.* Washington, DC: Albert Shanker Institute, 2000.

Emanuel, Rahm. *The Nation City: Why Mayors Are Now Running the World.* New York: Knopf Doubleday, 2020.

Enos, Evan. "How Greenwich Republicans Learned to Love Trump." *New Yorker,* May 3, 2020.

"Every Child, Every School: An Education Plan for the Chicago Public Schools." Working paper, Chicago Public Schools, Chicago, IL, September 2002.

Ewing, Eve L. *Ghosts in the Schoolyard: Racism and School Closings on Chicago's South Side.* Chicago: University of Chicago Press, 2018.

Fargo, Charles. "It Takes a Village to Raise a School." In "School Reform: What Matters Most," special series, *Catalyst,* December 1997.

Farrington, Camille A., David W. Johnson, Elaine Allensworth, Jenny Nagaoka, Melissa Roderick, Nicole Williams Beechu, and Tasha Senesca Keyes. *Teaching Adolescents to Become Learners: The Role of Noncognitive Factors in Shaping School Performance: A Critical Literature Review.* Chicago: University of Chicago, 2012.

Fendt, Carol, Elaine Allensworth, Jenny Nagaoka, Mark Smylie, Sara Hallman, Stacy A. Wenzel, and Stuart Luppescu. *The Chicago Annenberg Challenge: Successes, Failures, and Lessons for the Future.* Chicago: University of Chicago Consortium on Chicago School Research, 2003. https://consortium.uchicago.edu/publications/chicago-annenberg-challenge-successes-failures-and-lessons-future/.

Finn, Chester E., and Eli Broad. *Better Leaders for America's Schools: A Manifesto.* Washington, DC: The Broad Foundation and The Fordham Foundation, 2003.

Finnigan, Kay, and Jennifer O'Day. *External Support to Schools on Probation: Getting a Leg Up?* Chicago: University of Chicago Consortium on School Research, 2003.

Fitzpatrick, Lauren. "CPS Trying to Stanch Rapid Turnover of Principals." *Chicago Sun-Times,* November 14, 2016. https://chicago.suntimes.com/2016/11/14/18352057/cps-trying-to-stanch-rapid-turnover-of-principals.

Flexner, Abraham. *Medical Education in the United States and Canada: A Report to the Carnegie Foundation for the Advancement of Teaching.* New York: Carnegie Foundation for the Advancement of Teaching, 1910.

Gordon, David T. "Moving Instruction to Center Stage." In *School Reform in Chicago: Lessons in Policy and Practice,* edited by Alexander Russo, 47–54. Cambridge, MA: Harvard Education Press, 2004.

Gordon, Milly F., Marisa de la Torre, Jennifer R. Cowhy, Paul T. Moore, Lauren Sartain, and David Knight. *School Closings in Chicago.* Chicago: University of Chicago Consortium on School Research, 2018. https://consortium.uchicago.edu/sites/default/files/2018-10/School%20Closings%20in%20Chicago-May2018-Consortium.pdf.

Gorov, Lynda. "Hispanic Radio, TV Went All Out for Election." *Catalyst* 1, no. 1 (February 1990): 16–17.

Greenberg, Sharon. "Grounding a Theory of School Community Politics." PhD diss., University of Chicago, 1998.

Grissom, Jason A., Anna Egalite, and Constance A. Lindsay. *How Principals Affect Students and Schools: A Synthesis of Two Decades of Research.* New York: Wallace Foundation, 2021.

Gwynne, Julia, and Marisa de la Torre. *When Schools Close: Effects on Displaced Students in Chicago Public Schools.* Chicago: University of Chicago Consortium on School Research, 2009. https://consortium.uchicago.edu/publications/when-schools-close-effects-displaced-students-chicago-public-schools.

Gwynne, Julia A., and Paul T. Moore. *Chicago's Charter High Schools: Organizational Features, Enrollment, School Transfers, and Student Performance.* Chicago: University of Chicago Consortium on School Research, 2017.

Harr, Jenifer J., Tom Parrish, and Jay G. Chambers. "Special Education." In *Handbook of Research in Education and Finance,* edited by E. B. Fiske, 573–590. New York: Routledge, 2008.

Harris, Douglas N. *Charter School City: What the End of Traditional Public Schools in New Orleans Means for American Education.* Chicago: University of Chicago Press, 2020.

Hart, Holly M., Susan E. Sporte, Stephen M. Ponisciak, W. David Stevens, and Alissa Cambronne. *Teacher and Principal Leadership in Chicago: Ongoing Analyses of Preparation Programs.* Chicago: Consortium on Chicago School Research, 2008. https://consortium.uchicago.edu/sites/default/files/2018-10/T%20%20P%20Leadership%20CCSR%20064.pdf.

Hart, Holly, Christopher Young, Alicia Chen, Naureen Kheraj, and Elaine Allensworth. *5Essentials Survey in CPS: School Improvement and School Climate in High Poverty Schools.* Chicago: University of Chicago Consortium on School Research, 2021.

Hart, Holly M., Christopher Young, Alicia Chen, Andrew Zou, and Elaine Allensworth. *Supporting School Improvement: Early Findings from a Reexamination of the 5Essentials Survey.* Chicago: University of Chicago Consortium on School Research, 2020. https://consortium.uchicago.edu/publications/supporting-school-improvement.

Heath, Dan. *Upstream.* New York: Avid Reader Press 2020.

Hernandez, Donald J. *Double Jeopardy: How Third-Grade Reading Skills and Poverty Influence High School Graduation.* Baltimore: Annie E. Casey Foundation, 2011.

Herrick, Lynn. "Parents Learn to Read from Their Kids." *Chicago Tribune,* November 24, 1996.

"History of Chicago Public Schools." *Chicago Reporter,* 2022. https://www.chicagoreporter.com/cps-history/.

Hubbard, Lea, Hugh Mehan, and Mary Kay Stein. *Reform as Learning: School Reform, Organizational Culture, and Community Politics in San Diego.* New York: Routledge Taylor & Francis, 2016.

Hunt, Erika, Lisa Hood, Alicia Haller, and Maureen Kincaid. *Reforming Principal Prepara-tion at the State Level: Perspectives on Policy Reform from Illinois.* New York: Routledge, 2019.

Inter-American Magnet School. "History." https://iamschicago.com/apps/pages/index.jsp ?uREC_ID=348065&type=d.

Jiang, Jennie, and Susan Sporte. *Teacher Evaluation in Chicago: Key Findings from Consortium Research.* Chicago: University of Chicago Consortium on School Research, 2016. https://consortium.uchicago.edu/sites/default/files/2018-10/Teacher%20Evalua-tion%20Retrospective-Jan2016-Consortium.pdf.

Johnson, Dirk. "Illinois Legislature Moves to Give Parents Control of the Chicago Schools." *New York Times,* July 13, 1988, 7.

Joravsky, Ben. "Money Made the Difference in Voter Turn-Out." *Catalyst* 1, no. 1 (1990): 12.

Joyce Foundation. *Progress and Promise: Chicago's Nation-Leading Educational Gains.* Chi-cago: Joyce Foundation, 2018. https://www.joycefdn.org/research-reports/progress-and -promise-chicagos-nation-leading-educational-gains.

Kalata, Kasia, and Jelani McEwen. *Chicago: A Choice District.* Chicago: Illinois Network of Charter Schools, 2015.

Kapadia Matsko, Kavita, and Karen Hammerness. "Unpacking the 'Urban' in Urban Teacher Education: Making a Case for Context-Specific Preparation." *Journal of Teacher Education* (November 2013).

Karp, Sarah. "50 School Closings Approved at Raucous Board Meeting." *Catalyst,* May 22, 2013.

Karp, Sarah. "Grading Mayor Rahm Emanuel's Educational Legacy." WBEZ/NPR, May 16, 2019.

Karp, Sarah. "Minimal Cost Savings for Closing Schools: Analysis." *Catalyst,* October 31, 2012.

Karp, Sarah, and Catalyst Chicago. "Chicago's Social Promotion Ban Quietly Fades." *Education Week,* May 11, 2011.

Katz, Michael B. "Chicago School Reform as History." *Teachers College Record* 94, no. 1 (1992): 56–72.

Katz, Michael. "Teachers College Record: The Voice of Scholarship in Education." *Teachers College Record* 94, no. 1 (1992).

Keeping Chicago's Top Principals: A Look Back—The Path Forward. Chicago: Chicago Public Education Fund, 2016. https://thefundchicago.org/report/2016/keeping-chicagos-top -principals-look-back-path-forward/.

Kelleher, Maureen. "City, District Leaders Pivot from National Board Certification." *Chicago Reporter,* July 31, 2015. https://www.chicagoreporter.com/city-district-leaders-pivot-from -national-board-certification/.

Kelleher, Maureen. "CPS Gets Boost in Teachers Earning National Board Certification." *Chicago Reporter,* July 28, 2005. https://www.chicagoreporter.com/cps-gets-boost-in -teachers-earning-national-certification/.

Klugman, Joshua, Molly F. Gordon, and Penny Sebring. *A First Look at the 5Essentials in Illinois Schools.* Chicago: University of Chicago Consortium on School Research, 2015. https://consortium.uchicago.edu/sites/default/files/2018-10/Statewide%205E%20Report .pdf.

Knight, Meribah. "Five Big Ideas for Chicago's Troubled Schools. Idea One: Ax Middle Management." *Crain's*, December 7, 2015.

Koeneman, Keith. *First Son: The Biography of Richard M. Daley*. Chicago: University of Chicago Press, 2013.

Koetting, Nicole. "For the Record: Teachers Basic Skills Test." *Chicago Reporter*, July 27, 2012. https://www.chicagoreporter.com/record-teacher-basic-skills-test/.

Krone Phillips, Emily. *The Make or Break Year: Solving the Drop-Out Problem One Ninth Grader at a Time*. New York: New Press, 2019.

Langley, Gerald J., Ronald D. Moen, Kevin M. Nolan, Thomas W. Nolan, Clifford L. Norman, and Lloyd P. Provost. *The Improvement Guide*. San Francisco: Jossey-Bass, 2009.

Language Education: Preparing Chicago Public School Students for a Global Community: A Report of the Bilingual Education and World Language Commission. Chicago: Chicago Public Schools, 2010.

Lenz, Linda. "Missing in Action: The Chicago Teachers Union in School Reform in Chicago: Lessons in Policy and Practice." In *School Reform in Chicago: Lessons in Policy and Practice*, edited by Alexander Russo, 125–132. Cambridge, MA: Harvard Education Press, 2004.

Lenz, Linda. "Principal Selection Process Needs Fine-Tuning, Not Overhaul," with commentary from John Ayers, Sheila Castillo, and Beverly Tunney. *Chicago Reporter*, December 19, 2005. https://www.chicagoreporter.com/principal-selection-process-needs-fine-tuning-not-overhaul/.

Lenz, Linda. "So What's a School to Do?" *Chicago Reporter*, July 25, 2005. https://www.chicagoreporter.com/so-whats-school-do/.

Lenz, Linda. "To Our Readers." *Catalyst* 1, no. 1 (1990): 2.

Lenz, Linda. "What's in the New Law?" *Catalyst* (1995).

Lesnick, Joy, Robert M. Goerge, Cheryl Smithgall, and Julia Gwynne. *Reading on Grade Level in Third Grade*. Baltimore: Annie E. Casey Foundation, 2010. ED517805.

Levine, Arthur L. *Educating School Leaders*. Washington, DC: Education School Project, 2005.

Lewin, Kurt. Action Research and Minority Problems." *Journal of Social Issues* 2, no. 4 (1946): 34–46. https://doi.org/10.1111/j.1540-4560.1946.tb02295.x.

Lewin, Kurt, ed. *Resolving Social Conflict*. London: Harper & Row, 1946.

Lewis, Karen. "On Baseballs and Budgets." Speech to the City Club of Chicago, June 18, 2013. YouTube video, 30:19. https://www.youtube.com/watch?v=L3Anw3PQQ5k.

Lewis, Melissa, and Carlos Azcoitia. "For Equity in Alternative High Schools, We Must Build Community with Our Students." *Chicago Unheard* (blog), December 16, 2021. https://chicagounheard.org/blog/for-equity-in-alternative-high-schools-we-must-build-community-with-our-students/.

Lindblom, Charles E., and David K. Cohen. *Usable Knowledge: Social Science and Social Problem Solving*. New Haven, CT: Yale University Press, 1979.

Lipman, Pauline. "The Landscape of Education 'Reform' in Chicago; Neoliberalism Meets a Grassroots Movement." *Education Policy Analysis Archives* 25, no. 54 (2017).

Lipman, Pauline. "Making Sense of Renaissance 10 School Policy in Chicago: Race, Class and the Cultural Politics of Neoliberalism." UIC, A Great Cities Working Paper, 2009, GCP-09-02.

Malone, May, Shelby Mahaffie, Gisselle Hernandez, Alexandra Usher, and Jenny Nagaoka. *The Educational Attainment of Chicago Public Schools Students.* Chicago: University of Chicago Consortium on School Research, 2020. https://consortium.uchicago.edu /publications/the-educational-attainment-of-Chicago-Public-Schools-students-2020.

Manna, Paul, and Susan Moffitt. *New Education Advocacy Organizations in the U.S.: National Sample and a Case Study of Advance Illinois.* New York: Wallace Foundation, 2014.

Martinez, Michael. "City Teachers Rate Training as Ineffective." *Chicago Tribune,* February 7, 2001.

McDonald, Joseph P. *American School Reform: What Works, What Fails and Why.* Chicago: University of Chicago Press, 2014.

McGhee Hassrick, Elizabeth, Stephen W. Raudenbush, and Lisa Rosen. *The Ambitious Elementary School.* Chicago: University of Chicago Press, 2017.

McKersie, William S. "Strategic Philanthropy and Local Public Policy: Lessons from Chicago School Reform." PhD diss., University of Chicago, 1997. UMI 9829468

McKoy, Dominique, Alexandra Usher, Jenny Nagaoka, and Sanya Khatri. *Approaching Chicago Student Attainment from a Community Perspective.* Chicago: University of Chicago Consortium on School Research, 2021. https://consortium.uchicago.edu /publications/approaching-chicago-student-attainment-from-a-community-perspective.

Mehta, Jal. "Possible Futures: Toward a New Grammar of Schooling." *The Kappan,* January 24, 2022. https://kappanonline.org/possible-futures-new-grammar-0f-schooling -mehta/.

Menacker, Julius, Leslie Herzog, Emanuel Hurwitz, and Ward Weldon. "Most Principals, Councils Get Thumbs Up." *Catalyst* 1, no. 1 (1990): 2.

"Mission and History." WIDA. Wisconsin Center for Education Research, November 14, 2016. https://wida.wisc.edu/about/mission-history.

Moffitt, Terrie E., Louise Arseneault, and Daniel Belsky. "A Gradient of Childhood Self-Control Predicts Health, Wealth, and Public Safety." *Proceedings of the National Academy of Sciences of the United States of America* 108, no. 7 (2011): 2693–2698. DOI:10.1073/pnas.1010076108.

Morgan, Hani. "Review of Research: The Education System in Finland: A Success Story Other Countries Can Emulate." *Childhood Education* 90, no. 6 (2014): 453–457.

Murphy, Joseph, and Neil Shipman. "The Interstate School Leaders and Licensure Consortium: A Standards-Based Approach to Strengthening Educational Leadership." *Journal of Personnel Evaluation in Education* 13, no. 3 (1999): 205–224.

Nagaoka, Jenny, and Melissa Roderick. *Ending Social Promotion: The Effects of Retention.* Chicago: University of Chicago Consortium on School Research, 2004. https:// consortium.uchicago.edu/publications/ending-social-promotion-effects-retention.

National Commission on Excellence in Education. *A Nation at Risk: The Imperative for Educational Reform.* Washington, DC: US Department of Education, 1984.

"Network For College Success." University of Chicago. https://ncs.uchicago.edu.

Never Too Late to Learn: Lessons from the Teaching Academy for Math and Science. Chicago: Teachers Academy for Mathematics and Science and Project Exploration, 2009.

Newmann, Fred M., Anthony S. Bryk, and Jenny Nagaoka. *Authentic Intellectual Work and Standardized Tests: Conflict or Coexistence?* Chicago: University of Chicago Consortium on School Research, 2001.

Newmann, Fred M., Gudelia Lopez, and Anthony S. Bryk. *The Quality of Intellectual Work in Chicago Schools.* Chicago: University of Chicago Consortium on School Research, 1998.

Newmann, Fred M., BetsAnn Smith, Elaine Allensworth, and Anthony S. Bryk. "Instructional Program Coherence: What It Is and Why It Should Guide School Improvement Policy." *Educational Evaluation and Policy Analysis* 23, no. 4 (2001): 297–321.

Newmann, Fred M., and Associates. *Authentic Achievement: Restructuring Schools for Intellectual Quality.* San Francisco: Jossey Bass, 1996.

Nomi, Takako, Stephen Raudenbush, and Jake J. Smith. "Effects of Double-Dose Algebra on College Persistence and Degree Attainment." *Proceedings of the National Academy of Sciences* 118, no. 27 (2021), https://doi.org/10.1073/pnas.2019030118.

O'Connell, Mary. *School Reform Chicago Style: How Citizens Organized to Change Public Policy.* Chicago: Center for Neighborhood Technology, 1991.

O'Day, Jennifer, Catherine S. Bitter, and Louis M. Gomez. *Education Reform in New York City: Ambitious Change in the Nation's Most Complex School System.* Cambridge, MA: Harvard Education Press, 2011.

O'Day, Jennifer, and Marshall S. Smith. "Systemic Reform and Educational Opportunity." In *Designing Coherent Education Policy: Improving the System,* edited by Susan H. Fuhrman, 250–312. San Francisco: Jossey Bass, 1993.

Orfield, Gary, Albert Woolbright, and Helen Kim. *Neighborhood Change and Integration in Metropolitan Chicago: A Report of the Leadership Council for Metropolitan Open Communities.* Chicago: Leadership Council for Metropolitan Open Communities, 1984.

"Our Story: 10 Years of Art Education Progress." Ingenuity. https://www.ingenuity-inc.org /about/our-story/.

Payne, Charles M. *So Much Reform, So Little Change.* Cambridge, MA: Harvard Education Press, 2008.

Payne, Charles. *Still Crazy After All These Years: Race in the Chicago School System.* Chicago: University of Chicago Consortium on School Research, 2005.

Penuel, William R., Barry J. Fishman, Britte Haugan Cheng, and Nora Sabelli. "Organizing Research and Development at the Intersection of Learning, Implementation and Design." *Educational Researcher* 40 (2011): 331.

Performance Management in the Chicago Public Schools. Cambridge, MA: Harvard Educational Press, 2012.

Pick, Grant. "Business Group Launches Principal Assessment Center." *Chicago Reporter,* July 25, 2005. https://www.chicagoreporter.com/business-group-launches-principal -assessment-center/.

Pick, Grant. "A Tour of Duties: A Profile of Barbara Eason-Watkins, Principal of McCosh School." In "School Reform: What Matters Most," special series, *Catalyst,* December 1997.

Pitcher, Mary Ann, Sarah J. Duncan, Jenny Nagaoka, Eliza Moeller, Latesha Dickerson, and Nicole Beechum. *A Capacity Building Model for School Improvement.* Chicago: University of Chicago Consortium on School Research, 2016. https://consortium .uchicago.edu/sites/default/files/2018-10/A%20Capacity-Building%20Model-Nov2016 -Consortium.pdf.

Plan for Transformation: Improving Public Housing in Chicago and the Quality of Life. Chicago: Chicago Housing Authority, 2000.

Planty, Michael. *The Condition of Education.* Washington, DC: National Center for Education Statistics, Institute of Education Sciences, US Department of Education. NCES 2009-081

"The PLATO Protocol for Classroom Observations." MET Project, Bill and Melinda Gates Foundation, 2016. https://usprogram.gatesfoundation.org/-/media/dataimport/resources/pdf/2016/12/plato-10-29-101.pdf.

Powell, Arthur. *The Uncertain Profession: Harvard and the Search for Educational Authority.* Cambridge, MA: Harvard University Press, 1980.

Profiles in Excellence: Chicago, Illinois. Chicago: National Board for Professional Teaching Standards, 2009. https://files.eric.ed.gov/fulltext/ED508174.pdf.

Progress Report. Chicago: Chicago Public Education Fund, 2017.

Puckett, John L. Review of *School-University Partnerships in Action: Concepts, Cases, and Concerns,* by Kenneth A. Sirotnik and John I. Goodlad. *American Journal of Education* 97, no. 4 (1989): 443–448.

Raising the Achievement of Latino Students and English Language Learners in the Chicago Public Schools. Washington, DC: Council of the Great City Schools. https://www.chicagoreporter.com/wp-content/uploads/2017/06/Council_of_the_Great_City_Schools-Bilingual_Education_2015.pdf.

Reardon, Sean F., and Rebecca Hinze-Pifer. *Test Score Growth Among Chicago Public School Students, 2009–2014.* Stanford, CA: Stanford Center for Education Policy Analysis, 2017. https://cepa.stanford.edu/content/test-score-growth-among-chicago-public-school-students-2009-2014.

Report of the 1981 Special Task Force on Education. Chicago: Chicago United, 1981.

"Rhee Fires Principal." YouTube video, 2011. https://www.youtube.com/watch?v=FQ4N6UZbdxA.

Roberts, Penny. "Pride, Not Prejudice." *Chicago Tribune,* December 7, 1993. https://www.chicagotribune.com/news/ct-xpm-1993-12-07-9312070224-story.html.

Roderick, Melissa, Anthony S. Bryk, Brian A. Jacob, John Q. Easton, and Elaine Allensworth. *Ending Social Promotion: Results from the First Two Years.* Chicago: University of Chicago Consortium on School Research, 1999. https://consortium.uchicago.edu/publications/ending-social-promotion-results-first-two-years.

Roderick, Melissa, Vanessa Coca, and Jenny Nagaoka. "Potholes on the Road to College: High School Effects in Shaping Urban Students' Participation in College Application, Four-Year College Enrollment, and College Match." *Sociology of Education* 84, no. 3 (2011): 178–211.

Roderick, Melissa, Mimi Engel, Jenny Nagaoka, Brian A. Jacob, Alex Orfei, Sophia Degener, Susan Stone, and Jen Bacon. *Ending Social Promotion: Results from Summer Bridge.* Chicago: University of Chicago Consortium on School Research, 2003. https://consortium.uchicago.edu/publications/ending-social-promotion-results-summer-bridge.

Roderick, Melissa, Brian A. Jacob, and Anthony S. Bryk. "The Impact of High-Stakes Testing in Chicago on Student Achievement in Promotional Gate Grades." *Educational Evaluation and Policy Analysis* 24, no. 4 (2002): 333–357. https://doi.org/10.3102/01623737024004333.

Roderick, Melissa, Jenny Nagaoka, and Elaine Allensworth. *From High School to the Future: A First Look at the Chicago Public School Graduates' College Enrollment, College Preparation, and Graduation from Four-Year Colleges.* Chicago: Consortium on Chicago School Research, 2006. https://consortium.uchicago.edu/sites/default/files/2018-10/Postsecondary.pdf.

Roderick, Melissa, Jenny Nagaoka, and John Q. Easton. *Update: Ending Social Promotion— Passing, Retention, and Achievement Trends Among Promoted and Retained Students.* Chicago: University of Chicago Consortium on School Research, 2000. https://consortium.uchicago.edu/publications/update-ending-social-promotion-passing-retention-and-achievement-trends-among-promoted.

Rollow, Sharon, and Michael D. Bennett. *Parents' Participation and Chicago School Reform: Issues of Race, Class and Expectation.* Madison, WI: Center on the Organization and Restructuring of Schools, 1996. ED 412 635. EA 028 711.

Rollow, Sharon, and Maria J. Yanguas. *The Road to Emergent Restructuring and Strong Democracy.* Washington, DC: Office of Education Research and Improvement, 1996. ED 412625. EA 028.666.

Rossi, Rosalind, Becky Beaupre, and Kate N. Grossman. "Failing Teachers: A Sun-Times Investigation." *Chicago Sun-Times,* September 6, 2001, 6.

Russo, Alexander. "Branches of the Reading Initiative." *Chicago Reporter,* August 10, 2005.

Sakash, Karen, and Victoria Chou. "Increasing the Supply of Latino Bilingual Teachers for the Chicago Public Schools." *Teacher Education Quarterly* 34 (Fall 2007): 41–52.

Sampson, William A. *Chicago Charter Schools: The Hype and the Reality.* Charlotte, NC: Information Age, 2016.

Sanchez, Claudio. "Bilingual Education Returns to California. Now What?" NPR Ed, November 25, 2016.

Sartain, Lauren, Andrew Zou, Vanessa Gutierrez, Andria Shyjka, Ebony Hinton, Eric R. Brown, and John Q. Easton. *Teacher Evaluation in Chicago Public Schools: Analysis of the REACH Educator Evaluation and Support System, Five Years In.* Chicago: University of Chicago Consortium on School Research, 2020.

Sartain, Lauren, Andrew Zou, Venessa Gutierrez, Andria Shyjka, Ebony Hinton, Eric R. Brown, and John Q. Easton, *Teacher Evaluation in CPS: Perceptions of REACH Implementation, Five Years In.* Chicago: University of Chicago Consortium on School Research, 2020.

Schein, Edgar H. "Kurt Lewin's Change Theory in the Field and in the Classroom." *Systems Practice* 9, no. 1 (1996): 27–47.

Sebastian, James, and Elaine Allensworth, "Student Learning: A Study of Mediated Pathways to Learning: The Influence of Principal Leadership on Classroom Instruction." *Educational Administration Quarterly* 48 (2012).

Sebring, Penny B. *The Research Agenda, 2004–2008.* Chicago: University of Chicago Consortium on School Research, 2003. https://consortium.uchicago.edu/sites/default/files/2018-10/res_agenda.pdf.

Sebring, Penny B., Elaine Allensworth, Anthony S. Bryk, John Q. Easton, and Stuart Luppescu. *The Essential Supports for School Improvement.* Chicago: University of Chicago Consortium on Chicago School Research, 2006.

Sebring, Penny, Anthony S. Bryk, Melissa Roderick, Eric Camburn, Stuart Luppescu, Yeow M. Thum, BetsAnn Smith, and Joseph E. Kahne. *Charting Reform in Chicago: The Students Speak.* Chicago: University of Chicago Consortium on School Research, 1996.

Shipps, Dorothy. *School Reform, Corporate Style: Chicago 1880–2000.* Lawrence: University Press of Kansas, 2006.

Shipps, Dorothy, Karen Sconzert, and Holly Swyers. *The Chicago Annenberg Challenge: The First Three Years.* Chicago: University of Chicago Consortium on School Research, 1999. https://consortium.uchicago.edu/publications/chicago-annenberg-challenge-first-three -years.

Shohoni, Aneesh. "Teach for America Growth and Impact Snapshot: Chicago and NW Indiana." Teach For America website.

Shore, Debra. "Teachers Academy to Resume Training." *Catalyst* 4, no. 5 (February 1993).

Shouse, Roger C. "Academic Press and Sense of Community: Conflict, Congruence, and Implications for Student Achievement." *Social Psychology of Education* 1, no. 1 (1996): 47–88.

Sirotnik, Kenneth J., and John I. Goodlad. *School-University Partnerships in Action: Concepts, Cases, and Concerns.* New York: Teachers College Press, 1988.

Smith, BetsAnn. *It's About Time.* Chicago: University of Chicago Consortium on School Research, 1998.

Stake, Robert E. "Program Evaluation, Particularly Responsive Evaluation." *Journal of Multidisciplinary Services* 7, no. 15 (2010): 180–201.

Stein, Amanda G., Debra Pacchiano, and Stuart Luppescu. *Essential Organizational Supports for Early Education.* Chicago: University of Chicago Consortium on School Research, 2020. https://consortium.uchicago.edu/publications/essential-organizational-supports -early-education-development-new-survey-tool-measure.

Stoelinga, Sara R., and Melinda M. Mangin. *Examining Effective Teacher Leadership.* New York: Teachers College Press, 2010.

Stone, Clarence N. "Civic Capacity and Urban Education." *Urban Affairs Review* 36, no. 5 (2001): 595–619. https://doi.org/10.1177/10780870122185019.

Stone, Clarence N. "Rhetoric, Reality and Politics: The Neoliberal Cul-de-sac in Education." *Urban Affairs Review* 56, no. 3 (2020): 943–972. https://doi.org/10.1177 /1078087419867165.

Stone, Clarence N., Jeffrey R. Henig, Bryan D. Jones, and Carol Pierannunzi. *Building Civic Capacity: The Politics of Reforming Urban Schools.* Lawrence: University of Kansas Press, 2001.

Sutton, Robert, and Huggy Rao. *Scaling Up Excellence.* New York: Crown Business, 2014.

Taladrif, Stephani. "The Exclusion of Latinos from American Media and History Books." *New Yorker,* September 21, 2021.

Tepper Jacob, Robin, Susan Stone, and Melissa Roderick. *Ending Social Promotion: The Response of Teachers and Students.* Chicago: University of Chicago Consortium on School Research, 2004. https://consortium.uchicago.edu/publications/ending-social -promotion-response-teachers-and-students.

Todd-Breland, Elizabeth. *A Political Education: Black Politics and Education Reform in Chicago Since the 1960s.* Chapel Hill: University of North Carolina Press, 2018.

Tomorrow's Schools of Education: A Report of the Holmes Group. East Lansing, MI: Holmes Group, 1995.

Tomorrow's Teachers: A Report of the Holmes Group. East Lansing, MI: Holmes Group, 1986.

Tyack, David B. *The One Best System: A History of American Urban Education.* Cambridge, MA: Harvard University Press, 1974.

UCLA Center X. "UCLA Center X Prepares and Supports Educators." University of California Regents. https://centerx.gseis.ucla.edu/.

UIC Today. "I Made the Right Choice." University of Illinois at Chicago, November 19, 2018. https://today.uic.edu/cps-chief-janice-jackson-on-uic-i-made-the-right-choice.

"Urban Literacy: Partnerships for Improving Literacy in Urban Schools." *Reading Teacher* 61, no. 8 (May 2008): 674–680.

Verstegen, Deborah A. "Public Education Finance Systems in the United States and Funding Policies for Populations with Special Education Needs." *Education Policy Analysis Archives* 19, no. 21 (2011): 1–26. DOI: 10.14507/epaa.v19n21.2011.

Villarosa, Linda. "Black Lives Are Shorter in Chicago. My Family's History Shows Why." *New York Times Magazine*, April 27, 2021.

Wade, Andy. "Site-Based Management During a Time of Centralization." In *School Reform in Chicago: Lessons in Policy and Practice*, edited by Alexander Russo, 29–36. Cambridge, MA: Harvard Education Press, 2004.

Waiting for Superman. Directed by Davis Guggenheim. Produced by Leslie Chilcott. Documentary film, 2010.

Wakelyn, David, Jennifer O'Day, and Kara Finnigan. *External Support to Schools on Probation.* Chicago: University of Chicago Consortium on School Research, 2003. https://consortium.uchicago.edu/publications/external-support-schools-probation-getting-leg.

Walker, Lisa Jean, and Steven Tozer. "Towards the Continuous Improvement of Chicago Public Schools' High-Churn Elementary Schools" (Chicago, IL: University of Illinois Chicago Center for Urban Education Leadership, December, 2021)

Warnick, Bryan R. "Rethinking Education for Autonomy in Pluralistic Societies." *Educational Theory* 62, no. 4 (2012): 411–426. https://www.researchgate.net/publication/359717200_Toward_the_Continuous_Improvement_of_Chicago_Public_Schools'_High-churn_Elementary_Schools_Policy_and_Practice_Brief_UIC_Center_for_Urban_Education_Leadership

Weiss, Carol H., and Michael J. Bucuvalas. *Social Science Research and Decision Making.* New York: Columbia University Press, 1980.

Weissman, Daniel. "What's Next, Who's Next? Most People Want More Investment in Teachers and School Leaders." *Catalyst*, February 2001, 13.

Weyer, Matt. "Third-Grade Reading Legislation." National Conference of State Legislatures, July 2017. http://www.ncsl.org/research/education/third-grade-reading-legislation.aspx.

Whalen, Samuel P. *Transforming Central Office Practices for Equity, Coherence, and Continuous Improvement: Chicago Public Schools Under the Leadership of Dr. Janice K. Jackson.* Chicago: University of Illinois Chicago Center for Urban Education Leadership, 2020. https://urbanedleadership.org/wp-content/uploads/2021/01/CEOreport.pdf.

White, Terrenda C. "Teach For America's Paradoxical Diversity Initiative: Race, Policy, and Black Teacher Displacement in Urban Schools." *Education Policy Analysis Archives* 24, no. 16 (2016). http://dx.doi.org/10.14507/epaa.24.2100.

Wildavsky, Aaron. *Speaking Truth to Power: The Art and Craft of Policy Analysis.* New York: Taylor & Francis, 1979.

Wilkerson, Isabel. "New School Term Puts Parents in the Seat of Power." *New York Times,* September 3, 1989.

Williams, Debra. "Mid South: Linking Schools and Communities." *Catalyst,* June 1, 2004.

Williams, Debra. "Probation Stuns Schools That Raised State Test Scores." *Catalyst,* July 25, 2005. https://www.chicagoreporter.com/probation-stuns-schools-raised-state-test-scores/.

Wilson, William Julius. *The Truly Disadvantaged: The Inner City, the Underclass, and Public Policy.* Chicago: University of Chicago Press, 1987.

Wong, Ken. "The Big Stick." *Education Next* 3, no. 1 (2003): 44–49.

Zavitkovsky, Paul, and Steven Tozer. *Upstate/Downstate: Changing Patterns of Achievement, Demographics and School Effectiveness in Illinois Public Schools Under NCLB.* Chicago: Center for Urban Education Leadership, University of Illinois at Chicago, 2017. https://urbanedleadership.org/wp-content/uploads/2020/02/UPSTATE-DOWNSTATE -FINAL-w-Appendices-06.16.17.pdf.

Index